P9-CQX-081

ALSO BY THE EDITORS AT AMERICA'S TEST KITCHEN

The Science of Good Cooking

The Cook's Illustrated Cookbook

The America's Test Kitchen Menu Cookbook

The America's Test Kitchen Quick
Family Cookbook

The America's Test Kitchen Healthy
Family Cookbook

The America's Test Kitchen Family Baking Book

The America's Test Kitchen Family Cookbook

**THE AMERICA'S TEST KITCHEN LIBRARY
AND THE TEST KITCHEN HANDBOOK SERIES:**

Comfort Food Makeovers

The America's Test Kitchen D.I.Y. Cookbook

Pasta Revolution

Simple Weeknight Favorites

Slow Cooker Revolution

Slow Cooker Revolution Volume 2

The Best Simple Recipes

Pressure Cooker Perfection

THE COOK'S COUNTRY SERIES:

From Our Grandmothers' Kitchens

Cook's Country Blue Ribbon Desserts

Cook's Country Best Potluck Recipes

Cook's Country Best Lost Suppers

Cook's Country Best Grilling Recipes

The Cook's Country Cookbook

America's Best Lost Recipes

THE TV COMPANION SERIES:

The Complete Cook's Country
TV Show Cookbook

The Complete America's Test Kitchen
TV Show Cookbook 2001–2014

America's Test Kitchen: The TV Companion
Cookbook (2002–2009, 2011–2014 Editions)

AMERICA'S TEST KITCHEN ANNUALS:

The Best of America's Test Kitchen
(2007–2014 Editions)

Cooking for Two (2010–2013 Editions)

Light & Healthy (2010–2012 Editions)

THE BEST RECIPE SERIES:

The New Best Recipe

More Best Recipes

The Best One-Dish Suppers

Soups, Stews & Chilis

The Best Skillet Recipes

The Best Slow & Easy Recipes

The Best Chicken Recipes

The Best International Recipe

The Best Make-Ahead Recipe

The Best 30-Minute Recipe

The Best Light Recipe

The Cook's Illustrated Guide to
Grilling and Barbecue

Best American Side Dishes

Cover & Bake

Steaks, Chops, Roasts & Ribs

Baking Illustrated

Italian Classics

American Classics

**FOR A FULL LISTING OF ALL OUR BOOKS
OR TO ORDER TITLES:**

CooksIllustrated.com

AmericasTestKitchen.com

or call 800-611-0759

PRAISE FOR OTHER AMERICA'S TEST KITCHEN TITLES

"There are pasta books . . . and then there's this pasta book. Flip your carbohydrate dreams upside down and strain them through this sieve of revolutionary, creative, and also traditional recipes."
SAN FRANCISCO BOOK REVIEW ON *PASTA REVOLUTION*

"Ideal as a reference for the bookshelf . . . , this volume will be turned to time and again for definitive instruction on just about any food-related matter."
PUBLISHERS WEEKLY ON *THE SCIENCE OF GOOD COOKING*

"The perfect kitchen home companion. The practical side of things is very much on display. . . . cook-friendly and kitchen-oriented, illuminating the process of preparing food instead of mystifying it."
THE WALL STREET JOURNAL ON *THE COOK'S ILLUSTRATED COOKBOOK*

"If this were the only cookbook you owned, you would cook well, be everyone's favorite host, have a well-run kitchen, and eat happily every day."
THECITYCOOK.COM ON *THE AMERICA'S TEST KITCHEN MENU COOKBOOK*

"This book upgrades slow cooking for discriminating, 21st-century palates—that is indeed revolutionary."
THE DALLAS MORNING NEWS ON *SLOW COOKER REVOLUTION*

"Forget about marketing hype, designer labels and pretentious entrées: This is an unblinking, unbedazzled guide to the Beardian good-cooking ideal."
THE WALL STREET JOURNAL ON *THE BEST OF AMERICA'S TEST KITCHEN 2009*

"The strength of the Best Recipe series lies in the sheer thoughtfulness and details of the recipes."
PUBLISHERS WEEKLY ON *THE BEST RECIPE SERIES*

"Expert bakers and novices scared of baking's requisite exactitude can all learn something from this hefty, all-purpose home baking volume."
PUBLISHERS WEEKLY ON *THE AMERICA'S TEST KITCHEN FAMILY BAKING BOOK*

"If you're hankering for old-fashioned pleasures, look no further."
PEOPLE MAGAZINE ON *AMERICA'S BEST LOST RECIPES*

"This tome definitely raises the bar for all-in-one, basic, must-have cookbooks. . . . Kimball and his company have scored another hit."
PORTLAND OREGONIAN ON *THE AMERICA'S TEST KITCHEN FAMILY COOKBOOK*

"A foolproof, go-to resource for everyday cooking."
PUBLISHERS WEEKLY ON *THE AMERICA'S TEST KITCHEN FAMILY COOKBOOK*

"These dishes taste as luxurious as their full-fat siblings. Even desserts are terrific."
PUBLISHERS WEEKLY ON *THE BEST LIGHT RECIPE*

"Further proof that practice makes perfect, if not transcendent. . . . If an intermediate cook follows the directions exactly, the results will be better than takeout or mom's."
THE NEW YORK TIMES ON *THE NEW BEST RECIPE*

"Like a mini-cooking school, the detailed instructions and illustrations ensure that even the most inexperienced cook can follow these recipes with success."
PUBLISHERS WEEKLY ON *BEST AMERICAN SIDE DISHES*

"Makes one-dish dinners a reality for average cooks, with honest ingredients and detailed make-ahead instructions."
THE NEW YORK TIMES ON *COVER & BAKE*

6 Ingredient SOLUTION

HOW TO COAX More Flavor FROM FEWER INGREDIENTS

BY THE EDITORS AT
America's Test Kitchen

PHOTOGRAPHY BY
Carl Tremblay and Daniel J. van Ackere

Copyright © 2013
by the Editors at America's Test Kitchen

All rights reserved. No part of this book may
be reproduced or transmitted in any manner
whatsoever without written permission from
the publisher, except in the case of brief quo-
tations embodied in critical articles or reviews.

AMERICA'S TEST KITCHEN
17 Station Street, Brookline, MA 02445

Library of Congress
Cataloging-in-Publication Data
The six-ingredient solution : how to coax
more flavor from fewer ingredients / by the
editors at America's Test Kitchen ; photography by Daniel J. van Ackere ; additional
photography by Carl Tremblay. -- 1st edition.
    pages cm
  Includes index.
  ISBN 978-1-936493-44-9 (paperback)
1. Cooking, American. 2. Flavor. 3. Quick
and easy cooking. I. America's Test Kitchen
(Firm) II. Title: Six-ingredient solution.
  TX715.A1114 2013
  641.5'55--dc23
                                2013003383
Paperback: $26.95 US

Manufactured in the United States
of America

10 9 8 7 6 5 4 3 2 1

DISTRIBUTED BY
America's Test Kitchen
17 Station Street, Brookline, MA 02445

EDITORIAL DIRECTOR: Jack Bishop

EDITORIAL DIRECTOR, BOOKS: Elizabeth Carduff

EXECUTIVE FOOD EDITOR: Julia Collin Davison

EXECUTIVE EDITOR: Lori Galvin

SENIOR EDITOR: Suzannah McFerran

ASSOCIATE EDITORS: Kate Hartke, Alyssa King, Christie Morrison

TEST COOKS: Danielle DeSiato-Hallman, Rebecca Morris

ASSISTANT TEST COOK: Lainey Seyler

DESIGN DIRECTOR: Amy Klee

ART DIRECTOR: Greg Galvan

DESIGNER: Allison Pfiffner

FRONT COVER PHOTOGRAPH: Carl Tremblay

STAFF PHOTOGRAPHER: Daniel J. van Ackere

ADDITIONAL PHOTOGRAPHY: Keller + Keller, Steve Klise

FOOD STYLING: Catrine Kelty, Marie Piraino

PHOTOSHOOT KITCHEN TEAM:

    ASSOCIATE EDITOR: Chris O'Connor

    TEST COOKS: Daniel Cellucci, Sara Mayer

PRODUCTION DIRECTOR: Guy Rochford

SENIOR PRODUCTION MANAGER: Jessica Quirk

SENIOR PROJECT MANAGER: Alice Carpenter

PRODUCTION AND TRAFFIC COORDINATOR: Brittany Allen

WORKFLOW AND DIGITAL ASSET MANAGER: Andrew Mannone

SENIOR COLOR AND IMAGING SPECIALIST: Lauren Pettapiece

PRODUCTION AND IMAGING SPECIALISTS: Heather Dube, Lauren Robbins

COPYEDITOR: Debra Hudak

PROOFREADER: Elizabeth Wray Emery

INDEXER: Elizabeth Parson

PICTURED ON FRONT COVER: Meatloaf Florentine (page 109)

PICTURED OPPOSITE TITLE PAGE: Clams with Israeli Couscous, Chorizo, and Scallions (page 167)

PICTURED ON BACK OF JACKET: Roast Beef Sirloin with Caramelized Carrots and Potatoes (page 139), Chai-Infused Butternut Squash Soup (page 42), Cheddar Crumb–Crusted Chicken with Sautéed Cherry Tomatoes (page 65), Maryland-Style Grilled Shrimp and Corn (page 275), Six-Ingredient Spaghetti and Meatballs (page 195), Nutella Tart (page 289)

Contents

Preface by
Christopher Kimball
ix

Secrets to Six-Ingredient
Cooking
1

Effortless
Appetizers
4

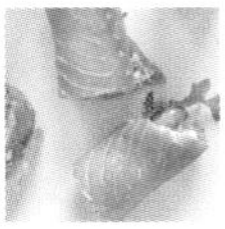

Simply Sensational
Soups
40

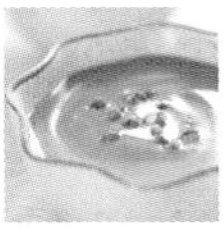

Chicken
58

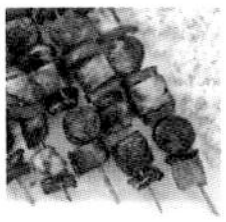

Beef, Pork, and
Lamb
92

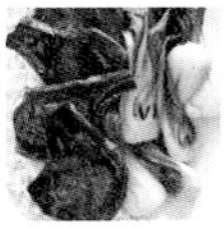

Slow and Easy
122

Seafood
144

Pasta
168

Vegetarian Mains
208

Fast-Lane
Casseroles
222

Easy Grilling
248

No-Fuss Desserts
280

Conversions &
Equivalencies
300

Index
302

Welcome to America's Test Kitchen

This book has been tested, written, and edited by the folks at America's Test Kitchen, a very real 2,500-square-foot kitchen located just outside of Boston. It is the home of *Cook's Illustrated* magazine and *Cook's Country* magazine and is the Monday-through-Friday destination for more than three dozen test cooks, editors, food scientists, tasters, and cookware specialists. Our mission is to test recipes over and over again until we understand how and why they work and until we arrive at the "best" version.

We start the process of testing a recipe with a complete lack of conviction, which means that we accept no claim, no theory, no technique, and no recipe at face value. We simply assemble as many variations as possible, test a half-dozen of the most promising, and taste the results blind. We then construct our own hybrid recipe and continue to test it, varying ingredients, techniques, and cooking times until we reach a consensus. The result, we hope, is the best version of a particular recipe, but we realize that only you can be the final judge of our success (or failure). As we like to say in the test kitchen, "We make the mistakes, so you don't have to."

All of this would not be possible without a belief that good cooking, much like good music, is indeed based on a foundation of objective technique.

Some people like spicy foods and others don't, but there is a right way to sauté, there is a best way to cook a pot roast, and there are measurable scientific principles involved in producing perfectly beaten, stable egg whites. This is our ultimate goal: to investigate the fundamental principles of cooking so that you become a better cook. It is as simple as that.

You can watch us work (in our actual test kitchen) by tuning in to America's Test Kitchen (AmericasTestKitchenTV.com) or Cook's Country from America's Test Kitchen (CooksCountryTV.com) on public television, or by subscribing to *Cook's Illustrated* magazine (CooksIllustrated.com) or *Cook's Country* magazine (CooksCountry.com). We welcome you into our kitchen, where you can stand by our side as we test our way to the "best" recipes in America.

Curious to see what goes on behind the scenes at America's Test Kitchen? The Feed features kitchen snapshots, exclusive recipes, video tips, and much more. **AmericasTestKitchenFeed.com**

f facebook.com/AmericasTestKitchen
t twitter.com/TestKitchen
You Tube youtube.com/AmericasTestKitchen

Preface

We recently hosted a group of girls from Junior League in our test kitchen for a Saturday morning cooking lesson. I told them that the simplest food is usually the best and that on the rare occasion when I have cooked with a well-known food personality, I am astonished that the menu is so simple. Julia Child once served me boiled new potatoes with a tin of caviar on the side (and lots of wine). James Beard was known for his love of bacon and simple picnics. Others have prepared a simple soup, an oyster stew, or a roast leg of lamb. And Jacques Pépin is famous for giving a final exam to his culinary students that is nothing more than a roast chicken, a side of potatoes, and a perfectly dressed salad.

The point is that recipes with a limited number of ingredients are often the best recipes. They also show off one's skills in the kitchen since one has to pay attention to each and every item. And that is the most satisfying way to cook—limit your menu, limit your ingredient list, and focus on the cooking and treating each food with the respect it deserves.

All of this has led us to publish the book you are holding in your hand, *The Six-Ingredient Solution*. We undertook this project not just to give you quick and easy recipes, but to celebrate the very best way to cook, making the most of every ingredient and every step. We also developed this book to refresh our own repertoire of cooking techniques. We were reminded of the benefits of high heat for flavor development, we explored new ingredients to enhance flavors (the liquid inside a jar of sun-dried tomatoes, for example), we bloomed spices in oil to bring out their rich flavors, we found new uses for old ingredients (hot pepper jelly made a terrific glaze for roast chicken), and we took a new look at lots of supermarket pantry ingredients, such as Thai curry paste.

At the end of this project, we came up with a whole new collection of simple but deeply satisfying recipes.

We made Chai-Infused Butternut Squash Soup with the addition of one chai tea bag. We braised chicken in a coconut-curry sauce. We cooked cod and potatoes on the same baking sheet for a terrific dish of Roasted Cod Fillets with Crispy Potatoes and Lemon. And, for a quick and easy dessert, we topped fresh berries with store-bought croissants processed with sugar, cinnamon, and butter.

Here at the test kitchen, we love good food, but most of all, we like to cook. We like it because there is nothing better than doing something well. Yes, this takes both patience and practice, but the little-known secret of the best cooks is simplicity. This is also true of music, of writing, and of most other artistic pursuits. It's what you don't put in the skillet that matters most.

This, of course, reminds me of the classic story of the flatlander who asked for directions from a Vermont farmer. The old-timer gave the man rather lengthy, involved directions and, a half hour later, the flatlander found himself back at the same place he had started. "Darn it," the city slicker said, "I asked for directions to East Barnard and here I am, right back where I started from!" The farmer looked straight at him and replied, "That's good. That's good. I wanted to find out first if you were capable of following directions. Now I can tell you how to get to East Barnard!"

Well, hopefully our recipe directions are clearer than that so you don't end up right where you started! Enjoy *The Six-Ingredient Solution*!

CHRISTOPHER KIMBALL
Founder and Editor,
Cook's Illustrated and *Cook's Country*
Host, *America's Test Kitchen* and
Cook's Country from America's Test Kitchen

Secrets to Six-Ingredient Cooking

Given how carefully scheduled and time-crunched most folks are these days, the appeal of cooking with fewer ingredients is undeniable. Fewer ingredients means less time shopping and less time prepping. But there's no point making a six-ingredient recipe unless the dish is really good. Thus, our goal wasn't just to simply provide recipes with short ingredient lists—we wanted to be able to transform a handful of ingredients into an impressive dish that's far more than the sum of its parts.

As the test kitchen worked on this project, we discovered new techniques that generate more flavor and we learned how to use familiar ingredients in new ways, which both save time and build flavor. During our testing, it quickly became obvious to us how important every ingredient is to a recipe. While we always encourage cooks to use quality ingredients, it really is imperative when cooking with just six ingredients—one subpar ingredient can drag down an entire dish. Throughout this book, we highlight important ingredients in Ingredient Spotlights, where we explain what you need to know when shopping, and often which brands we prefer.

Note that every recipe in this book requires no more than six ingredients (with the exceptions of water, salt, and pepper) from start to finish. Also, you'll see more than half of the recipes in this book highlighted as Fast Recipes—these can be on the table in about half an hour. Many of them require multitasking—you may need to slice meat and chop vegetables while bringing a pot of water to a boil—but this will help you pull together full-flavored dishes on even the busiest of weeknights.

Here are some general points we learned in the test kitchen about six-ingredient cooking. We hope you can apply some of our shopping and cooking strategies to your own kitchen.

LOOK BEYOND YOUR USUAL COOKING FATS

When our recipes include ingredients that contain flavorful fats—such as the oil packed inside a jar of sun-dried tomatoes, the oil in a jar of pesto, or even rich coconut milk—we use them for sautéing, which adds an extra boost of flavor to a number of dishes. For example, in our Coconut-Curry Braised Chicken (page 79) we used a couple tablespoons of coconut milk to pan-sear chicken breasts, a tablespoon to sauté the aromatics, and the remainder to braise the chicken until the meat cooked up moist and flavorful.

USE HIGH HEAT TO DEVELOP FLAVOR

High heat encourages meats and vegetables to brown, and browning is important for building flavor. In fact, browning is such a potent flavor builder that it is like having another ingredient (or two) in your arsenal. Pan searing, grilling, and broiling are all high-heat methods we employ in this book. Note that when we pan-sear food, we heat the oil in our skillet until just smoking. This ensures that when the food hits the pan, it will sear and brown upon contact. If the skillet isn't hot enough, your food will begin to steam and won't develop maximum flavor.

STOCK UP ON SPICE BLENDS

You probably have poultry seasoning or a basic chili powder blend in your pantry, but consider adding a few other useful blends to your collection, such as Cajun seasoning, herbes de Provence, five-spice powder, garam masala, and *za'atar*. These flavorful blends mean that you don't have to buy lots of individual spices and they often contain unique flavors that are otherwise hard to find. Five-spice powder gives simple broiled chicken thighs warmly spiced flavor; aromatic herbes de Provence (a combination of up to seven Mediterranean herbs) makes an easy, brightly flavored rub for pork tenderloin and lends sophisticated flavor to cheese coins when incorporated into the simple-to-mix dough.

UNLOCK THE FLAVOR OF SPICES AND HERBS

Many spices and spice blends will taste fuller and more complex if they are bloomed, or briefly cooked in oil. Blooming spices doesn't have to be complicated—it's as simple as heating the spices in oil a few seconds ahead of the other ingredients in your dish. Likewise, we often oil meat before we apply a rub. Yes, the oil helps the rub stick to the meat, but once heated, the flavor of the rub becomes richer and more fragrant than if it had been applied to the meat without any oil at all.

Cooking chili powder with ground beef works to bloom, or deepen, its flavor, resulting in a chili with complexity and intensity.

DISCOVER NEW USES FOR STORE-BOUGHT SAUCES

Using a store-bought sauce (such as a pesto, marinara sauce, or barbecue sauce) is an obvious way to streamline your cooking. But we've thought outside of the jar (or can) when considering their uses. Adding pesto to meatballs delivers flavor and richness in one shot; stirring barbecue sauce into skillet chicken and rice effortlessly infuses this weeknight workhorse with tangy, smoky flavor; and marinara sauce helps us give meatloaf an Italian character— poured over the loaf, it helps keep the exterior moist and accents the meat with rich tomato flavor.

Jarred marinara sauce adds robust flavor to our meatloaf and keeps the exterior moist in the oven.

BUILD GLAZES FOR MEAT WITH JAMS AND JELLIES

Caramelized onion jam, fig jam, and hot pepper jelly can be used for more than a cheese board. They each provide a quick route to a flavorful glaze—

Fig jam melts into a flavorful, clingy glaze when brushed onto a hot, roasted pork loin.

hot pepper jelly spread on chicken gives the meat sweet and spicy flavor, and also adds body, heat, and complexity to our beef teriyaki. Fig jam slathered over a hot pork roast melts into an earthy glaze that complements a flavorful fennel rub on the meat.

RETHINK PICKLES AND MARINATED VEGETABLES
We've always been a fan of the sweet, smoky flavor of jarred roasted red peppers and the flavor impact they can have on a dish, but we hadn't considered the other possibilities in the same grocery aisle until we worked on this book. Take *giardiniera*, Italian-style pickled vegetables. Tossed with fusilli, it gives the pasta bites of well-seasoned vegetables without any prep—and the packing liquid adds zesty punch to the sauce. Giardiniera also adds heft and bright flavor to sausage-stuffed peppers. And we don't stop there: Other ingredient multitaskers include marinated artichoke hearts, Peppadew peppers, and stuffed cherry peppers.

EXPLORE THE INTERNATIONAL AISLE
Every supermarket has one and if you don't know what's on those shelves then it's time to check it out. You'll find a variety of cuisines represented here, but the majority of the space is usually given to Latin American, Chinese, Japanese, and Thai products. For example, those small jars of Thai curry pastes are flavor powerhouses—and all the measuring and chopping is done for you. A typical curry paste

Just a tablespoon of Thai curry paste, a staple in the international aisle of any supermarket, can add potent, exotic flavor to many dishes.

contains several ingredients, including garlic and shallot, along with hard-to-find ingredients like galangal, lemon grass, and kaffir lime peel. Just a spoonful or two of curry paste infuses soups and braises with exotic flavor. And ditto for the value of rich, thick oyster sauce. This Chinese condiment helped us cut down on the notoriously long ingredient lists of stir-fries.

CONSIDER THE SNACK SHELF WHEN COOKING
Potato chips, tortilla chips, baked cheese sticks, and smoked almonds aren't just for eating out of hand, but can be used as a crisp coating for chicken or fish, as a thickener for soups and chilis, or as a topping for a casserole. Crumbled store-bought cookies also make it easy to whip up a last-minute trifle or parfait. Best of all, many of these snacks are already in your pantry.

Crushed store-bought cookies provide a crunchy layer in our easy parfaits, which come together in just minutes.

REMEMBER TO SEASON—AND TASTE
We didn't count salt and pepper among our six ingredients, but that doesn't mean that they are unimportant. In fact, seasoning when cooking and just before serving coaxes more flavor out of a dish, so do follow our seasoning instructions such as salting meat and poultry before cooking and be sure to taste your food before serving—and season again if necessary.

ENDIVE CUPS WITH APPLES AND BLUE CHEESE

Effortless Appetizers

6 Herbed Cheese Coins

7 Cheese Crisps (Frico)

9 Pink Peppercorn–Crusted Goat Cheese Log | FAST RECIPE

10 Feta-Dill Dip with Cucumber Chips | FAST RECIPE

11 Marinated Feta and Green Olives

13 Melted Brie with Honey and Herbs | FAST RECIPE

15 Herbed Ricotta Crostini

16 Crispy Spiced Chickpeas | FAST RECIPE

17 Serrano and Manchego Crostini with Orange Honey | FAST RECIPE

19 Caprese Skewers | FAST RECIPE

20 Endive Cups with Apples and Blue Cheese | FAST RECIPE

21 Prosciutto-Wrapped Figs with Gorgonzola | FAST RECIPE

23 Stuffed Mushrooms with Boursin and Prosciutto | FAST RECIPE

25 Warm Bacon-Wrapped Chorizo and Dates

26 Salami and Provolone-Stuffed Peppers | FAST RECIPE

27 Brie and Jam Phyllo Cups | FAST RECIPE

28 Tomato Tartlets

30 Ham and Cheese Palmiers

32 Kielbasa Bites

33 Naan Tarts with Artichokes, Pesto, and Goat Cheese | FAST RECIPE

35 Spicy Shrimp Cocktail Shooters

36 Citrusy Shrimp Cocktail | FAST RECIPE

37 Broiled Chipotle Shrimp | FAST RECIPE

39 Smoked Salmon Rolls | FAST RECIPE

Herbed Cheese Coins

MAKES 60 CRACKERS

½ teaspoon **herbes de Provence**

½ cup **walnuts**

2 cups (8 ounces) shredded
Gruyère cheese

1½ cups **all-purpose flour**

8 tablespoons softened
unsalted butter

¼ teaspoon **garlic powder**

INGREDIENT SPOTLIGHT
HERBES DE PROVENCE

Herbes de Provence, the aromatic
blend from the south of France,
combines dried lavender flowers with
rosemary, sage, thyme, marjoram,
and fennel, and sometimes chervil,
basil, tarragon, or savory. Herbes de
Provence makes a natural partner for
poultry and pork, and it contributes
complex herbal notes to our cheese
coins. You can find it in the spice aisle
of most supermarkets.

TO MAKE AHEAD
Dough logs can be refrigerated for up
to 2 days; slice before baking. Once
baked, crackers can be stored in airtight container for up to 2 days.

☑ WHY THIS RECIPE WORKS The duo of Gruyère cheese and
walnuts gives these simple crackers a robust flavor and easy elegance. To complement our bold-tasting ingredients, we selected
not one herb, but several, by including herbes de Provence, a
potent blend comprised of rosemary, sage, thyme, plus a few
additional herbs. For more oomph, we added a small amount
of garlic powder. Usually we call for blooming, or cooking, dry
herbs to bring out their flavor. Since we already needed water
to hydrate the dough, we combined the water and herbes de
Provence and gave the mixture a quick spin in the microwave
before adding it to the dry ingredients for crackers with a deeper
flavor. Although we prefer Gruyère cheese in this recipe, cheddar
can be substituted.

1. Combine herbes de Provence and 2 tablespoons water in small
bowl and microwave until hot, about 30 seconds; let cool. Pulse
walnuts in food processor until coarsely chopped, about 7 pulses.
Add Gruyère, flour, butter, and garlic powder to food processor
and pulse until just combined and uniform, about 8 pulses.

2. Transfer mixture to large bowl and sprinkle with herb-water
mixture. Squeeze mixture between hands to form ball, adding up
to 1 tablespoon more water as necessary. Form dough into two
10-inch logs and wrap tightly with plastic wrap. Refrigerate until
firm, about 1 hour.

3. Adjust oven racks to upper-middle and lower-middle positions and heat oven to 400 degrees. Line two baking sheets with
parchment paper. Slice logs into ¼-inch-thick coins and place on
prepared sheets. Bake until deep golden brown, 18 to 22 minutes,
switching and rotating sheets halfway through baking. Let crackers
cool on sheets for 3 minutes, then transfer to wire rack to cool
completely before serving.

TEST KITCHEN TIP
MAKING CHEESE COINS

After rolling and refrigerating
dough for 1 hour, slice logs into
¼-inch-thick coins and place
on prepared baking sheets.

Cheese Crisps (Frico)

1 pound
**Montasio or aged
Asiago cheese**

**INGREDIENT SPOTLIGHT
MONTASIO CHEESE**

Found mostly in specialty cheese shops, Montasio cheese is made from cow's milk and belongs to the big family of Alpine cheeses. It is made in only two regions of Italy—Friuli-Venezia Giulia and Veneto—and is said to be one of the many discoveries made by the local Benedictine monks back in the 1200s. Classified and sold according to its age, Montasio cheese can taste tangy and grassy (when aged for just a few months) or nutty with a deeper flavor (when aged 10 months or longer). Given its origin, it is not surprising that we found aged Asiago to be a good alternative in this recipe, as it is also a cow's-milk cheese from the northern Italian region of Veneto.

TO MAKE AHEAD
Frico can be stored in airtight container for up to 1 day.

✓ WHY THIS RECIPE WORKS This one-ingredient wonder is probably the simplest and most addictive snack you'll ever taste. A thin, golden, flavorful cheese crisp, traditionally made from Montasio cheese, *frico* is nothing more than grated cheese sprinkled into a pan, melted, and browned to form a crisp wafer. But though they might seem simple, coming up with a recipe that turned out perfect cheese crisps every time took a bit of work. First, we found it essential to use a nonstick skillet for easy release. Removing the pan from the heat after browning the first side allowed the frico to set up so it was easy to flip. The right level of heat was also key. When the pan was too hot, the cheese cooked too fast and turned bitter. But when cooked slowly over low heat, the cheese dried out. Using medium-high heat solved the problem. Aged Asiago is a good stand-in for Montasio; we don't recommend Parmesan because it gives the frico a salty, harsh taste.

1. Trim rind from Montasio then finely shred over small holes of box grater; you should have 4 cups shredded cheese. Sprinkle ½ cup cheese over bottom of 10-inch nonstick skillet. Cook over medium-high heat, shaking pan occasionally to ensure even distribution of cheese over pan bottom, until edges are lacy and toasted, about 4 minutes. As cheese begins to melt, use heatproof spatula to tidy lacy outer edges of cheese and prevent them from burning.

2. Remove pan from heat and allow cheese to set, about 30 seconds. Using fork and spatula, carefully flip cheese wafer over and return pan to medium-high heat. Cook until second side is golden brown, about 2 minutes. Slide cheese wafer out of pan onto plate. Repeat with remaining cheese. Serve.

**TEST KITCHEN TIP
MAKING FRICO**

Once first side is browned, remove pan from heat and let cool briefly. Then use fork and spatula to carefully flip cheese wafer over and return pan to medium-high heat to cook second side.

Pink Peppercorn–Crusted Goat Cheese Log

SERVES 8

1 teaspoon **fennel seeds**

4 teaspoons
whole pink peppercorns

Fresh thyme

1 (10-ounce) log **goat cheese**

¼ cup **extra-virgin olive oil**

INGREDIENT SPOTLIGHT
GOAT CHEESE

Goat cheese boasts an assertive, tangy flavor and a creamy yet crumbly texture that works well in many dishes, not just appetizers and salads. To find the best one, we tasted nine brands plain and baked. Our favorite goat cheese is **Laura Chenel's Chèvre Fresh Chèvre Log**, which tasters found to be "rich-tasting" with a "grassy" and "tangy" finish. This brand retained its "creamy, buttery" texture, even when baked.

TO MAKE AHEAD
Coated goat cheese can be refrigerated for up to 8 hours; drizzle with olive oil before serving.

⚗ WHY THIS RECIPE WORKS Goat cheese is often sold rolled in herbs, which is always more appealing than the naked log, but it seldom lives up to expectations. These herb coatings usually taste dusty or stale, plus they tend to overpower the flavor of the cheese itself. To liven up a plain log, we decided to make our own coating, starting with a base of bright, eye-catching pink peppercorns. Pink peppercorns have some of the familiar pungency of black peppercorns, but boast a much more delicate flavor that's a bit fruity and floral. Minced thyme and crushed fennel seeds rounded out the flavor of the coating and extra-virgin olive oil, drizzled over the top before serving, gave our attractive appetizer a little extra panache. Serve with baguette slices or crackers.

1. Toast fennel seeds in small skillet over medium heat, shaking pan, until first wisps of smoke appear, about 2 minutes. Let cool, then place in zipper-lock bag and crush coarsely with meat pounder. Place peppercorns in zipper-lock bag with fennel seeds and crush coarsely with meat pounder. Mince 4 teaspoons thyme, then combine with fennel seeds and peppercorns in shallow dish.

2. Roll goat cheese log in peppercorn mixture to coat thoroughly, pressing gently on mixture to adhere. Transfer goat cheese to serving platter, sprinkle with any remaining peppercorn mixture, and drizzle with olive oil. Serve.

TEST KITCHEN TIP PREPARING A GOAT CHEESE LOG

1. Place fennel seeds in zipper-lock bag and crush coarsely with meat pounder. Then add peppercorns to bag and crush again.

2. After combining fennel seeds, peppercorns, and minced thyme in shallow dish, roll goat cheese in mixture, pressing gently so it will adhere.

Feta-Dill Dip with Cucumber Chips

SERVES 8 TO 10

Fresh dill

1 **garlic clove**

2 cups (8 ounces) crumbled **feta cheese**

1 cup **plain Greek yogurt**

2 **seedless English cucumbers**

INGREDIENT SPOTLIGHT
FETA CHEESE

Within the European Union, only cheese made in Greece from a mixture of sheep's and goat's milk can be legally called feta, but most of the feta in American supermarkets is made from pasteurized cow's milk that has been curdled, shaped into blocks, sliced (*feta* is Greek for "slice"), and steeped in brine. Feta dries out quickly when removed from its brine, so always store it in the brine it's packed in (we do not recommend buying precrumbled feta, which is not only more expensive, but is also lacking in flavor and texture). Our favorite brand is **Mt. Vikos Traditional Feta**, which tasters found to be flavorful yet mild and to have a pleasing "creamy, crumbly" texture.

TO MAKE AHEAD

Dip can be refrigerated for up to 1 day; season with extra salt, pepper, and minced dill to taste before serving. Sliced cucumbers can be covered with wet paper towels and refrigerated for up to 8 hours before serving.

✔ **WHY THIS RECIPE WORKS** Supermarket and soup-mix dips might be convenient, but their lackluster, overprocessed taste hardly makes them worth the few seconds it takes to stir them together. We wanted a full-flavored, ultracreamy dip—and it had to be ready in almost no time. In the test kitchen, we often combine mayonnaise and yogurt for dips with the right balance of richness and tangy flavor, but now we wondered if both were really necessary. Eliminating the mayo and using whole-milk Greek yogurt gave us the body, richness, and velvety texture we were looking for. But our dip still needed a serious punch of flavor. We tried a variety of ingredients, but finally hit the jackpot with the combination of crumbled feta, fresh dill, and garlic. Mincing the garlic to a paste helped to mellow its raw, harsh taste and ensured it was evenly distributed. This dip is best made with whole Greek yogurt, although 2 percent can be used. Do not use 0 percent Greek yogurt as it will taste bland. Different brands of feta and Greek yogurt contain varying amounts of sodium so season this dip carefully.

1. Mince 2 tablespoons dill, mince garlic into paste, and combine with feta and yogurt in serving bowl. Season with salt and pepper to taste and refrigerate until needed.

2. Slice cucumbers thinly. Season chilled dip with salt and pepper to taste and adjust consistency with water as needed. Serve dip with cucumbers.

TEST KITCHEN TIP
MINCING GARLIC TO A PASTE

To make garlic paste, mince the garlic and then sprinkle it with a pinch of salt. Scrape the blade of a chef's knife across the garlic, mashing the garlic into the cutting board. After a few scrapes, the garlic will turn into a sticky paste.

Marinated Feta and Green Olives

SERVES 8

4 **garlic cloves**

1 **orange**

1¼ cups **extra-virgin olive oil**

½ teaspoon **red pepper flakes**

1 (12-ounce) block **feta cheese**

1½ cups assorted **pitted olives**

INGREDIENT SPOTLIGHT
EXTRA-VIRGIN OLIVE OIL

Extra-virgin olive oil has a uniquely fruity flavor that makes it a great choice for marinades, vinaigrettes, and pestos. Many things can impact the quality and flavor of olive oil, but the type of olives, the harvest (earlier means greener and more peppery; later, more golden and mild), and processing are the most important factors. The best-quality oil comes from olives picked at their peak and processed as soon as possible, without heat or chemicals (which can coax more oil from the olives but at the expense of flavor). In a tasting, our favorite oils were produced from a blend of olives and, thus, were well rounded. Our favorite brand is **Columela Extra Virgin Olive Oil** from Spain. This oil took top honors for its fruity flavor and excellent balance.

TO MAKE AHEAD
Marinated feta and olives can be refrigerated for up to 1 week; bring to room temperature before serving.

WHY THIS RECIPE WORKS We wanted a brightly flavored, chunky, spoonable mix of feta and olives worthy of any cocktail-hour spread. Thinly sliced garlic, orange zest, and a sprinkling of pepper flakes were all we needed to add complexity and brightness. The simple step of heating the mixture in oil deepened their flavors and the warm marinade easily infused the feta, which we'd cut into cubes, and chopped olives. Letting the feta and olives sit in the marinade for an hour allowed the flavors to meld. For more richness, we added a little extra oil just before serving. Don't use marinated olives here; choose only plain, brined olives, which can often be found in the deli section at most supermarkets. Serve with baguette slices, pita chips, or warm pita bread.

1. Thinly slice garlic, grate 1½ teaspoons orange zest, and combine with 1 cup oil and pepper flakes in small saucepan. Cook over low heat until garlic is softened, about 10 minutes.

2. Cut feta into ½-inch cubes and chop olives coarsely. Off heat, gently stir feta and olives into warm oil, cover, and let sit until mixture is room temperature, about 1 hour. Stir in remaining ¼ cup oil and serve.

TEST KITCHEN TIP
THINLY SLICING GARLIC

To slice garlic thinly, pick the flattest side of the peeled clove and hold it face down against the cutting board. Then carefully slice the garlic thinly, holding the clove securely. If there is a green stem in the middle of the clove, use the tip of a paring knife to pull it out.

Melted Brie with Honey and Herbs

SERVES 8

1 (8-ounce) wheel firm **Brie cheese**

2 tablespoons **honey**

Fresh thyme or rosemary

INGREDIENT SPOTLIGHT BRIE

Brie delivers an ultrarich, buttery interior, surrounded by a soft, pillowy rind that is also edible—and very flavorful. That's because the ripening process of Brie begins with the application of *Penicillium candidum*, a harmless white mold, on the surface of the immature cheese. Over the next several weeks, the mold grows into a tender white crust around the cheese that provides both textural contrast and concentrated flavor. The mold is also at work internally; as the cheese ages, the mold grows roots that make their way to the center of the Brie, breaking down the protein and softening the cheese as they go. If eating Brie out of hand, be sure that it is fully ripe; the center should feel soft and tender to the touch. But if using it in a recipe in which you are heating the cheese, be sure to use firm Brie.

✓ WHY THIS RECIPE WORKS Baked Brie is a cocktail party classic. Unfortunately, the puff pastry often turns out soggy on the bottom, and the assembled appetizer can hog the oven for up to 45 minutes, which is annoying when you're entertaining and need to get the entrée started. For our take on this dish, we ditched both the puff pastry and the oven. Microwaving the Brie ensured it delivered all the warm, gooey appeal of the original and guaranteed our appetizer was on the table in just a couple minutes. So the cheese could soften—but wouldn't ooze all over the serving platter—we cut the top rind off (starting with chilled Brie makes it easy to do this), but left the sides intact. To balance the rich flavor of the cheese, we drizzled honey over the top and sprinkled it with a bit of fresh thyme. And when the warm brie is served with crackers or a thinly sliced baguette, you won't miss the puff pastry.

1. Using serrated knife, carefully slice rind off top of Brie; leave rind on sides and bottom. Place Brie, cut side up, on microwave-safe platter.

2. Drizzle honey over top. Chop ½ teaspoon thyme and sprinkle over honey. Microwave until cheese is warm and just begins to bubble, 1 to 2 minutes. Serve immediately.

TEST KITCHEN TIP
CUTTING THE TOP RIND OFF BRIE

Using serrated knife, carefully slice top rind off wheel of chilled Brie, leaving rind on sides and bottom intact. Spray knife with vegetable oil spray to prevent sticking.

Herbed Ricotta Crostini

SERVES 8 TO 10

2 cups (1 pound)
whole-milk ricotta cheese

Fresh basil

2 **garlic cloves**

1 **lemon**

¼ cup **extra-virgin olive oil,**
plus extra for serving

2 (12-inch) **baguettes**

INGREDIENT SPOTLIGHT
RICOTTA CHEESE

Originally crafted from the whey byproduct of Romano cheese making, ricotta cheese has garnered fame as a delicious filling for baked pasta dishes, but it's also used as a simple rich spread, as in this easy appetizer. Our favorite brand of ricotta cheese is **Calabro**, which boasts a certain freshness that many commercial brands lack. It's made from fresh curds (drawn from nothing other than Vermont farm whole milk), skim milk, a starter, and a sprinkle of salt. If you can't find Calabro, look for another fresh ricotta without gums or stabilizers.

TO MAKE AHEAD
Ricotta can be left to drain, in refrigerator, for up to 1 day. Flavored ricotta can be refrigerated for up to 8 hours. Toasted bread can be stored in airtight container for up to 1 day.

✓ **WHY THIS RECIPE WORKS** Ricotta cheese doesn't have to be reserved for pasta dishes and casseroles. In this simple starter, it takes center stage as a creamy spread for crostini. Whole-milk ricotta delivered the clean, milky, rich flavor we were after, but the texture was a bit too watery. To remove some of the excess moisture, we put the ricotta in a coffee filter–lined strainer and let it sit for an hour. A little olive oil, stirred into the drained ricotta, added more richness and a luxurious texture, while garlic, lemon, and basil added bright, fresh flavors. To serve our herbed ricotta, we drizzled a bit more olive oil on top for extra richness and flavor, then served it with crisped baguette slices. We like to use baguettes for the crostini because their narrow shape makes toasts that are the perfect size. If you don't have coffee filters, you can use a triple layer of paper towels to drain the ricotta.

1. Line fine-mesh strainer with triple layer of coffee filters and place over bowl. Spoon ricotta into strainer, cover, and let drain for 1 hour.

2. Chop ⅓ cup basil and mince garlic. Grate 1 teaspoon zest from lemon, then squeeze for 1½ teaspoons juice. Combine drained ricotta, basil, garlic, lemon zest and juice, oil, ¼ teaspoon salt, and ¼ teaspoon pepper in bowl; refrigerate until needed.

3. Adjust oven rack 6 inches from broiler element and heat broiler. Slice baguettes on bias into ⅓-inch-thick pieces and lay on 2 rimmed baking sheets. Broil bread, 1 baking sheet at a time, until bread is golden brown on both sides, about 2 minutes per side.

4. Season ricotta with salt and pepper to taste and drizzle with extra oil as desired. Serve on crostini.

TEST KITCHEN TIP
DRAINING RICOTTA

Straight from the container, ricotta cheese can have a watery texture. To remove some of the excess moisture, drain the ricotta for at least 1 hour in a fine-mesh strainer lined with a triple-layer of coffee filters.

Crispy Spiced Chickpeas

SERVES 6

2 (14-ounce) cans **chickpeas**

1 teaspoon **smoked paprika**

1 teaspoon **sugar**

1 cup **olive oil**

INGREDIENT SPOTLIGHT
CANNED CHICKPEAS

Think all brands of canned chickpeas taste the same? So did we until we tried six brands in a side-by-side taste test. Once we peeled back the can lids and rinsed the beans, we found that many of them were incredibly bland or, worse yet, had bitter and metallic flavors. Tasters preferred those that were well seasoned and had a creamy yet "al dente" texture. **Pastene Chickpeas** came out on top for their clean flavor and firm yet tender texture.

TO MAKE AHEAD
Fried chickpeas can be stored in airtight container for up to 1 day.

WHY THIS RECIPE WORKS Chickpeas aren't just for salads and curries anymore. Tossed in oil and roasted, these beans become ultracrisp and deeply nutty in flavor, for the perfect cocktail snack. Most recipes call for roasting chickpeas in the oven, but we found they didn't become crisp enough. Switching to the stovetop and frying the chickpeas in olive oil gave us the big crunch factor we were seeking. A quick toss in a sweet and savory mixture of sugar and smoked paprika made our fried legumes incredibly addictive. Make sure to dry the chickpeas thoroughly with paper towels before placing them in the oil. In order to get crisp chickpeas, it is important to keep the heat high enough to ensure the oil is simmering the entire time. After about 12 minutes, test for doneness by removing a few chickpeas and placing them on a paper towel to cool slightly before tasting. If they are not quite crisp yet, continue to cook 2 to 3 minutes longer, checking occasionally for doneness.

1. Rinse chickpeas and pat thoroughly dry with paper towels. Combine paprika, sugar, ½ teaspoon salt, and ¼ teaspoon pepper in large bowl. Heat oil in large Dutch oven over high heat until just smoking.

2. Add chickpeas and cook, stirring occasionally, until deep golden brown and crisp, 12 to 15 minutes. Using slotted spoon, transfer chickpeas to paper towel–lined baking sheet to drain briefly, then toss with spices. Serve.

TEST KITCHEN TIP FRYING CHICKPEAS

1. Before frying the chickpeas, it is important to rinse off the canning liquid, then pat them dry thoroughly with paper towels to prevent splattering.

2. Once the oil in the Dutch oven is very hot, carefully add the chickpeas and let them fry until they are well browned and very crisp. Taste a few to test their doneness before removing them from the Dutch oven.

Serrano and Manchego Crostini with Orange Honey

SERVES 8

1 loaf
artisanal-style walnut or pecan bread

Fresh thyme

¼ cup **honey**

1 tablespoon **orange marmalade**

8 ounces thinly sliced **Serrano ham**

4 ounces thinly sliced **Manchego cheese**

INGREDIENT SPOTLIGHT
MANCHEGO CHEESE

This Spanish cheese has an ivory-yellow color and a dark brown or black rind marked with crosshatches. It tastes slightly sharp and full-flavored with a mild nuttiness. Manchego is made from sheep's milk and is sold at three stages of maturation: *fresco*, aged for 60 days; *curado*, aged for three to four months; and *viejo*, aged for nine months to a year. The majority of the Manchego available in the U.S. is curado, though any variety will work here.

TO MAKE AHEAD
Toasted bread can be stored in airtight container for up to 1 day. Assembled crostini should be eaten within several hours.

WHY THIS RECIPE WORKS Serrano ham, Manchego cheese, and artisanal bread come together to form an elegant yet stress-free Spanish-inspired starter. For the bread, we preferred a nutty artisanal loaf such as walnut or pecan with dried fruit. Toasting the bread intensifies its nutty flavor. Assembling the crostini is as easy as topping the bread with the ham and cheese and drizzling each toast with a mixture of honey, orange marmalade, and fresh thyme. The key to this recipe is using high-quality ingredients; be sure to use authentic Spanish Serrano ham and Manchego cheese. If you can't find walnut or pecan bread, any variety of hearty artisanal-style nut and fruit bread would work here.

1. Adjust oven rack 6 inches from broiler element and heat broiler. Slice bread into ¼-inch-thick pieces; cut larger pieces in half if necessary. Lay bread on 2 rimmed baking sheets. Broil bread, 1 baking sheet at a time, until golden brown on both sides, about 2 minutes per side.

2. Mince ½ teaspoon thyme and combine with honey and orange marmalade. Top toasts with ham and Manchego, then drizzle with honey mixture. Serve.

TEST KITCHEN TIP
TOASTING BREAD QUICKLY

For quickly crisped bread, we broil it rather than simply baking it. After laying the bread slices on a baking sheet, broil them until golden brown, about 2 minutes per side. This is long enough to dry them out and crisp the exterior.

Caprese Skewers

SERVES 8 TO 10

1 **garlic clove**

¼ cup **extra-virgin olive oil**

10 ounces **grape tomatoes**

8 ounces **baby mozzarella balls**

1 cup **fresh basil leaves**

INGREDIENT SPOTLIGHT
BABY MOZZARELLA BALLS

These smaller mozzarella balls, also sold as *ciliegini*, are about the size of a cherry tomato, but they deliver the same clean, milky flavor and tender texture as regular-size fresh mozzarella balls. They are generally packaged in water or whey, although sometimes they come in a marinade of olive oil, garlic, and other herbs or spices. For this recipe, we prefer the ciliegini packed in water or whey. You can find this cheese with the fresh mozzarella and other fresh cheeses in your supermarket.

TO MAKE AHEAD
Skewers can be assembled, covered, and refrigerated for up to 6 hours; bring to room temperature before drizzling with remaining garlic oil and serving.

✔ **WHY THIS RECIPE WORKS** To translate caprese salad into a festive appetizer, we used toothpicks to stand bite-size portions upright on a halved grape tomato pedestal. We found that a quick garlic-infused oil, which we made by mincing garlic into a paste and stirring it into fruity extra-virgin olive oil, boosted the flavor of our baby mozzarella balls and tomatoes, as did a bit of salt and pepper. Basil leaves, skewered onto our toothpicks whole, completed the caprese flavor profile and added a fresh touch. You will need about 30 sturdy wooden toothpicks for this recipe; avoid using very thin, flimsy toothpicks here. Placing a halved grape tomato, with its flat side facing down, on the bottom of the toothpick makes it easy to stand the skewers upright on a serving platter. You can use larger fresh mozzarella balls here, but they should be cut into ¾- to 1-inch pieces before marinating.

1. Mince garlic into paste (see page 10) and combine with oil in small bowl. Halve tomatoes, toss with mozzarella and 2 tablespoons garlic oil, and season with salt and pepper.

2. Skewer tomatoes, mozzarella, and basil leaves in following order from top to bottom: tomato half, basil leaf (folded if large), mozzarella ball, and tomato half with flat side facing down. Stand skewers upright on serving platter. Just before serving, drizzle remaining 2 tablespoons garlic oil over skewers, season with salt and pepper, and serve.

TEST KITCHEN TIP **MAKING CAPRESE SKEWERS**

1. After mincing garlic to paste and combining it with olive oil, toss halved tomatoes and mozzarella balls in garlic oil to infuse them with flavor.

2. Then skewer a tomato half, basil leaf (folded if large), mozzarella ball, and second tomato half, with flat side facing down, onto toothpick. Stand skewers on platter and drizzle with remaining garlic oil.

Endive Cups with Apples and Blue Cheese

SERVES 8 TO 10

⅓ cup **walnuts**

1 **Fuji, Braeburn, or Gala apple**

Fresh parsley

½ cup (2 ounces) crumbled **blue cheese**

1 tablespoon **extra-virgin olive oil**

2 (4-ounce) heads **Belgian endive**

INGREDIENT SPOTLIGHT
BELGIAN ENDIVE

Belgian endive, a member of the chicory family, has crisp, spear-shaped leaves that are white or pale yellow. It has a slightly bitter flavor. Though we generally think of endive in salads and appetizers similar to this one, it also takes well to the heat of the grill, which works to mellow its bitter flavor slightly. When shopping, look for heads of Belgian endive that are tight, firm, and blemish-free.

TO MAKE AHEAD
Endive cups can be assembled, covered, and refrigerated for up to 2 hours before serving.

✓ **WHY THIS RECIPE WORKS** Taking our inspiration from a popular hors d'oeuvre served at many wedding receptions, we used crisp, sturdy endive leaves as the serving vessel for a simple salad. For the filling, we tried a number of ingredients and finally settled on a mixture of apple, walnuts, and blue cheese. Tasters loved the combination of sweet, crisp apple, savory blue cheese, and toasted walnuts. In fact, they thought our endive cups were so flavorful that they didn't even require a full-on vinaigrette for more punch or brightness. All they needed was a drizzle of extra-virgin olive oil and a sprinkling of fresh parsley to bring all the components together. Be sure to buy medium heads of endive so they will have plenty of good-size leaves that won't be too small to fill, or too large to pick up once filled.

1. Toast and chop walnuts, core and chop apple, and chop 1 tablespoon parsley. Combine with blue cheese and oil; season with salt and pepper to taste.

2. Carefully remove leaves from endive and lay on large platter. Spoon about 1 tablespoon apple salad into each leaf. Serve.

TEST KITCHEN TIP
REMOVING ENDIVE LEAVES

Gently pull off endive leaves one at a time, continuing to trim root end as you work your way toward heart of endive.

Prosciutto-Wrapped Figs with Gorgonzola

SERVES 8 TO 10

16 **fresh figs**

2 ounces **Gorgonzola cheese**

1 tablespoon **honey**

8 thin slices (3 ounces) **prosciutto**

INGREDIENT SPOTLIGHT
GORGONZOLA

This Italian, cow's-milk blue cheese is creamy, rich, and assertive. Just a small amount adds big, potent flavor to many recipes. When it's the star of the show or one of just a handful of ingredients, we recommend seeking out authentic imported Gorgonzola at high-end or specialty markets. The inexpensive, mass-produced domestic Gorgonzola you'll find at the supermarket is somewhat salty and sour in flavor. When shopping, be sure to pass over the precrumbled Gorgonzola as well; it's often dry and flavorless.

TO MAKE AHEAD
Figs can be assembled, covered, and refrigerated for up to 8 hours; bring to room temperature before serving.

✓ WHY THIS RECIPE WORKS For this bite-size appetizer, we paired fresh, ripe figs with savory, salty prosciutto and bold, pungent blue cheese. We started by halving the figs so they'd be easy to eat, then wrapped them in thin slices of the ham. For more flavor and to play off the savory notes of the prosciutto, we added a bit of honey. Microwaving the honey briefly ensured it was easy to drizzle. For the cheese, tasters preferred creamy, assertive Gorgonzola. Small mounds of the cheese, placed in the center of each fig before adding the honey, offered a rich, bold counterpoint to the fig's tender flesh and sweet flavor. To guarantee the prosciutto stayed put, we stuck a toothpick through the center of each fig. Be sure to choose ripe figs for this recipe. They will not only taste best, but will also yield easily when mounding the blue cheese gently into the centers.

1. Remove stems from figs and cut in half lengthwise. Mound 1 teaspoon Gorgonzola into center of each fig half. Microwave honey in bowl to loosen, about 10 seconds, then drizzle over cheese.

2. Cut prosciutto slices in half lengthwise. Wrap prosciutto securely around figs, leaving fig ends uncovered. Secure prosciutto with toothpick and serve.

TEST KITCHEN TIP
ASSEMBLING PROSCIUTTO-WRAPPED FIGS

Mound 1 teaspoon of Gorgonzola in the center of each fig half, then drizzle honey over cheese. Wrap prosciutto around fig and secure with toothpick.

Stuffed Mushrooms with Boursin and Prosciutto

SERVES 8

24 (1½- to 2-inch wide)
white mushrooms

2 tablespoons **olive oil**

1 (5.2-ounce) package
Boursin Garlic and Fine Herbs cheese

3 thin slices (1 ounce) **prosciutto**

Fresh parsley or chives

INGREDIENT SPOTLIGHT
WHITE MUSHROOMS

The most common cultivated mushroom, the white button is recognizable for its pale color, broad cap, and stubby stem. Its flavor has been described as "mildly nutty" and its texture as "springy and moist." This variety of mushroom is quite versatile and great sautéed, grilled, roasted, and stuffed. When buying them for stuffing, look for those with caps that are 1½ to 2 inches in diameter. If they are much larger, they are too big to eat in a single bite, whereas smaller mushrooms are too hard to work with.

TO MAKE AHEAD
Stuffed mushrooms can be covered and held at room temperature for up to 2 hours before baking.

✔ **WHY THIS RECIPE WORKS** Stuffed mushrooms are iconic party fare, but they're a drag for the host, with their long ingredient lists and multistep procedures. We wanted flavorful stuffed mushrooms that were easy to assemble and ready in short order. Forgoing fussy stuffings that called for lots of chopping and sautéing, we filled our mushrooms with ultracreamy Boursin cheese, which also delivered potent herb and garlic flavors. For some crunch, we sprinkled a bit of chopped prosciutto over the top; after a quick stint in the oven, it crisped up nicely. Finally, to cut down on the baking time and to rid the mushrooms of excess moisture, we parcooked them in the microwave before filling them. This trick prevented our stuffed mushrooms from being soggy and ensured they hit the buffet table in no time. Be sure to buy mushrooms with caps that measure between 1½ and 2 inches in diameter; they will shrink substantially as they roast.

1. Adjust oven rack to lower-middle position and heat oven to 450 degrees. Remove stems completely from caps and discard, then toss caps with oil and season with salt and pepper. Lay mushrooms, gill side down, on plate lined with 2 layers of coffee filters. Microwave mushrooms until they release their moisture and shrink in size, about 10 minutes.

2. Line baking sheet with aluminum foil. Transfer mushrooms to prepared sheet, gill side up. Spoon Boursin into mushroom caps. Chop prosciutto and sprinkle over top.

3. Bake mushrooms until cheese is hot and prosciutto begins to crisp, 10 to 12 minutes. Transfer to serving platter. Chop 2 tablespoons parsley and sprinkle over top before serving.

TEST KITCHEN TIP
MICROWAVING MUSHROOMS

To remove the mushrooms' moisture, microwave them for 10 minutes before stuffing. Be sure to arrange the mushrooms gill side down so the moisture will drain away. Also, use coffee filters, not paper towels, to line the plate; the dyes on paper towels are not food-safe.

Warm Bacon-Wrapped Chorizo and Dates

SERVES 8 TO 10

18 slices **bacon**

18 **Medjool dates**

12 ounces **spicy chorizo sausage**

INGREDIENT SPOTLIGHT
MEDJOOL DATES

These plump, succulent, sweet dates are prized for their larger size. Traditionally, they are grown in Morocco and parts of the Middle East, but nowadays they are also cultivated in southern California, southern Florida, and Arizona. Medjool dates are usually packaged in small round plastic containers; at the supermarket you can find them with the specialty nuts and dried fruits, which is often located near the produce department.

TO MAKE AHEAD

Dates can be assembled, covered, and refrigerated for up to 1 day; bring to room temperature before baking.

WHY THIS RECIPE WORKS Virtually every bistro has a version of bacon-wrapped dates on its menu. But often, the dates are stuffed with nuts, which contribute a bit of crunch but not much else. For our take on this popular starter, we ditched the nuts and doubled up on the pork by reaching for smoky, spicy chorizo. Rather than stuff our dates, we halved them, placed a slice of the chorizo on top, then wrapped each one with half a slice of bacon. The dates and chorizo didn't need a long time in the oven—just 10 minutes to heat through—but the bacon was far from done by this point. We found that parcooking the bacon until some of the fat had rendered ensured everything was done and hot at the same time. Since half a strip of bacon was all we needed for each piece, we cut the bacon in half after parcooking it. It's important to fully skewer each bite with the toothpick so that it sits at an angle when placed on the baking sheet; this way, the bacon will get crispy on all sides.

1. Adjust oven racks to upper-middle and lower-middle positions and heat oven to 425 degrees. Line 2 rimmed baking sheets with aluminum foil. Lay bacon evenly over prepared sheets; bake until about half of fat has rendered but bacon is still pliable, 10 to 12 minutes. Let bacon cool slightly, then cut each slice in half crosswise.

2. Pit and halve dates. Slice chorizo on bias into ¼-inch-thick pieces. Top chorizo with date half, then wrap with piece of bacon. Secure bacon with toothpick and arrange on clean foil-lined baking sheet. Bake until bacon is crisp and chorizo is heated through, about 10 minutes. Let cool slightly before serving.

TEST KITCHEN TIP
ASSEMBLING BACON-WRAPPED CHORIZO AND DATES

Wrap each chorizo-date stack with 1 piece of bacon, secure bacon with toothpick, and place on foil-lined baking sheet.

Salami and Provolone–Stuffed Peppers

SERVES 6 TO 8

20 jarred **Peppadew peppers**

3 ounces **provolone cheese**

20 thin slices (3 ounces) **salami**

1 tablespoon **extra-virgin olive oil**

Fresh basil

INGREDIENT SPOTLIGHT
PEPPADEW PEPPERS

Peppadew is the brand name for the pickled grape-size red pepper known as Juanita. The plant was reportedly discovered in 1993 by Johannes Steenkamp, who found this spicy pepper growing in his garden in South Africa. To capitalize on the spicy flavor profile, he pickled the peppers in a simple sugar and vinegar mixture. Today, Peppadews are available in mild and hot varieties, as well as in a new yellow Goldew variety, which has less heat. In our testing we have found that the subtleties of the Peppadew flavor are lost in cooked sauces, so we recommend eating them raw on antipasto platters and in salads and relishes, or on cooked dishes such as pizza, where they can maintain their identity.

TO MAKE AHEAD
Peppers can be assembled, covered, and refrigerated for up to 1 day. Bring to room temperature and finish with oil and basil before serving.

✔ **WHY THIS RECIPE WORKS** Stuffed peppers are a mainstay on the antipasto table, and with good reason. They offer a bold flavor combination of salty, savory, and spicy, plus they come together in a snap. For ours, we decided to add sweetness to the mix, too, by using jarred Peppadew peppers. Tasters liked the duo of subtly tangy provolone and spicy salami for the filling. Folding each slice of salami in thirds before wrapping it around the cheese cubes ensured that both components were visible, and skewering the stuffed peppers with toothpicks made this flavor-packed snack easy to eat. A drizzle of extra-virgin olive oil and a sprinkling of fresh basil make these little bites an attractive addition to any party spread. Peppadews are available in mild and hot varieties, as well as in a new yellow Goldew variety, which has less heat; we prefer the spicy variety for this recipe. Peppadew peppers can be found in most grocery stores, but if you have a hard time finding them, pickled cherry peppers can be substituted. Be sure to get salami that is sliced very thin so that it will be easy to wrap around the cheese cubes and fit in the small opening of the peppers.

1. Rinse peppers and pat dry with paper towels. Cut provolone into ½-inch cubes. Fold each salami piece in thirds, wrap around cheese cubes, and stuff inside each pepper. Secure stuffed pepper with toothpick through side.

2. Arrange peppers on serving platter, drizzle with oil, and season with salt and pepper. Chop 2 tablespoons basil and sprinkle over top before serving.

TEST KITCHEN TIP **ASSEMBLING STUFFED PEPPERS**

1. Fold salami in thirds and wrap tightly around provolone cube. Repeat with remaining salami and provolone.

2. Stuff pepper with salami-wrapped cheese so that both cheese and salami peek out of pepper. Secure with toothpick.

Brie and Jam Phyllo Cups

SERVES 6

15 **mini phyllo shells**

4 ounces firm **Brie cheese**

4 teaspoons
**caramelized onion jam,
fig jam, or fig preserves**

Fresh chives or parsley

INGREDIENT SPOTLIGHT
MINI PHYLLO SHELLS

These small phyllo shells are the perfect starting point for a no-prep appetizer—they require no rolling, cutting, or shaping. You simply fill them and pop them into the oven. Once baked, they offer a shatteringly crisp crust with a light, flaky texture; in our testing, we had good luck using Athens Mini Fillo Shells. You can find them in the freezer section of your supermarket.

TO MAKE AHEAD
Phyllo cups can be assembled and held at room temperature for up to 2 hours before baking.

WHY THIS RECIPE WORKS Rich, buttery Brie and sweet yet savory caramelized onion jam come together in this elegant, easy appetizer. Mini phyllo shells, which require no prep whatsoever, made the perfect vessel to hold small cubes of Brie and teeny dollops of jam. Once baked in the oven, the phyllo was ultracrisp and the cheese was gooey. Though we loved the sweet and savory combination of caramelized onion jam paired with creamy Brie, fig jam worked equally well in place of the onion jam. A sprinkling of fresh chives added freshness and visual appeal to these savory little bites.

1. Adjust oven rack to middle position and heat oven to 350 degrees. Line rimmed baking sheet with parchment paper. Place phyllo shells on prepared sheet. Cut rind off cheese, then cut cheese into ½-inch cubes. Place 1 piece cheese inside each phyllo shell and top with about ¼ teaspoon jam.

2. Bake until cheese is melted and phyllo is golden, 6 to 8 minutes. Chop 1 tablespoon chives, sprinkle over top, and serve.

TEST KITCHEN TIP
CUTTING STICKY CHEESE

To prevent the Brie from smearing and sticking to the knife blade, simply spray the blade with vegetable oil spray.

Tomato Tartlets

SERVES 8

1 (9½ by 9-inch) sheet
puff pastry, thawed

1 **garlic clove**

1 tablespoon **extra-virgin olive oil**

3 **plum tomatoes**

½ cup (2 ounces) shredded
mozzarella cheese

½ cup (1 ounce) grated
Parmesan cheese

INGREDIENT SPOTLIGHT
PUFF PASTRY

Homemade puff pastry can be challenging and time-consuming to make, but fortunately premade puff pastry is available in virtually every supermarket and works really well in our easy appetizers and simple baked goods. In our testing, we had success using Pepperidge Farm Puff Pastry Sheets. Because the dough is frozen, it must be defrosted before you can use it; thawing the dough in the refrigerator overnight works best, although defrosting on the counter works fine. Depending on the temperature of your kitchen, it will take between 30 and 60 minutes. The dough should unfold easily once thawed, but still feel firm. If the seams crack, rejoin them by rolling them smooth with a rolling pin.

TO MAKE AHEAD
Tartlets can be assembled, covered, and refrigerated for up to 2 hours before baking.

✓ WHY THIS RECIPE WORKS For a fancy appetizer that pays homage to pizza night, we traded the dough for frozen puff pastry and created individual tomato and cheese tartlets. After cutting the puff pastry into tidy squares, we topped them with sliced tomatoes and shredded cheese. To give our sliced tomatoes a boost of flavor, we tossed them with garlic and extra-virgin olive oil and seasoned them with salt and pepper before laying them on the pastry. We opted for plum tomatoes because one slice fit perfectly on each square. As for the cheese, a mix of mozzarella and Parmesan gave us both rich, gooey bites and a salty, nutty flavor. Be sure to use a low-moisture supermarket mozzarella sold in block form, not fresh water-packed mozzarella, which will make the pastry soggy. To thaw frozen puff pastry, allow it to sit either in the refrigerator for 24 hours or on the counter for 30 minutes to 1 hour. If the dough becomes too warm and sticky to work with, cover it with plastic wrap and chill in the refrigerator until firm.

1. Adjust oven rack to middle position and heat oven to 400 degrees. Line two baking sheets with parchment paper. Roll puff pastry into 12-inch square, then cut into sixteen 3-inch squares. Transfer squares to prepared sheets.

2. Mince garlic into paste (see page 10) and combine with oil, ¼ teaspoon salt, and ⅛ teaspoon pepper in large bowl. Core tomatoes, slice ¼ inch thick, and toss gently with garlic oil. Place 1 tomato slice in center of each pastry square and sprinkle with mozzarella and Parmesan. Bake until pastry is golden, 20 to 25 minutes, switching and rotating sheets halfway through baking. Serve.

TEST KITCHEN TIP
CORING A TOMATO

To core a tomato, use the tip of a paring knife and cut around the stem, angling the tip of the knife slightly inward. When finished, you'll remove a cone-shaped piece of stem and hard core from the top.

Ham and Cheese Palmiers

SERVES 8 TO 10

1 (9½ by 9-inch) sheet
puff pastry, thawed

2 tablespoons **Dijon mustard**

Fresh thyme

4 ounces thinly sliced **deli ham**

1 cup (2 ounces) grated
Parmesan cheese

INGREDIENT SPOTLIGHT
DIJON MUSTARD

To be labeled Dijon, a mustard must adhere to the formula developed more than 150 years ago in Dijon, France: Finely ground brown or black mustard seeds are mixed with an acidic liquid (vinegar, wine, and/or grape must) and sparsely seasoned with salt and sometimes a hint of spice. Though it seems like the French might have the market cornered, when we sampled a variety of Dijon mustards, an American-made brand won over our tasters. "Potent" and "bold" **Grey Poupon Dijon Mustard** was our favorite for its "nice balance of sweet, tangy, and sharp" flavors.

TO MAKE AHEAD
Filled and rolled pastry log can be wrapped tightly in plastic wrap and refrigerated for up to 2 days or frozen for up to 1 month. If frozen, thaw completely before slicing. Baked palmiers can be held at room temperature for up to 8 hours.

✓ **WHY THIS RECIPE WORKS** Using store-bought puff pastry, rather than making our own from scratch, gave us an ultra-easy take on *palmiers*. But though they are usually a sweet treat, we opted for a savory palmier, perfect for an elegant dinner party. Once the frozen pastry was thawed, we brushed it with Dijon mustard, sprinkled it with minced thyme, and topped it with thinly sliced ham and Parmesan cheese. Then we rolled it into the classic palmier shape and set it to chill. When ready to serve, we simply sliced the log into thin pieces and baked them until golden brown and crisp. To thaw frozen puff pastry, allow it to sit either in the refrigerator for 24 hours or on the counter for 30 minutes to 1 hour.

1. Roll pastry into 12-inch square then brush with mustard. Mince 2 teaspoons thyme and sprinkle over top. Lay ham evenly over top to edge of pastry and sprinkle with Parmesan. Roll up both sides of dough until they meet in the middle. Wrap log of dough in plastic wrap and refrigerate until firm, about 1 hour.

2. Adjust oven rack to middle position and heat oven to 400 degrees. Line rimmed baking sheet with parchment paper. Trim ends of log, then slice into ⅓-inch-thick pieces with sharp knife. Lay on prepared sheet, spaced about 1 inch apart.

3. Bake until golden brown and crisp, about 25 minutes, rotating sheet halfway through baking. Transfer palmiers to wire rack and let cool completely before serving.

TEST KITCHEN TIP MAKING PALMIERS

1. After layering mustard, thyme, ham, and Parmesan on pastry, tightly roll up pastry from opposite sides until they meet in middle.

2. Once chilled, slice pastry into ⅓-inch-thick pieces. Be sure to slice dough evenly so that palmiers bake through at same rate.

Kielbasa Bites

SERVES 6 TO 8

1 (9½ by 9-inch) sheet
puff pastry, thawed

¼ cup **whole-grain mustard**

12 ounces **kielbasa sausage**

Fresh parsley

INGREDIENT SPOTLIGHT KIELBASA

Kielbasa, or Polish sausage, is a smoked pork sausage that sometimes has beef added and is usually sold precooked. We tested five national supermarket brands, and **Smithfield Naturally Hickory Smoked Polska Kielbasa** slightly outranked Wellshire Farms Polska Kielbasa, but both had a smoky, complex flavor and a hearty texture compared to the springy, hot dog–like textures of the others.

TO MAKE AHEAD

Kielbasa Bites can be assembled, covered, and refrigerated for up to 2 hours before baking.

✓ **WHY THIS RECIPE WORKS** We wanted a modern-day version of the retro classic pigs-in-a-blanket that kept all the flaky pastry and meaty bites, but was a touch more sophisticated. Slices of flavorful kielbasa sausage replaced the classic cocktail wieners, and whole-grain mustard stood in for the yellow variety. The kielbasa was overwhelmed when completely wrapped by store-bought puff pastry, so instead we took an open-faced approach. A mini muffin tin was the perfect vessel to cradle small squares of puff pastry in which we could dollop some mustard and gently sink a slice of kielbasa. In the oven, the flaky pastry perfectly puffed up around the sausage. With a garnish of fresh parsley, our update to this old-school standby of the party circuit was complete. To thaw frozen puff pastry, allow it to sit either in the refrigerator for 24 hours or on the counter for 30 minutes to 1 hour.

1. Adjust oven rack to middle position and heat oven to 400 degrees. Cut puff pastry into twenty-four 2½ by 1½-inch pieces. Firmly press pastry pieces into lightly greased 24-cup mini muffin tin.

2. Spoon ½ teaspoon whole-grain mustard into each muffin cup. Cut kielbasa into ½-inch-thick rounds and place on top of mustard. Bake until puffed and browned, 20 to 25 minutes, rotating muffin tin halfway through baking. Garnish with parsley leaves. Serve.

TEST KITCHEN TIP MAKING PUFF PASTRY CUPS

1. Lay pastry on cutting board and cut into twenty-four 2½ by 1½-inch pieces with sharp knife.

2. Firmly press 1 piece of dough into each cup of 24-cup mini muffin tin.

Naan Tarts with Artichokes, Pesto, and Goat Cheese

SERVES 6
1 tablespoon **olive oil**
2 (8-inch) **naan breads**
¾ cup (3 ounces) crumbled **goat cheese**
½ cup **prepared basil pesto**
½ cup **marinated artichokes**
Fresh parsley

INGREDIENT SPOTLIGHT PARSLEY

Though there are actually more than 30 varieties of parsley, you're likely to see only two at the market: curly-leaf and flat-leaf (also called Italian). Curly-leaf parsley is more popular, but in the test kitchen flat-leaf is by far the favorite; we find that it has a sweet, bright flavor that's much preferable to the bitter, grassy tones of curly-leaf. To help extend the shelf life of your parsley, gently rinse and dry it, then loosely roll it in a few sheets of paper towels. Put the roll of parsley in a zipper-lock bag and place it in your refrigerator's crisper drawer. Kept this way, your parsley will be fresh, washed, and ready to use for a week or longer.

TO MAKE AHEAD

Tarts can be assembled, covered, and held at room temperature for up to 2 hours before baking.

✓ WHY THIS RECIPE WORKS Baked *naan* (Indian flatbread) isn't just good for accompanying chicken curry or tikka masala. We used it as a prebaked crust on which we could build a savory appetizer pizza. Instead of reaching for standard pizza sauce and mozzarella, we combined store-bought pesto with tangy goat cheese to create a flavorful spread on which we layered marinated artichokes. Using jarred marinated artichokes rather than canned artichokes packaged in water or the plain frozen variety helped streamline our grocery list because they come already packed with flavor. The toppings needed only a brief stint in the oven to warm through, so we brushed the baking sheet with olive oil and baked the tart on the lowest rack to help the naan crisp up during the short baking time.

1. Adjust oven rack to lowest position and heat oven to 500 degrees. Brush rimmed baking sheet with oil and lay both naan on sheet. Combine goat cheese, pesto, and 1 tablespoon water, then spread evenly over naan, leaving ½-inch border around edge.

2. Drain artichokes, pat dry with paper towels, and scatter over top. Bake until naan are golden brown around edges, 8 to 10 minutes, rotating sheet halfway through baking. Sprinkle with parsley leaves, cut each tart into 6 wedges, and serve.

TEST KITCHEN TIP
LEAVING A BORDER ON NAAN TARTS

When spreading the filling over the top of the naan to make a tart, be sure to leave a ½-inch border at the edge for the crust.

Spicy Shrimp Cocktail Shooters

MAKES ABOUT 24

5 **limes**

Canned **chipotle chiles**

2½ cups **Bloody Mary mix**

¾ cup **tequila**

1 pound **extra-large shrimp**
(21 to 25 per pound)

Fresh cilantro

INGREDIENT SPOTLIGHT
BLOODY MARY MIX

Rather than load up the ingredient list for our shrimp cocktail shooters with numerous spices and dried herbs, plus an acidic, tomatoey base, we grabbed one ingredient off the shelf that had it all: Bloody Mary mix. Flavored with onion powder, paprika, and other spices and spiked with vinegar and lemon juice, this ingredient delivered a nicely bracing yet balanced mix of flavors, for a shooter that offered punch but didn't taste harsh.

TO MAKE AHEAD

Shrimp can be cooked, chilled, and refrigerated in airtight container for up to 1 day; toss with cilantro, salt, and pepper before serving. Tequila mixture can be refrigerated for up to 8 hours.

WHY THIS RECIPE WORKS Shrimp cocktail shooters, popular at many catered events, are a dressed-up take on a classic hors d'oeuvre. For our version of this lively starter, we began with tomato juice as the base, but it gave us a one-note, dull-tasting shooter. Luckily, we hit on an ingredient that packed a punch when it came to flavor and offered serious complexity: Bloody Mary mix. Preseasoned with spices and herbs, the Bloody Mary mix was just what we were looking for. For a bit more kick and smoky notes, we added some minced chipotles. Vodka gave our shooters an overly harsh taste, so we used tequila instead; it contributed a more mellow flavor, but still offered a subtly boozy taste. A healthy dose of lime juice livened up the mixture, and also tasted great squeezed over the shrimp, which we tossed with minced cilantro for freshness and a pop of color. You will need 24 plastic shot glasses for this recipe; look for them in party supply stores. To make a nonalcoholic version, substitute an equal amount of Bloody Mary mix for the tequila.

1. Squeeze 3 limes for 6 tablespoons juice, reserving spent lime rinds, and cut remaining 2 limes into wedges. Mince ½ teaspoon chipotle. Combine 2 tablespoons lime juice, chipotle, Bloody Mary mix, and tequila in pitcher and refrigerate until cold, about 1 hour.

2. Peel and devein shrimp (see page 37), leaving tails on. Stem and mince 2 tablespoons cilantro, reserving stems. Combine shrimp, remaining ¼ cup lime juice, lime rinds, reserved cilantro stems, 1 tablespoon salt, and 4 cups cold water in medium saucepan. Cook over medium heat, stirring occasionally, until shrimp are pink, firm to touch, and centers are no longer translucent, 8 to 10 minutes (water should be just bubbling around edge of pan; do not boil). Off heat, cover pan and let shrimp sit in broth for 2 minutes.

3. Fill medium bowl with ice water. Drain shrimp and add to ice water, discarding limes and cilantro, until no longer warm, about 3 minutes. Drain shrimp, pat dry with paper towels, and toss with minced cilantro, ½ teaspoon salt, and ½ teaspoon pepper; refrigerate until needed.

4. Season tequila mixture with salt and pepper to taste and pour evenly into 24 shot glasses. Arrange shrimp and lime wedges on edges of glasses and serve.

Citrusy Shrimp Cocktail

SERVES 4

1 pound **large shrimp**
(26 to 30 per pound)

---

3 **limes**

Fresh cilantro

---

1 **grapefruit**

---

1 **garlic clove**

¼ cup **hot pepper jelly**

INGREDIENT SPOTLIGHT
HOT PEPPER JELLY

In the test kitchen, we've found that hot pepper jelly is good for more than just spreading on biscuits and eating with cheese on crackers—it makes a great base for dressings, sauces, and glazes. Aside from its bold flavor, it has a thick texture, which gives dressings body and helps sauces and glazes stick to foods. Plus, it contains sugar, so it contributes a pleasant sweetness and helps foods caramelize nicely when cooked. In our testing, we had good luck using Stonewall Kitchen Hot Pepper Jelly.

TO MAKE AHEAD

Shrimp can be cooked, chilled, and refrigerated in airtight container for up to 1 day. Once assembled, shrimp cocktail can be covered and refrigerated for up to 4 hours before serving.

WHY THIS RECIPE WORKS Quick-cooking shrimp make this light, refreshing dish dotted with fresh grapefruit pieces and cilantro leaves a snap to prepare. Dressing our shrimp cocktail with an oil-based vinaigrette weighed down the components and dulled their flavors, so we looked for an alternative. We needed an ingredient with potent flavor and a bit of thickening power. After lots of testing, we ultimately landed on hot pepper jelly. Whisked together with 2 tablespoons of lime juice for a bit of acidity, the jelly gave us a flavorful dressing that clung perfectly to the shrimp and grapefruit, while still keeping the light, bright tones of our salad in place. To make the most of every ingredient, we added the spent lime halves and cilantro stems to our poaching liquid, which infused the shrimp with even more flavor.

1. Peel shrimp completely (including tails), devein (see page 37), and halve each shrimp lengthwise. Grate limes for 2 teaspoons zest, then squeeze for 6 tablespoons juice, reserving spent lime rinds. Stem ¼ cup cilantro leaves, reserving stems.

2. Combine shrimp, lime zest, ¼ cup lime juice, lime rinds, reserved cilantro stems, 2 teaspoons salt, and 4 cups cold water in medium saucepan. Cook over medium heat, stirring occasionally, until shrimp are pink, firm to touch, and centers are no longer translucent, 8 to 10 minutes (water should be just bubbling around edge of pan; do not boil). Off heat, cover pan and let shrimp sit in broth for 2 minutes.

3. Fill medium bowl with ice water. Drain shrimp and add to ice water, discarding limes and cilantro, until no longer warm, about 3 minutes. Drain shrimp and pat dry with paper towels; refrigerate until needed.

4. Cut away peel and pith from grapefruit, quarter, then slice each quarter crosswise into ¼-inch-thick pieces. Mince garlic and combine with remaining 2 tablespoons lime juice, hot pepper jelly, ¼ teaspoon salt, and ¼ teaspoon pepper in large bowl. Add shrimp, grapefruit, and cilantro leaves and toss gently. Season with salt and pepper to taste. Serve in small bowls or cups with cocktail forks.

Broiled Chipotle Shrimp

SERVES 8 TO 10

2 **limes**

Canned **chipotle chiles**

2 tablespoons **apple jelly**

1 tablespoon **honey mustard**

2 pounds **jumbo shrimp**
(16 to 20 per pound)

Fresh cilantro

INGREDIENT SPOTLIGHT
CHIPOTLE CHILES IN ADOBO SAUCE

Canned chipotle chiles are jalapeños that have been ripened until red and then smoked and dried. They are sold as is or packed in a tomato-based sauce. We prefer the latter since they are already reconstituted by the sauce, making them easier to use. Most recipes don't use an entire can, but these chiles can keep for two weeks in the refrigerator or be frozen. To freeze, puree the chiles and quick-freeze teaspoonfuls on a plastic wrap–covered plate. Once they are hard, peel them off the plastic and transfer them to a zipper-lock freezer bag. Then thaw what you need before use. They can be stored this way for up to two months.

TO MAKE AHEAD
Shrimp can be tossed with flavorings and refrigerated for up to 4 hours before broiling. Serve broiled shrimp immediately.

✔ WHY THIS RECIPE WORKS This sweet and spicy shrimp dish goes from the kitchen to the crowd in less than 10 minutes. Broiling our shellfish ensured it picked up some flavorful char, but we needed more than char to impress our tasters. A spicy chipotle-honey glaze added sweetness, plus smoky notes that echoed the char from the broiler, but the chipotles overpowered the honey. Switching to honey mustard helped, but tasters now found the glaze a bit too harsh. Scanning our pantry, we spotted a jar of apple jelly. Just 2 tablespoons lent ample sweetness and balanced the heat of the chipotle. As an added bonus, the sugar in the jelly helped the shrimp brown under the broiler, giving us even more appealing color. For a final flavor tweak, we stirred in a spoonful of lime juice. To boost the sweet and spicy flavors, we broiled our shrimp in half of the glaze, then tossed it in the remainder just before serving. A sprinkling of cilantro added freshness and ensured our tray of broiled shrimp looked as good as it tasted.

1. Squeeze 1 lime for 1 tablespoon juice and slice 1 lime into wedges for serving. Mince 2 teaspoons chipotle. Whisk lime juice, chipotle, apple jelly, honey mustard, and ½ teaspoon salt in small bowl.

2. Adjust oven rack 3 inches from broiler element and heat broiler. (If necessary, set upside-down rimmed baking sheet on oven rack to get closer to broiler element.) Peel and devein shrimp and pat dry with paper towels. Toss shrimp with half of lime-chipotle mixture and spread in even layer on aluminum foil–lined baking sheet. Broil shrimp until opaque and edges begin to brown, about 6 minutes.

3. Mince 2 tablespoons cilantro. Toss cilantro and remaining lime-chipotle mixture with cooked shrimp and transfer to serving platter. Serve with lime wedges.

TEST KITCHEN TIP
DEVEINING SHRIMP

To devein shrimp, hold shrimp firmly in one hand, then use paring knife to cut down back side of shrimp, about ⅛- to ¼-inch deep, to expose vein. Using tip of knife, gently remove vein. Wipe knife against paper towel to remove vein and discard.

Smoked Salmon Rolls

SERVES 6 TO 8

1 **lemon**

3 tablespoons
chive-flavored cream cheese

Fresh dill

8 ounces (9 slices)
smoked salmon

18 small sprigs **baby arugula**

INGREDIENT SPOTLIGHT
SMOKED SALMON

The translucent, mildly smoky slices piled on bagels and rye are produced by ever-so-slowly smoking (but not fully cooking) salt-cured fillets at roughly 60 to 90 degrees for at least 24 hours. This time-consuming process yields salmon that is glossy and silky, with a subtle smoke flavor. Once a specialty item, smoked salmon can now be found at most supermarkets. Note that you may need to buy more than one package of salmon; our recipe calls for 8 ounces, but most of the time, you'll see 4- or 6-ounce packages.

TO MAKE AHEAD
Salmon rolls can be assembled and refrigerated for up to 8 hours; garnish with arugula before serving.

☑ **WHY THIS RECIPE WORKS** We wanted to bring a classic brunch duo—savory smoked salmon and tangy cream cheese—to the cocktail hour in the form of a bite-size, hand-held appetizer. Though smoked salmon is paired with a variety of toppings (like red onions, chives, and dill) when served at breakfast, we were limited by our shopping list. Chive-flavored cream cheese provided both a rich, creamy texture and oniony flavor in just one ingredient. A bit of fresh dill and a splash of lemon juice brightened the cream cheese and complemented the flavor of the salmon. Rather than create the expected canapé, piling our ingredients on mini toasts, we spread the cream cheese mixture on pieces of smoked salmon and rolled them up. When cut in half and stood on end, they made the perfect one-bite appetizer. A sprig of fresh arugula added color to complete the presentation. Be sure to use good-quality, fresh smoked salmon for this recipe; it should glisten and have a bright, rosy color.

1. Squeeze lemon for ½ teaspoon juice, soften cream cheese, and combine with pinch pepper in bowl. Mince 1 teaspoon dill and stir into cream cheese mixture.

2. Lay salmon flat on cutting board and spread about 1 teaspoon cheese mixture evenly over top. Roll up salmon around cheese and slice in half with sharp knife. Stand each roll on its cut end and garnish with arugula sprigs. Serve.

TEST KITCHEN TIP **MAKING SMOKED SALMON ROLLS**

1. After spreading cream cheese mixture over slices of salmon, roll up salmon around filling. Using sharp knife, slice each salmon roll in half.

2. Stand up each roll on cut end and garnish with small sprig of arugula.

SAUSAGE AND TORTELLINI FLORENTINE SOUP

Simply Sensational Soups

42   Chai-Infused Butternut Squash Soup

44   Curried Cauliflower Soup | FAST RECIPE

45   Roasted Tomato Soup

47   Roasted Red Pepper Soup with Smoked Paprika and Basil Cream

49   Rustic Potato-Leek Soup with Kielbasa

50   Mushroom-Miso Soup with Shrimp and Udon | FAST RECIPE

52   Hearty Italian Chicken Soup with Kale and Gnocchi | FAST RECIPE

53   Thai Red Curry and Coconut Chicken Soup | FAST RECIPE

55   Black Bean Soup with Chorizo | FAST RECIPE

56   Sausage and Tortellini Florentine Soup | FAST RECIPE

57   Greek Egg and Lemon Soup with Rice | FAST RECIPE

Chai-Infused Butternut Squash Soup

SERVES 4 TO 6

3 pounds **butternut squash**

3 **scallions**

2 tablespoons **unsalted butter**

1 tablespoon packed **brown sugar**

1 **chai-flavored tea bag**

2 tablespoons **crème fraîche,**
plus extra for serving

INGREDIENT SPOTLIGHT CHAI TEA

Chai is a fragrant, Indian black-tea blend that often includes cardamom, cinnamon, clove, ginger, and black pepper, though the exact formulation can vary from brand to brand; you can find it in any supermarket. We tested this recipe with several brands of chai, both caffeinated and decaffeinated, and they all worked well.

✔ WHY THIS RECIPE WORKS Butternut squash soup derives much of its flavor from a wealth of warm spices. For big flavor from the outset, we started by sautéing our squash to coax out some of its natural sugars. Moving on to the spice factor, we landed on another ingredient that packed similar flavors: chai. By steeping a single chai-flavored tea bag with the squash while it simmered, we infused our soup with a melange of warm spice notes. (And our soup doesn't taste like tea. Really.) To finish, a modest amount of crème fraîche ensured a creamy texture and balanced the warm flavors with a tangy bite. If you can't find crème fraîche, substitute heavy cream; do not substitute sour cream.

1. Peel and seed squash, then cut into ½-inch pieces. Mince scallion whites and slice scallion greens; keep whites and greens separate. Melt butter in Dutch oven over medium-high heat. Add squash, scallion whites, sugar, ½ teaspoon salt, and ½ teaspoon pepper and cook, stirring occasionally, until squash is softened and lightly browned, about 8 minutes.

2. Stir in 5 cups water, scraping up any browned bits. Add tea bag. Bring to boil, then reduce heat to medium-low and simmer gently until squash is tender, about 20 minutes.

3. Remove tea bag. Working in batches, process soup in blender until smooth, 1 to 2 minutes. Return soup to clean pot and whisk in crème fraîche. Add extra water as needed to adjust soup's consistency. Heat mixture gently over low heat until hot (do not boil). Season with salt and pepper to taste. Sprinkle individual portions with scallion greens before serving.

TEST KITCHEN TIP CUTTING UP BUTTERNUT SQUASH

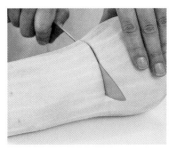 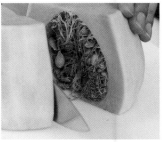

1. Peel squash using vegetable peeler, then cut in half, separating neck from curved bottom. Cut top into ½-inch pieces.

2. Cut bottom in half; scoop out and discard seeds. Then cut bottom halves into ½-inch pieces.

Curried Cauliflower Soup

SERVES 4 TO 6

1 head **cauliflower**
(2 pounds)

3 **scallions**

Fresh ginger

1 (14-ounce) can
light coconut milk

2 teaspoons **curry powder**

4 cups **chicken broth**

INGREDIENT SPOTLIGHT
CURRY POWDER

Though blends can vary dramatically, curry powders come in two basic styles—mild or sweet and a hotter version called Madras. The former combines as many as 20 different ground spices, herbs, and seeds, the staples being turmeric (which accounts for the traditional ocher color), coriander, cumin, black and red pepper, cinnamon, cloves, fennel seeds, cardamom, ginger, and fenugreek. Our favorite brand is **Penzeys Sweet Curry Powder**, which tasters praised for being neither too sweet nor too hot, and for delivering a balance of "sweet" and "earthy" notes.

✓ WHY THIS RECIPE WORKS We combined two ingredients popular in Indian cuisine—curry and cauliflower—in this boldly flavored soup. Coconut milk is often used in Indian cooking for its richness and sweetness, but regular coconut milk overpowered the delicate flavor of the cauliflower. Switching to the light variety worked better; it still provided a nice creaminess and subtle coconut flavor, but now we were able to taste the curry and cauliflower. Fresh ginger added spicy warmth to our soup, but it was calling out for more aromatic presence. Chopped scallion whites did the trick, plus we could use the scallion greens to garnish our finished soup. We'd typically cook the curry powder, ginger, and scallion whites in oil to deepen their flavors, but a portion of the coconut milk worked well in its place and kept our ingredient list down.

1. Core and coarsely chop cauliflower. Mince scallion whites and slice scallion greens; keep whites and greens separate. Grate 1 tablespoon ginger. Heat ¼ cup coconut milk in Dutch oven over medium heat until simmering. Add scallion whites, ginger, and curry powder and cook until fragrant, about 30 seconds. Stir in broth, cauliflower, ¼ teaspoon salt, and ¼ teaspoon pepper and simmer until cauliflower is tender, 15 to 20 minutes.

2. Working in batches, process soup in blender until smooth, 1 to 2 minutes. Return soup to clean pot and whisk in remaining 1½ cups coconut milk. Add extra water as needed to adjust soup's consistency. Heat mixture gently over low heat until hot (do not boil). Season with salt and pepper to taste. Sprinkle individual portions with scallion greens before serving.

TEST KITCHEN TIP CUTTING UP CAULIFLOWER

1. Pull off any leaves, then cut out cauliflower core using paring knife.

2. Separate florets from inner stem using tip of paring knife. If florets are too big, continue to cut them smaller as needed.

Roasted Tomato Soup

SERVES 4 TO 6

2 (28-ounce) cans
whole peeled tomatoes

1½ tablespoons packed
brown sugar

1 **onion**

2 tablespoons **unsalted butter**

2 cups **chicken broth**

⅓ cup **Boursin Garlic
and Fine Herbs cheese,**
plus extra for serving

**INGREDIENT SPOTLIGHT
CANNED WHOLE TOMATOES**

We prefer to use canned whole tomatoes in this recipe because they're easy to drain and roast in the oven (which deepens their flavor) and their soft texture turns especially silky when pureed in the soup. We found that whole tomatoes packed in juice rather than puree have a livelier, fresher flavor. Our top-rated brand is **Muir Glen Organic Whole Peeled Tomatoes**, which boast a "vibrant" flavor and "nice firm texture."

✓ **WHY THIS RECIPE WORKS** For a creamy tomato soup that's big on flavor (but not on ingredients) we started by roasting canned whole tomatoes to deepen their flavor and add complexity. Sprinkling them with a tablespoon of brown sugar aided in browning. Next we went to the stove and cooked a chopped onion with a bit of brown sugar until it was caramelized and intensely flavored. Most creamy tomato soup recipes call for heavy cream, but we were looking for more bang for our buck. Boursin cheese, which is flavored with garlic and herbs, was perfect; it gave our pureed soup a creamy, luxurious texture, and a bold aromatic presence as well. Make sure to use canned whole tomatoes that are packed in juice, not puree; you will need some of the juice to make the soup.

1. Adjust oven rack to upper-middle position and heat oven to 450 degrees. Drain tomatoes, reserving 3 cups juice. Lay tomatoes on aluminum foil–lined baking sheet and sprinkle with 1 tablespoon sugar. Bake until tomatoes begin to brown, about 30 minutes.

2. Finely chop onion. Melt butter in large saucepan over medium-high heat. Add onion, ¼ teaspoon salt, and ¼ teaspoon pepper and cook until just beginning to brown, about 5 minutes. Stir in remaining ½ tablespoon sugar and cook until onions are golden, about 5 minutes. Stir in ¼ cup broth and cook until onions are softened and deep golden brown, 3 to 5 minutes.

3. Add remaining 1¾ cups broth, reserved 3 cups tomato juice, and roasted tomatoes with any accumulated juice. Bring to boil, then reduce heat to medium-low and simmer gently until flavors meld, about 10 minutes.

4. Working in batches, process soup in blender until smooth, 1 to 2 minutes. Return soup to clean pot and whisk in Boursin. Heat mixture gently over low heat until hot (do not boil). Season with salt and pepper to taste. Sprinkle individual portions with extra Boursin before serving.

Roasted Red Pepper Soup with Smoked Paprika and Basil Cream

SERVES 4 TO 6
6 **red bell peppers**
½ cup **heavy cream**
¾ teaspoon **smoked paprika**
4 cups **chicken broth**
Fresh basil
2 **cheddar-flavored cheese sticks** (about ½ ounce), plus extra for serving

INGREDIENT SPOTLIGHT
CHEESE STICKS

These fancy little cheese sticks, found in the cheese section of most grocery stores, are a clever addition to our roasted red pepper soup. Taking a cue from old-fashioned soup recipes that use bread as a thickener, we found that these breadsticks made of sourdough and spiked with aged cheddar and Asiago added body to our soup, along with a wallop of cheese flavor. They also make a nice garnish for individual bowls of soup. We had good luck using John Wm. Macy's Original Cheddar CheeseSticks in this and other recipes in this book.

✓ **WHY THIS RECIPE WORKS** We wanted a red pepper soup with vibrant color and equally bold flavor. Jarred roasted red peppers didn't deliver big flavor, so we roasted our own peppers; smoked paprika played up their charred notes. To help thicken our soup, we decided to toss some of the crunchy cheese sticks we were serving on the side into the blender when we processed it. The soup now had more body, plus a boost of flavor. For a fancy finish, we whipped up an easy basil-infused cream, which we dolloped over individual servings.

1. Core and flatten bell peppers (see page 201). Adjust oven rack 6 inches from broiler element and heat broiler. Lay half of peppers on aluminum foil–lined baking sheet and broil until skin is charred but flesh is still firm, 8 to 10 minutes. Transfer peppers to bowl, cover, and let steam until skins peel off easily, about 10 minutes. Repeat with remaining peppers. Using paring knife, scrape off charred skin from softened peppers and discard. Chop peppers coarsely.

2. Cook 1 tablespoon cream and paprika together in large saucepan over medium-high heat until fragrant, about 30 seconds. Stir in broth and peppers and simmer until flavors meld, about 10 minutes.

3. Chop ¼ cup basil, combine with remaining 7 tablespoons cream in blender, and blend until cream is whipped to stiff peaks, 15 to 20 seconds. Transfer to bowl and season with salt and pepper to taste.

4. Working in batches, process soup and cheese sticks together in blender until smooth, 1 to 2 minutes. Return soup to clean pot and reheat gently over low heat. Season with salt and pepper to taste. Dollop individual portions with basil whipped cream and serve with extra cheese sticks.

TEST KITCHEN TIP
ROASTING RED PEPPERS

Place flattened peppers, tops, and bottoms on an aluminum foil–lined baking sheet; broil until skins are charred and puffed, 8 to 10 minutes. Transfer to bowl, cover, and let them steam for 10 minutes. Scrape off skins, keeping paper towels handy as this task can be messy.

Rustic Potato-Leek Soup with Kielbasa

SERVES 6 TO 8

4 pounds **leeks**

6 tablespoons **unsalted butter**

1¼ pounds **medium red potatoes**

1 tablespoon **all-purpose flour**

5¼ cups **chicken broth**

8 ounces **kielbasa sausage**

INGREDIENT SPOTLIGHT
RED POTATOES

Not all potatoes are created equal when it comes to many recipes, including this soup; we found that red potatoes worked best here. The reason is that they hold their shape better when simmered in the soup (thanks to their low-starch and high-moisture content), whereas other potatoes, such as Yukon Golds and russets, break down more quickly.

✓ WHY THIS RECIPE WORKS Most potato-leek soups suffer from two problems: They are severely lacking in leek flavor and they're not hearty enough. Our soup had to taste like leeks, not thin mashed potatoes, and it had to be thick and satisfying. For intense flavor, we started with 4 pounds of leeks and cooked them down in a covered pot until they were meltingly tender and offered a concentrated onion flavor. We left the leeks in fairly large pieces so that they not only contributed flavor but texture as well. For spoonable pieces of potato, we cut them into ¾-inch chunks; red potatoes were the best at holding their shape and didn't become waterlogged during cooking. Finally, we stirred in slices of kielbasa for big, meaty bites. Use medium red potatoes measuring 2 to 3 inches in diameter.

1. Trim and discard root and dark green leaves from leeks. Halve leeks lengthwise, then slice crosswise into 1-inch-thick pieces. Wash cut leeks thoroughly using salad spinner (see page 207). Melt butter in Dutch oven over medium heat. Stir in leeks, cover, and cook, stirring occasionally, until leeks are tender but not mushy, 15 to 20 minutes. Cut potatoes into ¾-inch pieces.

2. Stir in flour and cook for 1 minute. Gradually whisk in broth, smoothing out any lumps. Stir in potatoes. Cover, bring soup to boil, then reduce heat to medium-low and simmer gently until potatoes are almost tender, 5 to 7 minutes.

3. Slice kielbasa into ½-inch-thick rounds, add to soup, and let heat through, about 1 minute. Off heat, let stand until potatoes are tender and flavors meld, 10 to 15 minutes. Season with salt and pepper to taste and serve.

TEST KITCHEN TIP PREPPING LEEKS

1. Trim and discard root and dark green leaves. Cut trimmed leek in half lengthwise.

2. Slice or chop leek as desired; rinse thoroughly in salad spinner to remove dirt and sand.

Mushroom-Miso Soup with Shrimp and Udon

SERVES 4

12 ounces **udon noodles**

3 ounces (3 cups) **baby spinach**

10 ounces **shiitake mushrooms**

3½ cups **vegetable broth**

12 ounces **extra-large shrimp**
(21 to 25 per pound)

½ cup **white miso**

INGREDIENT SPOTLIGHT
UDON NOODLES

Udon are popular Japanese wheat noodles that have a hearty flavor and chewy texture. They can be purchased both fresh and dried, and although both will work in this recipe, we found the dried noodles to be more common. If using fresh noodles, the noodle cooking time may be shorter in step 1.

✓ WHY THIS RECIPE WORKS We wanted a deeply-flavored soup inspired by Japanese cuisine, but it couldn't take all day to make or rely on a two-page list of ingredients. Our first step was finding a substitute for the homemade *dashi*, a traditional Japanese soup base made of bonito flakes and seaweed. Store-bought vegetable broth worked well, providing vegetal notes and a subtle sweetness. To up the broth's savory depth, we added thin-sliced shiitakes and let them simmer for 10 minutes. White miso paste, stirred in at the end of cooking, provided complexity and a hint of nuttiness to our broth. Finished with chewy udon noodles, tender shrimp, and fresh spinach, this satisfying soup offered serious depth of flavor in a short amount of time. Don't be tempted to salt the noodle cooking water in step 1 or else the soup may taste too salty. See page 157 for more information on miso.

1. Bring 4 quarts water to boil in large pot. Add noodles and cook until al dente, 4 to 5 minutes. Drain noodles and rinse under warm water to remove excess starch. Drain noodles well, then portion into individual serving bowls and top with spinach.

2. Meanwhile, stem and thinly slice mushrooms. Bring broth, 2 cups water, and mushrooms to boil in large saucepan over medium–high heat. Reduce heat to medium–low and simmer gently until flavors meld and mushrooms are tender, about 10 minutes.

3. Peel shrimp completely (including tails), devein (see page 37), and cut each shrimp into 3 pieces. Whisk miso and ½ cup water together in bowl. Off heat, stir miso mixture and shrimp into soup, cover, and let sit until shrimp are just pink, 1 to 2 minutes. Ladle soup into prepared bowls and serve.

TEST KITCHEN TIP
MAKING SOUP WITH UDON

To make soup with udon, first boil, then rinse the noodles with warm water. Portion them right into the serving bowls and top them with spinach. To serve, simply ladle the hot broth over the top to gently wilt the spinach and reheat the noodles.

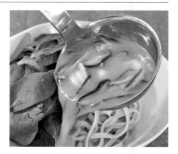

Hearty Italian Chicken Soup with Kale and Gnocchi

SERVES 4 TO 6

1 (14.5-ounce) can
diced fire-roasted tomatoes

3 tablespoons
prepared basil pesto,
plus extra for serving

4 cups **chicken broth**

1 pound
**boneless, skinless
chicken breasts**

8 ounces **kale**

8 ounces
vacuum-packed gnocchi

INGREDIENT SPOTLIGHT
CHICKEN BROTH

Starting with a high-quality store-bought chicken broth is paramount when making simple soups. Our favorite brand in the test kitchen is **Swanson Chicken Stock**, which was praised for its "complex," "chicken-y," "roasted" flavor. Tasters described this brand as having "nice depth" that was reminiscent of "turkey stuffing" and "dark meat."

✓ WHY THIS RECIPE WORKS Think a full-flavored chicken and vegetable soup is off the table when trying to keep groceries to a minimum? Think again. Our Italian-style chicken soup delivers big flavor and hearty bites, with just six ingredients. Fire-roasted tomatoes offered brightness and smoky complexity; after cooking them briefly, we mashed them and stirred in chicken broth for the base of our soup. Cooking the chicken was as easy as poaching it in our tomatoey broth before shredding the meat. Chopped kale added heartiness. Looking to add some aromatic backbone, we sautéed our tomatoes in pesto rather than olive oil alone. The result? Soup with complexity and depth. Adding more pesto at the end provided a big garlic-and-basil kick. Finally, we bypassed the usual potatoes and pasta in favor of light, pillowy gnocchi, which needed just a few minutes in the broth to become perfectly tender. We strongly prefer the flavor and texture of vacuum-packed gnocchi found in the pasta aisle; we don't recommend substituting refrigerated or frozen gnocchi.

1. Drain tomatoes, reserving juice. Heat 1 tablespoon pesto in large saucepan over medium-high heat until simmering. Add tomatoes and cook, stirring occasionally, until tomatoes are dry and darken slightly, about 5 minutes. Mash tomatoes with potato masher or back of spoon until crushed. Stir in broth and reserved tomato juice.

2. Trim chicken, add to soup, and bring to simmer. Reduce heat to medium, cover, and simmer gently until chicken registers 160 degrees, 10 to 12 minutes. Transfer chicken to cutting board, let cool slightly, then shred into bite-size pieces.

3. Stem and chop kale, then stir it into soup. Return soup to simmer and cook, stirring occasionally, until kale is wilted and just tender, 5 to 8 minutes. Add gnocchi and simmer until tender and floating, about 4 minutes.

4. Add chicken, any accumulated juices, and remaining 2 tablespoons pesto to saucepan and cook until heated through, about 1 minute. Season with salt and pepper to taste. Serve, passing extra pesto separately.

Thai Red Curry and Coconut Chicken Soup

SERVES 4 TO 6

1 (14-ounce) can **coconut milk**

3 tablespoons **Thai red curry paste**

1 pound **boneless, skinless chicken breasts**

8 ounces **white mushrooms**

⅔ cup **long-grain white rice**

Fresh cilantro

INGREDIENT SPOTLIGHT
THAI RED CURRY PASTE

Thai red curry paste combines a number of hard-to-find, authentic Thai aromatics—including galangal (Thai ginger), bird's eye chiles, lemongrass, and kaffir lime leaves—in one, easy-to-find ingredient. Look for it in the international section of the supermarket alongside other Thai ingredients. (See page 149 for more information on Thai green curry paste, which uses green chiles, not red chiles.)

WHY THIS RECIPE WORKS For an authentic-tasting Thai red curry soup, we skipped over the homemade Thai curry paste, which can be a time-consuming and ingredient-intensive endeavor, and reached for the store-bought variety. Using a generous amount of curry paste and blooming, or cooking, it in some coconut milk worked to deepen its flavor so we didn't need any extra aromatics. To infuse our chicken with rich flavor and ensure moist meat, we poached the chicken breasts right in the broth before shredding the meat; this also upped the savory notes of the broth. Stirring more coconut milk in at the end preserved its clean, fresh taste. To round out our Thai-style soup, we added white rice and mushrooms to the mix. You can substitute light coconut milk in this recipe, if desired.

1. Cook 1 tablespoon coconut milk, curry paste, and ½ teaspoon salt together in large saucepan over medium-high heat until fragrant, about 30 seconds. Stir in 4 cups water and ¾ cup coconut milk. Trim chicken and add to soup. Bring soup to simmer, then reduce heat to medium, cover, and simmer gently until chicken registers 160 degrees, 10 to 12 minutes. Transfer chicken to cutting board, let cool slightly, then shred into bite-size pieces.

2. Trim and quarter mushrooms, then add to soup with rice. Cover and continue to simmer soup gently until rice is tender, about 15 minutes. Stir in chicken with any accumulated juices and remaining coconut milk. Chop 2 tablespoons cilantro and stir into soup. Serve, topping individual portions with whole cilantro leaves.

TEST KITCHEN TIP
INFUSING THAI-STYLE CHICKEN SOUP WITH BIG FLAVOR

1. Cooking the curry paste with a little coconut milk provides a flavorful base for the broth.

2. Stirring some coconut milk into the soup at the end gives it a clean, fresh coconut flavor.

Black Bean Soup with Chorizo

SERVES 4 TO 6

8 ounces **chorizo sausage**

1 teaspoon **garam masala**

4 (15-ounce) cans **black beans**

3 cups **chicken broth**

1 cup **fresh salsa**

Fresh cilantro

INGREDIENT SPOTLIGHT
BLACK BEANS

Buying a good brand of black beans can make all the difference in this simple soup. Our favorite brand is **Bush's Best Black Beans**. These beans have a "clean," "mild," and "slightly earthy" flavor and "firm," "almost al dente" texture that tasters praised.

✔ WHY THIS RECIPE WORKS It doesn't take armfuls of ingredients and lots of time to make a great black bean soup—if you have the right tricks up your sleeve. To avoid the long process of soaking and simmering dried black beans, we went straight for the canned variety. Sliced chorizo and garam masala (a mixture of warm spices such as cumin, coriander, cinnamon, and cardamom) added flavor and richness without an exhausting amount of prep. Cooking the chorizo first provided rendered fat that we could use to bloom the garam masala and deepen its flavor, leading to a speedy soup with surprising intensity. Smashing a portion of the beans gave our soup body. Finally, for brightness, we stirred in a cup of fresh tomato salsa. Now our black bean soup offered all the rich, hearty flavor we expected—but in a fraction of the time and without much work. See page 286 for more information on garam masala.

1. Halve chorizo lengthwise then slice crosswise into ¼-inch-thick pieces. Cook chorizo in large saucepan over low heat until fat begins to render, 3 to 5 minutes. Increase heat to medium and cook until chorizo is lightly browned, about 5 minutes. Transfer chorizo to bowl.

2. Add garam masala to fat left in pot and cook over medium-high heat until fragrant, about 30 seconds. Rinse beans, then stir into pot with broth. Bring soup to simmer, scraping up any browned bits. Cook, stirring occasionally, until flavors meld, about 10 minutes.

3. Off heat, mash some beans against side of pot with spoon to thicken soup. Stir in chorizo and salsa and let heat through, about 1 minute. Chop ½ cup cilantro and stir into soup. Season with salt and pepper to taste. Serve.

TEST KITCHEN TIP
MASHING BEANS FOR A THICKER SOUP

Mashing some beans against the side of the pot helps to thicken the soup and add body, without the need for any extra ingredients.

Sausage and Tortellini Florentine Soup

SERVES 6

12 ounces
hot Italian sausage

2 **garlic cloves**

4 cups **V8 juice**

3 cups **chicken broth**

8 ounces **dried tortellini**

6 ounces (6 cups) **baby spinach**

INGREDIENT SPOTLIGHT V8 JUICE

Tasting brighter than canned tomatoes and more interesting than plain tomato juice, V8 juice gives this soup a bright, tomatoey taste, along with a big kick of vegetable flavor.

WHY THIS RECIPE WORKS A rich-tasting Italian soup, complete with pasta and lots of vegetables, not only requires loads of veggies, but lots of time for all the prep. For a streamlined version, we started with store-bought chicken broth and looked for ways to enhance its flavor. Hot Italian sausage offered big, meaty bites and a subtle heat. Browning the sausage, then sautéing minced garlic in the rendered fat, ramped up the flavor of our soup. While we didn't have room in our ingredient list for celery, onions, and tomatoes, we were able to get the flavors of all three in one supermarket staple that required no chopping whatsoever: V8 juice. The juice lent our soup a savory, vegetal backbone, and stirring some baby spinach in at the end added color and freshness. Sweet Italian sausage can be substituted in this recipe, if desired. You can substitute one 9-ounce package of fresh cheese tortellini for this recipe; the simmering time will be the same.

1. Brown sausages in large saucepan over medium heat, about 5 minutes. Mince garlic, add to pot, and cook until fragrant, about 30 seconds. Stir in V8 juice and broth, bring to gentle simmer, and cook until sausages are no longer pink in center, 12 to 15 minutes.

2. Transfer sausages to cutting board, let cool slightly, then slice into ½-inch-thick pieces. Meanwhile, stir tortellini into soup and simmer, stirring occasionally, until tender, about 10 minutes.

3. Return sliced sausage to pot and let heat through, about 1 minute. Off heat, stir in spinach and let wilt, about 1 minute. Season with salt and pepper to taste and serve.

TEST KITCHEN TIP COOKING SAUSAGE FOR SOUP

1. Browning sausage in the pot before adding the broth lends important flavor to the soup. Pork sausage is able to brown on its own, without any oil.

2. After the sausages are poached in the soup, transfer them to a cutting board and slice them into bite-size pieces, then add them back to the pot.

Greek Egg and Lemon Soup with Rice

SERVES 6 TO 8

2 **lemons**

4 **green cardamom pods**

8 cups **chicken broth**

½ cup **long-grain white rice**

2 **large eggs**
plus 2 **large yolks**

1 **scallion**

INGREDIENT SPOTLIGHT
CARDAMOM PODS

The delicate complexity of cardamom makes it a popular spice in several cuisines, most notably Middle Eastern, Indian, and Scandinavian. Green cardamom is the most commonly found variety in the United States and has a piney, sweet, and floral flavor with a peppery, warm finish. Crushing the pods gently (using the bottom of a skillet or broad side of a chef's knife) helps release their flavor before cooking. You can find cardamom with the other herbs and spices in well-stocked supermarkets or gourmet markets; you can also order it online.

✓ **WHY THIS RECIPE WORKS** Rich, soft, and luxurious, with a full, lemony flavor, this simple soup proves you don't need a lot of ingredients for a stand-out dish. After lots of testing, we discovered that adding two extra egg yolks was the trick to giving this soup a rich, silky texture. To prevent the eggs from curdling in the soup, we added a little hot broth to the eggs (a technique knowing as tempering), which worked to raise their temperature and help stabilize them for a smooth soup. For prominent, but not overwhelming, lemony flavor, we simmered strips of lemon zest in the broth; adding cardamom to the mix added warm, floral notes and complexity to this uncomplicated soup.

1. Remove 12 strips zest from lemons using vegetable peeler, then squeeze lemons for ¼ cup juice. Lightly crush cardamom pods. Bring broth to boil in large saucepan over high heat. Reduce heat to medium–low and add lemon zest, cardamom, rice, and 1½ teaspoons salt. Simmer until rice is tender, about 15 minutes. Using slotted spoon, remove cardamom and zest strips, then return broth to boil.

2. Whisk eggs, yolks, and lemon juice in medium bowl until combined. Reduce heat to low, and, whisking constantly, slowly pour 2 cups broth into egg mixture to temper. Pour tempered egg–broth mixture back into saucepan and cook, stirring constantly, until soup is slightly thickened and wisps of steam appear, 4 to 5 minutes (do not simmer). Divide soup among individual serving bowls. Slice scallion thinly and sprinkle over soup. Serve immediately.

TEST KITCHEN TIP TEMPERING EGGS

1. To temper the eggs so that they won't curdle when added to the hot soup, whisk them together in a bowl. Then, slowly whisk in some hot broth to gently warm them.

2. Once the eggs have been warmed, slowly whisk them into the pot and continue to cook gently, stirring constantly, until the soup is thickened.

CHEDDAR CRUMB–CRUSTED CHICKEN WITH SAUTÉED CHERRY TOMATOES

Chicken

60   Sweet and Spicy Glazed Chicken | FAST RECIPE

61   Porcini-Rubbed Chicken | FAST RECIPE

63   Prosciutto-Wrapped Chicken with Sage | FAST RECIPE

64   Cranberry-Ginger Chicken Bake | FAST RECIPE

65   Cheddar Crumb–Crusted Chicken with Sautéed Cherry Tomatoes | FAST RECIPE

67   Unstuffed Chicken Cordon Bleu | FAST RECIPE

68   Skillet Monterey Chicken with Rice | FAST RECIPE

69   Spicy Braised Chicken Abruzzo | FAST RECIPE

70   Chicken Pizzaiola with Pasta | FAST RECIPE

72   Chicken and Couscous with Dried Fruit and Smoked Almonds | FAST RECIPE

73   Simple Stuffed Chicken Breasts with Boursin

75   Pan-Roasted Chicken with Tomatoes and Olives

76   Pan-Roasted Chicken with Potatoes

77   Lemon-Braised Chicken with Fennel

79   Coconut-Curry Braised Chicken

81   Five-Spice Chicken Thighs with Snap Peas

82   Mustard-Glazed Drumsticks | FAST RECIPE

84   Braised Chicken with Onions, Mushrooms, and Bacon

85   Chicken Meatballs with Tomatoes and Cilantro

86   Aloha Kebabs with Sesame Rice | FAST RECIPE

89   Chicken and Sun-Dried Tomato Burgers | FAST RECIPE

91   Rustic Chicken and Brie Tart | FAST RECIPE

Sweet and Spicy Glazed Chicken

SERVES 4

1 tablespoon **vegetable oil**

4 (6- to 8-ounce)
**boneless, skinless
chicken breasts**

2 **oranges**

Fresh ginger

½ cup **hot pepper jelly**

Fresh cilantro

**INGREDIENT SPOTLIGHT
BONELESS, SKINLESS CHICKEN
BREASTS**

Boneless chicken breasts are an easy-to-find, no-fuss, virtually ready-to-use product, which makes them standard fare in many homes. To see if there was a difference in flavor among the various options at the supermarket, we tasted several brands. We sprinkled the chicken breasts with salt (except for one kosher brand, which is salted during processing) and baked them. In the end, tasters preferred **Bell & Evans Air Chilled Boneless, Skinless Chicken Breasts**, which they praised for having a "mega-juicy and tender" texture and "clean and chicken-y" taste.

✓ **WHY THIS RECIPE WORKS** Adding a glossy, flavor-packed glaze is a sure-fire way to liven up weeknight chicken breasts, but ensuring that the glaze clings to the meat is a challenge—and most glazes are often too sweet. But before we could tackle the flavor of our dish, we focused on the chicken. Browning the chicken first not only added flavor, but it also gave the glaze a rough surface to adhere to. To save time, we browned just one side before adding the sauce and letting the chicken cook through. Moving on to the glaze, we liked fresh-squeezed orange juice for a bold, bright backdrop. To cut the sweetness, we turned to an ingredient that contributed savory depth, heat, and thickening power: hot pepper jelly. A bit of fresh ginger added more spice, and minced cilantro offered a fresh finish and pop of color.

1. Heat oil in 12-inch skillet over medium–high heat until shimmering. Trim chicken, pat dry with paper towels, and season with salt and pepper. Lay chicken in skillet and cook until well browned on first side, 6 to 8 minutes.

2. Squeeze oranges for 1 cup juice, grate 1 tablespoon ginger, and whisk together with jelly. Flip chicken over, add orange juice mixture, and reduce heat to medium. Simmer chicken gently until it registers 160 degrees and sauce thickens slightly, 12 to 15 minutes. Transfer chicken to platter and cover to keep warm.

3. Increase heat to medium–high and simmer sauce until reduced to ½ cup, about 4 minutes. Mince 1 tablespoon cilantro and stir into sauce. Season with salt and pepper to taste and pour over chicken. Serve.

TEST KITCHEN TIP GRATING GINGER

1. To peel ginger easily, use edge of spoon to scrape away thin, brown skin. Don't use a knife; it will dig into ginger.

2. To grate ginger, use rasp-style grater or small holes of box grater.

Porcini-Rubbed Chicken

SERVES 4

¾ ounce
dried porcini mushrooms

1 tablespoon **vegetable oil**

4 (6- to 8-ounce)
**boneless, skinless
chicken breasts**

½ cup **dry sherry**

1 cup **heavy cream**

Fresh tarragon

INGREDIENT SPOTLIGHT
DRY SHERRY

Sherry, a wine fortified with brandy, can be made dry or sweet, with flavors that range from nutty and figlike to citrusy or melon-y. It originated in the Spanish city of Jerez de la Frontera and is still made in the region, but nowadays you can also find domestic brands. Recipes more often call for dry sherry, since sweet sherry concentrates in flavor as it cooks down and this sweetness can overpower other flavors. Our favorite brand is **Lustau Palo Cortado Península Sherry**, which offered "nice warmth" when sampled in savory recipes. Stay away from "cooking sherry" because it is loaded with salt and artificial caramel flavoring that will ruin the flavor of the food.

WHY THIS RECIPE WORKS The key to this chicken and mushroom dish was in rethinking the mushrooms. For a new take on classic mushroom cream sauce, we jettisoned the fresh mushrooms in favor of dried porcini. Though we usually rehydrate this umami-rich ingredient before using it in recipes, we decided to take advantage of its dried form and use it as a rub for our chicken breasts. A few pulses in the spice grinder turned the porcini into a fine powder, which easily clung to the chicken and added deep flavor upon searing. A rich yet delicate sherry-cream sauce enhanced with fresh tarragon completed the dish. Don't be alarmed by the color of the porcini powder; it darkens significantly as it cooks and will appear blackened, but it won't taste burned.

1. Adjust oven rack to upper-middle position and heat oven to 400 degrees. Process porcini in spice grinder to fine powder, about 15 seconds. Combine with ½ teaspoon salt and ½ teaspoon pepper; spread into shallow dish.

2. Heat oil in 12-inch skillet over medium-high heat until shimmering. Trim chicken, pat dry with paper towels, and coat completely with porcini mixture. Lay chicken in skillet and cook until lightly browned on both sides, 6 to 8 minutes.

3. Transfer chicken to baking sheet and bake until it registers 160 degrees, 10 to 12 minutes. Transfer chicken to platter and cover to keep warm.

4. Add sherry to now-empty skillet and simmer over medium heat, scraping up any browned bits, until reduced to ¼ cup, about 2 minutes. Whisk in cream and simmer until sauce thickens and measures ⅔ cup, 3 to 5 minutes. Mince 1 tablespoon tarragon, stir into sauce, and season with salt and pepper to taste. Pour over chicken and serve.

TEST KITCHEN TIP
PROCESSING PORCINI

To turn dried porcini into a flavorful dry rub, process them into a fine powder using a spice grinder. Alternatively, you can use a mortar and pestle to grind them to a powder.

Prosciutto-Wrapped Chicken with Sage

SERVES 4

4 (6- to 8-ounce)
**boneless, skinless
chicken breasts**

8 thin slices (3 ounces) **prosciutto**

1 tablespoon **olive oil**

Fresh sage

1 **lemon**

4 tablespoons **unsalted butter**

INGREDIENT SPOTLIGHT SAGE

Earthy, musky sage goes especially well with mild-tasting chicken and pork. Though it is available in three dried forms—ground, rubbed (finely chopped), and coarsely crumbled—we prefer fresh sage in any recipe where its flavor is at the forefront. Because of its "cottony texture" when raw, fresh sage should always be cooked.

WHY THIS RECIPE WORKS For a streamlined take on classic chicken saltimbocca, the Italian dish that marries tender chicken with rich prosciutto and woodsy sage, we ditched the annoying toothpicks typically required to hold the ham in place and simply wrapped it around the chicken breasts. Browning the breasts before transferring them to the oven worked to crisp the prosciutto and helped fuse it to the chicken. Finishing the chicken in the oven allowed it to cook through gently and ensured that the prosciutto didn't burn or become leathery in the meantime. To up the elegance quotient of our easy dinner, we created an effortless browned butter sauce and amped up its flavor with chopped sage and a splash of lemon juice. Make sure to buy prosciutto that is thinly sliced, not shaved.

1. Adjust oven rack to upper-middle position and heat oven to 400 degrees. Trim chicken, pat dry with paper towels, and season with salt and pepper. Slightly overlap 2 slices of prosciutto on cutting board and lay 1 chicken breast in center; fold prosciutto over chicken. Repeat with remaining prosciutto and chicken.

2. Heat oil in 12-inch nonstick skillet over medium-high heat until just smoking. Lay chicken in skillet and cook until lightly browned on both sides, 6 to 8 minutes. Transfer chicken to baking sheet and bake until it registers 160 degrees, 10 to 12 minutes. Transfer chicken to platter and cover to keep warm.

3. Mince 2 teaspoons sage and squeeze lemon for 1 teaspoon juice. Melt butter in now-empty skillet over medium-high heat, swirling occasionally, until butter is browned and has nutty aroma, about 1½ minutes. Off heat, stir in sage and cook until fragrant, about 1 minute. Stir in lemon juice, pinch salt, and ⅛ teaspoon pepper. Drizzle sauce over chicken and serve.

TEST KITCHEN TIP
WRAPPING CHICKEN IN PROSCIUTTO

To wrap prosciutto around chicken, place 1 breast in center of 2 overlapping slices of prosciutto. Fold prosciutto ends over chicken and press gently to adhere.

Cranberry-Ginger Chicken Bake

SERVES 4

1 **orange**

Fresh thyme

2 **garlic cloves**

Fresh ginger

2 (14-ounce) cans
whole berry cranberry sauce

4 (6- to 8-ounce)
**boneless, skinless
chicken breasts**

INGREDIENT SPOTLIGHT
WHOLE BERRY CRANBERRY SAUCE

Rustic, chunky whole berry cranberry sauce offers both an appealing texture and true cranberry flavor. Adding orange zest and juice and fresh thyme helps to add freshness and rid it of its canned flavor. We much prefer whole berry cranberry sauce to its jellied counterpart, which simply contributes a sugary taste and minimal cranberry flavor to recipes.

✓ WHY THIS RECIPE WORKS When it comes to convenience, it's hard to find an easier dish to pull together than a good old-fashioned chicken bake. Unfortunately, this dish has suffered the stigma of many pantry-ready meals: tinny, canned flavor in a watered-down, ersatz sauce. Our solution was to start with a base of intense flavor—sweet-tart cranberry sauce—that we could amp up with aromatics and herbs for a sauce that tasted out of this world, not out of a can. Orange zest and juice balanced the cranberries' tartness, and garlic and ginger added a touch of heat. We started the sauce in a skillet by blooming, or deepening, the flavor of the aromatics in a bit of water, then we added the orange zest and juice and cranberry sauce, plus some minced thyme, and reduced it all until slightly thickened. With such an intensely flavored sauce, browning the chicken was an unnecessary step; we simply poured the sauce over our seasoned chicken breasts and slid the casserole dish into the oven. Twenty minutes later, we had a deceptively easy, yet robustly flavored, dinner that was ready for the table.

1. Adjust oven rack to top position and heat oven to 450 degrees. Grate orange for ½ teaspoon zest, then squeeze for ½ cup juice. Mince 2 teaspoons thyme. Mince garlic, grate 2 teaspoons ginger, and combine with 2 tablespoons water in medium saucepan. Cook over medium heat until fragrant, about 1 minutes.

2. Stir orange zest and juice, thyme, cranberry sauce, ½ teaspoon salt, and ¼ teaspoon pepper into saucepan. Simmer, stirring often, until mixture is thickened, about 10 minutes.

3. Trim chicken, pat dry with paper towels, and season with salt and pepper. Lay chicken in 13 by 9-inch baking dish and pour cranberry mixture over top. Bake until chicken registers 160 degrees, about 20 minutes. Serve.

TEST KITCHEN TIP
GRATING ORANGE ZEST

Using rasp-style grater or small holes of box grater, grate orange peel from surface of fruit. Do not grate bitter, white pith under peel.

Cheddar Crumb–Crusted Chicken with Sautéed Cherry Tomatoes

12 **cheddar-flavored cheese sticks** (3 ounces)

2 tablespoons **olive oil**

4 (6- to 8-ounce) **boneless, skinless chicken breasts**

12 ounces **cherry tomatoes**

1 **garlic clove**

Fresh basil

INGREDIENT SPOTLIGHT
CHERRY TOMATOES

A supermarket staple, these small, round tomatoes are reliably good throughout the year, offering a sweet flavor and juicy texture, even in the winter months. They are good either raw or cooked. Don't confuse cherry tomatoes with grape tomatoes; cherry tomatoes are larger, with a rounder shape, and are juicier, which is why we prefer them in this recipe.

✓ WHY THIS RECIPE WORKS This riff on chicken Parmesan delivers the same intense cheesy flavor, tender bites of chicken, and crisp crust, but without the vat of oil or long list of ingredients. Our first step was finding a coating that baked up crisp in the oven and offered big flavor. We tried a number of the usual suspects (panko, bread crumbs, crushed Melba toast), but they lacked the flavor and texture of a fried crust. We found our solution in a cocktail-hour favorite: crunchy, cheddar-spiked cheese sticks. Crushed into fine crumbs and tossed with a tablespoon of oil, the crumbs formed a crisp, intensely flavored crust on the chicken that browned beautifully in the oven. Baking the crumb-coated chicken elevated on a wire rack ensured it stayed crisp all over, even on the bottom. Rather than weigh the chicken down with a heavy tomato sauce and ruin its crunchy exterior, we reached for cherry tomatoes and sautéed them with garlic and basil for a simple side dish. For more information on cheese sticks, see page 47.

1. Adjust oven rack to middle position and heat oven to 475 degrees. Spray wire rack with vegetable oil spray and set in rimmed baking sheet lined with aluminum foil. Crush cheese sticks into fine crumbs, toss with 1 tablespoon oil, and spread into shallow dish.

2. Trim chicken, pat dry with paper towels, season with salt and pepper, and coat with crumbs, pressing to adhere. Lay chicken on prepared rack. Bake until it registers 160 degrees, about 20 minutes.

3. Meanwhile, halve tomatoes. Heat remaining 1 tablespoon oil in 10-inch nonstick skillet over medium-high heat until shimmering. Add tomatoes and cook, stirring often, until softened and juicy, 2 to 4 minutes. Mince garlic, stir into skillet, and cook until fragrant, about 30 seconds. Chop 2 tablespoons basil, stir into tomatoes, and season with salt and pepper to taste. Serve with chicken.

TEST KITCHEN TIP
CRUSHING CHEESE STICKS INTO CRUMBS

To crush cheese sticks into even crumbs, place them in sealed zipper-lock bag and pound gently using meat pounder, rolling pin, or bottom of skillet.

Unstuffed Chicken Cordon Bleu

SERVES 4

1 tablespoon **olive oil**

4 (6- to 8-ounce)
**boneless, skinless
chicken breasts**

2 tablespoons **Dijon mustard**

4 slices (4 ounces) **deli ham**

1 cup (4 ounces) shredded
Gruyère cheese

15 **Ritz crackers**
(1¾ ounces)

**INGREDIENT SPOTLIGHT
RITZ CRACKERS**

Ritz crackers are known for their rich, buttery flavor and light, crisp texture—which, when crushed, made them the perfect topping for our Unstuffed Chicken Cordon Bleu. Though other toppings, like panko bread crumbs and fresh bread crumbs, provided a big crunch, they offered little in the way of flavor. We figured why bother doctoring them with butter or seasoning when easy-prep Ritz crackers, all on their own, offered not only crunch but a rich taste as well.

✔ **WHY THIS RECIPE WORKS** Most chicken cordon bleu recipes call for pounding the chicken breasts before stuffing them with ham and cheese, rolling them up, coating them with bread crumbs, and baking or frying the lot—not exactly weeknight-friendly dining. For an easier path to cordon bleu heaven, we arranged chicken breasts on a sheet pan and topped them with slices of ham and grated Gruyère for an inside-out approach that kept the work to a minimum. Brushing the chicken with mustard first added a tangy sharpness and also provided the "glue" to help the ham and cheese stay in place. For the crunchy, golden bread-crumb topping, we tested a variety of candidates, eventually ditching the panko and fresh bread crumbs in favor of crumbled Ritz crackers, which stayed crisp and offered a rich, buttery flavor. After about 20 minutes in a hot oven, our streamlined chicken cordon bleu delivered all the rich flavors and appealing textures of the authentic versions—but without all the work. Swiss cheese can be substituted for the Gruyère.

1. Adjust oven rack to lower-middle position and heat oven to 475 degrees. Brush rimmed baking sheet with oil. Trim chicken, pat dry with paper towels, season with pepper, and arrange on prepared sheet.

2. Spread mustard over top of chicken, then top each breast with 1 slice ham, folded in half, and ¼ cup Gruyère. Coarsely crush crackers and sprinkle over top, pressing on crumbs to adhere.

3. Bake until chicken registers 160 degrees, about 20 minutes, rotating sheet halfway through baking. Serve.

TEST KITCHEN TIP MAKING UNSTUFFED CHICKEN CORDON BLEU

1. After seasoning chicken, spread with Dijon mustard. Top with 1 slice ham, folded in half, and ¼ cup shredded Gruyère.

2. Sprinkle crushed Ritz crackers over top of cheese, pressing on crumbs to adhere. Bake chicken for 20 to 25 minutes.

Skillet Monterey Chicken with Rice

SERVES 4

1 cup **long-grain white rice**

4 slices **bacon**

4 (6- to 8-ounce)
**boneless, skinless
chicken breasts**

1 (11-ounce) can **Mexicorn**

½ cup **barbecue sauce,**
plus extra for serving

1 cup (4 ounces) shredded
Monterey Jack cheese

INGREDIENT SPOTLIGHT MEXICORN

This common supermarket item combines tender kernels of corn with pieces of red and green bell pepper, for a Mexican-inspired three-in-one ingredient that can add color, crunch, and flavor to many dishes. Look for it with the canned corn or Mexican ingredients.

✓ WHY THIS RECIPE WORKS We needed a strong punch of flavor to elevate this chicken and rice dish above the ordinary. Adding bacon to the mix was a good jumping-off point; it gave us a meaty, savory foundation. Plain white rice was fairly boring, so to add some interest, we stirred in a can of Mexicorn, which is a blend of sweet corn with red and green bell peppers. With this one ingredient, we'd added a pop of color and some texture to our chicken and rice. Though our dish was on the upswing, test after test yielded dry, flavorless chicken. Clearly, we needed a sauce to add some moisture and impart flavor. The smokiness of the bacon led us to brainstorm about other smoky, savory ingredients. In the end, we landed on barbecue sauce, which added tangy sweetness to the chicken and kept it moist. With a topping of melted Monterey Jack cheese, which we sprinkled over the chicken once it was cooked, we had a boldly flavored new dish guaranteed to wake up the weeknight dinner hour.

1. Rinse rice and combine with 1¾ cups water and ⅛ teaspoon salt in bowl. Cover and microwave until liquid is absorbed, about 10 minutes. Fluff rice with fork.

2. Meanwhile, chop bacon and cook in 12-inch nonstick skillet over medium heat until crisp, 5 to 7 minutes; transfer to paper towel–lined plate. Trim chicken, pat dry with paper towels, and season with salt and pepper. Heat bacon fat left in pan over medium heat until just smoking. Brown chicken lightly on both sides, about 5 minutes; transfer to plate.

3. Drain Mexicorn and stir into skillet with 1 cup water and microwaved rice, scraping up any browned bits. Nestle chicken and any accumulated juices into rice and brush chicken with ¼ cup barbecue sauce. Simmer gently, covered, until rice is tender and chicken registers 160 degrees, 10 to 15 minutes.

4. Off heat, brush chicken with remaining ¼ cup barbecue sauce and top with cheese. Cover and let sit until cheese melts, 2 to 3 minutes. Transfer chicken to platter. Gently fold bacon into rice and season with salt and pepper to taste. Serve with extra barbecue sauce.

Spicy Braised Chicken Abruzzo

SERVES 4

2 tablespoons **olive oil**

4 (6- to 8-ounce)
**boneless, skinless
chicken breasts**

2 **red bell peppers**

¼ cup jarred
sliced hot cherry peppers,
plus 2 teaspoons brine

3 **garlic cloves**

¾ cup **chicken broth**

INGREDIENT SPOTLIGHT
SLICED HOT CHERRY PEPPERS

In the test kitchen, we're big fans of this convenience product. We use the pickled peppers to add robust flavor, heat, and texture to dishes, but we also often include the brine to sauces to punch up the piquant, vinegary notes and add brightness. Plus, because these peppers are sold presliced, we don't even have to drag out a cutting board to use them.

✔ WHY THIS RECIPE WORKS The Abruzzo region in Italy, well known for its spicy cuisine and liberal use of hot peppers, is the inspiration for this lively dish, which gets its flavor from two different kinds of peppers. Pickled hot cherry peppers provided a complex heat and tang, while fresh red bell peppers added sweetness and a slight crunch. To reinforce the hot pepper flavor, we added some of the vinegary brine to the sauce. A few cloves of garlic offered warm complexity and contributed even more heat. To cook the chicken, we braised it right in the spicy sauce, which simultaneously kept the chicken moist and ensured it took on big flavor. This dish is not for the faint of heart (or palate); its sweet-hot pepper combo packs a wallop.

1. Heat 1 tablespoon oil in 12-inch skillet over medium-high heat until just smoking. Trim chicken, pat dry with paper towels, and season with salt and pepper. Brown chicken lightly on both sides, about 5 minutes; transfer to plate.

2. Core peppers and cut into ¼-inch strips (see page 201). Heat remaining 1 tablespoon oil in now-empty skillet over medium-high heat until shimmering. Stir in bell peppers and cherry peppers and cook until bell peppers begin to soften, about 5 minutes. Mince garlic, stir into skillet, and cook until fragrant, about 30 seconds.

3. Stir in broth and cherry pepper brine. Nestle chicken and any accumulated juices into skillet. Cover and simmer gently until chicken registers 160 degrees, 10 to 15 minutes.

4. Transfer chicken to platter and cover to keep warm. Return sauce to simmer and cook until slightly reduced, 2 to 4 minutes. Season with salt and pepper to taste. Pour over chicken and serve.

TEST KITCHEN TIP
**ADDING CHERRY PEPPER
BRINE FOR FLAVOR**

To brighten up the flavor of our sauce, we added 2 teaspoons of the brine that the sliced hot cherry peppers are packed in. While the peppers themselves offer heat and flavor, this liquid contributes acidity and brightness.

Chicken Pizzaiola with Pasta

SERVES 4

3 cups **tomato sauce**

1 cup (2 ounces) grated
Parmesan cheese

4 (6- to 8-ounce)
**boneless, skinless
chicken breasts**

1 cup (4 ounces) shredded
mozzarella cheese

2 ounces sliced **pepperoni**

8 ounces **spaghetti or penne**

INGREDIENT SPOTLIGHT PEPPERONI

More than just a pizza topping, pepperoni provides meaty, savory depth in a few of our dishes, from pastas to casseroles. In the test kitchen, our favorite brand is **Margherita Italian Style Pepperoni**, which tasters praised for its balance of "meatiness and spice" as well as its "tangy and fresh" flavor. Some tasters even picked up hints of "fruity licorice and peppery fennel."

✓ WHY THIS RECIPE WORKS For an effortless take on chicken pizzaiola that delivered rich, deep flavor, we started by amping up the flavor of the mild-tasting chicken. Coating boneless, skinless chicken breasts with a simple layer of grated Parmesan ensured that each bite was full of cheesy richness. For even more savory depth, spice, and gooey appeal, we topped off our chicken breasts with a sprinkling of shredded mozzarella cheese and sliced pepperoni. For the tomato sauce, we reached for the store-bought version, but added more flavor by using it to bake the chicken. This way, the sauce absorbed flavor from the chicken, plus the chicken stayed moist and tender. To complete our dish, we cooked some spaghetti, tossed it with the sauce, and served it alongside our chicken pizzaiola. Almost any of your favorite pizza toppings (such as crumbled sausage, peppers and onions, or mushrooms) can be substituted for the pepperoni. Our favorite brand of jarred pasta sauce is Victoria Marinara Sauce (see page 195).

1. Adjust oven rack to middle position and heat oven to 450 degrees. Spread tomato sauce into 13 by 9-inch baking dish. Spread Parmesan in shallow dish. Trim chicken, pat dry with paper towels, season with salt and pepper, and coat completely with Parmesan, pressing on cheese to adhere. Lay chicken on top of tomato sauce. Bake chicken for 15 minutes.

2. Sprinkle mozzarella and pepperoni over chicken. Increase oven temperature to 475 degrees and continue to bake until cheese melts and chicken registers 160 degrees, about 5 minutes longer.

3. Meanwhile, bring 4 quarts water to boil in large pot. Add pasta and 1 tablespoon salt and cook, stirring often, until al dente. Reserve ½ cup cooking water, then drain pasta and return it to pot.

4. Spoon some sauce from baking dish into pasta and toss to combine. Add reserved cooking water to pasta as needed to adjust consistency and season with salt and pepper to taste. Serve with chicken and remaining sauce.

Chicken and Couscous with Dried Fruit and Smoked Almonds

SERVES 4
2 tablespoons **olive oil**
4 (6- to 8-ounce) **boneless, skinless chicken breasts**
3 **scallions**
1 cup **couscous**
½ cup **dried mixed fruit**
¼ cup **smoked almonds**

INGREDIENT SPOTLIGHT
DRIED MIXED FRUIT

Dried mixed fruit gives the couscous a subtle sweetness and contributes some texture to this dish. There are a wide variety of dried fruit mixes at the supermarket; the one we used included a fairly standard combination of dried apricots, prunes, pears, and apples. You could use any blend of dried fruit, but avoid a mixture that's mainly berries, as it might impart an overly tart or acidic taste.

WHY THIS RECIPE WORKS This easy yet elegant chicken and couscous dish relies on just one pan to cook the chicken and then sauté the aromatics and simmer the couscous. Preparing the chicken first meant we were able to capitalize on the flavorful browned bits, or fond, left behind to infuse the couscous with deep, savory flavor. And since the couscous cooks so quickly, it comes together in a flash while the chicken rests. Toasting the couscous in a small amount of oil helped to develop its nutty flavor. To make the most of our ingredients, we bypassed the typical onions and garlic in favor of scallions; the sautéed whites gave our couscous an aromatic foundation, and the greens made for a bright, fresh-tasting garnish. Including another multitasking ingredient—dried mixed fruit—in our couscous gave it a subtle sweetness that tasters didn't find to be over-the-top or cloying. For some crunch and more savory depth, we stirred in a handful of chopped smoked almonds. The smoky flavor contrasted nicely with the sweetness of the fruit and added an unexpected twist to this simple dinner.

1. Heat 1 tablespoon oil in 12-inch nonstick skillet over medium-high heat until just smoking. Trim chicken, pat dry with paper towels, and season with salt and pepper. Brown chicken well on 1 side, 6 to 8 minutes. Flip chicken over, reduce heat to medium, and continue to cook until chicken registers 160 degrees, 6 to 8 minutes. Transfer to platter and cover to keep warm.

2. Mince scallion whites and slice scallion greens; keep whites and greens separate. Add remaining 1 tablespoon oil, scallion whites, and ½ teaspoon salt to now-empty skillet and cook over medium heat until scallions are softened, 3 to 5 minutes. Stir in couscous and cook for 30 seconds. Coarsely chop dried fruit and stir into couscous with 1½ cups water, scraping up any browned bits. Bring to brief simmer, then remove from heat, cover, and let sit until liquid is absorbed, about 3 minutes.

3. Chop almonds and gently fold into couscous with half of scallion greens. Season with salt and pepper to taste. Sprinkle remaining scallion greens over top and serve with chicken.

Simple Stuffed Chicken Breasts with Boursin

SERVES 4

4 (10- to 12-ounce)
bone-in split chicken breasts

1 (5.2-ounce) package
Boursin Garlic and Fine Herbs cheese

1 tablespoon **unsalted butter**

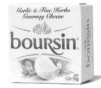

INGREDIENT SPOTLIGHT
BOURSIN CHEESE

Boursin is a soft, spreadable cheese that comes in several varieties and is widely available. We like the garlic and fine herbs variety and use it in many of our recipes. Besides stuffed chicken breasts, we also include Boursin in several pasta dishes and casseroles. This powerhouse ingredient not only contributes a nice creaminess and tangy taste, but because it is flavored with herbs and aromatics, we can cut back on our ingredient list without any loss in flavor.

✓ WHY THIS RECIPE WORKS Stuffed chicken breasts couldn't be easier—or more delicious. Rather than pull out a cutting board to chop aromatics and herbs, we started with a simple filling that didn't need any embellishment: Boursin cheese. This creamy, rich cheese is infused with the flavors of garlic and herbs, making additional ingredients (and extra prep work) unnecessary. Instead of cutting fussy pockets to hold the filling, we used the skin on the chicken as a natural pocket and placed a generous spoonful of the cheese underneath. The skin held the filling in place, and when the chicken emerged from the oven it was moist and tender with a creamy, flavorful filling. Brushing the skin with melted butter before moving our chicken to the oven ensured it came out with a rich-tasting, golden-brown exterior. It is important to buy chicken breasts with the skin still attached and intact, otherwise the stuffing will leak out.

1. Adjust oven rack to middle position and heat oven to 450 degrees. Line baking sheet with aluminum foil. Trim chicken, pat dry with paper towels, season with salt and pepper, and gently loosen center portion of skin covering each breast. Using spoon, place one-quarter of Boursin underneath skin over center of each chicken breast. Gently press on skin to spread out cheese.

2. Arrange chicken, skin side up, on prepared sheet. Melt butter and brush over chicken. Bake until chicken registers 160 degrees, about 30 minutes, rotating sheet halfway through baking. Serve.

TEST KITCHEN TIP STUFFING A CHICKEN BREAST

1. Using fingers, gently loosen center portion of skin covering each breast, making pocket for filling.

2. Using spoon, place Boursin underneath skin, over center of each breast. Gently press on skin to spread out cheese.

Pan-Roasted Chicken with Tomatoes and Olives

SERVES 4

4 (10- to 12-ounce)
bone-in split chicken breasts

2 tablespoons **olive oil**

1½ pounds **plum tomatoes**

¼ cup pitted **kalamata olives**

3 **garlic cloves**

Fresh rosemary

INGREDIENT SPOTLIGHT
KALAMATA OLIVES

These intensely colored olives are brine-cured, then packed in vinegar-heavy brine. We like them both as a snack and in cooked dishes. In sauces and tapenades, kalamatas contribute a deep, earthy, and briny, but not overpowering, flavor and a pleasantly creamy texture. You can purchase olives in jars—they're generally found near the pickles—or you can buy just what you need from the supermarket's olive bar.

WHY THIS RECIPE WORKS To take humble pan-roasted chicken breasts up a notch, we paired them with tomatoes and olives for a rustic supper with a Mediterranean bent. Our first task was to nail down the right kind of tomatoes. We initially tried canned whole tomatoes, but they lacked structure and broke down into an overly thick sauce that was reminiscent of pasta sauce. Canned diced tomatoes, on the other hand, cooked up too firm. Regular supermarket tomatoes were a no-go, since they are of mediocre quality most of the year and we wanted this dish to be a year-round option. We had the best luck with plum tomatoes, which broke down just enough, contributed ample juices, and offered plenty of sweetness and flavor. After browning the chicken in a skillet, we set it aside and combined the plum tomatoes, quartered, with kalamata olives in the pan, then tucked our chicken in. To add slow-cooked flavor, we added aromatic fresh rosemary and thinly sliced garlic, which melted into the tomatoes as they roasted.

1. Adjust oven rack to middle position and heat oven to 450 degrees. Trim chicken, pat dry with paper towels, and season with salt and pepper.

2. Heat 1 tablespoon oil in 12-inch nonstick, ovensafe skillet over medium-high heat until just smoking. Lay chicken, skin side down, in skillet and cook until well browned and crisp, 6 to 8 minutes. Transfer chicken to plate.

3. Core tomatoes and quarter lengthwise, quarter olives, thinly slice garlic, chop 2 teaspoons rosemary, and combine with remaining 1 tablespoon oil, ¼ teaspoon salt, and ¼ teaspoon pepper in now-empty pan. Nestle chicken, skin side up, into skillet. Transfer skillet to oven and bake until chicken registers 160 degrees and tomatoes are softened and lightly browned, 25 to 30 minutes. Serve.

Pan-Roasted Chicken with Potatoes

SERVES 4

1½ pounds
small or medium red potatoes

6 tablespoons **olive oil**

4 (10- to 12-ounce)
bone-in split chicken breasts

1 **lemon**

1 **garlic clove**

Fresh thyme

INGREDIENT SPOTLIGHT **THYME**

Thyme has a hearty, spicy, woodsy flavor and aroma that works well in many dishes with poultry and meat. It is often added early in cooking so it has time to infuse sauces, soups, and stews with flavor. Usually, the leaves are stripped from the stems and minced before being added to a recipe, but sometimes we call for adding whole sprigs directly to the pan or pot and then removing them before serving. Though we prefer fresh thyme, dried thyme can be used in long-cooking recipes.

WHY THIS RECIPE WORKS Sure, chicken and potatoes is a classic combination, but sometimes this duo is a little disappointing. For a satisfying, full-flavored dinner, we focused first on the chicken. For crisp skin and moist meat, we began with bone-in split breasts and seared them on the stovetop in a bit of olive oil before letting them cook through in a 450-degree oven. Moving on to the potatoes, we preferred small red potatoes over other, more starchy varieties, which broke down too much during cooking. After microwaving our spuds to jump-start their cooking, we transferred them to the skillet to sauté and pick up the flavorful browned bits left behind from searing the chicken. In lieu of a heavy pan sauce, we whisked together a quick, bright-tasting vinaigrette of olive oil, lemon juice, garlic, and thyme to drizzle over the chicken and potatoes. We prefer to use small or medium potatoes (1½ to 3 inches in diameter) because they are easier to cut into uniform pieces.

1. Adjust oven rack to middle position and heat oven to 450 degrees. Cut potatoes into 1-inch pieces and toss with 1 tablespoon oil, ¼ teaspoon salt, and pinch pepper in bowl. Microwave on high, uncovered, until potatoes soften but still hold their shape, about 10 minutes, gently stirring twice during cooking.

2. Trim chicken, pat dry with paper towels, and season with salt and pepper. Heat 1 tablespoon oil in 12-inch nonstick skillet over medium-high heat until just smoking. Lay chicken breasts, skin side down, in skillet and cook until well browned and crisp, 6 to 8 minutes. Transfer chicken, skin side up, to 13 by 9-inch baking dish and bake until thickest part of chicken registers 160 degrees, 25 to 30 minutes.

3. Drain microwaved potatoes well. Heat 1 tablespoon oil in now-empty skillet over medium-high heat until shimmering. Add potatoes in single layer and cook, turning as needed, until golden brown on both sides, 10 to 14 minutes.

4. Transfer potatoes and chicken to large platter. Squeeze lemon for 1 tablespoon juice, mince garlic, mince 1 tablespoon thyme, and whisk together with remaining 3 tablespoons oil and pinch pepper. Drizzle oil-lemon mixture over chicken and potatoes before serving.

Lemon-Braised Chicken with Fennel

SERVES 4

1 **lemon**

4 (10- to 12-ounce)
bone-in split chicken breasts

4 tablespoons **unsalted butter**

2 **fennel bulbs**

3 **garlic cloves**

1½ cups **chicken broth**

INGREDIENT SPOTLIGHT
BONE-IN SPLIT CHICKEN BREASTS

Boneless, skinless chicken breasts are great for an easy, speedy supper, but when we're preparing a braise or other slow-cooked dish, we reach for bone-in, skin-on breasts. The bone helps to insulate the meat, keeping it tender during a longer cooking time; it also infuses the meat with more flavor. And the skin is a bonus, too—it takes just minutes to brown, leading to fond that can contribute savory richness and depth to sauces.

✔ WHY THIS RECIPE WORKS Braising chicken breasts gives them savory depth in this rustic yet elegant dish. For the chicken, we opted for bone-in breasts; the bone works to insulate the meat and keep it moist during the long cooking time. But the bones do more than keep the meat moist—they also contribute serious depth and savory richness. To capitalize on this enhanced chicken flavor, we kept our braising medium on the simpler side: aromatic fennel and garlic brightened by the sweet, tart tang of lemon slices. Reducing the braising liquid helped to intensify the flavors, and whisking in a few tablespoons of butter at the end gave the sauce a silky richness. For a fancy finish, we minced some of the fennel fronds and sprinkled them over the chicken just before serving. Serve with buttered egg noodles.

1. Cut away peel and pith from lemon, then slice crosswise into ⅛-inch-thick rounds. Trim chicken, pat dry with paper towels, and season with salt and pepper. Melt 1 tablespoon butter in Dutch oven over medium-high heat. Brown 2 chicken breasts on both sides, 8 to 10 minutes; transfer to plate. Repeat with 1 tablespoon butter and remaining chicken.

2. Trim fennel stalks and fronds (see page 177); mince 2 tablespoons fronds and reserve. Trim bulb, cut in half, core, and slice into ¼-inch-thick strips. Add fennel and ¼ teaspoon salt to now-empty pot and cook over medium heat until softened, 5 to 7 minutes. Mince garlic, stir into pot, and cook until fragrant, about 30 seconds. Stir in broth, scraping up any browned bits.

3. Nestle chicken and any accumulated juices into pot. Add lemon slices and bring to simmer. Cover, reduce heat to medium-low, and simmer until chicken is fully cooked and tender and registers 160 degrees, 25 to 30 minutes.

4. Transfer chicken to serving dish; cover to keep warm. Remove fat from surface of sauce using large spoon, return sauce to simmer, and cook until slightly thickened, about 5 minutes. Off heat, stir in remaining 2 tablespoons butter and season with salt and pepper to taste. Pour sauce over chicken and sprinkle with fennel fronds. Serve.

Coconut-Curry Braised Chicken

SERVES 4

4 (10- to 12-ounce)
bone-in split chicken breasts

1⅔ cups **coconut milk**

3 **scallions**

1 **lime**

Fresh ginger

2 tablespoons **red curry paste**

INGREDIENT SPOTLIGHT
COCONUT MILK

Coconut milk is not the thin liquid found inside the coconut itself; that is called coconut water. Coconut milk is made by steeping equal parts shredded coconut meat with either warm milk or water. The meat is pressed or mashed to release as much liquid as possible, the mixture is strained, and the result is coconut milk. To find the best one, we tasted seven nationally available brands (five regular and two light) in coconut rice, a Thai-style chicken soup, chicken curry, and coconut pudding. In the savory recipes, tasters preferred **Chaokoh**, which boasted an incredibly smooth texture. When it came to the sweet recipes, tasters liked Ka-Me coconut milk best.

✔ **WHY THIS RECIPE WORKS** Thai curries are often elaborate dishes, requiring a considerable list of spices and aromatics to achieve maximum flavor and complexity. While we love the depth of flavor imparted by from-scratch curry powder, we don't love the time or effort involved. Fortunately, we found a convenient substitute in store-bought red curry paste, which made it easy to build big flavor with few ingredients and little effort. To bolster the flavor of the curry paste, we turned to scallions and grated ginger. Lime zest and juice added bright, citrusy notes. Coconut milk was a given for a Thai-style curry, but we used it for more than just the braising liquid. A tablespoon provided just enough fat in which to brown the chicken breasts and sauté the aromatics, and a big dash stirred in at the end of cooking contributed a fresh, clean creaminess to the reduced sauce. See page 53 for more information on red curry paste. Serve with rice.

1. Trim chicken, pat dry with paper towels, and season with salt and pepper. Heat 1 tablespoon coconut milk in Dutch oven over medium heat until hot. Brown 2 chicken breasts on both sides, 8 to 10 minutes; transfer to plate. Repeat with 1 tablespoon coconut milk and remaining chicken.

2. Mince scallion whites and slice scallion greens; keep whites and greens separate. Cook 1 tablespoon coconut milk and scallion whites in now-empty pot over medium heat until softened, 3 to 5 minutes. Grate lime for ½ teaspoon zest, then squeeze for 2 teaspoons juice. Grate 1½ tablespoons ginger, stir into pot with lime zest and curry paste, and cook until fragrant, about 1 minute.

3. Stir in 1 cup coconut milk and ½ cup water, scraping up any browned bits. Nestle chicken and any accumulated juices into pot and bring to simmer. Cover, reduce heat to medium-low, and simmer gently until chicken registers 160 degrees, 25 to 30 minutes.

4. Transfer chicken to serving dish; cover to keep warm. Continue to simmer sauce until reduced to 1 cup, about 4 minutes. Stir in remaining coconut milk and let heat through, about 2 minutes. Off heat, stir in lime juice and season with salt and pepper to taste. Pour sauce over chicken, sprinkle with scallion greens, and serve.

Five-Spice Chicken Thighs with Snap Peas

SERVES 4

4 tablespoons **unsalted butter**

Fresh ginger

1 **garlic clove**

½ teaspoon **five-spice powder**

8 (5- to 7-ounce) **bone-in chicken thighs**

1 pound **sugar snap peas**

INGREDIENT SPOTLIGHT
FIVE-SPICE POWDER

This pungent, aromatic blend contains five ingredients, namely cinnamon, clove, fennel seeds, Sichuan peppercorn, and star anise. Chinese culture values the balance of flavors that these spices represent. In recent years, Americans have taken to the spice, too, using it for both sweet and savory dishes. Our favorite brand of five-spice powder is **Dean & DeLuca**, which tasters described as having a "balanced heat and sweetness."

✔ WHY THIS RECIPE WORKS For a dish featuring golden, crisp skin and moist, tender dark meat, bone-in, skin-on chicken thighs were the obvious choice. Slashing the skin a few times before roasting the thighs allowed the fat in the skin to render, and turning on the broiler for the last few minutes of cooking ensured the skin crisped nicely. So the chicken thighs tasted as good as they looked, we rubbed a compound butter, enlivened with minced garlic, fresh ginger, and a bit of five-spice powder, under the skin. A pat of the compound butter also added richness and flavor to the snap peas we steamed in a skillet to round out the meal. Transfer the cooked snap peas to a serving dish immediately to avoid overcooking.

1. Adjust oven rack to middle position and heat oven to 450 degrees. Set wire rack in rimmed baking sheet lined with aluminum foil. Soften 3 tablespoons butter, grate 2 teaspoons ginger, mince garlic, and combine with five-spice powder in bowl; measure out and reserve 1 tablespoon butter mixture separately. Trim chicken, pat dry with paper towels, and gently loosen center portion of skin covering each thigh. Using spoon, place remaining 2 tablespoons butter mixture evenly underneath skin of thighs. Gently press on skin to spread out butter. Lay chicken, skin side up, on prepared rack.

2. Cut 3 diagonal slashes through skin of each thigh; do not cut into meat. Melt remaining 1 tablespoon butter, brush over chicken, and season with salt and pepper. Roast until chicken registers 165 degrees, 30 to 40 minutes.

3. Remove chicken from oven. Adjust oven rack 6 inches from broiler element and heat broiler. Broil chicken until skin is crisp and thighs register 175 degrees, 5 to 10 minutes. Transfer chicken to platter and cover to keep warm.

4. Remove strings from snap peas and combine with ⅓ cup water in 12-inch nonstick skillet. Cover and cook over medium-high heat until peas are almost crisp-tender, about 4 minutes. Uncover and continue to cook, stirring often, until skillet is dry and peas are crisp-tender, about 2 minutes longer. Stir in reserved 1 tablespoon butter mixture and season with salt and pepper to taste. Serve with chicken.

Mustard-Glazed Drumsticks

SERVES 4

2 **scallions**

½ cup **sugar**

⅓ cup **whole-grain mustard**

2 tablespoons **soy sauce**

4 teaspoons **cider vinegar**

8 (6-ounce) **chicken drumsticks**

INGREDIENT SPOTLIGHT
WHOLE-GRAIN MUSTARD

We love whole-grain mustard on sandwiches and sausage, but it also works to give the glaze for our drumsticks a bright, potent flavor and distinctive texture. In the test kitchen, our favorite brand is **Grey Poupon Harvest Coarse Ground Mustard**, which tasters praised for its "real burst of mustard flavor," "good heat," and "big, round, crunchy texture."

☑ WHY THIS RECIPE WORKS Perfecting our glazed drumsticks started with cooking them beyond 175 degrees, the point at which dark meat is done and considered safe to eat. Giving them extra time to simmer—until they registered 180 degrees—gave the collagen, the tough connective tissue abundant in dark chicken, time to break down, producing meltingly tender drumsticks. So we didn't have to deal with flabby, flavorless skin, we removed it prior to cooking. For an ultrasimple glaze that didn't call upon any special ingredients, we reached into our pantry. Whole-grain mustard, sugar, soy sauce, and cider vinegar delivered a bright, sweet, and tangy sauce that held its own against the richness of the drumsticks. For aromatic depth, we included a couple scallions, but made them pull double duty—we used the whites in the glaze for oniony depth, and stirred in the greens at the end for a pop of color and some crunch.

1. Mince scallion whites and slice scallion greens; keep whites and greens separate. Combine scallion whites, sugar, mustard, ¼ cup water, soy sauce, and vinegar in 12-inch nonstick skillet.

2. Remove skin from drumsticks and add drumsticks to skillet. Cover and simmer gently until chicken is tender and registers 180 degrees, 20 to 25 minutes, flipping drumsticks over halfway through cooking.

3. Uncover, increase heat to high, and simmer rapidly, turning drumsticks occasionally, until sauce is slightly thickened and reduced to about ½ cup, about 8 minutes. Transfer chicken to serving platter. Stir scallion greens into glaze, pour over chicken, and serve.

TEST KITCHEN TIP
REMOVING SKIN FROM CHICKEN DRUMSTICKS

The skin on drumsticks is often slippery, making it a challenge to remove by hand. To simplify the task, use a paper towel to provide extra grip while pulling.

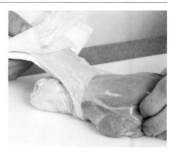

Braised Chicken with Onions, Mushrooms, and Bacon

SERVES 4
3 slices **bacon**
8 (3-ounce) **boneless, skinless chicken thighs**
2 **onions**
10 ounces **cremini mushrooms**
1 cup **chicken broth**
Fresh parsley

INGREDIENT SPOTLIGHT ONIONS

The workhorse of our kitchen, onions offer savory, aromatic backbone and well-rounded flavor to a wide variety of dishes, from braises and sauces to soups, stews, and chilis. Unless otherwise specified, we use yellow onions in our recipes; we go through onions quickly and stock the test kitchen with big bags of these onions. However, if you have white onions on hand, feel free to use those; in a tasting, we found that white and yellow onions can be used interchangeably in any recipe calling for "onions." When shopping, look for onions with dry skins and no signs of spotting or moistness; avoid those with soft spots. At home, be sure to store them in a cool, dry place with good air circulation.

✔ WHY THIS RECIPE WORKS To build big flavor in this minimalist braise, we started with two hearty, rich-tasting ingredients: bacon and mushrooms. Not only did the bacon contribute savory, smoky notes and crisp bites to the dish, but it also provided fat for browning the chicken thighs and cooking the mushrooms and onions, thereby creating unexpected depth with just a handful of ingredients. To streamline our recipe, we tried omitting the step of browning the thighs, but the shorter cooking time wasn't worth the loss in flavor. We were pleased to discover that simply browning the thighs on one side was a successful compromise; tasters were happy with the fuller flavor and promise of a relatively quick dish that tasted slow-cooked. Serve with mashed potatoes, buttered noodles, or polenta.

1. Chop bacon and cook in Dutch oven over medium heat until crisp, 5 to 7 minutes; transfer to paper towel–lined plate. Trim chicken, pat dry with paper towels, and season with salt and pepper. Heat bacon fat left in pot over medium heat until just smoking. Brown half of chicken lightly on 1 side, 3 to 5 minutes; transfer to plate. Repeat with remaining chicken.

2. Halve and thinly slice onions, trim and quarter mushrooms, and add to fat left in pot with ¼ teaspoon salt. Cover and cook over medium heat until softened and wet, about 5 minutes. Remove lid and continue to cook, stirring often, until onions and mushrooms are dry and well browned, 10 to 12 minutes. Stir in broth, scraping up any browned bits, and bring to simmer.

3. Nestle chicken and any accumulated juices into pot, cover, and simmer gently until chicken is very tender, 20 to 25 minutes. Transfer chicken to platter; cover to keep warm.

4. Return sauce to simmer and cook until thickened, about 5 minutes. Season with salt and pepper to taste and pour over chicken. Mince 2 tablespoons parsley, sprinkle parsley and bacon over top, and serve.

Chicken Meatballs with Tomatoes and Cilantro

SERVES 4

3 (14.5-ounce) cans
diced tomatoes with garlic and onion

6 **scallions**

Fresh cilantro

1 pound **ground chicken**

½ cup **panko bread crumbs**

2 tablespoons **olive oil**

INGREDIENT SPOTLIGHT
DICED TOMATOES WITH GARLIC AND ONION

The trio of tomatoes, garlic, and onions is the base for numerous Italian tomato sauces. But we don't always have room for all three in our ingredient list. Enter diced tomatoes flavored with garlic and onion. This convenient three-in-one product is made by several brands—you can use any of them here—and offers the firm yet tender texture and bright taste of diced tomatoes, enhanced by dried onion, dried garlic or garlic powder, and sometimes herbs. You can find it with the other tomato products in your supermarket.

✓ WHY THIS RECIPE WORKS We wanted a lighter, fresher alternative to the standard Italian-American meatball, so we swapped the usual meatloaf mix for ground chicken and the basil for cilantro. Looking to pack big flavor into our meatballs, but knowing we couldn't include too many ingredients, we hit on a convenience product that amped up the aromatic background *and* gave us our sauce: diced tomatoes flavored with garlic and onion. After breaking down the tomatoes in the food processor, we used a portion to liven up our mild-tasting chicken meatballs, and saved the rest for the sauce. Panko helped the meatballs hold together and absorbed excess moisture, and scallions provided an additional hit of flavor, plus a bit of color when sprinkled over the finished dish. Chilling the meatballs in the fridge before sautéing them ensured they didn't fall apart in the skillet, and simmering them in the sauce allowed both components to pick up rich flavor. Be sure to use ground chicken, not ground chicken breast (also labeled 99 percent fat free), in this recipe. You can substitute ground turkey if desired. Serve with rice.

1. Drain 1 can tomatoes, reserving juice, and pulse in food processor until coarsely chopped, about 4 pulses. Mince scallion whites and slice scallion greens; keep whites and greens separate. Chop 3 tablespoons cilantro. Gently mix ½ cup processed tomatoes, 1 tablespoon scallion whites, 1 tablespoon scallion greens, 2 tablespoons cilantro, chicken, panko, ¾ teaspoon salt, and ¾ teaspoon pepper together until uniform using hands. Shape mixture into 12 meatballs, transfer to large plate, cover, and refrigerate until firm, about 1 hour.

2. Pulse remaining 2 cans tomatoes, with their juice, until mostly smooth, about 12 pulses; combine with remaining chopped tomatoes and reserved juice.

3. Heat 1 tablespoon oil in 12-inch nonstick skillet over medium heat until just smoking. Brown meatballs well on all sides, about 10 minutes; transfer to paper towel–lined plate. Wipe out skillet with paper towels, add remaining 1 tablespoon oil and remaining scallion whites, and cook over medium heat until softened, 3 to 5 minutes. Stir in tomatoes and simmer until thickened, 18 to 20 minutes.

4. Add meatballs, cover, and simmer gently until cooked through, about 10 minutes. Stir in remaining scallion greens and season with salt and pepper to taste. Sprinkle with remaining 1 tablespoon cilantro; serve.

Aloha Kebabs with Sesame Rice

SERVES 4

2 teaspoons **sesame oil**

1 cup **long-grain white rice**

12 ounces
cooked chicken sausage

2 **red or green bell peppers**

2 cups **fresh pineapple chunks**

½ cup **hoisin sauce**

INGREDIENT SPOTLIGHT
LONG-GRAIN WHITE RICE

White rice is neutral in flavor, providing a great backdrop for other foods. Unlike medium- or short-grain white rice, long-grain white rice remains fluffy and separate after cooking. The reason for this is that long-grain white rice contains less of a starch called amylopectin, which is what makes rice stick together. Of all the brands found on supermarket shelves, our favorite is **Lundberg Organic Long-Grain White Rice**. Tasters enjoyed this brand's "smooth and distinct" grains, which tasted "nutty," "buttery," and "toasty" when sampled plain and in pilaf.

✔ **WHY THIS RECIPE WORKS** We wanted all the charred flavor and intensity of grilled kebabs—but without the fuss of waiting for the grill to heat. Broiling was the perfect solution, and it ensured our kebabs could be a year-round supper option. Although we lost the trademark grill marks, the meat still developed a nicely browned crust from the high heat. For a quick dinner, we found that cooked chicken sausage packed big flavor and required minimal prep. Paired with juicy pineapple chunks and crisp bell pepper, the precooked sausage simply needed to be heated through while the fruit and vegetables softened and caramelized. To bring the dish together, we brushed the kebabs with thick, rich hoisin sauce. The sweet Asian condiment browned quickly under the broiler, giving the kebabs a burnished, glazy sheen. Light and fluffy long-grain white rice rounded out our almost-effortless, grill-free dinner. We found that sautéing the rice in a small amount of sesame oil before cooking it in water added a rich dimension of flavor that played off the salty sweetness of the hoisin-coated kebabs. You will need eight 12-inch metal skewers for this recipe. See page 141 for more information on hoisin sauce.

1. Heat oil in medium saucepan over medium heat. Add rice and cook, stirring constantly, for 1 minute. Stir in 1½ cups water and ½ teaspoon salt and bring to boil. Reduce heat to low, cover, and cook until liquid is absorbed, about 15 minutes. Off heat, let rice sit, covered, until tender, about 15 minutes longer. Fluff rice with fork; cover to keep warm.

2. Meanwhile, adjust oven rack 6 inches from broiler element and heat broiler. Line rimmed baking sheet with aluminum foil. Cut sausage into 1-inch chunks; core bell peppers and cut into 1-inch pieces. Thread sausage, bell peppers, and pineapple onto eight 12-inch metal skewers.

3. Lay skewers on prepared sheet and brush with hoisin sauce. Broil skewers, turning occasionally, until vegetables are softened and well browned, 10 to 15 minutes. Serve with rice.

Chicken and Sun-Dried Tomato Burgers

SERVES 4

5 **hamburger buns**

⅓ cup
oil-packed sun-dried tomatoes,
plus 1 tablespoon oil

Fresh basil

1 **shallot**

1¼ pounds **ground chicken**

½ cup (2 ounces) crumbled
goat cheese

INGREDIENT SPOTLIGHT
SUN-DRIED TOMATOES

Sun-dried tomatoes are made by—not surprisingly—drying tomatoes in the sun or through other, artificial means, which turns the tomatoes dark red, makes their flesh chewy, and gives them an intense, concentrated flavor. Sun-dried tomatoes are sold either dry-packed in small plastic containers or bags or oil-packed in jars. We prefer to use oil-packed sun-dried tomatoes because the dry-packed variety are often leathery. Plus, the former provides a flavorful oil that can be used for cooking.

✔ WHY THIS RECIPE WORKS Chicken burgers never seem to measure up to their ground beef brethren in texture or taste. Since fat delivers flavor, the leanness of poultry burgers usually means a decrease in flavor, too. Our goal was to create a chicken burger with no excuses. First, we added richness and moisture with oil-packed sun-dried tomatoes. The tomatoes gave the patties a big bump in flavor, plus we now had a flavorful oil that we could use to cook the burgers. Many burger recipes call for bread crumbs to keep the patties moist and tender, but we opted for a panade made from a hamburger bun and a little water. Finally, rather than put our cheese on top of the patties, we put it inside. Crumbled goat cheese, mixed into the burgers, guaranteed creamy, tangy bites throughout. Be sure to use ground chicken, not ground chicken breast (also labeled 99 percent fat free), in this recipe. You can substitute ground turkey if desired. Serve with your favorite burger toppings.

1. Tear 1 hamburger bun into pieces, then using fork, mash into paste with 2 tablespoons water in large bowl. Chop tomatoes coarsely and add to bowl. Chop 2 tablespoons basil, mince shallot, and add to bowl.

2. Add chicken, goat cheese, ½ teaspoon salt, and ¼ teaspoon pepper and mix until uniform using hands. Divide meat mixture into 4 portions, form each into loose ball, then pat lightly into 1-inch-thick burger.

3. Heat tomato packing oil in 12-inch nonstick skillet over medium heat until just smoking. Lay burgers in skillet and cook until lightly browned and crusted on first side, 3 to 4 minutes. Flip burgers and continue to cook until second side is lightly browned, 3 to 4 minutes.

4. Reduce heat to low, partially cover, and continue to cook until burgers register 160 degrees, 8 to 10 minutes, flipping halfway through cooking. Serve on buns.

TEST KITCHEN TIP
MAKING A PANADE

To keep our chicken burgers moist and juicy, we added a panade, which is typically a paste of milk and bread. For our panade, we simply used a hamburger bun, mashed together with a bit of water.

Rustic Chicken and Brie Tart

SERVES 4

8 ounces
frozen chopped spinach

6 ounces firm **Brie cheese**

¼ cup **walnuts**

2 cups shredded
rotisserie chicken

¼ cup **chicken broth**

1 (9-inch) round store-bought
pie dough

INGREDIENT SPOTLIGHT
ROTISSERIE CHICKEN

While we prefer to roast our own bird when it is destined to be the dinner-time centerpiece, it's hard to beat the convenience of a supermarket-roasted rotisserie chicken for use in recipes like this tart. A typical rotisserie chicken weighs about 2½ pounds and yields anywhere from 3 to 4 cups of picked meat. While rotisserie chickens often have seasonings added (such as garlic and herbs) or are glazed, we prefer simply oven roasted for this recipe.

✓ WHY THIS RECIPE WORKS One glance at this elegant-looking tart, and your dinner guests will think you've been cooking for hours. With just a few carefully chosen ingredients, plus a store-bought pie crust and rotisserie chicken, it's possible to assemble and bake this rustic tart in less than half an hour. For savory flavor and to keep the tart moist, we added a small amount of chicken broth. Hearty spinach rounded out the flavor and chopped, toasted walnuts lent some crunch and textural contrast. Creamy and flavorful Brie pulled double-duty here: chopped, it melted into the filling and added richness; cut into pieces and placed on top before baking, it gave the finished tart lots of cheesy appeal. There are two crusts in a box of refrigerated pie crust; you will need only one crust for this recipe. The test kitchen's preferred store-bought crust is Wholly Wholesome 9-Inch Certified Organic Traditional Bake at Home Rolled Pie Dough; see page 289 for more information.

1. Adjust oven rack to middle position and heat oven to 475 degrees. Microwave spinach in covered bowl until completely thawed, about 5 minutes, stirring once; let cool slightly and thoroughly squeeze dry. Cut 4 ounces Brie into 1-inch pieces and finely chop remaining 2 ounces Brie. Toast walnuts (see page 297) and chop.

2. Chop chicken and combine with spinach, finely chopped Brie, walnuts, broth, ¼ teaspoon salt, and ⅛ teaspoon pepper in bowl. Cover and microwave until heated through, about 1 minute. Stir mixture to recombine and season with salt and pepper to taste.

3. Line rimmed baking sheet with parchment paper; place pie dough round in center. Spread chicken filling over dough, leaving 1-inch border at edges. Fold edge of dough over filling, pleating it every 2 to 3 inches as needed. Place remaining Brie pieces on top, with rind facing up. Bake tart until crust is golden and cheese is melted, about 15 minutes, rotating sheet halfway through baking. Let cool slightly; serve.

TEST KITCHEN TIP
ASSEMBLING A CHICKEN AND BRIE TART

Spread the filling over the crust, leaving a 1-inch border at the edge. Fold the dough over the filling, pleating it every few inches. The parchment paper–lined baking sheet will make it easy to slide the baked tart off.

PORK CHOPS WITH SPICY PEPPER RELISH AND CHEESY GRITS

Beef, Pork, and Lamb

95   Sirloin Steak with Boursin Mashed Potatoes | FAST RECIPE

96   Steak Salad with Arugula and Shaved Parmesan | FAST RECIPE

99   Spicy Chipotle Steak Soft Tacos

100   Teriyaki Steak Tips | FAST RECIPE

101   Philly Cheesesteak Sandwiches

102   Beef and Broccoli Stir-Fry | FAST RECIPE

105   Kimchi Fried Rice with Beef | FAST RECIPE

106   Lazy Man's Chili | FAST RECIPE

107   Easy Beef Empanadas | FAST RECIPE

109   Meatloaf Florentine

110   Sesame Pork Chops with Orange and Radish Salad | FAST RECIPE

112   Cola-Glazed Pork Chops with Bok Choy and Sticky Rice | FAST RECIPE

114   Cornflake-Crusted Pork Chops

115   Pork Chops with Spicy Pepper Relish and Cheesy Grits

117   Spicy Pork Tacos with Pineapple Salsa | FAST RECIPE

118   Mu Shu–Style Pork Wraps | FAST RECIPE

119   Sausage and Giardiniera–Stuffed Peppers | FAST RECIPE

121   Lamb Pitas with Roasted Red Pepper Sauce | FAST RECIPE

Sirloin Steak with Boursin Mashed Potatoes

SERVES 4

2 pounds **russet potatoes**

1 (2-pound)
boneless shell sirloin steak,
1 to 1¼ inches thick

1 tablespoon **vegetable oil**

1 cup **heavy cream**

½ (5.2-ounce) package
Boursin Garlic and Fine Herbs cheese

Fresh chives

INGREDIENT SPOTLIGHT **CHIVES**

Though chives are a member of the onion, or allium, family, they tend to be considered more an herb than a vegetable. Chives are mild-tasting with a grassy flavor and "garlicky" aftertaste. They offer a crisp texture and are best used raw so they can retain their fresh flavor and texture.

✓ **WHY THIS RECIPE WORKS** For the complete steakhouse experience at home, we looked to pair our juicy, rosy steak with creamy, rich mashed potatoes spiked with garlic and herbs. Starting with a boneless sirloin steak gave us plenty of beefy flavor and tender meat, and browning it in a smoking-hot pan ensured the formation of a nicely browned crust. Once the steak was well browned, we flipped it and turned down the heat so the meat could cook through gently to a nice medium-rare. As for the spuds, cream was essential for richness, but we didn't want to have to use both herbs and garlic. Instead we found both in garlicky, herb-laced Boursin cheese, which provided the potent aromatic and herbal flavor we were craving, plus additional creaminess. A few chives, minced and stirred into the potatoes, contributed a much-needed burst of fresh flavor and bright color. We prefer this steak cooked to medium-rare, but if you prefer it more or less done, see our guidelines on page 100.

1. Peel potatoes and slice ¾ inch thick. Cover potatoes by 1 inch water in large saucepan and bring to boil. Reduce to gentle simmer and cook until potatoes are tender, 15 to 20 minutes.

2. Meanwhile, trim steak and cut in half widthwise. Pat steaks dry with paper towels and season with salt and pepper. Heat oil in 12-inch skillet over medium-high heat until just smoking. Lay steaks in skillet and cook until well browned on first side, 3 to 5 minutes.

3. Flip steaks, reduce heat to medium, and continue to cook until steaks register 120 to 125 degrees (for medium-rare), 5 to 7 minutes. Transfer steaks to carving board, let rest for 5 to 10 minutes, then slice thinly against grain.

4. Drain potatoes and return to saucepan. Cook over low heat, stirring constantly, until potatoes are thoroughly dried, about 2 minutes. Off heat, mash potatoes with potato masher until smooth. Microwave cream and Boursin together until hot, about 1 minute, then gently fold into potatoes. Mince 2 tablespoons chives, fold into potatoes, and season with salt and pepper to taste. Serve with steak.

Steak Salad with Arugula and Shaved Parmesan

SERVES 4

4 (8-ounce)
boneless strip steaks,
1 inch thick

5 tablespoons **olive oil**

3 **garlic cloves**

⅓ cup jarred **Peppadew peppers,**
plus 3 tablespoons brine

8 ounces (8 cups) **baby arugula**

Shaved **Parmesan cheese**

INGREDIENT SPOTLIGHT
STRIP STEAKS

Available both boneless and bone-in, this steak is also called top loin, shell, sirloin strip, Kansas City strip, and New York strip. Cut from the middle of the steer's back, strip steaks are well-marbled and easy to trim of fat; they have a tight grain, pleasantly chewy texture, and big beefy flavor. We like them pan-seared, but they are also great on the grill.

✓ WHY THIS RECIPE WORKS For a full-flavored steak salad, we combined pan-seared strip steaks with peppery arugula. Rather than opt for a simple vinaigrette of olive oil and lemon juice, we prepared a more assertive vinaigrette that stood up to the rich-tasting meat and made use of the fond left behind from cooking our steaks. Minced garlic, cooked in olive oil until golden brown, picked up rich flavor from the browned bits and added depth. A handful of Peppadew peppers, coarsely chopped, contributed sweetness, some heat, and an appealing crunch, and a few spoonfuls of their brine (in lieu of the usual vinegar) provided brightness and acidity. We prefer this steak cooked to medium-rare, but if you prefer it more or less done, see our guidelines on page 100. See page 26 for more information on Peppadew peppers.

1. Trim steaks, pat dry with paper towels, and season with salt and pepper. Heat 1 tablespoon oil in 12-inch skillet over medium-high heat until just smoking. Lay steaks in skillet and cook until well browned on first side, 3 to 5 minutes.

2. Flip steaks, reduce heat to medium, and continue to cook until steak registers 120 to 125 degrees (for medium-rare), 5 to 7 minutes. Transfer steaks to carving board, let rest for 5 to 10 minutes, then slice thin.

3. Meanwhile, mince garlic and coarsely chop peppers. Combine remaining ¼ cup oil and garlic in now-empty skillet and cook over low heat, stirring constantly, until garlic is golden brown and sticky, about 1 minute. Off heat, stir in peppers, pepper brine, ⅛ teaspoon salt, and ¼ teaspoon pepper.

4. Transfer pepper mixture to large bowl, add arugula, and toss to coat. Divide arugula evenly among 4 dinner plates, top with sliced steak and Parmesan, and serve.

TEST KITCHEN TIP
SHAVING PARMESAN

To make thin shavings of Parmesan, simply run a sharp vegetable peeler along the top of the cheese to make paper-thin curls.

Spicy Chipotle Steak Soft Tacos

SERVES 6

1 (12-ounce) can
chipotle chiles

1 (1½-pound) **flank steak**

2 large **red onions**

12 (6-inch) **flour tortillas**

2 **avocados**

Fresh cilantro

INGREDIENT SPOTLIGHT AVOCADOS

This popular fruit has a pale yellow-green flesh that boasts a buttery, creamy texture. Avocados do well in tropical or subtropical climates; in the U.S., most avocados are grown in California or Florida. You'll see two main varieties at the supermarket. Hass avocados are more rounded and have dark purplish to black skin that is pebbly, while Fuerte avocados are pear-shaped and have greenish, smooth skin; in the test kitchen, we prefer Hass avocados for their richer, less fruity flavor. Though avocados can be stored on the counter or in the fridge, we prefer putting them in the fridge, which allows them to ripen slowly. In either case, the ripened fruit should be stored in the fridge to extend its shelf life. To test for ripeness, try to flick the small stem off the avocado. If it comes off easily and you can see green underneath it, the avocado is ripe. If it does not come off or if you see brown underneath, the avocado is not ripe yet.

✔ WHY THIS RECIPE WORKS Most steak taco recipes call for marinating the meat using a handful of ingredients—including oil or vinegar, herbs, and other seasonings—but we wanted to find just one item that could stand in for all of these. After numerous tests, we landed on an ingredient that delivered everything we were after, plus some spicy, smoky notes: chipotle chile in adobo sauce. Pureeing the chiles in a food processor gave us a smooth mixture that coated our flank steak nicely. After half an hour, we removed the steak from the marinade and cooked it under the broiler. Once cooked and sliced thin, the meat was flavorful and juicy, and we didn't even need to rub any oil on the steak thanks to the bit of sauce still clinging to it. With broiled red onions, cilantro leaves, and chunks of avocado for garnish, our chipotle steak tacos offered the perfect balance of bright, fresh flavor and rich, meaty bites. We prefer this steak cooked to medium, but if you prefer it more or less done, see our guidelines on page 100. Also, the flavor of this steak is fairly spicy; to make it milder, brush any extra marinade off the steak before broiling. If the steak begins to scorch before it is cooked through, adjust the rack further away from the broiler element and continue to cook.

1. Process chipotle in adobo sauce, ½ teaspoon salt, and ¼ teaspoon pepper in food processor until smooth, about 15 seconds. Trim steak, toss with sauce in zipper-lock bag, and let steak marinate for 30 minutes. Peel and slice onions into ¼-inch-thick rounds.

2. Adjust oven rack 6 inches from broiler element and heat broiler. Remove steak from marinade. Lay steak and onions on broiler pan top set over aluminum foil–lined broiler pan bottom. Broil, flipping steak and onions as needed, until onions are tender and lightly charred and steak registers 130 to 135 degrees (for medium), about 20 minutes. Transfer steak to carving board and let rest for 5 to 10 minutes.

3. Spread 6 tortillas onto baking sheet and broil until softened, about 2 minutes, flipping halfway through broiling. Wrap warm tortillas in foil and repeat with remaining tortillas. Halve and pit avocados; cut into ½-inch pieces.

4. Slice steak thinly against grain, separate onion rings, and toss together in bowl with any accumulated steak juices. Season with salt and pepper to taste. Divide steak mixture evenly among warm tortillas, top with avocado and cilantro leaves, and serve.

Teriyaki Steak Tips

SERVES 4

Fresh ginger

½ cup **hot pepper jelly**

½ cup **low-sodium soy sauce**

½ teaspoon **cornstarch**

1½ pounds **sirloin steak tips**

2 **scallions**

INGREDIENT SPOTLIGHT
SIRLOIN STEAK TIPS

Steak tips, also called flap meat or sirloin tips, have a big beefy flavor and tender texture (when sliced properly against the grain) that make this cut one of our favorite inexpensive steaks. But since "steak tips" is a catch-all phrase for almost any type of beef cut into strips, it can be tricky to identify. The easiest way is to look at the grain: Flap meat has a large-grained texture, similar to that of flank steak and skirt steak, unlike other beef cuts, which tend to have a finer, tighter grain. If you can, buy a whole steak, not strips or cubes, so you can cut it into evenly sized pieces that will cook through at the same rate.

✔ WHY THIS RECIPE WORKS For juicy, charred, teriyaki-inspired steak tips that boast a nice balance of sweet and salty elements, we knew we would need to get a little creative with our ingredient list. For a thick, glazy sauce that didn't need to simmer long on the stovetop, we added cornstarch to a mixture of soy sauce and fresh ginger. Though this sauce seemed promising, it needed a bit of heat and complexity. Hot pepper jelly amped up the flavor of our sauce and contributed some body. Thinly sliced scallions added fresh, crisp, grassy notes and brightness to the sweet yet savory steak tips. We prefer this steak cooked to medium, but if you prefer it more or less done, see our guidelines below.

1. Adjust oven rack 6 inches from broiler element and heat broiler. Line broiler pan bottom with aluminum foil and top with slotted broiler pan top.

2. Grate 1 tablespoon ginger. Whisk ginger, jelly, soy sauce, and cornstarch together in bowl to dissolve cornstarch. Transfer mixture to small saucepan and bring to simmer over medium–high heat. Reduce heat to medium-low and cook, stirring occasionally, until sauce is thickened and syrupy, about 5 minutes. Measure out and reserve ¼ cup glaze for serving.

3. Trim steak, cut into 2-inch chunks, and lay on prepared broiler pan. Brush with remaining glaze and broil, turning occasionally, until meat is charred around edges and registers 130 to 135 degrees (for medium), about 10 minutes.

4. Thinly slice scallions. Brush steak with reserved glaze, sprinkle with scallions, and serve.

TEST KITCHEN TIP
COOKING BEEF OR LAMB

Here are the temperatures at which beef or lamb should be removed from the pan, oven, or grill to meet your preferred level of doneness. Note that as the meat rests, its temperature will climb 5 to 10 degrees.

LEVEL OF DONENESS	COOK UNTIL IT REGISTERS
Rare	115 to 120 degrees
Medium-rare	120 to 125 degrees
Medium	130 to 135 degrees
Medium-well	140 to 145 degrees
Well-done	150 to 155 degrees

Philly Cheesesteak Sandwiches

SERVES 4

2 pounds **skirt steak**

4 (8-inch) **Italian sub rolls**

2 tablespoons **vegetable oil**

¼ cup grated **Parmesan cheese**

8 slices (8 ounces)
American cheese

**INGREDIENT SPOTLIGHT
SKIRT STEAK**

This long, thin steak is cut from the underside of the cow. Also known as fajita or Philadelphia steak, it has distinctive striations and an especially beefy taste. Commonly used in fajitas, skirt steak was a good pick for our Philly Cheesesteak Sandwiches because it's easy to slice it into small pieces. Plus, it's well-marbled and reasonably priced.

✓ WHY THIS RECIPE WORKS Two things are key for great Philly cheesesteaks: the right meat and the right cheese. Many sandwich shops use rib-eye steak, which is very expensive, and a meat slicer to shave it incredibly thin. Hunting for a more affordable cut that was easy to slice by hand, we landed on skirt steak. When partially frozen, skirt steak's thin profile made it a snap to shave the steak into thin pieces, and its flavor was nearest to rib-eye, but without the sticker shock. For the cheese, we preferred American, which melted into the steak when placed on top in the hot pan. A sprinkling of grated Parmesan boosted the cheesy flavor, and we tossed the hot steak with the cheeses right in the skillet to evenly distribute their flavors. If skirt steak is unavailable, substitute sirloin steak tips (also called flap meat). Top these sandwiches with chopped pickled hot peppers, sautéed onions or bell peppers, sweet relish, or hot sauce, if desired.

1. Trim steak. Slice steak crosswise, with grain, into 3-inch-wide strips. Place steak on large plate and freeze until very firm, about 1 hour. Using sharp knife, shave frozen steak as thinly as possible against grain. Mound meat on cutting board and chop coarsely with knife, 10 to 20 times.

2. Adjust oven rack to middle position and heat oven to 400 degrees. Split rolls open, spread on baking sheet, and toast until lightly browned, 5 to 10 minutes.

3. Heat 1 tablespoon oil in 12-inch nonstick skillet over high heat until just smoking. Add half of meat in even layer and cook, without stirring, until well browned, 4 to 5 minutes. Stir and continue to cook until meat is no longer pink, 1 to 2 minutes; transfer meat to colander to drain. Wipe out skillet with paper towels and repeat with remaining 1 tablespoon oil and chopped meat.

4. Return now-empty skillet to medium heat. Drain excess moisture from meat, return meat to skillet, and add ½ teaspoon salt and ⅛ teaspoon pepper. Cook, stirring constantly, until meat is warmed through, 1 to 2 minutes.

5. Reduce heat to low, sprinkle with Parmesan, and lay American cheese over top. Let cheeses melt, about 2 minutes. Fold melted cheese into meat thoroughly. Divide mixture evenly among toasted rolls and serve.

Beef and Broccoli Stir-Fry

SERVES 4

1 (1-pound) **flank steak**

2 tablespoons **oyster sauce**

1½ pounds **broccoli**

1 **red bell pepper**

3 tablespoons **sweet chili sauce**

2 tablespoons **toasted sesame oil**

INGREDIENT SPOTLIGHT
OYSTER SAUCE

This thick, salty, strong brown sauce is a concentrated mixture of oysters, soy sauce, brine, and seasonings. It is used to enhance the flavor of many dishes and is the base for many Asian dipping sauces; we use it in our stir-fry for both complex flavor and its thick, clingy texture. Our favorite brand is **Lee Kum Kee's Premium Oyster Flavored Sauce**. Tasters found this oyster sauce to offer intense, deep flavor and a nice balance of saltiness and sweet caramel undertones.

✔ WHY THIS RECIPE WORKS Most stir-fry sauces have several components, but we were limited to two for our beef and broccoli stir-fry. After trying a wide variety of Asian condiments, looking for a duo that would deliver both complex flavor and a thick, clingy texture, we had luck with oyster sauce, which gave us the right texture plus depth, and sweet chili sauce, which tasted sweet, spicy, and bright. For more flavor, we used toasted sesame oil rather than vegetable oil to sauté our meat and vegetables and infuse our stir-fry with nutty flavor and more richness. Serve with rice.

1. Trim steak. Cut lengthwise, with grain, into 2-inch-wide strips, then slice crosswise against grain into ⅛-inch-wide slices. Toss beef with 1 tablespoon oyster sauce. Cut broccoli florets into bite-size pieces. Trim and peel broccoli stalks, then slice crosswise ¼ inch thick. Core red pepper and cut into 2-inch-long matchsticks. Whisk remaining 1 tablespoon oyster sauce, chili sauce, 2 teaspoons oil, and 2 tablespoons water together in bowl.

2. Heat 1 teaspoon oil in 12-inch nonstick skillet over high heat until just smoking. Add half of beef, break up any clumps, and cook, without stirring, for 1 minute. Stir beef and continue to cook until browned, about 2 minutes; transfer to bowl and cover. Repeat with 1 teaspoon oil and remaining beef.

3. Add remaining 2 teaspoons oil to now-empty skillet and return to high heat until just smoking. Add broccoli florets and stalks and bell pepper and cook for 30 seconds. Add ½ cup water, cover, and reduce heat to medium. Steam vegetables until slightly tender, about 2 minutes. Remove lid and continue to cook until broccoli is tender and liquid has evaporated, about 2 minutes.

4. Return cooked beef and any accumulated juices to skillet and toss to combine. Whisk sauce to recombine, then add to skillet. Cook, stirring constantly, until sauce is slightly thickened and coats beef and vegetables, about 1 minute. Serve.

TEST KITCHEN TIP
SLICING BEEF FOR STIR-FRIES

Using sharp chef's knife, slice steak with grain into 2-inch-wide pieces (freezing steak for 15 minutes first will make it easier to slice). Then cut each piece across grain into very thin slices.

Kimchi Fried Rice with Beef

SERVES 4

1 (1-pound) **flank steak**

½ cup **oyster sauce**

5 teaspoons **toasted sesame oil**

2 cups medium-spicy or spicy **cabbage kimchi,** plus ¼ cup kimchi liquid

5 cups **cooked rice**

4 **large eggs**

INGREDIENT SPOTLIGHT KIMCHI

Kimchi is a pickled vegetable condiment found at nearly every meal in Korea and used in many Korean stews and fried rice dishes. There are more than 100 different varieties of kimchi, but the most popular variety consists primarily of napa cabbage, scallions, garlic, and ground chiles in brine; carrots, radishes, and peppers are sometimes included as well. It is packed in jars, where it is allowed to ferment and build its spicy and pungent flavor. Because it includes a handful of vegetables and aromatics, using kimchi in our fried rice helped us cut down on prep time. And rather than drain away the piquant brine, we saved some and added it to the dish for even more flavor.

✓ WHY THIS RECIPE WORKS Our inspiration for this dish came from the Korean rice bowl known as *bibimbap*, which is topped off with meat, veggies, and a fried egg. For our streamlined version, we tossed thinly sliced flank steak in a little oyster sauce before cooking; this kept it moist and gave it a deep, savory flavor. Instead of chopping and cooking a pile of vegetables, we reached for a jar of spicy cabbage kimchi, which includes cabbage and scallions, plus aromatics like garlic and ground chiles. Using precooked rice helped us further simplify our recipe. Rather than keeping the elements separate and layered, we tossed it all together like fried rice so the flavors could meld. Stirring in a few spoonfuls of the kimchi liquid reinforced the spicy, piquant notes of the kimchi, and topping each bowl with a fried egg lent richness and made this loose interpretation of a Korean favorite feel complete. Kimchi can be found in spicy or mild varieties, but we prefer the medium-spicy or spicy variety in this dish. See page 102 for more information on slicing beef for stir-fries.

1. Adjust oven rack to middle position and heat oven to 200 degrees. Trim steak. Cut lengthwise, with grain, into 2-inch-wide strips, then slice crosswise against grain into ⅛-inch-thick slices. Toss beef with 2 tablespoons oyster sauce.

2. Heat 1 teaspoon oil in 12-inch nonstick skillet over high heat until just smoking. Add half of beef, break up any clumps, and cook, without stirring, for 1 minute. Stir beef and continue to cook until browned, about 2 minutes; transfer to bowl and cover. Repeat with 1 teaspoon oil and remaining beef; transfer to bowl.

3. Thoroughly drain kimchi. Add kimchi and 2 tablespoons kimchi liquid to now-empty skillet and cook over medium heat until warmed through, about 2 minutes. Stir in rice, remaining 6 tablespoons oyster sauce, and remaining 2 tablespoons kimchi liquid. Continue to cook, stirring constantly, until mixture is hot, about 3 minutes. Stir in beef and any accumulated juices and let heat through, about 1 minute. Divide rice mixture evenly among 4 ovensafe bowls and keep warm in oven.

4. Crack eggs into 2 small bowls (2 eggs in each). Wipe out now-empty skillet with paper towels, add remaining 1 tablespoon oil, and heat over low heat until shimmering. Gently add eggs to skillet and season with salt and pepper. Cover and cook until whites are set, 2 to 3 minutes. Remove bowls from oven, top each with fried egg, and serve.

Lazy Man's Chili

SERVES 4 TO 6

1½ pounds 85 percent lean **ground beef**

1 tablespoon **chili powder**

2 (15-ounce) cans **kidney beans**

3 cups jarred chunky **tomato salsa**

1½ cups **beef broth**

Fresh cilantro

INGREDIENT SPOTLIGHT
CHILI POWDER

Chili powder is a seasoning blend made from ground dried chiles and an assortment of other ingredients. Much like curry powder, there is no single recipe, but cumin, garlic, and oregano are traditional additions. Be sure to check the label because some chili powders are made from chiles alone and don't include the additional spices, which we like in this dish. Chili powder is not to be confused with the lesser-known chile powder (also often spelled chili powder), made solely from chiles without additional seasonings. Besides its obvious use—to add spicy depth and heat to chili—we also use it in spice rubs and marinades. Our favorite brand is **Morton & Bassett Chili Powder**, which has a deep, roasty, and complex flavor; subtle sweetness; and just the right amount of heat.

☑ WHY THIS RECIPE WORKS Most recipes for chili call for a long list of ingredients and hours of simmering—not ours. We achieved a rich-tasting, meaty chili with just a few main ingredients, and in less than half an hour. Bypassing dried beans in favor of the canned variety was an obvious move, and rinsing the beans helped wash away their canned flavor. We added the chili powder to the pot with the beef so its flavor would bloom, or deepen, as the beef cooked. Canned diced tomatoes held their shape well, but didn't give our chili much body. A simple trick—mashing some beans against the side of the pot—worked wonders, giving us a nicely thickened chili. But the flavor was still lacking. Reviewing the ingredient list, we knew we were missing the aromatic backbone from some onion, garlic, and extra spices. What if we swapped out the canned tomatoes for jarred salsa? Bingo! Now our chili offered bright and balanced, yet still intensely beefy, flavor. A final addition of minced cilantro gave this lazy man's chili surprising depth of flavor and freshness. Do not use leaner ground beef here; the chili won't be as rich-tasting.

1. Combine beef and chili powder in Dutch oven and cook over medium-high heat until beef is no longer raw, about 5 minutes.

2. Rinse beans. Stir beans, salsa, and broth into pot and bring to simmer. Cook, mashing some of the beans against side of pot, until flavors meld and chili is slightly thickened, about 15 minutes.

3. Mince ¼ cup cilantro, stir into chili, and season with salt and pepper to taste. Serve.

TEST KITCHEN TIP
RINSING CANNED BEANS

Canned beans are made by pressure-cooking dried beans directly in the can with water, salt, and preservatives. The resulting starchy canning liquid doesn't taste great, so we like to drain and rinse the beans before using them in a recipe.

Easy Beef Empanadas

SERVES 4

1 pound 85 percent lean
ground beef

1 cup jarred chunky **tomato salsa**

4 **garlic cloves**

Fresh cilantro

1 cup (4 ounces) shredded
Monterey Jack cheese

1 package store-bought **pie dough**

INGREDIENT SPOTLIGHT
JARRED TOMATO SALSA

Though homemade salsa is best, the jarred stuff wins out for convenience every time. We used jarred salsa to make the filling of our empanadas flavorful, moist, and a little spicy. In the test kitchen, **Chi-Chi's Medium Thick and Chunky Salsa** is our favorite brand. Tasters preferred this salsa for its bright, vibrant flavor, which they found to be "spicy, fresh, and tomatoey."

✓ **WHY THIS RECIPE WORKS** Empanadas are essentially the savory Latin-American version of a turnover. Traditional recipes often instruct the cook to stuff a pastry crust (often made with *masa* or corn flour) with a ground or shredded meat filling, but we decided to pass on all the work required to make the pastry and used store-bought pie dough instead, for empanadas with a light and flaky crust. For the filling, ground beef and melt-worthy Monterey Jack cheese were a must, and for flavor and spice we tried everything from tomato paste to Ro-tel tomatoes, which are flavored with chiles. In the end, we settled on jarred salsa plus a few cloves of garlic, which gave us chunky, tender tomatoes, a bit of spice, and an aromatic backbone. You will use both rounds of pie dough in the package and cut them in half to yield 4 empanadas. See page 289 for more information on our favorite pie dough.

1. Adjust oven rack to middle position and heat oven to 450 degrees. Line rimmed baking sheet with parchment paper.

2. Cook beef and salsa together in 12-inch nonstick skillet over medium-high heat until beef is no longer raw, about 5 minutes. Mince garlic, stir into skillet, and cook until fragrant, about 30 seconds, then remove from heat. Mince ¼ cup cilantro; stir into filling with cheese. Season filling with salt and pepper to taste; let cool slightly.

3. Cut each dough round in half. Spread one-quarter of filling over 1 side of each piece of dough, leaving ½-inch border around edges. Brush edges of dough with water, fold over filling, and crimp edges to seal. Transfer to prepared sheet. Using fork, pierce several steam vents in top of dough. Bake empanadas until hot and golden, 15 to 20 minutes. Serve.

TEST KITCHEN TIP **MAKING EASY BEEF EMPANADAS**

 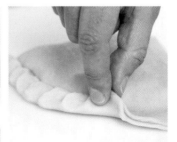

1. Cut each dough round in half. Spread ¼ of filling over 1 side of dough, leaving ½-inch border.

2. Brush dough edges with water, fold over filling, and crimp edges to seal.

Meatloaf Florentine

SERVES 6

1 (25-ounce) jar **tomato sauce**

¾ cup **panko bread crumbs**

⅓ cup **prepared basil pesto**

1½ pounds **meatloaf mix**

3 ounces (3 cups) **baby spinach**

5 thin slices (3 ounces) deli **provolone cheese**

INGREDIENT SPOTLIGHT
PREPARED PESTO

When it comes to versatile, flavor-packed ingredients, one of our favorites is store-bought basil pesto. Of course it can be used as a sauce for pasta, but why stop there? Made from olive oil, pine nuts, basil, garlic, and Parmesan cheese, basil pesto is a highly potent product that can easily add big flavor while streamlining prep and cutting down on the grocery list. When used in meatloaf and meatballs, it also works to contribute moisture and richness.

✔ WHY THIS RECIPE WORKS Some dishes, such as meatloaf, can be hard to dress up. Add a cheesy layer and some greens, however, and you've got a company-worthy take on this comfort-food classic. For ours, we started with meatloaf mix, which is a blend of ground pork, beef, and veal, and combined it with panko bread crumbs for structure. Two convenience products—store-bought tomato sauce and pesto—gave our meatloaf a decidedly Italian feel and robust flavor, and more sauce kept the exterior of our loaf moist in the oven. For the filling, tasters like the combination of thinly sliced provolone and baby spinach; the provolone melted into a nice, gooey layer and the fresh spinach balanced the richness of the meat and cheese. Our effortless meatloaf Florentine, which required no chopping or prep, tasted great and looked just as impressive on the plate—not bad for six ingredients.

1. Adjust oven rack to middle position and heat oven to 350 degrees. Mash ¾ cup tomato sauce, panko, and pesto together in medium bowl with fork. Gently mix in meatloaf mix, ¼ teaspoon salt, and ¼ teaspoon pepper with hands until thoroughly combined.

2. Shape half of meat mixture into 10 by 6-inch rectangle in center of 13 by 9-inch baking dish. Lay half of spinach on top, leaving ½-inch border at edges. Shingle provolone over spinach; top with remaining spinach. Form remaining meat mixture into 9 by 5-inch rectangle; gently transfer to baking dish on top of meatloaf. Reshape top layer as needed and tuck in edges of filling, leaving ½ inch of bottom meat layer exposed. Fold bottom edge of meatloaf over top layer; pinch edges together to seal.

3. Spread ½ cup tomato sauce on top of meatloaf; bake until meatloaf registers 145 degrees, about 45 minutes. Remove from oven; spoon off fat. Add remaining tomato sauce to dish and continue to bake meatloaf until it registers 160 degrees, 10 to 15 minutes. Skim fat from surface of sauce using spoon. Slice meatloaf and serve with sauce.

TEST KITCHEN TIP
MAKING MEATLOAF FLORENTINE

Shape half of meat into 10 by 6-inch rectangle inside baking dish. Layer with half of spinach, provolone, and remaining spinach, leaving ½-inch border. Form remaining meat into 9 by 5-inch rectangle; place on top.

Sesame Pork Chops with Orange and Radish Salad

SERVES 4
8 **radishes**
5 **oranges**
2 tablespoons **sweet chili sauce,** plus extra for serving
½ cup **sesame seeds**
6 (3- to 4-ounce) **boneless pork chops,** ½ inch thick
¼ cup **vegetable oil**

INGREDIENT SPOTLIGHT
SWEET CHILI SAUCE

Often served with barbecued chicken in Thailand, this sweet, thick sauce is mildly flavored and made primarily from palm sugar, pickled chiles, vinegar, and garlic. Though used here as a flavorful "glue" to help sesame seeds adhere to our pork chops, it also works well as a dipping sauce for egg rolls or dumplings. You can find it with the Asian ingredients at the supermarket.

✔ **WHY THIS RECIPE WORKS** To liven up our boneless pork chops for an exciting weeknight dinner, we decided to coat them with crunchy, nutty sesame seeds. With our limited ingredient list, we didn't have room for the typical flour and egg coating to keep the meat moist and help the sesame seeds adhere. We tried brushing Dijon mustard on our chops to get the seeds to stick, but tasters found the flavor overpowering. Looking for a different "glue," we decided to try a few Asian condiments. Oyster sauce was too salty for the mild pork, and Sriracha sauce was too spicy and harsh. A light coating of sweet chili sauce did the trick, providing a subtle sweetness and plenty of sticking power. A refreshing salad of oranges, radishes, and more sweet chili sauce made the perfect bright and lively counterpoint to our sesame seed–encrusted pork chops.

1. Thinly slice radishes. Cut away peel and pith from oranges, then quarter them. Slice each quarter crosswise into ¼-inch-thick pieces. Toss radishes, oranges, 2 teaspoons chili sauce, ⅛ teaspoon salt, and ⅛ teaspoon pepper together in bowl.

2. Spread sesame seeds in shallow dish. Cut 2 small slits, about 2 inches apart, through fat and silverskin on side of each pork chop. Pat chops dry with paper towels and season with salt and pepper. Working with 1 chop at a time, coat evenly with remaining 4 teaspoons chili sauce, then dredge in sesame seeds, pressing on seeds to adhere.

3. Heat oil in 12-inch nonstick skillet over medium heat until shimmering. Fry chops until golden on both sides and meat registers 145 degrees, 2 to 3 minutes per side. Transfer to carving board, let rest for 5 to 10 minutes, then slice into ⅓-inch-thick pieces. Arrange salad and pork among 4 dinner plates and serve with extra chili sauce.

TEST KITCHEN TIP
PREVENTING CURLED PORK CHOPS

To prevent pork chops from curling while cooking, cut two small slits, about 2 inches apart, into the fat and silverskin of each chop (this method works for both bone-in and boneless chops).

Cola-Glazed Pork Chops with Bok Choy and Sticky Rice

SERVES 4

1¾ cups **sushi rice**

4 heads **baby bok choy**

2 tablespoons **vegetable oil**

4 (8-ounce)
bone-in pork rib chops,
¾ inch thick

1 cup **cola**

⅓ cup **hoisin sauce**

INGREDIENT SPOTLIGHT SUSHI RICE

Sushi rice boasts a trademark tacky yet toothsome texture because it is a short-grain rice. Short-grain rice has a higher percentage of starch than other varieties, which translates into its unique texture. Be warned that short-grain rice can get very sticky, if not downright gluey, if overhandled, so be sure to treat it gently once cooked. Look for sushi rice with the other Asian ingredients at the supermarket.

✓ WHY THIS RECIPE WORKS In this Asian-inspired dinner, rich-tasting glazed pork chops and crisp-tender baby bok choy are served on a bed of sticky rice for a truly impressive dinner from six ingredients. For the pork, we started with bone-in rib chops and seared them in a skillet, then set them aside until we had our glaze together in the pan. Looking for something that would give us a sweet yet peppery flavor profile, we hit on cola, which is sometimes used in barbecue sauces. A bit of hoisin added complexity, and a quick simmer ensured the glossy sauce clung nicely to our chops. To make this a meal, we made some sticky rice using short-grain sushi rice and quickly sautéed a few heads of baby bok choy. See page 110 for more information on cutting slits in pork chops.

1. Rinse rice, combine with 2¼ cups water and ½ teaspoon salt in large saucepan, and bring to boil. Cover, reduce heat to low, and cook for 10 minutes. Remove rice from heat and let sit, covered, until tender, about 15 minutes.

2. Meanwhile, halve bok choy lengthwise. Heat 1 tablespoon oil in 12-inch skillet over high heat until shimmering. Add bok choy, cut side down, and cook until lightly browned on bottom, about 2 minutes. Add 2 tablespoons water, cover, and continue to cook until stems are crisp-tender, about 1 minute. Transfer to serving platter and cover to keep warm.

3. Cut 2 small slits, about 2 inches apart, through fat and silverskin on side of each pork chop. Pat chops dry with paper towels and season with ½ teaspoon pepper. Wipe out now-empty skillet with paper towels, add remaining 1 tablespoon oil, and heat over medium-high heat until just smoking. Add chops and cook until well browned and meat registers 145 degrees, 3 to 5 minutes per side. Transfer to plate.

4. Whisk cola, hoisin, and 2 tablespoons water into now-empty skillet and simmer until slightly thickened, about 3 minutes. Return chops and any accumulated juices to skillet and continue to simmer until chops are coated with glaze, 1 to 2 minutes. Transfer to serving platter with bok choy and drizzle with glaze left in pan. Serve with rice.

Cornflake-Crusted Pork Chops

SERVES 4 TO 6

⅔ cup **cornstarch**

1 cup **buttermilk**

2 tablespoons **Dijon mustard**

3 cups **cornflakes**

8 (3- to 4-ounce)
boneless pork chops,
½ to ¾ inch thick

⅔ cup **vegetable oil**

**INGREDIENT SPOTLIGHT
BONELESS PORK CHOPS**

It's hard to deny the convenience of boneless pork chops. They're a super-market staple, they cook in a jiffy, and they require no prep whatsoever. Plus, there's no bone to work around at the dinner table. However, since there's also no bone to help keep the meat juicy or add flavor, it's critical to keep a close eye on the cooking time. When buying pork chops, try to buy chops of a similar size so they will cook through at the same rate. Also, always buy chops that are the thick-ness specified in the recipe; thinner chops will cook through more quickly than the given time and may be dry, while thicker chops will require a longer stint on the stovetop or in the oven and may be underdone by the end of the stated cooking time.

☑ **WHY THIS RECIPE WORKS** For these pork chops, we rethought our standard breading procedure to make every ingredient count. First, we used cornstarch in place of the typical flour; the cornstarch worked to absorb moisture, ensuring our coating was extra-crisp. Rather than use eggs to help the breading adhere, we opted for buttermilk doctored with Dijon mustard, which contributed a savory tang. Finally, crushed cornflakes upped the crunch factor in a big way. To help the cornflakes stay put, we lightly scored the chops before coating them; this way, they released moisture and proteins that the coating could adhere to.

1. Spread ⅓ cup cornstarch into shallow dish. In second shallow dish, whisk buttermilk and mustard together. Process cornflakes, ½ teaspoon salt, ½ teaspoon pepper, and remaining ⅓ cup corn-starch in food processor until finely ground, about 10 seconds; transfer to third shallow dish.

2. Adjust oven rack to middle position and heat oven to 200 degrees. Trim chops completely and score both sides in ½-inch crosshatch pattern, about ¹⁄₁₆ inch deep. Season chops with salt and pepper. Working with 1 chop at a time, dredge in cornstarch and shake off excess. Using tongs, coat with buttermilk mixture, letting excess drip off. Coat with cornflake mixture, gently pat off excess, and transfer to wire rack set in rimmed baking sheet. Let chops sit for 10 minutes.

3. Heat ⅓ cup oil in 12-inch nonstick skillet over medium-high heat until shimmering. Lay 4 chops in skillet and cook until golden and crisp, 2 to 5 minutes. Carefully flip chops and continue to cook until second side is crisp and registers 145 degrees, 2 to 5 minutes longer.

4. Transfer chops to paper towel–lined plate, let drain for 30 sec-onds on each side, then transfer to clean wire rack set over rimmed baking sheet; keep warm in oven. Discard oil in now-empty skillet, wipe it clean with paper towels, and repeat with remaining ⅓ cup oil and breaded pork chops. Serve.

**TEST KITCHEN TIP
SCORING THE CHOPS**

Making shallow cuts in the pork chops' surface releases juices and sticky meat proteins that dampen the cornstarch and help the coating adhere.

Pork Chops with Spicy Pepper Relish and Cheesy Grits

SERVES 4

1 cup **old-fashioned grits**

1 cup (4 ounces) shredded **sharp cheddar cheese**

3 tablespoons **unsalted butter**

4 (6- to 8-ounce) **bone-in pork rib chops,** ½ to ¾ inch thick

4 **red bell peppers**

6 jarred **Peppadew peppers,** plus 2 tablespoons brine

INGREDIENT SPOTLIGHT **GRITS**

Corn grits are cornmeal, or ground-up dried corn. Though grits seem like an easy thing to shop for, it's not hard to confuse them with Italian polenta, which is also made from cornmeal, or cornmeal itself. When shopping, be sure to look for "grits" on the label. Our favorite brand is **Anson Mills Pencil Cobb Grits**, which have an intense, rich flavor but are available via mail order only. For an easier-to-find alternative, we also like Arrowhead Mills Organic Yellow Corn Grits.

WHY THIS RECIPE WORKS A boldly flavored pepper relish brings unexpected flair to this Southern-style supper. Red bell peppers gave the relish a nice sweetness, but for more punch, we added sliced Peppadews; a couple spoonfuls of their brine contributed brightness and much-needed acidity. To infuse our chops with big flavor, we seared them first, then set them aside to cook the peppers and added them back to the pan to finish in the sauce. Finally, for grits with serious richness, we stirred in a full cup of shredded cheddar. See page 110 for more information on cutting slits in pork chops and page 26 for more information on Peppadew peppers.

1. Bring 4 cups water to boil in medium saucepan. Slowly pour in grits while whisking constantly in circular motion. Cover, reduce heat to low, and cook, stirring often, until grits are thick and creamy, 10 to 15 minutes. Off heat, stir in cheddar and 1 tablespoon butter until melted and season with salt and pepper to taste; cover to keep warm.

2. Cut 2 small slits, about 2 inches apart, through fat and silverskin on side of each pork chop. Pat chops dry with paper towels and season with salt and pepper. Core bell peppers and cut into ¼-inch-wide strips. Rinse and thinly slice Peppadews. Melt 1 tablespoon butter in 12-inch skillet over medium-high heat. Add chops and cook until one side is well browned, about 5 minutes. Transfer to plate.

3. Add bell peppers and Peppadews to now-empty skillet and cook, stirring occasionally, until just beginning to soften, about 3 minutes. Add Peppadew brine and 1 cup water and bring to boil, scraping up any browned bits with wooden spoon.

4. Nestle pork chops, browned side up, and any accumulated juices into skillet. Bring to simmer and cook until meat registers 145 degrees, about 5 minutes. Transfer chops to platter. Continue to simmer peppers until liquid is reduced to about ⅓ cup, about 5 minutes. Off heat, stir in remaining 1 tablespoon butter. Season with salt and pepper to taste and pour over chops. Serve with grits.

Spicy Pork Tacos with Pineapple Salsa

SERVES 4

9 ounces
fresh peeled and cored pineapple

1 small **red onion**

Fresh cilantro

1 (10-ounce) can
Ro-tel Diced Tomatoes and Green Chilies

1 pound **ground pork**

8 store-bought **taco shells**

INGREDIENT SPOTLIGHT

TACO SHELLS

Packaged taco shells simplify the process of taco-making tremendously, but do any of them deliver the flavor and texture of home-fried shells? We tasted six brands to find out. Though most of the shells tasted dry and stale, we did find one we liked. **Old El Paso Taco Shells** were deemed the winner, thanks to their solid crispness and corny sweetness.

✔ WHY THIS RECIPE WORKS Looking to tacos *al pastor* for inspiration, we set out to create a recipe for easy pork tacos that were moist and flavorful, with a subtle heat, and boasted the bright, lively notes of fresh pineapple. Rather than using the traditional pork butt, we started with quick-cooking ground pork. To keep the pork moist and infuse it with flavor, we tried cooking it with some chopped onion, tomato sauce, canned tomatoes, and pineapple. Unfortunately, the resulting tacos tasted one-note and overly tomatoey. Next we tried a can of Ro-tel tomatoes, which are flavored with chiles and offered some heat, and pureed them in the food processor along with some pineapple chunks. After a quick simmer in the sauce, the pork was tender and richly flavored. A simple pineapple salsa, flavored with red onion and cilantro, made the perfect garnish and bright-tasting finish to our easy pork tacos.

1. Cut 6 ounces pineapple into ¼-inch pieces and coarsely chop remaining 3 ounces pineapple. Finely chop red onion and mince ¼ cup cilantro. Toss diced pineapple, half of red onion, and cilantro in bowl and season with salt and pepper to taste.

2. Process tomatoes with their juice and coarsely chopped pineapple in food processor until smooth, about 15 seconds. Cook remaining onion and pork together in 12-inch nonstick skillet over medium-high heat until pork is no longer raw, about 5 minutes. Stir in tomato mixture and simmer until thickened, 8 to 10 minutes. Season with salt and pepper to taste.

3. Warm taco shells as directed on package. Divide pork evenly among taco shells and serve with pineapple salsa.

TEST KITCHEN TIP

INFUSING PORK TACOS WITH FLAVOR

To make our own simple but flavorful taco seasoning, we processed Ro-tel tomatoes and fresh pineapple together in the food processor.

Mu Shu–Style Pork Wraps

SERVES 4

1 (1-pound) **pork tenderloin**

8 ounces **shiitake mushrooms**

¼ cup **hoisin sauce,**
plus extra for serving

2 tablespoons **toasted sesame oil**

1 (14-ounce) bag **coleslaw mix**

8 (6-inch) **flour tortillas**

INGREDIENT SPOTLIGHT
COLESLAW MIX

Shredding a head of cabbage and carrots isn't difficult, but it is time-consuming and tedious, especially when you're trying to get a weeknight dinner on the table. Fortunately, there's a two-in-one ingredient that's easy to find at most grocery stores: coleslaw mix. Not only does it cut back on prep time, but it also frees up a space on the shopping list.

WHY THIS RECIPE WORKS Mu shu pork can often be a disappointment with dull, leathery meat and overcooked vegetables. For mu shu–style pork wraps that were faster than delivery and full of fresh flavor, we relied on a package of coleslaw mix, which gave us both shredded cabbage and carrots in one convenient package. We beefed it up with some sliced shiitake mushrooms, which were crucial for imparting an *umami* richness to this simple dish. We reached for the traditional mu shu sauce, hoisin, for a sweet and tangy flavor punch. Toasted sesame oil helped to round out its flavor and provided subtle nutty notes when used to sear the pork.

1. Trim pork and cut into ¼-inch-wide strips. Stem and thinly slice mushrooms. Combine hoisin, 1 tablespoon water, 1 teaspoon oil, and ⅛ teaspoon salt in small bowl.

2. Heat 1 teaspoon oil in 12-inch nonstick skillet over high heat until just smoking. Add half of pork, breaking up any clumps, and cook, without stirring, for 1 minute. Stir pork and continue to cook until lightly browned, about 1 minute; transfer to clean bowl. Repeat with 1 teaspoon oil and remaining pork.

3. Add remaining 1 tablespoon oil to now-empty skillet and return to high heat until just smoking. Add mushrooms and cook until browned, about 3 minutes. Stir in coleslaw mix and cook until vegetables are crisp-tender, about 3 minutes.

4. Return cooked pork and any accumulated juices to skillet. Stir in hoisin mixture and cook, stirring constantly, until sauce is thickened, about 30 seconds; transfer stir-fry to bowl. Stack tortillas on plate, cover, and microwave until soft and hot, about 2 minutes. Serve pork and vegetables with warm tortillas and extra hoisin sauce.

TEST KITCHEN TIP
SLICING PORK FOR STIR-FRIES

Using a sharp chef's knife, slice pork tenderloin into ¼-inch-thick medallions (freezing pork for 15 minutes first will make slicing easier). Then slice each medallion into ¼-inch-wide strips.

Sausage and Giardiniera–Stuffed Peppers

SERVES 4

4 **red bell peppers**

12 ounces **sweet Italian sausage**

2 cups **giardiniera pickled vegetables**

3 **scallions**

2 cups **cooked rice**

2 cups (8 ounces) shredded **Monterey Jack cheese**

INGREDIENT SPOTLIGHT
PRECOOKED RICE

We've found the ease and convenience of precooked rice to be a real asset when trying to save time in the kitchen. Though we prefer the flavor and texture of freshly cooked rice when served alongside chicken or pork chops, when precooked rice is used as an ingredient and combined with other flavors and seasonings (as in our stuffed peppers), we find it a worthy stand-in. In a recent taste test, our preferred brand was **Minute Ready to Serve White Rice**, which had a buttery flavor and an "al dente" bite. Note that one package yields 2 cups of rice.

WHY THIS RECIPE WORKS For a speedy take on stuffed peppers that didn't rely on loads of ingredients, we started by microwaving our peppers to soften them and cut down on the oven time. Looking for a multitasker to ensure our peppers were both filling and flavorful, we tried a frozen vegetable medley, which we cooked with ground beef, but tasters were disappointed with the lack of flavor. *Giardiniera,* the classic Italian combination of pickled celery, cauliflower, and carrots, worked much better, making our filling bright-tasting and lively. But it overpowered the ground beef, so we swapped in sweet Italian sausage, which held its own against the strongly flavored vegetables and provided an intense, savory backbone. With the addition of some shredded Monterey Jack cheese and white rice, these stuffed peppers, which needed just a brief stint under the broiler so the cheese could melt and brown, were as richly flavored as they were satisfying.

1. Adjust oven rack 6 inches from broiler element and heat broiler. Line rimmed baking sheet with aluminum foil. Halve peppers lengthwise and remove core and seeds. Place peppers, cut side down, on large plate and microwave until just tender, about 8 minutes. Pat peppers dry with paper towels.

2. Meanwhile, remove sausage from casing. Rinse and finely chop giardiniera. Cook sausage and giardiniera together in 12-inch nonstick skillet over medium-high heat, breaking sausage into small pieces with wooden spoon, until sausage is no longer raw, 5 to 8 minutes. Thinly slice scallions and stir into skillet with rice and 1 cup cheese. Season with salt and pepper to taste.

3. Place peppers, cut side up, on prepared sheet and fill with sausage mixture. Sprinkle with remaining 1 cup cheese. Broil peppers until cheese is melted and spotty brown, about 3 minutes. Serve.

TEST KITCHEN TIP
MICROWAVING PEPPERS

Jump-starting the cooking of our peppers in the microwave ensures they are soft and tender in a shorter amount of time and need just a brief stint in the oven.

Lamb Pitas with Roasted Red Pepper Sauce

SERVES 4

½ cup jarred **roasted red peppers**

¼ cup plus 2 tablespoons crumbled **marinated feta,** plus 1 tablespoon marinade

4 (8-inch) **pita breads**

1 pound **ground lamb**

1 **romaine lettuce heart** (6 ounces)

1 small **cucumber**

INGREDIENT SPOTLIGHT
MARINATED FETA

Marinated feta combines several ingredients—feta, olive oil, herbs, spices, and peppercorns—in one. This multitasker came in handy when we needed not just tangy bites of cheese, but also an aromatic backbone and a flavorful fat (the marinade) for cooking. You can find marinated feta at supermarket olive bars or packed in jars near the olives.

✅ WHY THIS RECIPE WORKS Rather than use bread crumbs to help bind our lamb patties, we had a better idea. Since we were serving them in pita breads, we simply used part of the pita. Processing the extra pita bits with some marinated feta helped to ensure that the patties were moist and full of flavor, thanks to the cheese and herbs in the marinade. Besides flavoring the patties, the marinade also served as their cooking oil. To top things off, we whipped up a simple roasted red pepper and feta sauce, and for crunch we added sliced cucumber and romaine lettuce. You can substitute 85 percent lean ground beef for the lamb.

1. Rinse peppers, pat dry with paper towels, and process with ¼ cup feta in food processor until completely smooth, about 20 seconds. Season with salt and pepper to taste; transfer to bowl.

2. Cut top 2 inches off each pita bread, reserving 2 scrap pieces. Process reserved pita scrap pieces, 2 tablespoons water, remaining 2 tablespoons feta, ¼ teaspoon salt, and ½ teaspoon pepper in now-empty food processor (no need to clean bowl) until mixture is completely smooth, about 15 seconds. Transfer to large bowl, add lamb, and mix together using hands until combined. Pinch off and roll lamb into 12 balls, then press into ½-inch-thick patties.

3. Heat feta marinade in 12-inch nonstick skillet over medium-high heat until just smoking. Brown patties well on first side, about 4 minutes. Flip patties, reduce heat to medium, and cook until well browned and cooked through, about 5 minutes; transfer to paper towel–lined plate.

4. Shred romaine and thinly slice cucumber. Stack pitas on plate; microwave, covered, until warm, about 30 seconds. Nestle patties, lettuce, and cucumber inside warm pitas, drizzle with pepper sauce, and serve.

TEST KITCHEN TIP
CUTTING THE TOPS OFF PITA

Cut top 2 inches off each pita and reserve 2 trimmed pieces to use as binder in lamb patties.

FIG-GLAZED PORK LOIN WITH ROASTED POTATOES AND BACON

Slow and Easy

125 Cajun Roast Chicken with Sautéed Corn and Bell Pepper

126 Za'atar-Rubbed Butterflied Chicken with Roasted Shallots

127 Chicken with 40 Cloves of Garlic

128 Pomegranate-Glazed Chicken with Couscous

131 Turkey Breast en Cocotte with Pan Gravy

132 Roast Pork Tenderloin with Herbes de Provence and

Warm Fennel Salad

133 Fig-Glazed Pork Loin with Roasted Potatoes and Bacon

135 Easy Stuffed Pork Loin with Sun-Dried Tomato Vinaigrette

136 Roast Pork Loin with Cilantro Sauce

137 Slow-Roasted Pork with Cherry Sauce

139 Roast Beef Sirloin with Caramelized Carrots and Potatoes

140 Braised Beef with Red Wine and Cherries

141 Ginger and Soy–Braised Short Ribs

142 Easiest Sunday Pot Roast

Cajun Roast Chicken with Sautéed Corn and Bell Pepper

SERVES 4
1 (3½- to 4-pound) **whole chicken**
1 tablespoon **olive oil**
1 tablespoon **Cajun seasoning**
4 **scallions**
1 **red bell pepper**
4 ears **corn**

INGREDIENT SPOTLIGHT
CAJUN SEASONING

This ingredient combines the spices, aromatics, and other seasonings found in Cajun cuisine in one convenient spice blend. Though there's no set formula, these blends generally include garlic, onion, paprika, celery seed, and black pepper. You can find Cajun blends with the other spices and herbs at the supermarket.

☑ WHY THIS RECIPE WORKS Roast chicken seems like a simple dish, until you consider that most recipes call for a roasting pan, a V-rack, and rotating the hot bird several times. We found we could skip both the extra equipment and the annoying flipping by using a preheated skillet and placing the bird breast side up in the pan; this gave the thighs a jump start on cooking. Starting the chicken in a 450-degree oven, then turning the oven off while it finished, slowed the evaporation of juices, ensuring moist meat. For flavorful skin, we rubbed the bird with zesty Cajun seasoning before cooking. A maque choux–inspired side dish of sautéed fresh corn, red bell pepper, and scallions, made in the same pan, completed our dish.

1. Adjust oven rack to middle position, place 12-inch ovensafe skillet on rack, and heat oven to 450 degrees. Pat chicken dry with paper towels, tuck wing tips behind back, and tie legs together with kitchen twine. Rub chicken evenly with oil, then Cajun seasoning.

2. Lay chicken, breast side up, in preheated skillet and roast until breast registers 120 degrees and thighs register 135 degrees, 25 to 35 minutes. Turn off oven and leave chicken in oven until breast registers 160 degrees and thighs register 175 degrees, 25 to 35 minutes. Transfer chicken to carving board and let rest for 20 minutes.

3. Mince scallion whites and thinly slice scallion greens; keep whites and greens separate. Core pepper and cut into ¼-inch pieces (see page 201) and cut corn kernels from cobs (see page 181). Carefully (handle will be hot), using spoon, discard all but 1 tablespoon fat left in skillet leaving any fond. Add scallion whites and bell pepper and cook over medium-high heat until soft, about 2 minutes. Stir in corn and cook until lightly browned, about 3 minutes. Off heat, stir in scallion greens and season with salt and pepper to taste. Carve chicken and serve with corn.

TEST KITCHEN TIP
TUCKING THE WINGS

Tucking the wings back behind the chicken before cooking helps prevent the wing tips from burning and allows the skin on the breast to brown more evenly.

Za'atar-Rubbed Butterflied Chicken with Roasted Shallots

SERVES 4

1 (3- to 3½-pound) **whole chicken**

¼ cup crumbled **marinated feta,**
plus 2 tablespoons marinade

1 tablespoon plus ¼ teaspoon
za'atar seasoning

Fresh mint

¾ cup **plain yogurt**

8 **shallots**

INGREDIENT SPOTLIGHT
ZA'ATAR SEASONING

In Arabic, *za'atar* can refer to a specific herb (*Thymbra spicata*); to several herbs that are related to thyme, savory, and oregano; or to a blend of spices that contain these herbs, along with sesame seeds, salt, and sumac. The latter is what we use to flavor our chicken and also what you're most likely to find at your local market. Look for za'atar in the international foods section of your supermarket; you can also find it at Middle Eastern markets.

✓ WHY THIS RECIPE WORKS To add some spice to the weeknight dinner hour, we butterflied our bird and crisped the skin in a skillet before brushing it with a mix of oil and *za'atar*, a Middle Eastern spice blend. Then we tossed some shallots in the hot skillet, returned the chicken to the pan, and roasted the lot in a hot oven. A refreshing yogurt, mint, and feta sauce made the perfect creamy garnish. Using marinated feta let us cut back on the herbs, plus we used the richly flavored oil to sear the chicken.

1. Adjust oven rack to lowest position and heat oven to 450 degrees. Butterfly chicken, pat dry with paper towels, and season with salt and pepper. Heat 1 teaspoon feta marinade in 12-inch ovensafe nonstick skillet over medium-high heat until just smoking. Lay chicken, skin side down, in pan, reduce heat to medium, and place heavy pot on chicken to press it flat. Cook, checking often, until crisp and browned, about 25 minutes. (If chicken is not crisp after 20 minutes, increase heat to medium-high.)

2. Combine 1 tablespoon za'atar and remaining 5 teaspoons feta marinade in bowl. Chop 3 tablespoons mint and combine with feta, yogurt, and remaining ¼ teaspoon za'atar in separate bowl; season with salt and pepper to taste. Peel and halve shallots.

3. Using tongs, transfer chicken, skin side up, to clean plate. Pour off fat in pan, add shallots, and season with salt and pepper. Lay chicken, skin side up, on shallots and brush with za'atar oil. Transfer skillet to oven and roast until breast registers 160 degrees and thighs register 175 degrees, 10 to 20 minutes.

4. Transfer chicken to carving board; let rest for 10 minutes. Continue to roast shallots until tender and browned, 5 to 10 minutes; transfer to serving bowl with slotted spoon. Carve chicken; serve with shallots and yogurt-feta sauce.

TEST KITCHEN TIP
BUTTERFLYING A CHICKEN

Lay chicken on its breast and use poultry shears to cut out backbone. Then, flip chicken over and use heel of your hand to flatten breastbone.

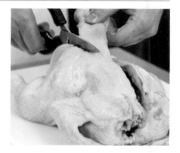

Chicken with 40 Cloves of Garlic

SERVES 4 TO 6

3 **garlic heads**

⅓ cup **olive oil**

4 pounds **bone-in chicken pieces**

¾ cup **chicken broth**

¾ cup
dry vermouth or white wine

1 sprig **fresh rosemary**

INGREDIENT SPOTLIGHT **GARLIC**

Heads of garlic vary in quality, and it can be hard to pick one that's flavorful. Here's our advice: Go for the loose garlic, not the heads sold packaged in little cellophane-wrapped boxes that don't allow for close inspection. Look for heads with no spots of mold or signs of sprouting. Also, it shouldn't smell unusually fragrant or fermented—those are signs of spoilage. Finally, squeeze the head in your hand. If you feel hollow skins where cloves used to reside or if the head feels at all spongy or rubbery, pass it up—it should feel firm and solid. When cooking, be sure to prep your garlic just before you're going to use it as it can lose its potency over time. If your garlic has sprouted, remove the green sprouts prior to cooking; we've found they can impart a bitter taste, even in cooked dishes.

☑ **WHY THIS RECIPE WORKS** In most versions of this French classic, the garlic flavor is minimal, the chicken is dry, and the skin is flabby. We wanted a rich-tasting dish that lived up to its name—it had to offer moist, tender meat and golden, crisp skin, all infused with the nutty, sweet flavor of roasted garlic. For this recipe, we preferred chicken pieces, which took less time in the oven than a whole bird. Browning the chicken before braising it kept the meat moist and allowed the exposed skin to retain its crust in the oven. A sprig of rosemary added depth and freshness, and equal parts chicken broth and dry vermouth made for a bright, perfectly balanced braising liquid. For big garlic flavor, we roasted our cloves first, then smashed them into a paste and added them to the sauce. Not only did the garlic paste contribute flavor, but it also helped thicken the sauce to the right consistency. Leaving a few cloves whole gave our chicken and sauce a rustic appearance. Serve the dish with slices of crusty baguette; you can dip the bread into the sauce and use the whole roasted garlic cloves as a spread. For the chicken, we like to use a combination of split breasts, drumsticks, and thighs.

1. Adjust oven rack to middle position and heat oven to 400 degrees. Separate and peel garlic cloves, then combine with oil, ¼ teaspoon salt, and ½ teaspoon pepper in small baking dish. Cover with aluminum foil and bake, stirring occasionally, until garlic is caramelized and soft, about 20 minutes. Let cool slightly, then drain off and reserve oil. Reserve 12 cloves separately. Mash remaining cloves with 1 tablespoon reserved oil into paste with fork.

2. Increase oven temperature to 450 degrees. Trim chicken, pat dry with paper towels, and season with salt and pepper. Heat 2 tablespoons reserved oil in 12-inch ovensafe skillet over medium-high heat until just smoking. Brown half of chicken on both sides, 5 to 8 minutes per side; transfer to plate. Repeat with remaining chicken and oil left in pan.

3. Pour off fat in now-empty skillet. Add broth, vermouth, and rosemary; bring to simmer over medium heat, scraping up any browned bits. Return chicken, skin side up, to pan with any accumulated juices. Transfer skillet to oven and roast until breasts register 160 degrees and thighs register 175 degrees, 12 to 22 minutes.

4. Transfer chicken to serving dish, tent loosely with foil, and let rest while finishing sauce. Discard rosemary. Carefully (skillet handle will be hot), whisk in garlic paste and reserved cloves. Simmer over medium-high heat until sauce has reduced to 1 cup, about 3 minutes. Season with salt and pepper to taste. Serve with chicken.

Pomegranate-Glazed Chicken with Couscous

SERVES 6 TO 8

2 (3- to 3½-pound)
whole chickens

1 cup **pomegranate molasses,**
plus extra for serving

¼ cup **pine nuts**

2 tablespoons **unsalted butter**

2 teaspoons **curry powder**

1½ cups **couscous**

INGREDIENT SPOTLIGHT
POMEGRANATE MOLASSES

Thick and syrupy, pomegranate molasses is a reduction of pomegranate juice; it has a distinctly rich, tart, and slightly sweet flavor and is an ingredient used in Mediterranean and Middle Eastern cooking. It makes a great glaze for our chicken because it clings nicely and its sugars help the skin brown. You can find pomegranate molasses at well-stocked supermarkets and Middle Eastern markets.

✅ **WHY THIS RECIPE WORKS** Rather than reaching for an armful of ingredients to create an intensely flavored, nicely thickened glaze for our roast chicken, we found one that did the trick: pomegranate molasses. Its bold, sweet-tart flavor made the perfect complement to the mild-tasting meat and clung nicely to our birds, which we butterflied, then halved, for easy maneuvering and even exposure to the heat. Applying the glaze in stages gave each layer a chance to thicken and brown before we added another coating. A simple side dish of couscous, spruced up with curry powder and toasted pine nuts, rounded out the dish. Do not use chickens larger than 3½ pounds in this recipe; they won't fit on the baking sheet.

1. Adjust oven rack to middle position and heat oven to 450 degrees. Line rimmed baking sheet with aluminum foil, top with wire rack, and coat with vegetable oil spray. Pour ½ cup water into pan.

2. Butterfly chickens (see page 126), then split in half. Pat dry with paper towels, season with salt and pepper, and arrange, skin side up, on prepared rack; position pieces as needed to fit. Roast until skin begins to brown, about 25 minutes.

3. Reduce oven temperature to 350 degrees; continue to roast until breasts register 160 degrees and thighs register 175 degrees, 20 to 30 minutes, brushing with ¼ cup molasses every 10 minutes. Transfer to carving board, brush with remaining molasses, and let rest 15 minutes.

4. Toast pine nuts (see page 297). Melt butter in 12-inch nonstick skillet over medium heat. Stir in curry powder and cook until fragrant, about 1 minute. Stir in couscous and cook until fragrant, about 30 seconds. Stir in 2¼ cups water, bring to simmer, then remove from heat. Cover and let sit until liquid is absorbed, about 3 minutes. Stir in pine nuts and season with salt and pepper to taste. Carve chicken and serve with couscous and extra molasses for drizzling.

TEST KITCHEN TIP
SPLITTING A WHOLE CHICKEN

After cutting out backbone and flipping chicken over (see page 126), cut in half through breastbone using chef's knife.

Turkey Breast en Cocotte with Pan Gravy

SERVES 6 TO 8

1 (6- to 7-pound) **bone-in turkey breast**

2 tablespoons **olive oil**

2 **onions**

2 tablespoons **Bell's Poultry Seasoning**

¼ cup **all-purpose flour**

4 cups **chicken broth**

INGREDIENT SPOTLIGHT
BELL'S POULTRY SEASONING

Invented by William G. Bell in Boston in 1867, this seasoning mix combines several herbs and aromatics—rosemary, oregano, sage, ginger, and marjoram—for bold flavor, complexity, and depth in just one ingredient. Though Bell's Poultry Seasoning is most commonly used to flavor turkey and chicken, it can also be used to add herbal notes to stuffing and other side dishes. You can find it in the herb and spice aisle at the supermarket.

WHY THIS RECIPE WORKS Roasting an entire turkey can be tedious. After all, the whole bird has to be turned or flipped, then there's the complicated carving to deal with. But we didn't want to relegate roast turkey to a holidays-only dish. So we could enjoy our turkey year-round, we opted for a bone-in breast, which was easier to maneuver and required no fancy carving, and set out to cook it *en cocotte* (in a covered pot over low heat for an extended period of time) so the meat would be moist and tender. We started by browning the turkey in our Dutch oven to build flavor, added onions and a convenient herb blend—Bell's Poultry Seasoning—for savory depth, then covered the pot and moved it to the oven for easy, hands-off cooking. After setting the cooked turkey aside for a brief rest, we used the spent onions and drippings left behind in the pot, plus some chicken broth and flour, to make a rich gravy. Be sure to use a 7- to 8-quart Dutch oven here. Don't buy a turkey breast larger than 7 pounds; it won't fit in the pot.

1. Adjust oven rack to lowest position and heat oven to 250 degrees. Trim turkey, pat dry with paper towels, and season with salt and pepper. Heat oil in large Dutch oven over medium-high heat until just smoking. Brown breast side of turkey, 5 to 10 minutes; transfer to plate.

2. Chop onions, add to fat left in pot, and cook over medium-high heat until softened, 5 to 7 minutes. Off heat, stir in seasoning and add turkey, skin side up. Place large sheet of aluminum foil over pot and press to seal, then cover tightly with lid. Transfer pot to oven and cook until turkey registers 160 degrees, 1½ to 2 hours.

3. Remove pot from oven. Transfer turkey to carving board, tent loosely with foil, and let rest while making gravy. Place pot with juices and onions over medium-high heat and simmer until almost all liquid has evaporated, 15 to 20 minutes.

4. Stir in flour and cook, stirring constantly, until browned, 2 to 5 minutes. Slowly whisk in chicken broth and simmer, stirring often, until gravy is thickened and has reduced to 2½ cups, 10 to 15 minutes. Strain gravy through fine-mesh strainer and season with salt and pepper to taste. Carve turkey and serve with gravy.

Roast Pork Tenderloin with Herbes de Provence and Warm Fennel Salad

SERVES 4 TO 6

2 large **fennel bulbs**

½ cup pitted
niçoise or kalamata olives

2 tablespoons
extra-virgin olive oil

2 (1-pound) **pork tenderloins**

2 teaspoons **herbes de Provence**

1 **orange**

INGREDIENT SPOTLIGHT
PORK TENDERLOIN

Pork tenderloin is an easy-to-find, quick-cooking cut that has a mild flavor and is easily embellished with a spice rub or simple glaze. But be careful when cooking pork tenderloin; this lean, delicate, boneless meat has little marbling so it can dry out faster than fattier cuts. A thin, tough membrane called the silverskin covers part of the tenderloin and is best removed before cooking.

✓ WHY THIS RECIPE WORKS Mild-tasting pork tenderloin makes the perfect showcase for many flavors. To dress up ours, we looked to the Mediterranean for inspiration. A rub of herbes de Provence, usually a mix of basil, fennel seed, lavender, marjoram, rosemary, sage, and thyme, contributed depth. Subtly sweet, anise-scented fennel and briny olives added more flavor and substance. Giving the fennel a head start in the microwave before popping it into the oven with the pork tenderloin ensured it was tender and nicely caramelized by the end of the cooking time. A bit of orange zest and orange pieces, stirred into the fennel and olives, worked to reinforce the bright and sunny Mediterranean tone of our dish.

1. Adjust oven rack to lower-middle position; heat oven to 450 degrees. Line rimmed baking sheet with aluminum foil. Trim fennel stalks and fronds (see page 177); mince fronds and reserve. Trim bulb, cut in half, core, and cut crosswise into ½-inch-thick slices. Combine fennel and 2 tablespoons water in bowl and microwave, covered, until softened, about 5 minutes; drain well. Halve olives, toss with fennel and oil, and season with salt and pepper to taste.

2. Trim pork, pat dry with paper towels, and season with herbes de Provence, salt, and pepper. Lay pork in center of prepared sheet. Arrange fennel mixture around pork and roast until pork registers 145 degrees, 20 to 25 minutes, turning tenderloins over halfway through roasting. Transfer pork to carving board, tent loosely with foil, and let rest for 10 minutes.

3. Grate orange for 1 teaspoon zest, stir into vegetables, and continue to roast until fennel is tender, about 10 minutes. Cut away peel and pith from orange, then quarter and slice crosswise into ¼-inch-thick pieces. Stir orange into roasted vegetables and sprinkle with fennel fronds. Cut pork into ½-inch-thick slices and serve with salad.

TEST KITCHEN TIP
REMOVING PORK SILVERSKIN

To remove silverskin, simply slip a knife under it, angle knife slightly upward, and remove it using a gentle back-and-forth motion.

Fig-Glazed Pork Loin with Roasted Potatoes and Bacon

4 slices **bacon**

2 pounds **small red potatoes**

1 (2- to 2½-pound)
boneless pork loin roast

1 tablespoon **ground fennel seeds**

¼ cup **fig jam or preserves**

Fresh chives

**INGREDIENT SPOTLIGHT
FIG JAM OR PRESERVES**

This thick, rich-tasting condiment of cooked figs contains sugar plus an acidic ingredient, such as vinegar or citrus, to keep it from tasting overly sweet. The balanced sweetness and the figs' subtle earthy notes make this jam perfect for savory recipes. You'll find fig jam or preserves at the supermarket; you can also find it at high-end or gourmet markets.

✔ WHY THIS RECIPE WORKS This one-pan meal has it all—it's simple, elegant, and flavorful. After microwaving chopped bacon to render its fat, we tossed it with red potatoes for a robustly flavored side dish. Brushing the pork with bacon fat added flavor and moisture, and helped the seasoning—we liked sweet, aniselike ground fennel—adhere to the roast. To ensure that our halved potatoes became nicely browned and crisp, we placed them cut side down on the baking sheet with the pork. For a final flourish, we brushed the hot pork roast with fig jam; while the pork rested, the jam melted into a sweet glaze. We prefer to use small red potatoes measuring about 1 inch in diameter in this recipe, but you can substitute larger red potatoes, cut into ¾-inch chunks. Using a nonstick baking sheet helps the potatoes crisp more; a regular baking sheet can be used but the potatoes won't be as crisp. You can substitute orange marmalade or caramelized onion jam in this recipe if desired.

1. Adjust oven rack to upper-middle position and heat oven to 375 degrees. Chop bacon and microwave in bowl until it is slightly shriveled and fat has rendered, 1 to 3 minutes. Reserve 1 teaspoon bacon fat. Halve potatoes, toss with remaining bacon fat, and season with salt and pepper.

2. Trim pork, pat dry with paper towels, and brush with reserved bacon fat. Combine fennel seeds, ¼ teaspoon salt, and ½ teaspoon pepper and rub evenly over pork. Lay roast in center of nonstick baking sheet. Lay potatoes, cut side down, around pork and scatter bacon pieces over potatoes. Roast until pork registers 140 degrees, 30 to 45 minutes, rotating sheet halfway through roasting.

3. Transfer pork to carving board, brush with fig jam, and let rest for 15 minutes. Continue to roast potatoes and bacon until potatoes are browned and bacon is crisp, about 8 minutes. Cut pork into ½-inch-thick slices. Mince 2 tablespoons chives, toss with roasted potatoes and bacon, and serve with pork.

Easy Stuffed Pork Loin with Sun-Dried Tomato Vinaigrette

SERVES 6

1 (3-pound)
boneless pork loin roast

⅓ cup **olive tapenade**

¼ cup
oil-packed sun-dried tomatoes,
plus 3 tablespoons oil

Fresh basil

1 small **shallot**

4 teaspoons **red wine vinegar**

INGREDIENT SPOTLIGHT
OLIVE TAPENADE

Olive tapenade, sometimes sold as olive spread, is a robustly flavored condiment made from olives, garlic, olive oil, and sometimes capers and anchovies. Woodsy herbs, such as oregano or rosemary, are often included as well. This rich-tasting spread makes a great dip for crackers and crudités, and a good relish for sandwiches, meat, and fish. At the supermarket, you may see both green olive and black olive (usually kalamata) varieties; either one will work in this recipe.

✓ WHY THIS RECIPE WORKS For a convenient, one-ingredient filling for stuffed pork loin roast, we went with prepared olive tapenade, which offered intense flavor and aromatic notes and helped to keep the pork moist. For a bright vinaigrette to serve with the roast, we started with sun-dried tomatoes, which fit the Mediterranean theme and provided oil that we could use to brown our pork. Basil added freshness, and red wine vinegar contributed fruity notes.

1. Adjust oven rack to lower-middle position and heat oven to 375 degrees. Set wire rack inside rimmed baking sheet lined with aluminum foil. Trim pork, pat dry with paper towels, and butterfly (see photos). Spread tapenade evenly over roast, leaving ¼-inch border at edges. Roll and tie pork with kitchen twine at 1½-inch intervals. Season with salt and pepper.

2. Heat 1 tablespoon tomato oil in 12-inch skillet over medium-high heat until just smoking. Brown pork well on all sides, 8 to 10 minutes. Transfer pork to prepared wire rack and roast until pork registers 140 degrees, 40 to 60 minutes. Transfer pork to carving board, tent loosely with foil, and let rest for 15 minutes.

3. Coarsely chop tomatoes, chop 3 tablespoons basil, and mince shallot; combine with vinegar, 3 tablespoons water, and remaining 2 tablespoons tomato oil in bowl and season with salt and pepper to taste. Remove twine from pork, cut pork into ½-inch-thick slices, and serve with tomato vinaigrette.

TEST KITCHEN TIP BUTTERFLYING A PORK LOIN

1. Slice roast open down middle, from end to end, about two-thirds through meat. Gently open up roast with your hands to expose interior.

2. There will be two distinct lobes of meat on either side of initial cut. Carefully slice open each lobe, from end to end, until roast lays flat, being careful not to cut through meat.

Roast Pork Loin with Cilantro Sauce

SERVES 6

1 (3-pound)
boneless pork loin roast

2 teaspoons **ground cumin**

½ cup plus 1 tablespoon **olive oil**

2 bunches **fresh cilantro**

2 **garlic cloves**

4 teaspoons
Rose's Sweetened Lime Juice

INGREDIENT SPOTLIGHT
ROSE'S SWEETENED LIME JUICE

This cocktail-mixer's staple was invented in the late 1800s by a family of shipbuilders as a way to combat scurvy, but nowadays it is called for in many cocktails and stocked not only at liquor stores, but also many supermarkets. Though there are many flavor variations of this cocktail mixer, we prefer the classic sweetened lime juice in our roast pork loin recipe for the sweet and tart notes it contributes.

✔ WHY THIS RECIPE WORKS To take our roast pork dinner from ordinary to extraordinary, we took a hint from Caribbean cuisine, which adds bright, lively notes to pork in the form of herbs, garlic, and citrus, usually combined in a sauce. For our own potently flavored sauce, we started by pulsing cilantro, olive oil, and garlic in a food processor until the cilantro was minced but still retained some texture. Fresh lime juice added much-needed acidity, but we really hit the jackpot when we swapped the lime juice for Rose's Sweetened Lime Juice. This bartender's staple added a nice citrusy punch and sweet flavor to our sauce. As for the pork, rubbing it with cumin prior to cooking it gave it warm spice notes and stayed true to the flavor profile of our dish. A moderate oven kept the meat from drying out during roasting, ensuring rosy, tender slices of pork. This sauce uses two entire bunches of cilantro, including the stems. Do not substitute extra-virgin olive oil for the regular olive oil because it will impart a bitter flavor to the sauce.

1. Adjust oven rack to lower-middle position and heat oven to 375 degrees. Set wire rack inside rimmed baking sheet lined with aluminum foil. Trim pork, tie at 1½-inch intervals with kitchen twine, and pat dry with paper towels. Season pork with cumin, salt, and pepper.

2. Heat 1 tablespoon oil in 12-inch skillet over medium-high heat until just smoking. Brown pork well on all sides, 8 to 10 minutes. Transfer pork to prepared wire rack and roast until pork registers 140 degrees, 40 to 60 minutes, turning roast over halfway through roasting.

3. Trim cilantro stems and mince garlic. Pulse cilantro, garlic, remaining ½ cup oil, and lime juice in food processor until cilantro is finely chopped, 10 to 15 pulses, scraping down bowl as needed. Season with salt and pepper to taste.

4. Transfer pork to carving board, tent loosely with foil, and let rest for 15 minutes. Cut pork into ¼-inch-thick slices and serve with cilantro sauce.

Slow-Roasted Pork with Cherry Sauce

SERVES 8 TO 12

1 (6- to 8-pound)
bone-in pork butt roast

⅔ cup packed **light brown sugar**

10 ounces
fresh or frozen pitted cherries

2 cups **dry red wine**

5 tablespoons **red wine vinegar**

¼ cup **ruby port**

INGREDIENT SPOTLIGHT
FROZEN CHERRIES

Since cherry season is so short, a bag of frozen cherries can come in handy if you want to cook or bake with this fruit any other time of the year. Our favorite brand is **Cascadian Farm Organic Premium Organic Sweet Cherries**. These large, glossy, dark cherries were consistent in both size and appearance—unlike other brands we sampled—and tasted as good as they looked, with tasters describing them as "sweet, ripe, and fruity."

WHY THIS RECIPE WORKS Pork butt isn't just for barbecue—we used it for our hearty, old-fashioned roast. This cut is loaded with intramuscular fat that builds flavor and bastes the meat during roasting; on the outside, its top layer of fat renders to form a perfectly bronzed crust. We didn't need much to enhance the roast's texture and flavor; a simple rub of kosher salt and brown sugar did the trick, and scoring the meat first helped the rub penetrate. For an accompanying sauce, we combined cherries, red wine, port, red wine vinegar, and a tad more brown sugar with the drippings, then reduced it all. To round out the sweetness and punch up the brightness, we finished it with an extra spoonful of vinegar. We prefer natural to enhanced pork, though either will work in this recipe. We also prefer to use kosher salt in step 1, but 2½ tablespoons of table salt can be substituted if necessary. Add more water to the roasting pan as necessary during the last hours of cooking to prevent the drippings from burning.

1. Using sharp knife, cut slits 1 inch apart in crosshatch pattern in fat cap of roast, being careful not to cut into meat. Combine ⅓ cup kosher salt and ⅓ cup sugar and rub over entire roast and into slits. Wrap meat tightly with plastic wrap, place in large bowl, and refrigerate for 12 to 24 hours.

2. Adjust oven rack to lowest position; heat oven to 325 degrees. Lightly coat V-rack with vegetable oil spray and set in large roasting pan. Brush off any excess salt and sugar from roast, blot dry, and season with pepper. Lay roast in prepared V-rack; add 6 cups water to pan.

3. Roast pork until meat is extremely tender and registers 190 degrees, 5 to 6 hours, basting twice during cooking and adding more water to pan as needed to keep juices from burning. Transfer pork to carving board, tent loosely with aluminum foil, and let rest for 1 hour. Pour drippings from roasting pan into fat separator. Let liquid settle for 5 minutes, then pour off and reserve ¼ cup defatted liquid; discard fat and remaining liquid.

4. Bring ¼ cup defatted liquid, cherries, wine, remaining ⅓ cup brown sugar, ¼ cup vinegar, and port to simmer in small saucepan over medium heat. Cook, stirring occasionally, until reduced to 1½ cups, about 45 minutes. Off heat, stir in remaining 1 tablespoon vinegar; cover to keep warm.

5. Using paring knife, cut around inverted T-shaped bone of pork until it can be pulled from roast (use clean dish towel to grasp bone). Using serrated knife, thinly slice pork and serve with cherry sauce.

Roast Beef Sirloin with Caramelized Carrots and Potatoes

Fresh thyme

2 tablespoons **unsalted butter**

1½ pounds **red potatoes**

1½ pounds **carrots**

1 (2-pound)
boneless top sirloin roast

3 tablespoons **vegetable oil**

INGREDIENT SPOTLIGHT
TOP SIRLOIN ROAST

Also known as a top butt or center-cut roast, the top sirloin roast is our favorite inexpensive roast in the test kitchen; it offers big, beefy flavor and a tender texture at a reasonable price. Look for a roast with at least a ¼-inch fat cap on top; the fat renders in the oven, basting the roast and helping to keep it moist.

☑ **WHY THIS RECIPE WORKS** You don't need a long list of ingredients to make a truly great roast beef dinner. We started with a top sirloin roast, which offers ultra-beefy flavor and a tender texture. After searing the roast for a nicely browned exterior, we moved it to a low oven so it could cook through gently and evenly. Finishing the beef in a super-hot oven guaranteed it had a nice crust that contrasted with the rosy, juicy interior. An easy compound butter, infused with fresh thyme, made the perfect finishing touch to our beef. Because no roast beef dinner is complete without some vegetables, we added carrots and potatoes to the mix and jump-started their cooking in the microwave before adding them to the pan to cook alongside the roast.

1. Mince 1 tablespoon thyme. Soften butter and stir in 1 teaspoon thyme, pinch salt, and pinch pepper. Place butter in center of piece of plastic wrap, shape into log, then wrap tightly. Refrigerate until firm, about 1 hour.

2. Adjust oven rack to lower-middle position and heat oven to 250 degrees. Cut potatoes into 1½-inch pieces. Peel carrots, halve lengthwise, and cut into 1½-inch pieces. Combine potatoes and carrots with ¼ cup water in large bowl, cover, and microwave until vegetables are mostly tender, about 10 minutes.

3. Trim fat on beef roast to ⅛ inch thick and tie roast at 1½-inch intervals with kitchen twine. Pat beef dry with paper towels and season with salt and pepper. Heat 1 tablespoon oil in 12-inch skillet over medium-high heat until just smoking. Brown beef well on all sides, 7 to 10 minutes; transfer to large roasting pan.

4. Drain vegetables well, toss with remaining 2 tablespoons oil and remaining 2 teaspoons thyme, and season with salt and pepper. Spread vegetables into roasting pan around beef. Roast beef and vegetables until meat registers 110 degrees, 50 to 55 minutes. Increase oven temperature to 500 degrees and continue to roast beef and vegetables until meat registers 120 degrees (for rare) to 125 degrees (for medium-rare), 10 to 15 minutes longer.

5. Transfer beef to carving board, tent loosely with aluminum foil, and let rest for 15 minutes. Continue to roast vegetables until nicely browned, about 15 minutes. Remove twine from beef and slice ¼ inch thick. Unwrap butter, slice into 4 pieces, and place on top of beef. Serve with vegetables.

Braised Beef with Red Wine and Cherries

SERVES 4 TO 6

6 slices **bacon**

1 (3½- to 4-pound) **boneless beef chuck-eye roast**

3 **onions**

2 cups **red wine**

1½ cups (6 ounces) **dried cherries**

Fresh parsley

INGREDIENT SPOTLIGHT
RED WINE FOR COOKING

We recently tested more than 30 bottles of wine—from $5 jug wines to a $30 Bordeaux—cooked in a hearty tomato sauce, a pan sauce, and a slow-simmered beef stew. What did we learn? First, save the expensive wine for drinking; wines that cost $10 and under were fine for cooking. Second, stick with blends like Côtes du Rhône or generically labeled "table" wines that use a combination of grapes to yield a balanced, fruity finish. If you prefer single grape varietals, choose medium-bodied wines, such as Pinot Noir and Merlot; oaky wines, like Cabernet Sauvignon, turned bitter when cooked. Finally, avoid the "cooking wines" sold in supermarkets. These low-alcohol concoctions have little flavor, a high-pitched acidity, and enormous amounts of salt.

✓ WHY THIS RECIPE WORKS Beef chuck-eye roast may be the go-to cut for beef stews, but it doesn't need to be flanked by carrots and potatoes to deliver a satisfying dinner. We put this economical cut to work in a simple braise with a sweet and savory sauce. Smoky bacon laid down a base of flavor and provided ample fat for sautéing thinly sliced onions. Braising our beef chunks in red wine in a low oven worked to infuse them with intense flavor and allowed them to cook through gently. Uncovering the pot halfway through the cooking time enabled the exposed beef to brown, thereby eliminating the time-consuming step of searing it beforehand. Dried cherries, stirred in toward the end of cooking, infused the sauce with their sweet, tart flavor. To finish our dish and brighten the flavor of the sauce, we added more red wine; minced parsley added freshness. Serve with mashed potatoes or buttered noodles.

1. Adjust oven rack to middle position and heat oven to 300 degrees. Finely chop bacon and cook in Dutch oven over medium heat until crisp, 5 to 7 minutes. Using slotted spoon, transfer bacon to paper towel–lined plate. Trim beef, cut into 2-inch pieces, and season with 1 teaspoon salt and ½ teaspoon pepper.

2. Halve and thinly slice onions; add to fat left in pot. Add ¼ teaspoon salt and cook over medium heat until onions are softened, 5 to 7 minutes. Slowly whisk in 1¾ cups wine, scraping up any browned bits. Stir in beef and half of bacon. Cover, bring to simmer, transfer to oven, and cook for 1 hour.

3. Stir in cherries and continue to cook stew in oven, uncovered, until meat is tender, 1½ to 2 hours longer. Stir in remaining ¼ cup wine and season with salt and pepper to taste. Mince 2 tablespoons parsley, sprinkle over stew with remaining bacon, and serve.

TEST KITCHEN TIP
TRIMMING AND CUTTING A ROAST

Pull apart roast at its major seams delineated by lines of fat and silverskin, using a knife as necessary. Then trim off excess fat and silverskin and cut meat into cubes or chunks as directed in recipe.

Ginger and Soy–Braised Short Ribs

SERVES 6
6 **scallions**
1 (3-inch) piece **ginger**
1 tablespoon **vegetable oil**
¾ cup **hoisin sauce**
2 tablespoons **soy sauce**
3½ pounds **boneless beef short ribs**

INGREDIENT SPOTLIGHT
HOISIN SAUCE

Hoisin is a thick, reddish-brown mixture of soybeans, sugar, vinegar, garlic, chiles, and spices, the most predominant of which is five-spice powder. It is used in many classic Chinese dishes, such as Peking duck and kung pao shrimp, and as a table condiment, but we've also found it to be a great asset in the six-ingredient pantry because it gives sauces both a sweet, tangy flavor and a rich, thick texture. Our favorite brand is **Kikkoman Hoisin Sauce**; tasters praised its initial "burn," which mellowed into a harmonious blend of sweet and savory flavors.

☑ **WHY THIS RECIPE WORKS** Braised short ribs have a rich flavor and fork-tender texture, but their excess fat can weigh them down and make for an overly greasy dish. We found that less fat is rendered from boneless short ribs, so we opted to use those, although bone-in short ribs will work fine, too. To balance the richness of our short ribs, we turned to an Asian-influenced braising liquid, spiked with fresh ginger and scallions. To boost the flavor further and achieve the right consistency, we turned to thick, sticky hoisin sauce, which also gave the sauce a sweet backbone. A couple spoonfuls of soy sauce, along with some smashed ginger and minced scallion whites, rounded out the sauce; we sprinkled the scallion greens on at the end for a fresh hit of allium flavor and bright color. After defatting the braising liquid, we reduced it to concentrate the flavors and thicken it slightly, so we would have a rich, luxurious sauce for our fork-tender meat. Make sure that the ribs are at least 4 inches long and 1 inch thick. If boneless short ribs are unavailable, buy 7 pounds of bone-in beef short ribs (at least 4 inches long with 1 inch of meat above the bone) and remove the bones yourself.

1. Adjust oven rack to lower-middle position and heat oven to 300 degrees. Mince scallion whites and slice scallion greens on bias; keep whites and greens separate. Peel ginger, slice into ¼-inch-thick rounds, and smash with back of knife. Heat oil in Dutch oven over medium–high heat until shimmering. Add scallion whites and cook, stirring occasionally, until softened, 3 to 5 minutes. Stir in ginger and cook until fragrant, about 1 minute. Stir in hoisin, soy sauce, and 3 cups water, scraping up any browned bits.

2. Trim beef, season with 1 teaspoon pepper, and add to pot. Cover, bring to simmer, transfer to oven, and cook for 1 hour. Stir meat thoroughly and continue to cook in oven, covered, until meat is tender, 1 to 1½ hours longer.

3. Using tongs, transfer meat to serving platter and tent with aluminum foil. Strain cooking liquid through fine-mesh strainer into fat separator, pressing on solids to extract as much liquid as possible; discard solids. Return defatted liquid to pot and simmer over medium heat until reduced to 2 cups, about 15 minutes. Stir in scallion greens, pour over meat, and serve.

Easiest Sunday Pot Roast

SERVES 4 TO 6

1 (3½- to 4-pound)
boneless beef chuck-eye roast

1 tablespoon **vegetable oil**

2 **garlic cloves**

Fresh thyme

1 (10.5-ounce) can
condensed French onion soup

2½ pounds **small red potatoes**

INGREDIENT SPOTLIGHT
CONDENSED FRENCH ONION SOUP

Condensed soups have been used in casseroles for years to help add both flavor and moisture. But we found we could use this convenient multitasker—specifically, condensed French onion soup—to give our easy pot roast intense flavor and a liquid base, without calling for a slew of extra ingredients.

WHY THIS RECIPE WORKS For a hearty pot roast with fall-apart meat and a savory sauce, we started with a chuck-eye roast; its fat and connective tissue broke down and kept the meat moist in the oven. Separating the roast into two lobes helped shorten the cooking time. Browning the meat first added flavor as well as color. Minced garlic and fresh thyme offered depth. For the braising liquid, we used condensed French onion soup for an intense flavor base and added enough water for the liquid to come up the sides of the roast and prevent it from drying out. Small red potatoes (about 1 to 2 inches in diameter) completed our easy roast.

1. Adjust oven rack to lower-middle position and heat oven to 300 degrees. Pull roast apart into 2 pieces and trim, tie each piece with kitchen twine, pat dry with paper towels, and season with pepper. Heat oil in Dutch oven over medium-high heat until just smoking. Brown roasts on all sides, 7 to 10 minutes; transfer to large plate.

2. Mince garlic and 1 teaspoon thyme; add to fat left in pot. Cook over medium heat until fragrant, about 30 seconds. Stir in soup and 2 cups water, scraping up any browned bits, and bring to simmer. Add roasts and any accumulated juices to pot; bring to simmer. Cover, transfer pot to oven, and cook for 2 hours, turning roasts every hour.

3. Halve potatoes, stir into pot, and continue to cook in oven, covered, until meat and potatoes are very tender, 1 to 1½ hours longer. Remove pot from oven. Transfer potatoes to serving platter; cover to keep warm. Transfer roasts to carving board, tent loosely with aluminum foil, and let rest for 15 minutes.

4. Pour braising liquid into fat separator, then return defatted liquid to pot and simmer over medium heat until reduced to 1½ cups, about 10 minutes. Season sauce with salt and pepper to taste. Remove twine, cut roasts into ½-inch-thick slices, and transfer to platter. Pour 1 cup sauce over top and serve with remaining sauce.

TEST KITCHEN TIP
SEPARATING AND TYING A ROAST

Pull roast apart into 2 pieces and trim. Then tie each piece with kitchen twine.

ROASTED SALMON WITH TANGERINE RELISH

Seafood

147   Baked Cod with Artichokes, Olives, and Sun-Dried Tomatoes

148   Braised Cod with Leeks and Cherry Tomatoes | FAST RECIPE

149   Thai-Style Fish and Creamy Coconut Rice Packets | FAST RECIPE

151   Roasted Cod Fillets with Crispy Potatoes and Lemon

152   Swordfish en Cocotte with Fennel and Pesto

153   Catfish in Salty-Sweet Caramel Sauce

154   Sesame-Crusted Tuna with Wasabi Dressing | FAST RECIPE

156   Roasted Salmon with Tangerine Relish | FAST RECIPE

157   Miso-Glazed Salmon

158   Crispy Potato-Crusted Salmon with Herb Salad | FAST RECIPE

160   Spicy Pan-Seared Shrimp with Tomatoes and Scallions | FAST RECIPE

161   Greek-Style Shrimp with Orzo and Feta

163   Pan-Seared Scallops with Butternut Squash Puree | FAST RECIPE

164   Pan-Seared Scallops with Tomato-Ginger Relish | FAST RECIPE

165   Bistro-Style Steamed Mussels with White Wine
and Garlic | FAST RECIPE

167   Clams with Israeli Couscous, Chorizo, and Scallions | FAST RECIPE

Baked Cod with Artichokes, Olives, and Sun-Dried Tomatoes

SERVES 4

¾ cup
oil-packed sun-dried tomatoes

1 pound **frozen artichoke hearts**

1 **lemon**

½ cup pitted **kalamata olives**

4 (6-ounce) **skinless cod fillets,**
1 to 1½ inches thick

Fresh basil

INGREDIENT SPOTLIGHT
FROZEN ARTICHOKES

Frozen artichokes are a convenient alternative to the fresh variety, which can be labor-intensive and time-consuming to prepare. (Jarred artichokes, which are usually packed in marinade, are useful when we need the seasonings to play a role and help flavor a dish.) You can thaw frozen artichokes in the microwave. Or, if you have time, you can thaw them overnight in the refrigerator.

✓ **WHY THIS RECIPE WORKS** Wanting to infuse baked cod with the zesty flavors of the Mediterranean, we turned to artichoke hearts (frozen for convenience), kalamata olives, and chopped tomatoes. The dish was good, but needed a flavor boost. Switching from regular tomatoes to sun-dried tomatoes solved the problem, plus the flavorful packing oil provided brightness and aromatic notes to our artichokes, which we roasted before adding the fish, tomatoes, and olives, to ensure that they were nicely browned and deeply flavored. Fresh lemon zest and juice along with fresh basil added brightness. You can substitute haddock or halibut for the cod. To thaw the frozen artichokes quickly, microwave them, covered, for 3 to 5 minutes, then drain them thoroughly in a colander.

1. Adjust oven rack to middle position and heat oven to 450 degrees. Drain sun-dried tomatoes, reserving ¼ cup tomato oil. Thaw artichokes, pat dry, and toss with 2 tablespoons tomato oil; season with salt and pepper. Spread artichokes into 13 by 9-inch baking dish and roast until lightly browned, about 15 minutes.

2. Grate lemon for 1 teaspoon zest, then squeeze for 1 tablespoon juice. Chop olives. Remove baking dish from oven and carefully stir in lemon zest, olives, tomatoes, and 1 tablespoon tomato oil.

3. Pat cod dry with paper towels. Nestle cod into artichoke mixture, brush with remaining 1 tablespoon tomato oil, and season with salt and pepper. Bake until fish flakes apart when gently prodded with paring knife and registers 140 degrees, 15 to 18 minutes. Chop 2 tablespoons basil. Drizzle fish with lemon juice, sprinkle with basil, and serve.

TEST KITCHEN TIP
TUCKING THE TAIL

If you end up with a piece of fish with a thinner tail end, simply tuck the thinner end under before cooking so that it will cook at the same rate as the other pieces.

Braised Cod with Leeks and Cherry Tomatoes

SERVES 4

1 pound **leeks**

12 ounces **cherry tomatoes**

4 **garlic cloves**

3 tablespoons **unsalted butter**

½ cup
**dry white wine or
dry vermouth**

4 (6-ounce) **skinless cod fillets,**
1 to 1½ inches thick

INGREDIENT SPOTLIGHT **LEEKS**

A member of the onion family, leeks have a mild, sweet flavor and a melt-ingly tender texture when sautéed or braised. When preparing leeks for a recipe, don't forget to wash them thoroughly (see page 207); they trap dirt as they grow. When shopping, look for leeks that have a larger portion of white at the bottom; this is the usable part, along with some of the light green portion. The dark green tops can be reserved and used for stock.

WHY THIS RECIPE WORKS Braising is a great way to add flavor to mild-tasting fish, such as cod, plus it's mess-free (no oil splatter-ing on the stovetop). Pairing our cod with cherry tomatoes and a white wine sauce added brightness and freshness, and thinly sliced leeks provided a subtle, sweet flavor. After sautéing our leeks until they were tender, we stirred in a good amount of minced garlic and halved tomatoes, plus a big splash of wine, and nestled the cod into the pan. To ensure the cod cooked through gently and evenly, we turned down the heat and covered the skillet with a tight-fitting lid so that the fish partially simmered and partially steamed. A pat of butter, stirred into the vegetables, contributed some much-needed richness. If you don't have a lid that fits your skillet, you can use a sheet of aluminum foil and crimp it around the edges of the skillet. Halibut, snapper, tilapia, bluefish, monkfish, or sea bass fillets are all good substitutions for the cod.

1. Trim and discard root and dark green leaves from leeks (see page 49). Halve leeks lengthwise, then slice crosswise into ¼-inch-thick pieces. Wash cut leeks thoroughly using salad spinner (see page 207). Halve tomatoes and mince garlic.

2. Melt 2 tablespoons butter in 12-inch nonstick skillet over medium-high heat. Add leeks and ¼ teaspoon salt and cook until softened, about 5 minutes. Stir in garlic and cook until fragrant, about 30 seconds. Add tomatoes, wine, and ¼ teaspoon pepper and bring to a simmer.

3. Pat cod dry with paper towels and season with salt and pep-per. Nestle cod into skillet and spoon some vegetables and sauce over top. Cover and reduce heat to medium-low. Cook until fish flakes apart when gently prodded with paring knife and registers 140 degrees, 10 to 12 minutes.

4. Carefully transfer fish to platter. Stir remaining 1 tablespoon butter into vegetables, season with salt and pepper to taste, and spoon over fish. Serve.

Thai-Style Fish and Creamy Coconut Rice Packets

SERVES 4

1 **lime**

Fresh cilantro

¾ cup **coconut milk**

2 tablespoons
Thai green curry paste

4 (6- to 8-ounce)
skinless halibut fillets,
¾ to 1 inch thick

4 cups **cooked rice**

INGREDIENT SPOTLIGHT
THAI GREEN CURRY PASTE

Reaching for store-bought green curry paste, rather than making our own, helps add potent flavor quickly and saves us from having to hunt down a number of hard-to-find ingredients. Made from fresh green Thai chiles, lemon grass, galangal (Thai ginger), garlic, and other spices, green curry paste adds rich herbal flavor, complexity, and a bit of heat. It is usually sold in small jars with the other Thai ingredients at the supermarket. (See page 53 for more information on Thai red curry paste, which uses dried red chiles instead of fresh green chiles.)

WHY THIS RECIPE WORKS Cooking fish *en papillote*, or in a pouch, is a classic French technique. In addition to being incredibly easy, it allows the fish to steam in its own juices and thus emerge from the oven moist and flavorful. Plus, you can cook a side right along with the entrée in the pouch for a complete meal that's mostly hands-off. For our fish en papillote, we combined meaty halibut fillets with rice and gave the dish a Thai spin with a quick yet potent sauce made from coconut milk, green curry paste, lime zest, and a little cilantro, which we simply whisked together. The sauce did more than infuse the fish with flavor—it also provided a burst of color and transformed the rice into a rich, creamy partner for our hearty halibut fillets. Any white fish will work here, but we prefer the thickness and meaty texture of halibut or cod. You can use leftover rice or precooked rice here.

1. Adjust oven rack to middle position and heat oven to 400 degrees. Grate lime for 2 teaspoons zest, then cut into wedges. Mince ½ cup cilantro. Whisk lime zest, ¼ cup cilantro, coconut milk, and curry paste together in bowl. Pat halibut dry with paper towels and season with salt and pepper.

2. Lay four 14-inch lengths of aluminum foil flat on counter. Pile rice in center of foil pieces, then lay fish on top and spoon sauce over fish. Fold foil over fish and rice into packets and crimp edges to seal.

3. Place foil packets on rimmed baking sheet and bake until fish flakes apart when gently prodded with paring knife and registers 140 degrees, 16 to 19 minutes. Carefully open packets and sprinkle with remaining ¼ cup cilantro. Serve with lime wedges.

TEST KITCHEN TIP
PREPARING FISH AND RICE PACKETS

Lay four 14-inch lengths of aluminum foil flat on counter and pile rice in center. Lay fish on top of rice; spoon sauce over top. Fold foil over fish and rice to make packets, then fold edges together tightly to seal.

Roasted Cod Fillets with Crispy Potatoes and Lemon

SERVES 4

1½ pounds **russet potatoes**

5 tablespoons **unsalted butter**

3 **garlic cloves**

Fresh thyme sprigs

4 (6-ounce) **skinless cod fillets,**
1 to 1½ inches thick

1 **lemon**

INGREDIENT SPOTLIGHT COD

Cod is a medium-firm, meaty white fish. Because of its clean, mild flavor, it is suited to a variety of preparations and flavor combinations. Cod is great roasted, baked, and braised, but it's also a good choice for soups and stews; once cooked, cod has a flaky texture, so it's not a good pick for sautéing or grilling, as the fillets can break apart easily when moved around the pan or on the grate. Though you might see both skin-on and skinless fillets at the supermarket, we prefer the latter in this recipe; be sure to remove the skin before cooking if you buy skin-on fillets.

WHY THIS RECIPE WORKS This dish features flaky, moist fish roasted atop a bed of thinly sliced potatoes, for an elegant take on a classic duo. Cooking both the fish and potatoes together on a baking sheet allowed their juices to mingle for more flavor and kept the cleanup to just one pan. After slicing the potatoes and piling them on the baking sheet, we popped them into the oven to give them a head start so both elements would finish cooking at the same time. Then we laid our cod fillets on top and placed butter, thyme sprigs, and lemon slices on the fish; the butter and lemon basted the fish as it baked, and the thyme added subtle flavor to the mild-tasting cod. Halibut and haddock are good substitutes for the cod.

1. Adjust oven rack to lower-middle position and heat oven to 425 degrees. Slice potatoes into ¼-inch-thick rounds and place in large bowl. Melt 2 tablespoons butter, mince garlic, and mince 1 teaspoon thyme; toss with potatoes and season with salt and pepper.

2. Shingle potatoes into four 4 by 6-inch rectangular piles on parchment paper–lined rimmed baking sheet. Roast potatoes until spotty brown and just tender, 30 to 35 minutes, rotating sheet halfway through roasting.

3. Pat cod dry with paper towels and season with salt and pepper. Cut remaining 3 tablespoons butter into small pieces and thinly slice lemon. Lay cod, skinned side down, on top of each potato pile and top with butter, thyme sprig, and lemon slices. Continue to bake until fish flakes apart when gently prodded with paring knife and registers 140 degrees, about 15 minutes.

4. To serve, slide spatula underneath potatoes and fish and gently transfer to individual plates.

TEST KITCHEN TIP
JUMP-STARTING ROASTED POTATOES

Shingle potato slices into four 4 by 6-inch rectangular piles on parchment paper–lined baking sheet, then roast until spotty brown and just tender, 30 to 35 minutes, before adding fish.

Swordfish en Cocotte with Fennel and Pesto

SERVES 4
1 **fennel bulb**
2 **shallots**
2 tablespoons **extra-virgin olive oil**
¼ cup **prepared basil pesto**
4 (6-ounce) **swordfish steaks,** 1¼ inches thick
1 **lemon**

INGREDIENT SPOTLIGHT SWORDFISH

Swordfish boasts a firm, meaty texture and assertive flavor that works well in robustly flavored dishes. It takes especially well to the grill, but we also like it broiled or pan-seared. When shopping, be sure to buy swordfish steaks that are the same size so they will cook through at the same rate.

✔ **WHY THIS RECIPE WORKS** For a hearty, slow-cooked seafood dinner with intense flavor, we started with meaty swordfish steaks and cooked them *en cocotte*, a method that calls for roasting meat or poultry in a covered pot in a low oven to develop big flavor. For a richly flavored aromatic base, we sautéed some thinly sliced fennel and shallots in olive oil. To pump up the flavor of our dish, we stirred in a small amount of nutty, garlicky pesto. Finally, we placed our swordfish steaks on the sautéed vegetables, put the lid on top, and moved it all to a 250-degree oven. Covering the pot with a sheet of aluminum foil before placing the lid on top helped prevent any steam from escaping. As the fish cooked, the fennel, shallots, and pesto created a rich sauce that complemented the meaty fish. Stirring in a bit of lemon juice at the end of cooking contributed bright notes and brought the elements of the dish together. Make sure your swordfish steaks are of equal size to ensure even cooking; if your steaks are thicker or thinner than 1¼ inches, be sure to adjust the cooking time as needed. You can substitute halibut steaks for the swordfish.

1. Adjust oven rack to lowest position and heat oven to 250 degrees. Remove fennel stalks and fronds (see page 177). Trim fennel bulb, cut in half, core, and cut crosswise into ½-inch-thick slices. Thinly slice shallots. Heat oil in Dutch oven over medium heat until shimmering. Add fennel and shallots and cook until softened, 6 to 8 minutes. Off heat, stir in pesto.

2. Pat swordfish dry with paper towels and season with salt and pepper. Lay swordfish on top of fennel mixture. Press large sheet of aluminum foil over pot to seal, then cover tightly with lid. Transfer pot to oven and cook until fish flakes apart when gently prodded with paring knife and registers 140 degrees, 35 to 40 minutes.

3. Gently transfer swordfish to platter. Cook fennel mixture over medium-high heat until thickened slightly, about 1 minute. Squeeze lemon for 2 teaspoons juice. Off heat, stir in lemon juice and season with salt and pepper to taste. Spoon fennel mixture over swordfish and serve.

Catfish in Salty-Sweet Caramel Sauce

SERVES 4 TO 6

⅓ cup **sugar**

2 pounds **skinless catfish fillets**

5 **garlic cloves**

¼ cup **vegetable oil**

¼ cup **fish sauce**

Fresh cilantro

INGREDIENT SPOTLIGHT FISH SAUCE

Fish sauce is a salty amber-colored liquid made from fermented fish. It is used as an ingredient and condiment in certain Asian cuisines, most commonly in the foods of Southeast Asia. In very small amounts, it adds a well-rounded, salty flavor to sauces, soups, and marinades. Note that the lighter the color of the fish sauce, the milder its flavor. You can find fish sauce with the other Asian ingredients at the supermarket.

✓ WHY THIS RECIPE WORKS Catfish simmered in a salty-sweet caramel sauce is a popular southern Vietnamese dish that is uniquely satisfying and utterly addictive. We wanted a simple recipe for this exotic dish that wouldn't require hunting down any specialty ingredients. First, we made a basic caramel right in a skillet using sugar and water; pouring the water into the skillet first then sprinkling the sugar over the top prevented the sugar from crystallizing on the pan's sides. To this mixture, we added a hefty dose of garlic and oil for potent flavor and richness. A good pour of fish sauce provided the perfect amount of salty, savory notes to balance the sweetness of the caramel, and a generous amount of black pepper added a subtle heat. After cutting our catfish fillets into smaller, 2-inch pieces, we added them to the pan. In just half an hour, the sauce had become nicely thickened and the fish had absorbed its sweet and savory flavors. A handful of fresh cilantro added a bright, grassy touch. Though catfish is the traditional pick for this recipe, any thin, medium-firm white fish fillets can be substituted. You will need boiling water for this recipe; for an accurate measurement of boiling water, bring a full kettle of water to boil, then measure out the desired amount. Serve with rice.

1. Measure ¼ cup water into 12-inch nonstick skillet and sprinkle sugar evenly into water. Cook over medium heat, gently swirling pan occasionally (do not stir), until sugar melts and mixture turns color of maple syrup, about 10 minutes.

2. Pat catfish dry with paper towels and slice crosswise into 2-inch-wide pieces. Mince garlic and mix with oil in bowl. Carefully stir garlic mixture into skillet and cook until fragrant, about 30 seconds. Off heat, slowly whisk in 2 cups boiling water (the sauce will bubble slightly). Return skillet to medium heat and stir in fish sauce and 1½ teaspoons pepper.

3. Nestle catfish pieces into skillet without overlapping and spoon sauce over top. Bring to simmer, reduce heat to medium-low, and cook, uncovered, until fish is tender and sauce has thickened to thick, syrupy consistency, about 25 minutes.

4. Gently transfer catfish to platter and pour sauce over top. Sprinkle with 1 cup cilantro leaves and serve.

Sesame-Crusted Tuna with Wasabi Dressing

SERVES 4
1 **lime**
¼ cup **mayonnaise**
1 tablespoon **wasabi paste**
½ cup **sesame seeds**
4 (6-ounce) **tuna steaks,** 1 inch thick
2 tablespoons **vegetable oil**

INGREDIENT SPOTLIGHT
WASABI PASTE

Hot and pungent, wasabi is commonly used as a condiment for sushi and sashimi but is also useful as an ingredient in other Japanese dishes. Fresh wasabi root (also known as Japanese horseradish) is hard to find and expensive (about $8 per ounce). More widely available is wasabi that is sold in paste or powder form (the powder is mixed with water to form a paste). Because fresh wasabi root is so expensive, most pastes and all powders contain no wasabi at all, but instead a mixture of garden-variety horseradish, mustard, cornstarch, and food coloring, so check the label carefully. We advise seeking out wasabi paste made from real wasabi root for its complex flavor.

WHY THIS RECIPE WORKS In our opinion, pan-seared tuna should have a nice crust, a rare to medium-rare center, and simple, complementary flavors. We found that a coating of sesame seeds helped us accomplish all of these things in one fell swoop. Our sesame seed–coated tuna steaks developed a crisp exterior much faster than an uncoated tuna steak, which in turn minimized the time the fish needed to spend in the skillet and all but eliminated the risk of overcooking the interior. Once toasted, the sesame seeds also contributed great nutty flavor but were still mild enough that they didn't compete with the flavor of the fish. A creamy, spicy dressing of wasabi paste, mayonnaise, and lime juice, thinned with water, made the perfect finishing touch. We prefer the flavor and texture of yellowfin tuna here; however, any type of fresh tuna will work. Try to purchase tuna steaks that are about 1 inch thick; if the steaks are thicker or thinner, be sure to adjust the cooking time as needed.

1. Squeeze lime for 1 tablespoon juice and whisk together with mayonnaise, wasabi, and 2 tablespoons water in bowl; season with salt and pepper to taste. Spread sesame seeds into shallow dish. Pat tuna dry with paper towels, coat with 1 tablespoon oil, and season with salt and pepper. Coat both sides of tuna with sesame seeds and press gently to adhere.

2. Heat remaining 1 tablespoon oil in 12-inch nonstick skillet over medium-high heat until just smoking. Gently lay tuna in skillet and cook until seeds are golden, about 2 minutes. Carefully flip fish with two spatulas and continue to cook until just golden, opaque at perimeter, translucent red at center when checked with tip of paring knife, and fish registers 110 degrees (for rare), about 1½ minutes, or reddish pink at center when checked with tip of paring knife and fish registers 125 degrees (for medium-rare), about 3 minutes.

3. Gently transfer fish to carving board and immediately slice on bias. Serve with wasabi dressing.

Roasted Salmon with Tangerine Relish

SERVES 4
4 **tangerines**
1 **scallion**
1 **lemon**
Fresh ginger
4 teaspoons **olive oil**
4 (6-ounce) **center-cut skin-on salmon fillets**

INGREDIENT SPOTLIGHT SALMON

Setting environmental and sustainability issues aside, we wanted to know if there was a difference between wild-caught and farm-raised salmon fillets, so we sampled them pan-seared and prepared in salmon cakes. In general, tasters preferred the flavor and texture of the wild salmon; however, high-quality wild-caught salmon is available only from late spring through the end of summer. Fortunately, tasters found farmed salmon, which is available year-round, to be perfectly acceptable in both recipes.

✔ WHY THIS RECIPE WORKS For oven-roasted salmon with a nicely browned exterior and a silky, moist interior, we preheated the oven to 500 degrees with a baking sheet set on the lowest rack, then turned down the heat to 275 just before placing the fish on the hot sheet. The initial blast of heat firmed the exterior, while the slowly dropping temperature cooked the fish gently and kept it moist. Keeping the skin on the salmon prevented it from falling apart and losing moisture as it cooked, but we found it essential to score the skin to allow the fat to render. An easy tangerine relish contributed brightness. Use center-cut salmon fillets of similar thickness so that they cook at the same rate. The best way to ensure uniformity is to buy a 1½-pound whole center-cut fillet and cut it into 4 pieces.

1. Adjust oven rack to lowest position, place rimmed baking sheet on rack, and heat oven to 500 degrees.

2. Cut away peel and pith from tangerines, quarter, then slice each quarter crosswise into ½-inch-thick pieces. Drain tangerines through strainer set over bowl for 15 minutes; reserve 2 tablespoons juice. Thinly slice scallion, squeeze lemon for 2 teaspoons juice, and grate 1½ teaspoons ginger; whisk together with reserved tangerine juice and 2 teaspoons oil in bowl. Add tangerines and season with salt and pepper to taste.

3. Pat salmon dry with paper towels and cut several shallow slashes, about 1 inch apart, on diagonal through skin. Rub fish evenly with remaining 2 teaspoons oil and season with salt and pepper. Reduce oven temperature to 275 degrees and remove baking sheet. Carefully lay salmon, skin side down, on hot baking sheet. Roast until center is still translucent when checked with tip of paring knife and registers 125 degrees (for medium-rare), 9 to 13 minutes. Serve with tangerine relish.

TEST KITCHEN TIP
SCORING SALMON FILLETS

Using sharp knife, cut 4 or 5 shallow slashes diagonally, about 1 inch apart, through skin of salmon, being careful not to cut into flesh.

Miso-Glazed Salmon

Fresh ginger

1 cup **white miso**

½ cup **sugar**

½ cup **sake**

4 (6-ounce)
**center-cut skin-on
salmon fillets**

Fresh cilantro

INGREDIENT SPOTLIGHT MISO

Miso is the Japanese word for "bean paste." Commonly found in Asian—most notably Japanese—cuisines, miso is a fermented paste of soybeans and rice, barley, or rye. Miso paste is incredibly versatile, suitable for use in soups, braises, dressings, and sauces, as well as for topping grilled foods. This salty, deep-flavored paste ranges in strength and color from a mild, pale yellow (referred to as white) to stronger-flavored red or brownish-black, depending on the fermentation method and ingredients. Avoid miso labeled "light," as this is an American low-sodium product whose flavor pales in comparison to the real thing. Miso can be found in well-stocked grocery stores and Japanese or Asian markets. It will keep for up to a year in the refrigerator.

✔ **WHY THIS RECIPE WORKS** For our take on this classic Japanese dish, which promises salty, sweet, and rich-tasting salmon with a deeply caramelized, almost candylike exterior, we started with the marinade. After a number of tests, we worked out the perfect ratio of white miso, sugar, and sake that offered intense flavor and a texture thick enough that it clung nicely to our fillets. Fresh grated ginger, though not traditional, helped to brighten the dish. Authentic Japanese recipes call for marinating the salmon for up to two days, but we found that a minimum of five hours gave the salmon plenty of time to absorb the flavors. Broiling was the best way to achieve the caramelized crust we were after; in less than 10 minutes, our salmon was perfectly done. A sprinkle of minced cilantro contributed fresh, grassy notes that offset the richness of the dish. When removing the salmon from the marinade, do not wipe away any excess marinade clinging to the fish; the excess marinade will turn to a sweet-salty crust during cooking. Use center-cut salmon fillets of similar thickness so that they cook at the same rate. The best way to ensure uniformity is to buy a 1½-pound whole center-cut fillet and cut it into 4 pieces. Be sure to buy white miso, but do not buy light or low-sodium white miso; these will not work in this recipe. Note that you'll have to read the label carefully to know if the miso is light or low-sodium.

1. Grate 1½ teaspoons ginger and whisk together with miso, sugar, and sake in medium bowl to dissolve sugar and miso. Cut several shallow slashes, about 1 inch apart, on diagonal through skin of salmon (see page 156); place fillets in 1-gallon zipper-lock bag and pour marinade into bag. Seal bag, pressing out as much air as possible, and refrigerate at least 5 hours or up to 24 hours, flipping bag occasionally to help fish marinate evenly.

2. Adjust oven rack 6 inches from broiler element and heat broiler. Line broiler pan bottom with aluminum foil and top with slotted broiler pan top. Remove fish from marinade and lay on broiler pan top, skin side down. Spoon 1 tablespoon marinade over each fillet; discard extra marinade.

3. Broil salmon until center is still translucent when checked with tip of paring knife and registers 125 degrees (for medium-rare), 7 to 10 minutes. Mince 2 tablespoons cilantro, sprinkle over top, and serve.

Crispy Potato-Crusted Salmon with Herb Salad

SERVES 4

4 ounces
**salt-and-vinegar
kettle-cooked potato chips**

4 (6-ounce)
center-cut salmon fillets

2 tablespoons plus ½ teaspoon
Dijon mustard

2 **lemons**

2 tablespoons
extra-virgin olive oil

6 ounces (6 cups)
mesclun greens with herbs mix

**INGREDIENT SPOTLIGHT
KETTLE-COOKED POTATO CHIPS**

Kettle-cooked potato chips are thick-cut chips that are cooked in small batches and spend more time in the cooking oil. A thicker cut means more potato mass—and thus more potato flavor—and longer cooking times result in crunchier chips. When crushed to coarse crumbs, these chips added a big crunch to our salmon fillets, and using the salt-and-vinegar variety ensured the chip coating offered robust flavor.

✔ WHY THIS RECIPE WORKS In search of a supremely crunchy and flavorful coating for our salmon fillets, we bypassed the fresh bread crumbs, which didn't provide ample crunch, and panko bread crumbs, which were light on flavor, in favor of super-crunchy, kettle-cooked potato chips. Crushed into small crumbs, they created the perfect rich and crunchy topping—and for even more flavor, we swapped out plain chips for the salt-and-vinegar variety. A bit of Dijon mustard helped the crumbs adhere and delivered more tang, and another two-for-one ingredient—mesclun greens mixed with herbs—gave us a simple, refreshing side salad when tossed in a lemon vinaigrette. Use center-cut salmon fillets of similar thickness so that they cook at the same rate. The best way to ensure uniformity is to buy a 1½-pound whole center-cut fillet and cut it into 4 pieces. You can use either skin-on or skinless salmon fillets here.

1. Adjust oven rack to upper-middle position and heat oven to 450 degrees. Crush potato chips to coarse crumbs and spread into shallow dish. Pat salmon dry with paper towels. Brush top of salmon evenly with 2 tablespoons mustard and season with salt and pepper. Coat salmon with potato chips and press gently to adhere.

2. Lay salmon on rimmed baking sheet lined with aluminum foil. Bake until crumbs are golden and center of salmon is still translucent when checked with tip of paring knife and registers 125 degrees (for medium-rare), 12 to 14 minutes.

3. Meanwhile, squeeze 1 lemon for 1 tablespoon juice and whisk together with remaining ½ teaspoon mustard, ⅛ teaspoon salt, and ⅛ teaspoon pepper in large bowl. Whisking constantly, drizzle in oil. Add mesclun greens to bowl and toss gently to coat. Cut remaining 1 lemon into wedges and serve with salmon and salad.

**TEST KITCHEN TIP
CUTTING SALMON FILLETS**

If you can't buy similar-sized fillets, buy a single 1½ pound fillet and cut it into four evenly sized portions.

Spicy Pan-Seared Shrimp with Tomatoes and Scallions

SERVES 4

4 **scallions**

1 (10-ounce) can
**Ro-tel Diced Tomatoes
& Green Chilies**

1½ pounds **extra-large shrimp**
(21 to 25 per pound)

2 tablespoons **vegetable oil**

2 **limes**

1 **avocado**

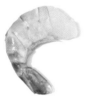

INGREDIENT SPOTLIGHT SHRIMP

Virtually all of the shrimp sold today in supermarkets have been previously frozen, either in large blocks of ice or by a method called "individually quick frozen," or IQF for short. Supermarkets simply defrost the shrimp before displaying them on ice at the fish counter, where they look as though they are freshly plucked from the sea. As a general rule, we highly recommend purchasing bags of still-frozen, shell-on IQF shrimp and defrosting them as needed at home, since there is no telling how long "fresh" shrimp may have been kept on ice at the market. IQF shrimp also have a better flavor and texture than shrimp frozen in blocks. IQF shrimp are available both with and without their shells, but we find the shell-on shrimp to be firmer and sweeter.

☑ WHY THIS RECIPE WORKS For pan-seared shrimp that were nicely browned on the outside and moist and tender on the inside, we had to nail the cooking method. Using a ripping-hot skillet allowed for a little browning on the shrimp, and cooking them in a single layer in the pan also aided in browning; if the shrimp were crowded, they steamed and didn't sear. Thus, it was necessary to cook them in two batches. We also finished the shrimp off the heat to prevent them from overcooking. After we set the shellfish aside, we made a quick and easy sauce right in the same skillet. With a nod toward the classic dish of Mexican griddle-seared shrimp, we combined Ro-tel tomatoes with scallions and lime juice, then let the shrimp finish in the sauce. Chunks of avocado, thinly sliced scallion greens, and lime wedges made the perfect garnishes to our saucy, spicy pan-seared shrimp. If your shrimp are larger or smaller, be sure to alter the cooking time in step 2 accordingly.

1. Thinly slice scallion whites and scallion greens; keep whites and greens separate. Combine tomatoes and their juice, scallion whites, and ¼ teaspoon salt in bowl. Peel shrimp (including tails) and devein (see page 37). Pat shrimp dry with paper towels and season with salt and pepper.

2. Heat 1 tablespoon oil in 12-inch nonstick skillet over high heat until just smoking. Add half of shrimp in single layer and cook, without stirring, until spotty brown and edges turn pink, about 1 minute. Remove skillet from heat, flip shrimp, and let sit off heat until opaque in very center, about 30 seconds; transfer to bowl. Repeat with remaining 1 tablespoon oil and remaining shrimp.

3. Return now-empty skillet to high heat, add tomato mixture, and cook until tomatoes soften slightly, about 2 minutes. Off heat, stir in shrimp, cover, and let sit until shrimp are cooked through, 1 to 2 minutes. Squeeze 1 lime for 2 teaspoons juice and stir into shrimp; season with salt and pepper to taste. Transfer shrimp to platter. Dice avocado and sprinkle over top with scallion greens. Cut remaining 1 lime into wedges and serve with shrimp.

Greek-Style Shrimp with Orzo and Feta

SERVES 4

1 pound **medium-large shrimp** (31 to 40 per pound)

1 (14.5-ounce) can **diced tomatoes with garlic and onion**

12 ounces (2 cups) **orzo**

1 pinch **saffron threads**

2 cups (8 ounces) crumbled **marinated feta**

3 **scallions**

INGREDIENT SPOTLIGHT SAFFRON

Sometimes known as "red gold," saffron is the world's most expensive spice. It's made from the dried stigmas of *Crocus sativus* flowers; the stigmas are so delicate they must be harvested by hand in a painstaking process. Luckily, a little saffron goes a long way, adding a distinct reddish-gold color, notes of honey and grass, and a slight hint of bitterness to dishes like bouillabaisse, paella, and risotto. You can find it as powder or threads, but we've found threads are more common. The major producers are Iran and Spain; the saffron you find in the supermarket is usually Spanish. Look for bottles that contain dark red threads—saffron is graded, and the richly hued, high-grade threads from the top of the stigma yield more flavor than the lighter, lesser-grade threads from the base.

✔ **WHY THIS RECIPE WORKS** To pay homage to the classic Greek duo of shrimp and orzo, we toasted our orzo, then cooked it in shrimp broth (made in the microwave with the shrimp shells) and tomato juice from canned tomatoes. After stirring in the shrimp (scattering them on top left them exposed to the heat), we moved them to the oven. Diced tomatoes flavored with garlic and onion added acidity and aromatic notes. Saffron, though not traditional, gave the dish a sunny hue, and feta added salty, tangy bites. Make sure that the orzo is al dente, or slightly firm to the bite; otherwise it may overcook in the oven. If your shrimp are larger or smaller, be sure to alter the cooking time in step 4 accordingly. The small amount of saffron makes a big difference to the flavor and look of the dish; do not omit it.

1. Adjust oven rack to middle position and heat oven to 400 degrees. Peel shrimp (including tails) and devein (see page 37); reserve shells. Pat shrimp dry with paper towels, season with salt and pepper, and transfer to bowl; cover and refrigerate.

2. Combine shrimp shells, 3½ cups water, ¼ teaspoon salt, and ¼ teaspoon pepper in bowl, cover, and microwave until liquid is hot and shells are pink, about 6 minutes. Drain broth, discarding shells. Drain tomatoes, reserving juice.

3. Toast orzo in 12-inch ovensafe nonstick skillet over medium heat until lightly browned, about 4 minutes. Stir in shrimp broth, tomato juice, and crumbled saffron. Bring to a simmer and cook, stirring often, until orzo is al dente, 10 to 12 minutes.

4. Off heat, stir in shrimp and tomatoes. Sprinkle feta over top. Transfer skillet to oven and bake until shrimp are cooked through and cheese is lightly browned, about 20 minutes. Thinly slice scallions, sprinkle over top, and serve.

TEST KITCHEN TIP
TOASTING ORZO

Toasting the orzo in a dry skillet before adding the liquid helps to deepen its flavor and prevent it from becoming gummy when cooked. Be sure to use a nonstick skillet or the orzo will stick to the pan bottom when the liquid is added.

Pan-Seared Scallops with Butternut Squash Puree

SERVES 4

1½ pounds **large sea scallops**
(10 to 20 per pound)

2 pounds **butternut squash**

4 tablespoons **unsalted butter**

¾ teaspoon **curry powder**

2 tablespoons **vegetable oil**

3 **scallions**

INGREDIENT SPOTLIGHT
PRECUT BUTTERNUT SQUASH

Butternut squash can be time-consuming and tedious to cut up, but are you any better off using the precut, pre-peeled squash that many supermarkets carry nowadays? The test kitchen has found that whole squash that you peel and cube yourself can't be beat in terms of flavor or texture, but when you are trying to speed up dinner, already peeled, halved squash is perfectly acceptable. Just be sure to avoid the precut chunks; tasters found these to be dry and stringy, with barely any squash flavor.

WHY THIS RECIPE WORKS For an elegant, restaurant-style dinner, we paired sweet, briny scallops with earthy, nutty butternut squash. To match the buttery texture of the scallops, we opted for a silky-smooth squash puree. After microwaving the squash for about 10 minutes, we moved it to the food processor, added a pat of butter and a bit of curry powder for bold flavor, and processed it all until perfectly smooth. Then we pan-seared the scallops in two batches; this ensured they weren't crowded in the skillet and browned nicely. Resting the scallops on dish towels for 10 minutes before cooking also helped guarantee a golden-brown crust; the towels absorbed excess moisture that would have caused the scallops to steam. A simple sauce of browned butter and sautéed scallions added more richness and completed our fancy, yet incredibly easy, dinner. We recommend buying "dry" scallops, which don't have chemical additives and taste better than "wet." Dry scallops will look ivory or pinkish; wet scallops are bright white; see page 164 for more information.

1. Remove and discard tendons from scallops (see page 164), place on rimmed baking sheet lined with dish towel, and top with another towel. Blot moisture gently and let sit with towels for 10 minutes.

2. Meanwhile, peel and seed squash, then cut into 1-inch chunks (see page 42). Place squash in bowl, cover, and microwave until tender, 8 to 12 minutes, stirring halfway through cooking. Drain squash and transfer to food processor. Add 1 tablespoon water, 1 tablespoon butter, curry powder, and ½ teaspoon salt and process until smooth, about 30 seconds; transfer to bowl and cover.

3. Season scallops with salt and pepper. Heat 1 tablespoon oil in 12-inch nonstick skillet over high heat until just smoking. Lay half of scallops in skillet in single layer and cook, without moving, until well browned, 1½ to 2 minutes. Flip scallops and continue to cook until sides are firm and centers are opaque, 30 to 90 seconds; transfer to platter and tent with aluminum foil. Wipe out now-empty skillet with paper towels and repeat with remaining 1 tablespoon oil and scallops.

4. Thinly slice scallions. Add remaining 3 tablespoons butter to now-empty skillet and cook over medium-low heat until melted and just starting to brown, about 30 seconds. Add scallions and cook until fragrant, about 1 minute. Season with salt and pepper to taste. Pour sauce over scallops and serve with pureed squash.

Pan-Seared Scallops with Tomato-Ginger Relish

1½ pounds **large sea scallops**
(10 to 20 per pound)

2 **scallions**

3 **plum tomatoes**

Fresh ginger

¼ cup **olive oil**

1 **lemon**

INGREDIENT SPOTLIGHT SCALLOPS

You may have noticed scallops labeled as "dry," but what exactly does this mean? Some scallops are dipped in a phosphate-water mixture to extend their shelf life; these are known as "wet" scallops. Dry scallops taste fresher and develop a better crust when browned since they aren't pumped full of water, so they're always our top choice. When you are at the market, remember that unprocessed (dry) scallops have a natural ivory or pinkish hue rather than the stark white of wet scallops. If you can only find "wet" scallops, soak them in a solution of 1 quart cold water, ¼ cup lemon juice, and 2 tablespoons table salt for 30 minutes before cooking.

✔ **WHY THIS RECIPE WORKS** For another dressed-up take on sweet, tender pan-seared scallops, we paired them with a boldly flavored relish. We started by sautéing chopped plum tomatoes, which contributed brightness and acidity. We then added minced scallions for mild oniony flavor and fresh ginger for spicy notes. After a couple minutes, the tomatoes had softened slightly and released a little juice. A squeeze of lemon added freshness and brought the elements of our tomato-ginger relish together. All we had left to do was sear the scallops. In a matter of 20 minutes, we had an effortless, yet impressive, dinner on the table.

1. Remove and discard tendons from scallops, place on rimmed baking sheet lined with dish towel, and top with another towel. Blot moisture gently and let sit with towels for 10 minutes.

2. Meanwhile, mince scallions, core and finely chop tomatoes, and grate 1 tablespoon ginger. Heat 2 tablespoons oil in small saucepan over medium heat until shimmering. Add scallions and cook until softened, about 2 minutes. Stir in tomatoes and ginger and cook until tomatoes are slightly softened, about 2 minutes; remove from heat. Squeeze lemon for 1 tablespoon juice, stir into tomatoes, and season with salt to taste; cover to keep warm.

3. Season scallops with salt and pepper. Heat 1 tablespoon oil in 12-inch nonstick skillet over high heat until just smoking. Lay half of scallops in skillet in single layer and cook, without moving, until well browned, 1½ to 2 minutes. Flip scallops and continue to cook until sides are firm and centers are opaque, 30 to 90 seconds; transfer to platter and tent with aluminum foil.

4. Wipe out now-empty skillet with paper towels and repeat with remaining 1 tablespoon oil and scallops. Serve immediately with tomato-ginger relish.

TEST KITCHEN TIP
PREPPING SCALLOPS

The small, crescent-shaped muscle that is sometimes attached to the scallop will be incredibly tough when cooked. Use your fingers to peel this muscle away from the side of each scallop before cooking.

Bistro-Style Steamed Mussels with White Wine and Garlic

SERVES 4
4 pounds **mussels**
3 **shallots**
6 **garlic cloves**
5 tablespoons **unsalted butter**
2 cups **dry white wine**
Fresh parsley

INGREDIENT SPOTLIGHT MUSSELS

The most common varieties of mussels are the North Atlantic blue, which are found mostly on the East Coast, and the "Mediterranean," which are grown along the Mediterranean and on the Pacific Coast. No matter which variety you have, the mussels should be scrubbed with a stiff brush to remove any grit and then debearded, if necessary, prior to cooking. When you get home from the supermarket or fish market, you can store mussels in the refrigerator in a colander of ice set over a bowl, discarding any water that accumulates in the bowl so that the shellfish are never submerged. Be sure to discard any mussels that won't close when tapped; these may be dead and should not be eaten.

☑ **WHY THIS RECIPE WORKS** The indulgent pairing of sweet, tender mussels with a velvety, rich-tasting sauce is what makes this bistro standby so popular. After sautéing a generous amount of garlic and a few shallots in butter, we stirred in a big dose of white wine and let it reduce. Then we tossed in the mussels and covered the pot so they'd steam open and absorb the rich flavors. Once the mussels were cooked (and we had discarded any that hadn't opened), we transferred them to a serving bowl and enriched the flavorful broth with more butter. A handful of minced parsley added fresh floral notes to round out the dish. These mussels can be served either as a main course or as an appetizer that serves 6 to 8. Serve with crusty bread for soaking up the rich sauce.

1. Scrub and debeard mussels. Mince shallots and garlic. Melt 2 tablespoons butter in Dutch oven over medium-high heat. Add shallots and cook until softened, about 2 minutes. Stir in garlic and cook until fragrant, about 30 seconds. Stir in wine; simmer for 3 minutes.

2. Add mussels to pot, increase heat to high, and cover. Cook, stirring occasionally, until mussels open, 4 to 9 minutes. Using slotted spoon, transfer mussels to large serving bowl; discard any that refuse to open.

3. Mince ½ cup parsley. Whisk remaining 3 tablespoons butter and parsley into broth left in pot, pour over mussels, and serve.

TEST KITCHEN TIP
DEBEARDING MUSSELS

Occasionally, mussels have a harmless weedy piece (known as a beard) protruding from their shells. To remove it before cooking, simply hold the beard between your thumb and a butter knife or the flat side of a paring knife and tug gently.

Clams with Israeli Couscous, Chorizo, and Scallions

SERVES 4

2 cups **Israeli couscous**

6 ounces **chorizo sausage**

6 **scallions**

2 tablespoons **unsalted butter**

4 pounds **littleneck clams**

1 cup
**dry white wine or
dry vermouth**

**INGREDIENT SPOTLIGHT
ISRAELI COUSCOUS**

Also known as pearl couscous, Israeli couscous is much larger than traditional, fine-grain couscous. This variety is about the size of a caper and is not precooked like the fine-grain variety, which steams through in a matter of minutes in a small amount of liquid. Instead, it must be cooked like pasta in a large amount of water and drained. We found that the unique, nutty taste of Israeli couscous gave this dish just the right flavor boost.

WHY THIS RECIPE WORKS To infuse this simple clam dish with big flavor, we added chorizo and scallions to white wine for a potent broth that we could use to steam our shellfish. Thinly sliced half-moons of chorizo added richness and savory, spicy notes to the broth, and several scallions gave this dish an aromatic backbone. A couple pats of butter contributed ample richness to counter the bright, briny notes of the wine and clams. To make this dish a complete meal, we added some couscous to our shopping list. Using larger-grained Israeli couscous instead of the more traditional, small-grain Moroccan couscous gave our dish texture and visual appeal. To cook the couscous, we simmered it like pasta, drained it, and then tossed it into the broth after the clams had steamed open so it could absorb the bright, briny flavors. Small quahogs or cherrystones are good alternatives to the littleneck clams. We like the punch that dry vermouth adds to this dish, but dry white wine will also work well. Be sure to use Israeli couscous in this dish; regular (or fine-grain) couscous won't work here.

1. Bring 2 quarts water to boil in large saucepan. Stir in couscous and 1 teaspoon salt and cook until al dente, about 8 minutes; drain couscous well.

2. Meanwhile, halve chorizo lengthwise and slice thin. Thinly slice scallion whites and thinly slice scallion greens on bias; keep whites and greens separate. Melt butter in Dutch oven over medium-high heat. Add chorizo and scallion whites and cook, stirring occasionally, until chorizo is lightly browned, about 4 minutes.

3. Scrub clams. Stir wine into Dutch oven and cook, scraping up any browned bits, until slightly reduced, about 1 minute. Stir in clams, cover, and cook, stirring occasionally, until clams open, 8 to 10 minutes.

4. Using slotted spoon, transfer clams to large bowl; discard any that refuse to open. Stir drained couscous and scallion greens into liquid left in pot and season with salt and pepper to taste. Portion couscous into bowls, top with clams, and serve.

ROTINI WITH BRUSSELS SPROUTS, BLUE CHEESE, AND BACON

Pasta

170 Spaghetti with Garlic, Olive Oil, and Marinated Artichokes | FAST RECIPE

171 Spaghetti with Quickest Tomato Sauce | FAST RECIPE

173 Penne with Fire-Roasted Tomato and Roasted Red Pepper Sauce | FAST RECIPE

174 Campanelle with Porcini Cream Sauce | FAST RECIPE

175 Penne with Zucchini, Cherry Tomatoes, and Boursin Cheese | FAST RECIPE

177 Farfalle with Fennel, Cream, and Herbs | FAST RECIPE

179 Spaghetti with Fried Eggs and Bread Crumbs

180 Farfalle with Sautéed Mushrooms and Truffle Oil

181 Farfalle with Bacon, Toasted Corn, Cherry Tomatoes, and Basil | FAST RECIPE

183 BLT Pasta | FAST RECIPE

184 Shells with Blue Cheese, Radicchio, and Walnuts | FAST RECIPE

185 Rotini with Brussels Sprouts, Blue Cheese, and Bacon | FAST RECIPE

187 Ziti with Fire-Roasted Tomatoes, Pepperoni, and Smoked Mozzarella | FAST RECIPE

188 Gemelli with Caramelized Onions, Kale, and Bacon

189 Ziti with Stuffed Cherry Peppers, Pepperoni, and Tomato Sauce | FAST RECIPE

191 Campanelle with Roasted Garlic, Chicken Sausage, and Arugula

192 Easy Tortellini Gratin

193 Creamy Tortellini with Vegetables | FAST RECIPE

195 Six-Ingredient Spaghetti and Meatballs | FAST RECIPE

196 Ziti with Italian Sausage, Broccoli, and Sun-Dried Tomatoes | FAST RECIPE

197 Ziti with Fennel and Italian Sausage | FAST RECIPE

199 Fusilli with Giardiniera and Sausage | FAST RECIPE

200 Brats with Beer and Mustard on Egg Noodles

201 Ziti with Cajun Shrimp, Andouille Sausage, and Bell Pepper | FAST RECIPE

203 Linguine with Clams and Chorizo | FAST RECIPE

204 Mediterranean Penne with Tuna and Nicoise Olives | FAST RECIPE

205 Fettuccine with Shrimp, Tarragon, and Cream | FAST RECIPE

207 Farfalle with Salmon and Leeks | FAST RECIPE

Spaghetti with Garlic, Olive Oil, and Marinated Artichokes

SERVES 4 TO 6

12 **garlic cloves**

7 tablespoons
extra-virgin olive oil

3 cups (14 ounces)
marinated artichokes

1 pound **spaghetti**

Fresh parsley

½ cup (1 ounce) grated
Parmesan cheese,
plus extra for serving

INGREDIENT SPOTLIGHT
MARINATED ARTICHOKES

A given on any antipasto platter, marinated artichokes not only cut back on prep time, but they also come packed with flavor, thanks to the herbs, aromatics, and olive oil they're packaged in—meaning they can play the role of multiple ingredients. Sometimes we call for draining the marinade to remove excess liquid or if we don't want the extra flavors in a dish. Also, patting the artichokes dry is key if they need to be browned; if thrown into a pan wet, they'll steam, not brown.

✔ **WHY THIS RECIPE WORKS** Called *aglio e olio* in the old country, spaghetti with garlic and olive oil proves that just a handful of ingredients—especially lots of garlic—can really pack a punch. For our spaghetti, we used a whopping 12 cloves and cooked them slowly over low heat until the garlic was golden, nutty-tasting, and subtly sweet. To add more oomph to this simple dish, we called on a staple of the antipasto platter—marinated artichokes—which provided a flavorful backbone and meant we didn't need any other dried herbs or aromatics. For some textural contrast, we browned the artichokes until crisp around the edges. Stirring some raw garlic into the sauce before tossing it with the browned artichokes and cooked pasta ensured a hit of potent garlic flavor in each bite. To make this dish a bit spicy, consider adding a pinch of red pepper flakes to the skillet with the garlic.

1. Mince garlic. Cook 1 tablespoon garlic, 3 tablespoons oil, and ½ teaspoon salt in 10-inch nonstick skillet over low heat, stirring, until garlic is foamy, sticky, and straw-colored, about 10 minutes. Transfer to bowl and stir in 3 tablespoons oil and remaining garlic.

2. Drain artichokes and pat dry with paper towels. Heat remaining 1 tablespoon oil in now-empty skillet over high heat until shimmering. Add artichokes and cook until golden, about 6 minutes.

3. Meanwhile, bring 4 quarts water to boil in large pot. Add pasta and 1 tablespoon salt and cook, stirring often, until al dente. Reserve ½ cup cooking water, then drain pasta and return it to pot.

4. Stir 2 tablespoons reserved cooking water into garlic mixture to loosen. Mince 3 tablespoons parsley, add to pasta with garlic mixture, artichokes, and Parmesan, and toss to combine. Season with salt and pepper to taste and add remaining reserved cooking water as needed to adjust consistency. Serve with extra Parmesan.

TEST KITCHEN TIP
SLOW-COOKING GARLIC

Cook garlic gently in skillet until it is foamy, sticky, and straw-colored, about 10 minutes. Do not overcook or garlic will turn bitter.

Spaghetti with Quickest Tomato Sauce

SERVES 4 TO 6

3 **garlic cloves**

3 tablespoons
extra-virgin olive oil

1 (28-ounce) can
crushed tomatoes

1 (14.5-ounce) can **diced tomatoes**

1 pound **spaghetti**

Fresh basil

INGREDIENT SPOTLIGHT
CRUSHED TOMATOES

Our experience in the test kitchen has taught us that the brand of crushed tomatoes you choose really matters; we've found that their consistency can vary widely depending on the manufacturer. Our favorite brand is **Tuttorosso Crushed Tomatoes in Thick Puree with Basil**; tasters found it "chunky, with dimensional flavor and a bright tomato taste."

✔ **WHY THIS RECIPE WORKS** You don't need a laundry list of ingredients or a ton of time to create a tomato sauce with robust, bright flavor. The secret is using the right mix of tomato products. After lots of testing, we determined that the duo of crushed and diced tomatoes gave us the ideal texture; the former provided the slightly thickened texture we wanted, while the latter offered tender bites of tomato. Less than 20 minutes on the stovetop gave our "canned" sauce serious depth of flavor, and chopped basil gave it a fresh taste and feel. Serve with grated Parmesan.

1. Mince garlic and cook with oil in medium saucepan over medium heat, stirring often, until fragrant but not browned, about 2 minutes. Stir in crushed tomatoes and diced tomatoes with their juice and simmer until slightly thickened, 15 to 20 minutes.

2. Meanwhile, bring 4 quarts water to boil in large pot. Add pasta and 1 tablespoon salt and cook, stirring often, until al dente. Reserve ½ cup cooking water, then drain pasta and return it to pot.

3. Chop 3 tablespoons basil, add to pasta with sauce, and toss to combine. Season with salt and pepper to taste and add reserved cooking water as needed to adjust consistency. Serve.

TEST KITCHEN TIP
RESERVING PASTA COOKING WATER

Before draining the pasta, be sure to reserve about ½ cup cooking water. This flavorful water can be used to help loosen a thick sauce.

Penne with Fire-Roasted Tomato and Roasted Red Pepper Sauce

SERVES 4 TO 6

3 cups jarred
roasted red peppers

1 (28-ounce) can
fire-roasted whole tomatoes

3 **garlic cloves**

3 tablespoons
extra-virgin olive oil

¾ cup **heavy cream**

1 pound **penne**

INGREDIENT SPOTLIGHT
FIRE-ROASTED TOMATOES

Long gone are the days when canned tomatoes came in only one flavor. Now you can get them with garlic and herbs and even fire-roasted. We're big fans of the latter variety, as they can add an intense, smoky flavor and complexity to a wide range of dishes—from pasta sauces to chilis and stews—in a short amount of time.

WHY THIS RECIPE WORKS For an easy tomato sauce with a kick, we reached for a can of fire-roasted tomatoes, which offer intense, smoky flavor. Roasted red peppers added sweet character and echoed the charred notes of the tomatoes, and a few cloves of garlic provided a subtle aromatic background. Pulsing the tomatoes and roasted peppers in the food processor gave the sauce a nice thickness. To tame the acidity and bring some richness to the sauce, we stirred in a generous pour of heavy cream. If necessary, you can substitute regular canned whole tomatoes for the fire-roasted tomatoes.

1. Drain red peppers, pat dry with paper towels, and chop coarsely. Pulse red peppers and tomatoes with their juice together in food processor until coarsely ground, about 12 pulses.

2. Mince garlic and cook with oil in medium saucepan over medium heat, stirring often, until fragrant but not browned, about 2 minutes. Stir in pepper-tomato mixture and simmer until slightly thickened, 15 to 20 minutes. Stir in cream and simmer for 3 minutes. Off heat, season with salt and pepper to taste.

3. Meanwhile, bring 4 quarts water to boil in large pot. Add pasta and 1 tablespoon salt and cook, stirring often, until al dente. Reserve ½ cup cooking water, then drain pasta and return it to pot. Add sauce and toss to combine. Season with salt and pepper to taste and add reserved cooking water as needed to adjust consistency. Serve.

TEST KITCHEN TIP
PROCESSING TOMATOES AND
RED PEPPERS FOR SAUCE

For a sauce with some texture, pulse the roasted red peppers and tomatoes until coarsely ground. Don't overprocess them, or the sauce will be too smooth.

Campanelle with Porcini Cream Sauce

SERVES 4 TO 6

2 ounces
dried porcini mushrooms

2 **onions**

3 tablespoons **unsalted butter**

½ cup **heavy cream**

1 pound **campanelle**

1 cup (2 ounces) grated
Parmesan cheese,
plus extra for serving

INGREDIENT SPOTLIGHT
DRIED PORCINI

Like fresh fruits and vegetables, the quality of dried porcini can vary dramatically from package to package and brand to brand. Always inspect the mushrooms before you buy. Avoid those with small holes, which indicate that the mushroom was perhaps home to pinworms. Instead, look for large, smooth porcini, free of worm holes, dust, and grit.

✔ WHY THIS RECIPE WORKS We started with dried porcini for concentrated, robust flavor in this easy recipe. To eke out the most flavor from the mushrooms, we used a two-step approach: First, after softening our porcini in the microwave with water, we sautéed them with chopped onions for a rich foundation. Second, we saved the liquor leftover from rehydrating the dried mushrooms and used it as the base of the sauce; this way, none of the hearty porcini flavor went down the drain. Heavy cream enriched the sauce, while grated Parmesan thickened it and added a salty tang that enhanced the meaty, savory flavor of the porcini.

1. Rinse mushrooms, then combine with 2 cups water in bowl. Cover and microwave until steaming, about 1 minute, then let sit until softened, about 5 minutes. Drain mushrooms through fine-mesh strainer lined with coffee filter; reserve liquid and chop mushrooms into ¾-inch pieces.

2. Finely chop onions. Melt butter in large saucepan over medium heat. Add onions and ¼ teaspoon salt and cook until softened and lightly browned, 10 to 12 minutes.

3. Stir in mushrooms and cook until fragrant, about 2 minutes. Stir in strained mushroom liquid, scraping up any browned bits, and simmer until thickened, about 10 minutes. Stir in cream and simmer until thickened, about 2 minutes.

4. Meanwhile, bring 4 quarts water to boil in large pot. Add pasta and 1 tablespoon salt and cook, stirring often, until al dente. Reserve ½ cup cooking water, then drain pasta and return it to pot. Add sauce and Parmesan and toss to combine. Season with salt and pepper to taste and add reserved cooking water as needed to adjust consistency. Serve with extra Parmesan.

TEST KITCHEN TIP
REHYDRATING DRIED PORCINI

Rinse the dried porcini thoroughly, then place in bowl and cover with water. Cover bowl and microwave until steaming, about 1 minute. Let sit until mushrooms are softened, about 5 minutes. Drain through fine-mesh strainer lined with coffee filter; reserve liquid and chop as directed.

Penne with Zucchini, Cherry Tomatoes, and Boursin Cheese

SERVES 4 TO 6

¼ cup **extra-virgin olive oil**

1½ pounds **zucchini**

1 pound **penne**

1 pound **cherry tomatoes**

Fresh basil

1 (5.2-ounce) package
Boursin Garlic and Fine Herbs cheese

INGREDIENT SPOTLIGHT PENNE

Wanting to know if the best penne is pricey and imported or inexpensive and domestic, we tasted eight different brands, including samples from both categories. Though the fancier brands from Italy boasted traditional techniques and ingredients (such as slow kneading, mixing cold mountain spring water with hard durum semolina, and extruding the dough through traditional bronze cast dies for a coarse texture), we found they didn't necessarily translate into better-tasting pasta. In the end, our favorite brand was a domestic pasta. **Mueller's Penne Rigate** won top honors for its "hearty," "wheaty" flavor.

✓ WHY THIS RECIPE WORKS For a streamlined version of pasta and veggies in a flavorful cream sauce, we condensed the shopping list for the sauce to just one shortcut ingredient: garlic-and-herb–flavored Boursin cheese. This single ingredient provided both the creamy texture and rich, tangy flavor we were after, plus some herbal and aromatic notes. Zucchini and tomatoes provided the perfect mix of quick-cooking, fresh-flavored vegetables. The tomatoes required no prep, but the zucchini needed some cooking to draw out excess moisture. Broiling proved optimal, as it also encouraged the development of some flavorful char on the vegetable's surface. The zucchini should be slightly undercooked after broiling in step 1; it will continue to soften as it sits.

1. Adjust oven rack 4 inches from broiler element and heat broiler. Line rimmed baking sheet with aluminum foil and brush with 1 tablespoon oil. Quarter zucchini lengthwise, then slice crosswise into ¾-inch pieces. Toss zucchini with 1 tablespoon oil, season with salt and pepper, and spread evenly onto prepared sheet. Broil zucchini, stirring occasionally, until lightly charred around edges but still firm in center, about 10 minutes; let cool slightly on sheet.

2. Meanwhile, bring 4 quarts water to boil in large pot. Add pasta and 1 tablespoon salt and cook, stirring often, until al dente. Reserve 1 cup cooking water, then drain pasta and return it to pot.

3. Quarter tomatoes and chop ½ cup basil. Add tomatoes, Boursin, and ¼ cup reserved cooking water to pasta and toss to combine. Gently stir in zucchini, basil, and remaining 2 tablespoons oil. Season with salt and pepper to taste and add remaining cooking water as needed to adjust consistency. Serve.

TEST KITCHEN TIP
BROILING ZUCCHINI

To jump-start the cooking of the zucchini and help drive off some of its moisture, we broil it for about 10 minutes, just until it starts to take on some flavorful char. Brushing the baking sheet with olive oil first ensures that the zucchini doesn't stick to the pan.

Farfalle with Fennel, Cream, and Herbs

SERVES 4 TO 6

2 **fennel bulbs**

3 tablespoons **unsalted butter**

8 **scallions**

2 cups **heavy cream**

1 pound **farfalle**

Fresh tarragon or mint

INGREDIENT SPOTLIGHT FENNEL

Fennel adds an unmistakably bright flavor to many dishes. Raw fennel has a fairly strong anise flavor, but cooking works to mellow out its licorice notes. No matter how it is cooked, fennel is slightly sweet. Although each part—the bulb, stalks, and fronds—has a different culinary use, for most recipes only the white bulb is used. The stalks can be reserved for making vegetable broth, while the fronds can be minced and used as a garnish for dishes made with the bulb. When shopping, look for fennel with its long, thin stalks still attached and be sure that the fennel bulb is creamy white and not bruised or discolored.

☑ WHY THIS RECIPE WORKS For an ultracreamy, intensely flavored dish, we started by sautéing thinly sliced fennel in butter until deeply caramelized and meltingly tender. Scallions provided a double dose of flavor—the minced whites, which we sautéed with the fennel, gave the sauce an aromatic backbone, while the thinly sliced greens added a bright, crisp touch and pop of color when stirred in at the end. Applying the same two-for-one philosophy to our fennel, we reserved the fronds, minced them, and stirred them in with the scallion greens for a delicate, herbal finish. Heavy cream turned our simple pasta dish into a luxurious, rich main course. When shopping, look for fennel that has the fronds still attached; the fronds add significant flavor to the final dish.

1. Trim fennel stalks and fronds; mince fronds and reserve. Trim bulb, cut in half, core, and slice into thin strips. Melt butter in 12-inch nonstick skillet over medium heat. Add fennel and ½ teaspoon salt and cook until soft and golden, about 20 minutes.

2. Mince scallion whites and thinly slice scallion greens; keep whites and greens separate. Stir scallion whites into skillet and cook until fragrant, about 30 seconds. Stir in cream and simmer until thickened, about 8 minutes.

3. Meanwhile, bring 4 quarts water to boil in large pot. Add pasta and 1 tablespoon salt and cook, stirring often, until al dente. Reserve ½ cup cooking water, then drain pasta and return it to pot. Chop ¼ cup tarragon, add to pasta with sauce, fennel fronds, and scallion greens, and toss to combine. Season with salt and pepper to taste and add reserved cooking water as needed to adjust consistency. Serve.

TEST KITCHEN TIP PREPARING FENNEL

1. After removing stalks, trim bulb bottom, then cut in half.

2. Remove pyramid-shaped core, then slice into thin strips.

Spaghetti with Fried Eggs and Bread Crumbs

SERVES 4

2 slices
hearty white sandwich bread

10 tablespoons
extra-virgin olive oil

4 **garlic cloves**

1 pound **spaghetti**

½ cup (1 ounce) grated
Parmesan cheese,
plus extra for serving

4 **large eggs**

INGREDIENT SPOTLIGHT SPAGHETTI

Does it really matter which brand of spaghetti you buy at the supermarket? We sampled six Italian imports and two domestic brands dressed simply with olive oil and tossed with a tomato sauce to find out. Though flavor differences from brand to brand were subtle, texture was another story, with some brands being downgraded for a mushy, gummy texture. Tasters preferred **De Cecco Spaghetti no. 12**, which they praised for its "clean wheat flavor" and "firm" strands with "good chew."

✔ WHY THIS RECIPE WORKS This rustic Italian specialty of garlicky spaghetti topped with fried eggs and crunchy bread crumbs shows how something simple can be really spectacular. The key is adding the eggs to the skillet all at once, rather than cracking them in one by one, to ensure that they finish cooking at the same time. Covering the skillet during cooking helped the surface of the eggs set so they didn't have to be flipped. But our perfectly fried eggs couldn't wait for the pasta—if they sat around for even a minute, the yolks firmed up, so we made sure to prepare the bread crumbs, garlic, and pasta before tackling the eggs.

1. Adjust oven rack to middle position and heat oven to 375 degrees. Process bread in food processor into coarse crumbs, about 10 pulses. Toss crumbs with 2 tablespoons oil, season with salt and pepper, and spread over rimmed baking sheet. Bake, stirring often, until golden, 8 to 10 minutes.

2. Mince garlic and cook with 3 tablespoons oil and ¼ teaspoon salt in 12-inch nonstick skillet over low heat, stirring often, until garlic is foamy, sticky, and straw-colored, 8 to 10 minutes; transfer to bowl.

3. Meanwhile, bring 4 quarts water to boil in large pot. Add pasta and 1 tablespoon salt and cook, stirring often, until al dente. Reserve 1 cup cooking water, then drain pasta and return it to pot. Add garlic mixture, 3 tablespoons oil, Parmesan, and ½ cup reserved cooking water and toss to combine; cover and set aside.

4. About 5 minutes before pasta is ready, wipe now-empty skillet clean with paper towels and place over low heat for 5 minutes. Crack eggs into 2 small bowls (2 eggs per bowl). Add remaining 2 tablespoons oil to skillet, swirl to coat pan, then quickly add eggs. Season with salt and pepper, cover, and cook until whites are set but yolks are still runny, 2 to 3 minutes.

5. Season pasta with salt and pepper to taste and add reserved cooking water as needed to adjust consistency. Top individual portions with bread crumbs and fried egg. Serve with extra Parmesan.

Farfalle with Sautéed Mushrooms and Truffle Oil

SERVES 4 TO 6

6 tablespoons **unsalted butter**

1½ pounds **cremini mushrooms**

4 **garlic cloves**

1 pound **farfalle**

1 cup (2 ounces) grated
Parmesan cheese,
plus extra for serving

4 teaspoons **white truffle oil,**
plus extra to taste

INGREDIENT SPOTLIGHT
TRUFFLE OIL

This pungent oil is made by adding flavor molecules (either fresh
or synthetic) to oil (usually olive
or safflower). Truffle oil is typically
used as a finishing touch, as its flavor
becomes dulled with cooking. Given
that it has such a bold flavor, all that's
needed is a mere drizzle to provide
maximum impact. Though you may
see both white and black truffle oil,
we prefer the flavor of white truffle oil.
White truffle oil has a pleasant, earthy,
rich aroma, while black truffle oil has
an overpowering, unpleasant aroma.

WHY THIS RECIPE WORKS Perfectly sautéed mushrooms and
rich, earthy truffle oil come together in this incredibly indulgent,
yet surprisingly effortless, dish. For mushrooms with the ideal
texture, we cooked them covered to draw out their moisture,
then removed the lid so they could brown. To deglaze the pan
and loosen the flavorful browned bits left behind, we added water
from our already-boiling pot of pasta cooking water. The hot
water, plus a generous amount of butter, formed an ultrarich sauce
that coated each piece of pasta perfectly. To keep the flavor of
the truffle oil pure and intense, we stirred it in at the end, off the
heat—cooking would have muted its flavor. We prefer the flavor
of white truffle oil to black truffle oil. You can substitute white
mushrooms for the cremini mushrooms if necessary.

1. Bring 4 quarts water to boil in large pot for pasta. Cut 4 tablespoons butter into ¼-inch pieces and refrigerate. Trim mushrooms
and slice ¼ inch thick. Melt remaining 2 tablespoons butter in
12-inch skillet over medium heat. Add mushrooms and ½ teaspoon
salt, cover, and cook until mushrooms have released their liquid,
about 8 minutes. Uncover and continue to cook until mushrooms
are dry and well browned, 10 to 15 minutes.

2. Mince garlic, stir into skillet, and cook until fragrant, about
30 seconds. Add ¾ cup boiling water, scraping up any browned bits,
and bring to simmer. Stir in chilled butter, then remove from heat.

3. Meanwhile, add pasta and 1 tablespoon salt to boiling water
and cook, stirring often, until al dente. Reserve ½ cup cooking
water, then drain pasta and return it to pot. Add mushroom mixture, Parmesan, and truffle oil and toss to combine. Season with
salt, pepper, and extra truffle oil to taste and add reserved cooking
water as needed to adjust consistency. Serve with extra Parmesan.

TEST KITCHEN TIP
COOKING MUSHROOMS

Cooking mushrooms with
a pinch of salt in a covered
pan helps to draw out their
moisture. Then, after they've
released their liquid, the pan
can be uncovered so the liquid
can evaporate and the mushrooms can brown.

Farfalle with Bacon, Toasted Corn, Cherry Tomatoes, and Basil

SERVES 4 TO 6
8 slices **bacon**
4 ears **corn**
1 pound **cherry tomatoes**
1 pound **farfalle**
Fresh basil
1 cup (2 ounces) grated **Parmesan cheese,** plus extra for serving

INGREDIENT SPOTLIGHT CORN

Generally, it's best to eat corn on the cob the same day you buy it, as its sugars start converting to starches as soon as it is harvested, causing the corn to lose sweetness. But if you buy corn and don't plan to cook it the same day, it should be stored in the refrigerator until you're ready to use it. We recommend storing corn unshucked and wrapped in a wet paper bag to slow down the conversion from sugar to starch, then placing the wet paper bag in a plastic bag (any shopping bag will do). Because corn on the cob is sensitive to chill injury, it should be placed in the front of the fridge, where the temperatures tend to be higher.

WHY THIS RECIPE WORKS Ripe, in-season corn and cherry tomatoes need little adornment in this rustic sauce. Toasting the corn in a skillet just until slightly brown gave it a nutty flavor and played up its sweetness. Adding the halved tomatoes to the pan for a few minutes ensured that they softened slightly. And cooking a good amount of bacon beforehand gave us plenty of rendered fat that we could use to sauté our vegetables. A full cup of grated Parmesan brought the elements together and infused the dish with a salty, nutty tang. Adding the crisped bacon at the end guaranteed every forkful offered crunchy, smoky bites and sweet, tender corn and tomatoes. This dish depends on the flavor of fresh corn; do not substitute frozen corn.

1. Chop bacon and cook in 12-inch nonstick skillet over medium-high heat until crisp, about 5 minutes; transfer to paper towel–lined plate. Pour off all but 2 tablespoons fat left in skillet. Cut corn kernels from cobs, add to bacon fat left in skillet, and cook over medium-high heat until browned, about 10 minutes. Halve tomatoes, add to skillet, and cook until just softened, about 3 minutes.

2. Meanwhile, bring 4 quarts water to boil in large pot. Add pasta and 1 tablespoon salt and cook, stirring often, until al dente. Reserve ½ cup cooking water, then drain pasta and return it to pot. Chop ½ cup basil, add to pasta with bacon, tomato mixture, and Parmesan, and toss to combine. Season with salt and pepper to taste and add reserved cooking water as needed to adjust consistency. Serve with extra Parmesan.

TEST KITCHEN TIP TOASTING CORN

1. To remove corn kernels, place cob in large bowl and cut off kernels using sharp knife.

2. Toast corn in hot skillet until it turns spotty brown, about 10 minutes.

BLT Pasta

SERVES 4 TO 6

12 slices **bacon**

2 **garlic cloves**

12 ounces **cherry tomatoes**

1 pound **orecchiette**

5 ounces (5 cups) **baby arugula**

1 cup (2 ounces) grated
Parmesan cheese,
plus extra for serving

INGREDIENT SPOTLIGHT BACON

We love the smoky, savory flavor and crunchy texture that bacon contributes to cooked dishes. But we don't use it just as a garnish or finishing touch; we also use its rendered fat to sauté aromatics or other ingredients—making extra fats, like oil and butter, unnecessary. Our favorite brands of bacon are **Applegate Farms Uncured Sunday Bacon** (shown) and **Farmland/Carando Apple Cider Cured Bacon, Applewood Smoked**. Tasters praised them both for good meaty flavor and mild smokiness.

✔ WHY THIS RECIPE WORKS We wanted to transform the traditional BLT into a pasta dish that was just as addictive as the sandwich. Starting with the bacon, we cooked it until crisp and then stirred it in at the end so it would keep its big crunch. Then we used the rendered fat to sauté the tomatoes and add even more smoky flavor to the dish. Halved cherry tomatoes cut back on prep time; cooking them briefly brought out their sweetness and allowed them to soften slightly. Baby arugula made the perfect stand-in for the usual iceberg lettuce—the arugula offered a welcome spicy bite, and it wilted nicely when added to the hot pasta just before serving.

1. Chop bacon and cook in 12-inch nonstick skillet over medium-high heat until crisp, about 5 minutes; transfer to paper towel–lined plate. Pour off all but 2 tablespoons fat left in skillet. Mince garlic, halve tomatoes, and add both to bacon fat left in skillet. Cook over medium-high heat until tomatoes are slightly softened, about 2 minutes.

2. Meanwhile, bring 4 quarts water to boil in large pot. Add pasta and 1 tablespoon salt and cook, stirring often, until al dente. Reserve 1½ cups cooking water, then drain pasta and return it to pot. Add bacon, garlic-tomato mixture, arugula, Parmesan, and 1 cup reserved cooking water and toss to combine. Season with salt and pepper to taste and add reserved cooking water as needed to adjust consistency. Serve with extra Parmesan.

TEST KITCHEN TIP
SOFTENING CHERRY TOMATOES

Cooking the cherry tomatoes briefly in the rendered bacon fat along with some garlic works to flavor and soften them. Don't overcook the tomatoes; they should be just slightly softened.

Shells with Blue Cheese, Radicchio, and Walnuts

SERVES 4 TO 6

3 **garlic cloves**

2 cups **heavy cream**

1 head **radicchio**

½ cup (2 ounces) crumbled **blue cheese**

1 cup **walnuts**

1 pound **medium pasta shells**

INGREDIENT SPOTLIGHT RADICCHIO

Though it tends to show up in salads most of the time, radicchio also works well in many cooked dishes, such as our blue cheese–spiked pasta, where it cuts the richness of the sauce. Radicchio is a member of the chicory family that boasts an assertive flavor and a peppery bitterness. It's fairly noticeable in the produce section thanks to the intense reddish-purple hue of its leaves. When shopping for radicchio, be sure to look for heads that are tight and firm.

WHY THIS RECIPE WORKS Starting out with blue cheese for this recipe gave us an elegant, bistro-worthy entrée with big flavor. Turning the cheese into a luxurious, potently flavored sauce was as easy as simmering it with heavy cream for just a few minutes. Adding a few cloves of garlic contributed aromatic complexity. Slightly bitter radicchio played off the richness of the sauce and gave our dish more substance, and toasted walnuts added crunch. For a sauce with just the right thickness, we turned to an ingredient that was already right in front of our noses: the starchy pasta cooking water. Use either a mild blue cheese (like Stella brand) or a slightly sweet blue cheese (like Gorgonzola dolce).

1. Mince garlic, combine with cream in 12-inch skillet, and cook over medium-high heat, whisking often, until thickened, about 5 to 7 minutes. Core radicchio and cut into ½-inch pieces. Stir radicchio and ¼ cup blue cheese into skillet and cook until radicchio is wilted, 3 to 5 minutes; cover and set aside.

2. Meanwhile, toast walnuts (see page 297) and chop. Bring 4 quarts water to boil in large pot. Add pasta and 1 tablespoon salt to boiling water and cook, stirring often, until al dente. Reserve 1½ cups cooking water, then drain pasta and return it to pot. Add cream mixture and ½ cup reserved cooking water and toss to combine. Season with salt and pepper to taste and add remaining cooking water as needed to adjust consistency. Sprinkle individual portions with nuts and remaining ¼ cup blue cheese before serving.

TEST KITCHEN TIP PREPPING RADICCHIO

1. Remove any blemished outer layers, then cut radicchio in half and remove pyramid-shaped core.

2. With cut side facing down, cut each piece radicchio lengthwise and widthwise into square-shaped, ½-inch pieces.

Rotini with Brussels Sprouts, Blue Cheese, and Bacon

SERVES 4 TO 6

6 slices **bacon**

1 pound **Brussels sprouts**

1 cup **heavy cream**

1 cup (4 ounces) crumbled **blue cheese**

¼ cup **pine nuts**

1 pound **rotini**

INGREDIENT SPOTLIGHT
BRUSSELS SPROUTS

Brussels sprouts don't need to be saved for the holiday dinner table; this cruciferous vegetable works well to add complexity and nutty flavor to a variety of dishes, from salads to pastas. Brussels sprouts, which grow in clusters on long stalks, are so named because they originated in Belgium. We've found that smaller sprouts can be more tender and sweeter than larger sprouts (more than an inch across), which can be bitter. Before cooking, be sure to trim the stem ends and remove any discolored leaves.

☑ **WHY THIS RECIPE WORKS** For another streamlined pasta recipe featuring tangy, piquant blue cheese, we decided to add nutty, slightly bitter Brussels sprouts and rich-tasting pine nuts to the mix. Rather than halve our Brussels sprouts, we decided to thinly slice them; this way, they were evenly distributed throughout the dish. Cooking some bacon until crisp provided enough rendered fat that we didn't need any oil to sauté our sprouts, and adding the crunchy pieces of bacon back at the end delivered a rich, creamy dish with crispy, smoky bits throughout. Small, firm Brussels sprouts (about 1 inch in diameter) work best here. Slicing the Brussels sprouts in a food processor can help to cut down on their prep time.

1. Chop bacon and cook in 12-inch nonstick skillet over medium-high heat until crisp, about 5 minutes; transfer to paper towel–lined plate. Pour off all but 2 tablespoons fat left in skillet.

2. Trim and thinly slice Brussels sprouts, add to bacon fat left in skillet with ½ teaspoon salt and ¼ teaspoon pepper, and cook over medium-high heat until they begin to soften, about 5 minutes. Stir in cream, cover, and simmer until sprouts are tender, about 3 minutes. Off heat, stir in blue cheese.

3. Meanwhile, toast pine nuts (see page 297) and bring 4 quarts water to boil in large pot. Add pasta and 1 tablespoon salt to boiling water and cook, stirring often, until al dente. Reserve ½ cup cooking water, then drain pasta and return it to pot. Add sprouts mixture and bacon and toss to combine. Season with salt and pepper to taste and add reserved cooking water as needed to adjust consistency. Sprinkle individual portions with pine nuts before serving.

TEST KITCHEN TIP
SLICING BRUSSELS SPROUTS

You could slice the Brussels sprouts for this recipe by hand, but we like to use a food processor fitted with the slicing disk. First, trim the stem ends from the Brussels sprouts. Then, working in batches, fill the feed tube with sprouts and press them through with the feed tube plunger.

Ziti with Fire-Roasted Tomatoes, Pepperoni, and Smoked Mozzarella

SERVES 4 TO 6
6 ounces sliced **pepperoni**
3 **garlic cloves**
3 (14.5-ounce) cans **fire-roasted diced tomatoes**
6 ounces **smoked mozzarella**
1 pound **ziti**
Fresh basil

INGREDIENT SPOTLIGHT
SMOKED MOZZARELLA

We've found that quality can vary when it comes to smoked mozzarella. Don't bother with the supermarket variety; it's usually made with rubbery, low-quality block mozzarella and has a fake smoky flavor. Instead, seek out good-quality smoked mozzarella at high-end food markets or Italian markets.

✓ WHY THIS RECIPE WORKS This smoky, spicy dish relies on pepperoni for heat and smoked mozzarella and canned fire-roasted tomatoes for a hint of char. Pulsing the tomatoes in the food processor before simmering them ensured our sauce had just the right texture. To keep our cheese from melting and forming a gummy wad when tossed with the pasta, we cut it into cubes and froze it for about 10 minutes; this ensured that it softened properly when mixed with the hot pasta. With just a few cloves of garlic and some chopped basil, this easy sauce boasted surprising depth and flavor. Regular canned whole tomatoes can be substituted for the fire-roasted tomatoes.

1. Finely chop pepperoni and cook in 12-inch skillet over medium-high heat until rendered and crisp, about 5 minutes. Mince garlic, stir into skillet, and cook until fragrant, about 30 seconds. Pulse tomatoes with their juice in food processor until coarsely ground, about 12 pulses, then stir into skillet. Simmer sauce until slightly thickened, 15 to 20 minutes.

2. Cut mozzarella into ½-inch cubes and freeze until slightly firm, about 10 minutes.

3. Meanwhile, bring 4 quarts water to boil in large pot. Add pasta and 1 tablespoon salt to boiling water and cook, stirring often, until al dente. Reserve ½ cup cooking water, then drain pasta and return it to pot. Chop ½ cup basil, add to pasta with sauce and frozen mozzarella, and toss gently to combine. Season with salt and pepper to taste and add reserved cooking water as needed to adjust consistency. Serve.

TEST KITCHEN TIP
FREEZING MOZZARELLA

To keep the mozzarella from becoming rubbery and clumping together when tossed with the hot pasta, dice it and freeze it for 10 minutes.

Gemelli with Caramelized Onions, Kale, and Bacon

SERVES 4 TO 6
8 slices **bacon**
3 **onions**
1 pound **kale**
4 **garlic cloves**
1 pound **gemelli**
1 cup (2 ounces) grated **Parmesan cheese,** plus extra for serving

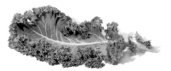

INGREDIENT SPOTLIGHT KALE

Kale is a hearty green that has a cabbage-y, slightly sweet flavor. We recommend discarding the thick stems; even when cooked, these remain tough and fibrous. Kale makes a great addition to many soups and stews, as it softens slightly but doesn't completely disintegrate the way more delicate greens might with a long simmering time.

✓ WHY THIS RECIPE WORKS Glossy caramelized onions, braised kale, and crisped bacon give this pasta dish a sweet, savory, and highly addictive flavor profile. We jump-started the caramelization of our onions by cooking them covered so they'd release their moisture, then we removed the lid and sautéed them to let the liquid evaporate and give the onions a chance to become deeply browned and tender. For the kale, we simply added it to the pan with the onions. The pasta cooking water did double duty—before adding the pasta, we added a scoop of the boiling water to the pan to braise the kale. Grated Parmesan cheese brought the sauce together and reinforced the meaty, salty notes of the bacon. Don't dry the kale completely after washing; a little extra water clinging to the leaves will help them wilt when cooking in step 2.

1. Bring 4 quarts water to boil in large pot for pasta. Cut bacon into ½-inch pieces and cook in 12-inch nonstick skillet over medium-high heat until crisp, about 5 minutes; transfer to paper towel–lined plate. Halve and thinly slice onions, add to bacon fat left in skillet with ½ teaspoon salt, cover, and cook over medium-high heat until soft, 5 to 8 minutes. Remove lid, reduce heat to medium, and continue to cook onions, stirring often, until well browned, 20 to 25 minutes.

2. Stem kale and chop leaves into 1-inch pieces. Mince garlic, stir into skillet, and cook until fragrant, about 30 seconds. Stir in half of kale and cook until it begins to wilt, about 2 minutes. Add remaining kale and 1½ cups boiling pasta water (skillet will be very full). Cover and simmer, tossing occasionally, until kale is tender, about 15 minutes.

3. Meanwhile, add pasta and 1 tablespoon salt to boiling water and cook, stirring often, until al dente. Reserve ½ cup cooking water, then drain pasta and return it to pot. Add kale mixture, bacon, and Parmesan and toss to combine. Season with salt and pepper to taste and add reserved cooking water as needed to adjust consistency. Serve with extra Parmesan.

Ziti with Stuffed Cherry Peppers, Pepperoni, and Tomato Sauce

SERVES 4 TO 6

6 ounces sliced **pepperoni**

2 **onions**

8 **oil-packed stuffed hot cherry peppers**

3 **garlic cloves**

1 (15-ounce) can **tomato sauce**

1 pound **ziti**

INGREDIENT SPOTLIGHT
STUFFED CHERRY PEPPERS

These peppers, which are stuffed with provolone and prosciutto, make a great addition to an antipasto platter, but they also contribute several layers of flavor to our sauce when chopped and sautéed with onion and garlic. They offer a zingy, peppery flavor along with the richness of a little cheese and the meaty flavor of prosciutto. You can find them in the supermarket either in jars alongside the pickles, or sold loose at the olive bar.

✔ **WHY THIS RECIPE WORKS** A classic antipasto star—stuffed peppers—brings big flavor to this pasta dish. Filled with provolone and prosciutto, this three-in-one ingredient provided spicy, savory, and salty notes—and all we had to do was chop them. Pepperoni reinforced the peppery heat, and cooking it first gave us rendered fat that we could use to sauté the peppers, plus some chopped onions and minced garlic for an aromatic backbone. To bring everything together, we stirred in a can of tomato sauce and let it all simmer until the flavors melded. Look for stuffed cherry peppers at the olive bar in the supermarket or next to the jarred pickles; one (12-ounce) jar of peppers will yield plenty for this recipe.

1. Finely chop pepperoni and cook in 12-inch skillet over medium-high heat until rendered and crisp, about 5 minutes. Finely chop onions, stir into skillet, and cook until softened and lightly browned, 8 to 10 minutes.

2. Rinse cherry peppers, pat dry with paper towels, and finely chop. Mince garlic, stir into skillet with cherry peppers, and cook until fragrant, about 1 minute. Stir in tomato sauce and simmer until thickened, about 10 minutes.

3. Meanwhile, bring 4 quarts water to boil in large pot. Add pasta and 1 tablespoon salt and cook, stirring often, until al dente. Reserve ½ cup cooking water, then drain pasta and return it to pot. Add sauce and toss to combine. Season with salt and pepper to taste and add reserved cooking water as needed to adjust consistency. Serve.

TEST KITCHEN TIP
COOKING PEPPERONI

Cooking the chopped pepperoni in a skillet helps it crisp and provides rendered fat that is used to sauté aromatics and add flavor to the dish.

Campanelle with Roasted Garlic, Chicken Sausage, and Arugula

SERVES 4 TO 6

16 **garlic cloves**

⅓ cup plus 1 tablespoon **olive oil**

12 ounces
cooked chicken sausage

1 pound **campanelle**

5 ounces (5 cups) **baby arugula**

1 cup (4 ounces) crumbled
goat cheese

INGREDIENT SPOTLIGHT
PREPEELED GARLIC

This pasta dish calls for a whopping 16 cloves of garlic—that's a lot of peeling. Fortunately, we found that prepeeled cloves from the supermarket make a fine—and convenient—stand-in for cloves from a fresh head of garlic, though cloves from a fresh head have the best flavor. When buying prepeeled garlic, look for packages of unblemished cloves that look firm and white and have a matte finish, and always store prepeeled cloves in the refrigerator, as they are more prone to spoilage than whole heads.

✓ **WHY THIS RECIPE WORKS** Roasted garlic gives this dish a sweet, intensely flavored foundation. Though roasting a head of garlic can take up to an hour, we found we could roast it more quickly when the cloves were separated. Combining the peeled garlic cloves (removing the skins made it easier to handle them once they were cooked) with oil, salt, and pepper in a small baking dish made it a snap to both roast and mash them into a paste, and cranking the oven up to 425 degrees cut the roasting time to 20 minutes. With some crumbled goat cheese, we had a thick and creamy coating for our campanelle. Lightly browned chicken sausage and baby arugula made this flavorful dish filling, too. Chicken sausage is available in a wide variety of flavors; feel free to choose a flavor that you think will pair well with the other flavors in this dish.

1. Adjust oven rack to upper-middle position; heat oven to 425 degrees. Peel garlic and combine with ⅓ cup oil, ½ teaspoon salt, and ½ teaspoon pepper in 8-inch square baking dish. Cover with aluminum foil; bake, stirring occasionally, until garlic is caramelized and soft, about 20 minutes. Let cool, then mash into paste with fork.

2. Slice sausage ½ inch thick on bias. Heat remaining 1 tablespoon oil in 12-inch skillet over medium-high until shimmering. Add sausage and cook until lightly browned, about 4 minutes. Off heat, stir in caramelized garlic mixture.

3. Meanwhile, bring 4 quarts water to boil in large pot. Add pasta and 1 tablespoon salt and cook, stirring often, until al dente. Reserve 1½ cups cooking water, then drain pasta and return it to pot. Add sausage mixture, arugula, goat cheese, and ½ cup reserved cooking water and toss to combine. Season with salt and pepper to taste and add remaining cooking water as needed to adjust consistency. Serve.

TEST KITCHEN TIP
EASY ROASTED GARLIC

To speed up the process of roasting garlic, we separate and peel the cloves before placing them in a baking dish with some olive oil and roasting them in a super-hot oven.

Easy Tortellini Gratin

SERVES 4

12 ounces **dried cheese tortellini**

1 (25-ounce) jar **tomato sauce**

¼ cup **heavy cream**

4 ounces **fresh mozzarella**

Fresh basil

INGREDIENT SPOTLIGHT
STORE-BOUGHT TORTELLINI

Handmade tortellini is a rich-tasting, albeit time-consuming, kitchen project. Store-bought tortellini makes a great runner-up, offering both good flavor and tender texture in a fraction of the time. Our favorite tortellini is a dried brand, **Barilla Three Cheese Tortellini**, which beat out several refrigerated and frozen competitors, plus one other dried brand, in our tasting. The Barilla tortellini was praised for a filling that tasters called "creamy," "pungent," and "tangy," thanks to its bold mixture of ricotta, Emmentaler, and Grana Padano cheeses. Another factor in Barilla's win was the texture of the pasta: The delicate wrapper of these petite tortellini was strong enough to contain the filling during boiling, but not overly gummy or prone to blowouts like other brands.

✔ WHY THIS RECIPE WORKS Store-bought tortellini and tomato sauce is usually a default dinner. But exciting? We'd have to say no. For a livelier take on this simple supper, we decided to move our tortellini to a baking dish, top it with cheese, and bake it like a gratin. To add some richness and a velvety texture to our jarred pasta sauce, we stirred in a bit of heavy cream. After cooking the tortellini, we tossed it with our no-cook sauce, then moved it to a 13 by 9-inch baking dish. Thin slices of fresh mozzarella spread over the top of the pasta provided more richness and a fresh cheese flavor. After 15 minutes, the mozzarella had melted into a nice, gooey layer. With a garnish of shredded basil, our simple gratin easily elevated two supermarket staples to new heights.

1. Adjust oven rack to middle position and heat oven to 450 degrees. Bring 4 quarts water to boil in large pot. Add tortellini and 1 tablespoon salt and cook, stirring often, until tender. Drain tortellini and transfer to 13 by 9-inch baking dish.

2. Combine tomato sauce and heavy cream, then pour over tortellini. Slice mozzarella very thinly and lay on top. Bake until cheese is melted and sauce is hot throughout, about 15 minutes. Shred 2 tablespoons basil, sprinkle over top, and serve.

TEST KITCHEN TIP **SHREDDING BASIL**

1. To shred basil, stack three or four clean, dry leaves.

2. Roll leaves up tightly like a cigar, then slice them thin.

Creamy Tortellini with Vegetables

SERVES 4

2 ounces thinly sliced **prosciutto**

2 cups **chicken broth**

12 ounces **dried cheese tortellini**

1 (5.2-ounce) package
Boursin Garlic and Fine Herbs cheese

5 ounces (5 cups)
baby spinach

1 cup **frozen peas**

INGREDIENT SPOTLIGHT
PROSCIUTTO

Though Italy invented the method used to produce this salt-cured and air-dried ham, our favorite brand is a domestic prosciutto. In a recent tasting, **La Quercia Prosciutto Americano**, which is made in Iowa, bested a handful of Italian competitors, thanks to its "deep," "earthy" flavor and "creamy" texture.

WHY THIS RECIPE WORKS Most tortellini dishes featuring a cheese sauce and vegetables go too heavy on the former and too light on the latter. We wanted a well-balanced dish with plenty of richness, but lots of fresh bites as well. For the vegetables, we opted for prep-free baby spinach and frozen peas; both needed just a few minutes over the heat to wilt and warm through, respectively. Looking for a boldly flavored ingredient to give our sauce an identity, we hit on Boursin cheese, which delivered potent aromatic flavor and a creamy texture. Adding chicken broth to the pasta cooking water upped the savory notes of the dish, and gave us a head start on the sauce. Once the tortellini was tender, we stirred in the cheese and vegetables, making this an easy one-pan supper. Topped off with crisped prosciutto, this pasta dinner offers an addictive mix of flavors and textures.

1. Chop prosciutto and cook in Dutch oven over medium heat until crisp, 5 to 7 minutes; transfer to paper towel–lined plate.

2. Add broth, 1½ cups water, and tortellini to now-empty pot and simmer vigorously over medium-high heat, stirring often, until tortellini is tender, 6 to 9 minutes.

3. Reduce heat to low. Stir in Boursin, spinach, peas, and ½ cup water and cook until spinach is wilted, about 2 minutes. Off heat, season with salt and pepper to taste. Top with prosciutto and serve.

TEST KITCHEN TIP
COOKING TORTELLINI IN BROTH

Cooking the tortellini in a combination of water and chicken broth adds deep, savory flavor to the dish, plus there's no need to drain the pot—the tortellini soaks up a good amount of the liquid, and the remaining liquid provides a flavorful base for our sauce.

Six-Ingredient Spaghetti and Meatballs

SERVES 4 TO 6

1½ pounds **meatloaf mix**

⅔ cup
prepared basil pesto

⅔ cup **panko bread crumbs**

1 (25-ounce) jar **tomato sauce**

1 pound **spaghetti**

Grated **Parmesan**

INGREDIENT SPOTLIGHT
JARRED TOMATO SAUCE

We lean on jarred pasta sauce to help us reduce the prep work in our Six-Ingredient Spaghetti and Meatballs as well as other pasta and casserole recipes. But with so many options on supermarket shelves, what should you buy? We have a few favorites in the test kitchen. **Victoria Marinara Sauce** (shown) is our favorite premium brand; it has a short ingredient list (just tomatoes, olive oil, fresh onions, fresh basil, fresh garlic, salt, and spices) and, accordingly, boasts a "robust" flavor that tastes like "homemade." For a runner-up, we also like Classico Marinara with Plum Tomatoes and Olive Oil. For a traditional, everyday sauce, we prefer **Bertolli Tomato and Basil Sauce**. Though not as fresh-tasting as the top-rated premium brand, this sauce offers a "good balance of flavors."

☑ **WHY THIS RECIPE WORKS** Classic spaghetti and meatballs can take hours to make, and usually calls for piles of ingredients. To help speed things up without losing any flavor, we added a secret ingredient to our meatballs: pesto. The pesto eliminates the need for garlic, cheese, and even the egg yolk in a standard meatball recipe, making ours nearly prep-free; with a sprinkling of salt and pepper, plus some bread crumbs (we liked super-crisp panko), they were ready to go. Starting the meatballs in a cold skillet meant we didn't need any oil, and prevented the finished dish from tasting too greasy. Browning the meatballs also works to give the sauce a big boost of flavor. Once the meatballs were browned, we simply added jarred sauce and simmered them until cooked through. Meatloaf mix is a combination of equal parts ground beef, pork, and veal and is available at most grocery stores. If you cannot find meatloaf mix, substitute equal parts 90 percent lean ground beef and ground pork. You will need a 12-inch nonstick skillet with a tight-fitting lid for this recipe; do not substitute a smaller skillet here.

1. Mix meatloaf mix, pesto, bread crumbs, ½ teaspoon salt, and ¼ teaspoon pepper together in bowl using hands until uniform. Lightly shape mixture into 18 meatballs (scant ¼ cup each). Lay meatballs in 12-inch nonstick skillet. Place skillet over medium-high heat and cook meatballs, turning as needed, until browned on all sides, about 10 minutes.

2. Pour sauce over meatballs and bring to simmer. Cover, reduce heat to medium-low, and simmer until meatballs are cooked through, about 10 minutes.

3. Meanwhile, bring 4 quarts water to boil in large pot. Add pasta and 1 tablespoon salt and cook, stirring often, until al dente. Reserve ½ cup cooking water, then drain pasta and return it to pot.

4. Add several large spoonfuls of tomato sauce (without meatballs) to pasta and toss to combine. Add reserved cooking water as needed to adjust consistency and season with salt and pepper to taste. Divide pasta among individual bowls, top with remaining sauce and meatballs, and sprinkle with Parmesan. Serve.

Ziti with Italian Sausage, Broccoli, and Sun-Dried Tomatoes

SERVES 4 TO 6

1 pound
sweet or hot Italian sausage

¾ cup
oil-packed sun-dried tomatoes

1 cup **chicken broth**

12 ounces **broccoli florets**

1 pound **ziti**

1 cup (2 ounces) grated
Parmesan cheese,
plus extra for serving

INGREDIENT SPOTLIGHT
BROCCOLI FLORETS

Broccoli florets add a nice crunch and bright green color to this ziti dish. Most supermarkets sell broccoli florets already trimmed and ready to go, which helps cut back on prep time and waste. But note that if the florets you've purchased are large or unevenly cut, you may need to trim them further before cooking.

☑ **WHY THIS RECIPE WORKS** For a fresher take on the traditional chicken, broccoli, and ziti, we first ditched the chicken in favor of spiced Italian sausage. The hearty sausage gave our sauce a rich, bold flavor. Adding sun-dried tomatoes was our second change to the ingredient lineup. To soften the tomatoes, we sliced them thinly and simmered them, with the sausage, in some chicken broth. A little Parmesan and some pasta cooking water was all it took to transform this mixture into a nicely clingy sauce. Finally, we blanched our broccoli florets in the boiling water, before cooking the pasta, until crisp-tender but still bright green. Now our pasta dish not only tasted but also looked brighter and fresher than its traditional counterpart.

1. Remove sausage from casing (see page 199) and cook in 12-inch nonstick skillet over medium-high heat, breaking up meat with wooden spoon, until no longer pink, about 4 minutes. Rinse sun-dried tomatoes, pat dry with paper towels, and slice thinly. Stir sun-dried tomatoes and broth into skillet and simmer until tomatoes soften, about 2 minutes.

2. Meanwhile, bring 4 quarts water to boil in large pot. Add broccoli and 1 tablespoon salt and cook until crisp-tender, about 2 minutes; transfer broccoli to paper towel–lined plate.

3. Return water to boil, add pasta, and cook, stirring often, until al dente. Reserve ½ cup cooking water, then drain pasta and return it to pot. Add sausage mixture, broccoli, and Parmesan and toss to combine. Season with salt and pepper to taste and add reserved cooking water as needed to adjust consistency. Serve.

TEST KITCHEN TIP
BLANCHING THE BROCCOLI

Blanching the broccoli in the boiling pasta water for 2 minutes kept it fresh and crisp in the finished dish. The key is to remove the broccoli while it is still slightly underdone, as it will continue to soften slightly as it cools.

Ziti with Fennel and Italian Sausage

SERVES 4 TO 6

1 pound
sweet or hot Italian sausage

2 **onions**

1 **fennel bulb**

1 (6-ounce) can **tomato paste**

1 pound **ziti**

½ cup (1 ounce) grated
Pecorino Romano cheese,
plus extra for serving

INGREDIENT SPOTLIGHT
TOMATO PASTE

Because it's naturally full of gluta-mates, which stimulate taste buds, tomato paste brings out subtle depths and savory notes, which is why we use it in a variety of recipes, from quick-cooking pasta dishes to longer-cooking stews and braises. Our preferred brand is **Goya Tomato Paste**, for its bright, robust tomato flavor. Tasters liked its sweetness, yet found it well-balanced.

✅ WHY THIS RECIPE WORKS We wanted a rich, hearty pasta dish with cooked-all-day flavor—but we wanted it pronto. Starting with Italian sausage ensured our sauce offered big, meaty flavor in short order and meant we could cut back on aromatics and spices. Caramelized onions and fennel provided a sweet richness that didn't overshadow the sausage, and cooking them covered for a few minutes sped up the caramelization process; once they had softened, we uncovered the pan and let our onions and fennel cook until golden and meltingly tender. For savory depth and intensity, we stirred in a full can of tomato paste; toasting it briefly brought out its flavor even more. Starchy pasta cooking water and grated Pecorino Romano helped to thicken the sauce and make it cling.

1. Bring 4 quarts water to boil in large pot for pasta. Remove sausage from casing (see page 199) and cook in large Dutch oven over medium-high heat, breaking up meat with wooden spoon, until no longer pink, about 4 minutes.

2. Halve and thinly slice onions. Trim fennel stalks and fronds; mince fronds and reserve. Trim bulb, cut in half, core, and slice into ½-inch-thick strips (see page 177). Stir onions and fennel into skillet, cover, and cook until softened, about 5 minutes. Uncover, reduce heat to medium, and cook until vegetables are golden, 10 to 12 minutes.

3. Add tomato paste and cook until darkened, about 3 minutes. Stir in 2 cups boiling pasta water and simmer until thickened, about 5 minutes.

4. Meanwhile, add pasta and 1 tablespoon salt to boiling water and cook, stirring often, until al dente. Reserve 1½ cups cooking water, then drain pasta and return it to pot. Add sausage mixture, Pecorino, and 1 cup reserved cooking water and toss to combine. Season with salt and pepper to taste and add remaining cooking water as needed to adjust consistency. Sprinkle individual portions with fennel fronds and extra Pecorino before serving.

TEST KITCHEN TIP
GRATING HARD CHEESE

When grating hard cheeses, such as Parmesan and Pecorino Romano, we use a rasp grater because it produces lighter, fluffier shreds of cheese that melt seamlessly into pasta dishes and sauces.

Fusilli with Giardiniera and Sausage

SERVES 4 TO 6

1 pound **sweet Italian sausage**

2 **onions**

3 cups
giardiniera pickled vegetables

1 (15-ounce) can **tomato sauce**

1 pound **fusilli**

Fresh basil

INGREDIENT SPOTLIGHT
GIARDINIERA

In Italy, giardiniera refers to pickled vegetables that are typically eaten as an antipasto. But here in the United States, it's most recognized as a combination of pickled cauliflower, carrots, celery, and sweet and hot peppers that is served alongside sandwiches or other lunch fare. Our favorite brand is **Pastene**. It includes a good mix of crunchy vegetables (some brands are mostly peppers) and boasts a "sharp, vinegary tang."

✓ **WHY THIS RECIPE WORKS** This dish derives its big flavor from a surprising yet easy-to-find convenience product: pickled Italian vegetables, also known as *giardiniera*. Here, we called upon the giardiniera to do double duty: The vegetables themselves added crunch and flavor—and saved us from having to prep a number of ingredients—while the brine added bright, tangy notes to the sauce. Browned Italian sausage, sautéed onions, chopped giardiniera vegetables, and canned tomato sauce gave us a boldly flavored sauce in little time. Chopped basil added a fresh finishing touch. Look for giardiniera either at the olive bar in the supermarket or next to the jarred pickles; one (16-ounce) jar of giardiniera will yield enough for this recipe.

1. Remove sausage from casing and cook in 12-inch nonstick skillet over medium-high heat, breaking up meat with wooden spoon, until no longer pink, about 4 minutes. Finely chop onions, stir into skillet, and cook until softened and lightly browned, 10 to 12 minutes.

2. Drain giardiniera, reserving 6 tablespoons brine, and chop coarsely. Stir giardiniera, 4 tablespoons brine, and tomato sauce into skillet and simmer until thickened, about 10 minutes.

3. Meanwhile, bring 4 quarts water to boil in large pot. Add pasta and 1 tablespoon salt and cook, stirring often, until al dente. Reserve ½ cup cooking water, then drain pasta and return it to pot. Chop ½ cup basil, add to pasta with sausage mixture and 1 tablespoon brine, and toss to combine. Season with salt, pepper, and remaining 1 tablespoon brine to taste and add reserved cooking water as needed to adjust consistency. Serve.

TEST KITCHEN TIP
REMOVING SAUSAGE FROM ITS CASING

After cutting off one end of casing, hold sausage firmly and squeeze sausage out of casing through open end.

Brats with Beer and Mustard on Egg Noodles

SERVES 4 TO 6
2 tablespoons **vegetable oil**
1 pound **bratwurst**
2 **onions**
1 (12-ounce) bottle **mild beer**
⅓ cup **Dijon mustard**
12 ounces (7¾ cups) **egg noodles**

INGREDIENT SPOTLIGHT BRATWURST

Authentic versions of these pale, mild German sausages made from pork and veal have a smooth, almost emulsified texture, with all the fat blended thoroughly with the meat. But this type of bratwurst can be hard to find. At your local supermarket, you're more likely to see bratwurst with a coarser texture, like the Johnsonville Brats shown above, which worked well in our recipe. Note that either style will work fine.

✓ **WHY THIS RECIPE WORKS** To transform the Midwestern classic of bratwurst and beer—a popular tailgating dish that adds onions for a saucy topping—into a sit-down supper, we started by getting rid of the buns in favor of egg noodles. Browning the bratwurst left us with flavorful bits in the pan that we could use to build the sauce. Thinly sliced onions and mustard added flavor, and picked up the rich, meaty notes of the sausage when they mingled with the fond in the skillet. A bottle of beer formed the bulk of the sauce, which we used to cook the brats through and instill them with complex flavor. Tossed with tender egg noodles, this dish was perfect for halftime feasting.

1. Heat 1 tablespoon oil in 12-inch skillet over medium heat until shimmering. Add sausage and cook until well browned, about 5 minutes; transfer to plate.

2. Halve and thinly slice onions. Add remaining 1 tablespoon oil, onions, and ⅛ teaspoon salt to now-empty skillet and cook, stirring often, until softened and lightly browned, about 15 minutes. Whisk in beer and mustard until smooth. Nestle sausages, with any accumulated juices, into pan, cover, and simmer gently until sausages are cooked through, about 10 minutes.

3. Transfer sausages to cutting board, let cool slightly, then slice ½ inch thick on bias. Return sausage to skillet and season with salt and pepper to taste.

4. Meanwhile, bring 4 quarts water to boil in large pot. Add pasta and 1 tablespoon salt and cook, stirring often, until al dente. Reserve ½ cup cooking water, then drain pasta and return it to pot. Add sausage mixture and toss to combine. Season with pepper to taste and add reserved cooking water as needed to adjust consistency. Serve.

Ziti with Cajun Shrimp, Andouille Sausage, and Bell Pepper

SERVES 4 TO 6

1 pound **andouille sausage**

2 **red bell peppers**

1 (28-ounce) can
crushed tomatoes

1 pound **extra-large shrimp**
(21 to 25 per pound)

1 pound **ziti**

Fresh parsley

INGREDIENT SPOTLIGHT
ANDOUILLE SAUSAGE

Traditional andouille (pronounced an-DOO-ee) sausage from Louisiana is made from ground pork, salt, and garlic—and seasoned with plenty of black pepper—then slowly smoked over pecan wood and sugarcane for up to 14 hours. Used in a wide range of Cajun dishes, such as gumbo, jambalaya, and red beans and rice, it bolsters any dish with its intense smoky, spicy, earthy flavor. Our favorite brand is **Jacob's World Famous Andouille**, a sausage straight from Louisiana. Tasters liked its smoky, spicy flavor and chewy texture, which comes from cubing the pork instead of grinding it.

✔ WHY THIS RECIPE WORKS For a supper boasting the best flavors of the Bayou, we combined sweet, tender shrimp with smoky, spicy andouille sausage. Building the sauce around the browned sausage ensured that its flavors permeated the dish—no extra aromatics or dried spices needed. Chopped red bell peppers added sweetness, while crushed tomatoes offered up rich flavor quickly and delivered a thick, clingy sauce. Rather than sauté the shrimp separately, we poached it right in the sauce, which ensured moist, tender shrimp and kept the method easy and streamlined. If your shrimp are larger or smaller, be sure to alter the cooking time in step 1 accordingly. If your andouille seems very dry and crumbly when cooking in step 1, add 1 tablespoon olive oil to the pan.

1. Slice andouille ½-inch thick and cook in 12-inch nonstick skillet over medium-high heat until well browned, about 5 minutes. Core and cut peppers into ½-inch pieces, add to skillet, and cook until softened, about 3 minutes. Add tomatoes and simmer until thickened, about 10 minutes. Peel shrimp completely (including tails) and devein (see page 37). Stir shrimp into skillet, cover, and simmer gently until shrimp are cooked through, about 5 minutes.

2. Meanwhile, bring 4 quarts water to boil in large pot. Add pasta and 1 tablespoon salt and cook, stirring often, until al dente. Reserve ½ cup cooking water, then drain pasta and return it to pot. Chop ¼ cup parsley, add to pasta with shrimp mixture, and toss to combine. Season with salt and pepper to taste and add reserved cooking water as needed to adjust consistency. Serve.

TEST KITCHEN TIP CUTTING UP A BELL PEPPER

1. Slice off top and bottom of pepper, remove seeds, and slice down through side.

2. Lay pepper flat, carefully trim away ribs, and cut into pieces or strips as desired.

Linguine with Clams and Chorizo

SERVES 4 TO 6

8 ounces **chorizo sausage**

4 pounds
littleneck or cherrystone clams

½ cup **dry white wine**

6 tablespoons **unsalted butter**

Fresh parsley

1 pound **linguine**

INGREDIENT SPOTLIGHT CHORIZO

When shopping for chorizo, you may come across several different styles, including Spanish, Colombian/Argentinean, and Mexican. Though they all will work in this recipe, they will have distinctly different flavors and textures. The dry-cured Spanish chorizo (shown) has a coarsely ground texture and a bright red color and smoky flavor from the inclusion of smoked paprika; depending on the paprika, the chorizo can be sweet (dulce) or hot (picante). Colombian/Argentinean chorizo can be either raw or cooked and is very coarsely ground and seasoned with garlic and herbs (think Italian sausage). Mexican chorizo is raw and made from either pork or beef, is very finely ground, and has a spicy tanginess due to the inclusion of chili powder and vinegar.

✔ **WHY THIS RECIPE WORKS** This gutsy, bold dish puts a new spin on classic clam sauce by adding spicy chorizo. We started by sautéing the chorizo, then added clams and white wine to the pot and let the clams steam; the rendered fat from the chorizo offered our sauce big flavor, and the wine contributed much-needed brightness. Finishing the sauce with butter gave it a rich, velvety texture and stirring in some chopped parsley added a fresh touch. If your chorizo seems very dry and crumbly when cooking in step 1, add 1 tablespoon olive oil to the pan. When shopping for clams, choose the smallest ones you can find. Be sure to scrub the clams thoroughly of grit and sand before cooking. Note that the clams can be very briny, so be sure to taste the final dish before seasoning with additional salt.

1. Slice chorizo into ½-inch-thick pieces on bias and cook in large Dutch oven over medium heat, stirring often, until well browned, about 6 minutes. Scrub clams and stir into pot with wine. Cover and simmer, shaking pan occasionally, until clams begin to open, about 6 minutes. Uncover and continue to simmer until all clams have opened and sauce is slightly reduced, about 2 minutes.

2. Discard any clams that refuse to open; if cooking liquid is sandy, remove clams and strain sauce into clean pot. Cut butter into small pieces, chop ½ cup parsley, and gently stir both into pot. Off heat, season with pepper to taste.

3. Meanwhile, bring 4 quarts water to boil in large pot. Add pasta and 1 tablespoon salt; cook, stirring often, until al dente. Reserve ½ cup cooking water, then drain pasta and return it to pot. Add clam mixture; toss to combine. Season with salt and pepper to taste and add reserved cooking water as needed to adjust consistency. Serve.

TEST KITCHEN TIP
SCRUBBING CLAMS

Before cooking clams, use a soft brush to scrub away any bits of sand trapped in the shell.

Mediterranean Penne with Tuna and Niçoise Olives

SERVES 4 TO 6

10 ounces
oil-packed solid white tuna

6 **garlic cloves**

3 (14.5-ounce) cans
diced tomatoes

¾ cup pitted **niçoise olives**

¼ cup **capers**

1 pound **penne**

INGREDIENT SPOTLIGHT
PREMIUM TUNA

Ultra-premium ventresca tuna is cut from the fatty belly of either the bonita del norte or yellowfin species, and the buttery, tender, olive oil–packed slices make a luxe addition to salads and tapas. Our favorite brand is **Nardin Bonito Del Norte Ventresca Fillets** (shown). But though the fillets taste rich, fresh, and "tender" yet "firm," they also cost a pretty penny at $35 for 8.5 ounces. For a more affordable alternative, we also like Tonnino Tuna Ventresca Yellowfin in Olive Oil, which costs $8 for 6.7 ounces.

✓ WHY THIS RECIPE WORKS For a zesty, Mediterranean-inspired pasta dish, we combined meaty chunks of tuna and piquant niçoise olives in a simple yet speedy sauce. Oil-packed tuna not only provided a richer flavor than the water-packed variety, it also gave us some oil that we could use to sauté the aromatics (several cloves of garlic provided a potent flavor base). Canned tomatoes offered us a chunky sauce, and including some of their juice imparted a nice, fresh flavor. Finally, we turned to one more boldly flavored ingredient—capers—to give our dish just a little more punch. Serve with grated Parmesan cheese and extra-virgin olive oil. If necessary, you can substitute olive oil for the reserved oil from the cans of tuna.

1. Drain tuna, reserving ½ cup drained oil, and flake gently with fork. Mince garlic and cook with reserved oil in large saucepan over medium heat until fragrant, 1 to 2 minutes. Drain tomatoes, reserving 1½ cups juice, and stir both tomatoes and juice into pot. Simmer until tomatoes soften and sauce thickens, about 15 minutes.

2. Chop olives; rinse and mince capers. Stir olives, capers, and tuna into pot and simmer until heated through, about 5 minutes.

3. Meanwhile, bring 4 quarts water to boil in large pot. Add pasta and 1 tablespoon salt and cook, stirring often, until al dente. Reserve ½ cup cooking water, then drain pasta and return it to pot. Add sauce and toss to combine. Season with salt and pepper to taste and add reserved cooking water as needed to adjust consistency. Serve.

TEST KITCHEN TIP PITTING OLIVES

1. To pit olives, place them between paper towels and pound gently with a mallet.

2. Once all the olives have been cracked open, use your fingers to remove the pits.

Fettuccine with Shrimp, Tarragon, and Cream

SERVES 4 TO 6

1¼ pounds **medium-large shrimp**
(31 to 40 per pound)

2 tablespoons **unsalted butter**

2 **garlic cloves**

2 cups **heavy cream**

2 (9-ounce) packages
fresh fettuccine

Fresh tarragon

INGREDIENT SPOTLIGHT **TARRAGON**

In France, this slender-leafed herb is called "little dragon" because of its fiery quality. Its flavor is very assertive, with a "mouth-numbing, anesthetic quality" and a sweet "orange-anise" aroma. Because of its bold presence, we use tarragon sparingly in recipes; it works well in fish, egg, and chicken dishes. In the test kitchen, we prefer fresh tarragon to dried tarragon for its fresher, brighter flavor.

WHY THIS RECIPE WORKS Elegant yet easy, this rich, creamy dish features the complementary flavors of tender, briny shrimp and sweet, aniselike tarragon. Searing the shrimp in butter infused it with rich flavor. After setting the shrimp aside (we stirred it in at the end to warm through), we simmered heavy cream in the pan until slightly thickened. Then we added the reduced cream and some minced tarragon to the cooked fettuccine; heating the mixture for a moment ensured that the pasta absorbed the sauce, and it kept the tarragon flavor from becoming muted. Note that it is important to cook the pasta until it is not quite al dente because it will continue to cook after being tossed and heated with the sauce. We prefer to use fresh fettuccine in this dish; however, you can substitute 12 ounces of dried fettuccine if necessary.

1. Peel shrimp completely (including tails), devein (see page 37), pat dry with paper towels, and season with salt and pepper. Melt butter in 12-inch skillet over medium-high heat until just beginning to brown, about 2 minutes. Add shrimp and cook, stirring occasionally, until just pink at edges, about 1½ minutes. Mince garlic, stir into skillet, and cook until fragrant, about 30 seconds; transfer to bowl and cover.

2. Add cream to now-empty skillet and simmer over medium-high heat until slightly thickened and measures 1½ cups, about 8 minutes; cover and remove from heat.

3. Meanwhile, bring 4 quarts water to boil in large pot. Add pasta and 1 tablespoon salt and cook, stirring often, until nearly al dente. Reserve ½ cup cooking water, then drain pasta and return it to pot. Mince 2 tablespoons tarragon and add to pasta with cream. Cook pasta over low heat until sauce clings lightly to pasta, about 1 minute. Off heat, stir in shrimp along with any accumulated juices. Season with salt and pepper to taste and add reserved cooking water as needed to adjust consistency. Serve.

Farfalle with Salmon and Leeks

SERVES 4 TO 6

2 pounds **leeks**

2 tablespoons **unsalted butter**

2 (6-ounce)
skinless salmon fillets,
1¼ inches thick

1 cup **dry white wine**

¾ cup **heavy cream**

1 pound **farfalle**

INGREDIENT SPOTLIGHT
WHITE WINE FOR COOKING

When a recipe calls for dry white wine, it's tempting to grab whatever open bottle is in the fridge. Chardonnay and Pinot Grigio may taste different straight from the glass, but how much do those distinctive flavor profiles really come through in a cooked dish? To find out, we tried four varietals and a supermarket "cooking wine" in five recipes. Only Sauvignon Blanc consistently boiled down to a "clean" yet sufficiently acidic flavor that worked well with the other ingredients. Vermouth is acceptable in some recipes, but because its flavor is stronger, we don't recommend using it unless it is listed as an option in the recipe.

✓ WHY THIS RECIPE WORKS In this dish, moist, buttery salmon and meltingly tender leeks come together with al dente pasta in a velvety cream sauce. For perfectly tender leeks, we sautéed them in butter until softened. Shallow-poaching the salmon right in the pan with the leeks—we used white wine for the cooking liquid—kept the fish moist and the procedure streamlined. Cream, added directly to the pan, thickened nicely and absorbed the subtle oniony flavor of the leeks. To prevent the salmon from breaking apart into tiny shreds, we set it aside while the cream simmered, then stirred it into the pasta with the sauce so the fillets would separate into fork-friendly bites. Be careful to handle the salmon gently after it's cooked, or it will break apart into very fine pieces.

1. Trim and discard root and dark green leaves from leeks. Halve leeks lengthwise, then slice crosswise into ½-inch-thick pieces (see page 49). Wash cut leeks thoroughly using salad spinner. Melt butter in 12-inch nonstick skillet over medium-high heat. Add leeks and ¼ teaspoon salt and cook until tender, about 7 minutes.

2. Season salmon with salt and pepper and nestle into skillet. Add wine, cover, and cook until salmon is just cooked through, about 6 minutes. Transfer salmon to plate and cover to keep warm. Stir cream into skillet and simmer until thickened, about 2 minutes; remove from heat and cover.

3. Meanwhile, bring 4 quarts water to boil in large pot. Add pasta and 1 tablespoon salt and cook, stirring often, until al dente. Reserve ½ cup cooking water, then drain pasta and return it to pot. Add sauce and salmon, along with any accumulated juices, and toss gently to combine, breaking salmon into bite-size pieces. Season with salt and pepper to taste and add reserved cooking water as needed to adjust consistency. Serve.

TEST KITCHEN TIP
WASHING LEEKS

To wash leeks, cut them as desired and place them in a salad spinner with water, swishing them thoroughly to remove any dirt or sand. Then lift them out of the water; the dirt and sand will drain away.

CRISPY TOFU WITH COCONUT-LIME RICE

Vegetarian Mains

211 Roasted Tomato and Corn Tostadas

212 Portobello and Spinach Strudel

213 Parmesan Polenta with Eggplant Ragu

215 Skillet Pizza with Broccolini and Sun-Dried Tomatoes

216 Orzo Primavera with Feta

217 Roasted Poblano and Black Bean Enchiladas

218 Baked Quinoa with Roasted Kale and Chickpeas

220 Easy Stuffed Zucchini

221 Crispy Tofu with Coconut-Lime Rice

Roasted Tomato and Corn Tostadas

SERVES 4

1½ pounds **cherry tomatoes**

2 ears **corn**

2 tablespoons **chili oil**

1 cup
vegetarian refried black beans

8 (6-inch) **corn tostadas**

1 cup (4 ounces) crumbled
queso fresco

INGREDIENT SPOTLIGHT
CORN TOSTADAS

The Mexican tostada is a close relative of the tortilla chip—only bigger, flatter, and less salty. Traditionally, tostadas are made from stale corn tortillas that are toasted (the literal translation of the word) or deep-fried to make them not only more flavorful but also sturdy enough to support a generous topping of refried beans or shredded meat. Most supermarkets keep them in stock nowadays, so it's not necessary to go to such lengths to enjoy them at home. Looking for store-bought tostadas that delivered a shatteringly crisp texture and full, nutty corn flavor, we sampled five brands, both plain and with refried beans. Our favorite brand was **Mission Tostadas Estilo Casero**; its "clean corn flavor," "rustic crunch," and "substantial" texture made it the hands-down favorite.

✓ WHY THIS RECIPE WORKS Topped with a flavorful combination of fresh tomatoes and corn, these tostadas are a pleasant departure from your typical taco dinner. To bring out the sweet flavors of our star vegetables, we roasted them until the tomatoes began to brown and break down. Rather than roasting the vegetables in flavorless vegetable oil, we added a spicy kick with a little bit of chili oil, which we also stirred into vegetarian refried beans to boost their flavor. Premade corn tostadas helped this dish come together in a snap, but they needed a short stint in the oven to warm through along with the beans. To bring the entire dish together at once, we made use of the lower oven rack to warm the tostadas and beans while the vegetables finished roasting. A sprinkling of *queso fresco*, a crumbly, mild Mexican cheese, added brightness and a mild tang. If you can't find queso fresco, you can substitute feta cheese. You can use any kind of spicy chili oil here.

1. Adjust oven racks to upper-middle and lower-middle positions and heat oven to 450 degrees. Halve tomatoes, cut corn kernels from cobs (see page 181), and toss with 1½ tablespoons chili oil, ½ teaspoon salt, and ¼ teaspoon pepper in bowl. Spread vegetables onto rimmed baking sheet. Bake on upper-middle rack, stirring occasionally, until tomatoes are softened and begin to brown, 20 to 25 minutes.

2. Combine refried beans, remaining 1½ teaspoons chili oil, and ¼ teaspoon salt and spread evenly over tostadas; arrange on rimmed baking sheet. During final minutes of vegetable roasting time, bake tostadas on lower-middle rack until beans are warm, about 5 minutes. Divide vegetables evenly among warm tostadas, sprinkle with queso fresco, and serve.

TEST KITCHEN TIP
ROASTING VEGETABLES

Roasting the tomatoes and corn in a hot oven works to drive off moisture and intensify their flavor.

Portobello and Spinach Strudel

SERVES 4

1½ pounds
portobello mushroom caps

5 tablespoons **olive oil**

10 ounces
frozen chopped spinach

1 cup (4 ounces) crumbled
herbed goat cheese

¼ cup **heavy cream**

10 (14 by 9-inch) sheets
phyllo, thawed

INGREDIENT SPOTLIGHT
FROZEN PHYLLO DOUGH

Frozen packaged phyllo dough makes it easy to prepare traditional Greek dishes such as baklava and spana-kopita, but it also works as a light, flaky crust or wrapper for both savory and sweet fillings. However, working with phyllo can be a challenge, as the paper-thin sheets tend to tear, dry out quickly, and stick together. We've found a few tricks for helping with these problems. To prevent cracking, phyllo must be kept moist until you're ready to work with it; covering it with plastic wrap, then a damp dish towel, solves this problem, and prevents the dough from getting too wet. If your phyllo does tear or have cracks, you don't need to discard it. Just be sure to adjust the orientation of the sheets as you stack them so that cracks don't line up. Also, phyllo sheets can emerge from the box fused at their edges; to separate them, trim the fused portion and discard it.

✅ **WHY THIS RECIPE WORKS** For a streamlined savory strudel, we kept the ingredients simple and our method straightforward. Meaty portobello mushrooms formed the base of the filling, and earthy spinach added bulk; herbed goat cheese contributed rich flavor. For the pastry, sheets of phyllo dough kept things super easy. To avoid a soggy pastry, be sure to squeeze the spinach dry before mixing it with the mushrooms. Phyllo dough is also available in larger 18 by 14-inch sheets; if using, cut them in half to make 14 by 9-inch sheets. Don't thaw the phyllo in the microwave; let it sit in the refrigerator overnight or on the counter for four to five hours.

1. Adjust oven rack to middle position and heat oven to 400 degrees. Scrape out gills from portobellos and cut portobellos into ½-inch pieces. Heat 2 tablespoons oil in 12-inch nonstick skillet over medium-high heat until shimmering. Add mushrooms and ¼ teaspoon salt, cover, and cook until mushrooms have released their moisture, 8 to 10 minutes. Remove lid and cook until mushrooms are deep golden brown, 8 to 10 minutes; transfer to large bowl.

2. Microwave spinach in covered bowl until completely thawed, about 5 minutes; let cool slightly and thoroughly squeeze dry. Combine spinach, goat cheese, cream, ¼ teaspoon salt, and ¼ teaspoon pepper with mushrooms.

3. Lay 1 phyllo sheet on counter; brush thoroughly with oil. Repeat, 1 sheet at a time, with remaining phyllo and oil. Mound mushroom mixture into narrow log along bottom edge of phyllo, leaving 2-inch border at bottom and ½-inch border on sides. Fold bottom edge of dough over filling, then continue rolling dough tightly around filling, leaving ends open.

4. Transfer strudel, seam side down, to parchment paper–lined baking sheet. Cut four 1½-inch vents diagonally across top of strudel. Bake until strudel is golden brown, 20 to 25 minutes. Let strudel cool slightly on sheet, then slice and serve.

TEST KITCHEN TIP
MAKING STRUDEL

Mound mushroom mixture along bottom edge of phyllo, leaving 2-inch border at bottom and ½-inch border on sides. Fold bottom edge of dough over filling, then roll dough around filling into tight log.

Parmesan Polenta with Eggplant Ragu

SERVES 4

1 pound **eggplant**

2 tablespoons **olive oil**

2 (14.5-ounce) cans
**diced tomatoes with garlic,
basil, and oregano**

1½ cups **coarse-ground polenta**

1½ cups (3 ounces) grated
Parmesan cheese,
plus extra for serving

Fresh basil

INGREDIENT SPOTLIGHT EGGPLANT

At the supermarket, the eggplant varieties you're most likely to see are the globe or the Italian (which is a little smaller than the globe); well-stocked supermarkets may also carry the long and slender Chinese or Japanese eggplants or the apple-shaped Thai eggplant, which has a nice flavor and crunch and is the only eggplant we recommend eating raw. In general, we prefer using the globe eggplant in recipes. In tests, we've found this variety to be a true multitasker, suitable for all dishes and responding well to all cooking methods.

✓ WHY THIS RECIPE WORKS For a rich and hearty eggplant ragu to spoon over our Parmesan polenta, we needed to concentrate the flavors of the key ingredients: eggplant and tomatoes. Microwaving salted eggplant to drive off its moisture was our first step; this move ensured we could brown the eggplant in a skillet to add deep flavor. Canned diced tomatoes flavored with garlic, basil, and oregano served as the base for the sauce, and browning the drained tomatoes added another layer of flavor. Deglazing the pan with the reserved tomato juice and simmering the sauce for just 20 minutes gave us a rich-tasting ragu with little effort. Do not use fine-ground, stone-ground, or instant polenta in this recipe. The polenta should do little more than release wisps of steam as it cooks; if it bubbles or sputters even slightly after the first 10 minutes, the heat is too high.

1. Line large plate with double layer of coffee filters and spray with vegetable oil spray. Cut eggplant into ½-inch pieces, toss with ½ teaspoon salt, and spread onto plate. Microwave eggplant, uncovered, until dry to touch and slightly shriveled, 8 to 12 minutes, tossing halfway through cooking.

2. Heat oil in Dutch oven over high heat until shimmering. Add eggplant and cook until browned, about 2 minutes. Drain tomatoes, reserving juice. Stir in tomatoes and cook until beginning to brown, about 5 minutes. Stir in tomato juice, 1 cup water, ¼ teaspoon salt, and ½ teaspoon pepper, scraping up any browned bits, and bring to boil. Reduce heat to medium, cover, and gently simmer until eggplant is completely broken down, 20 to 25 minutes.

3. Meanwhile, bring 4 cups water and ½ teaspoon salt to boil in medium saucepan over medium-high heat. Slowly add polenta, whisking constantly in circular motion to prevent clumping. Bring to simmer, stirring constantly, about 1 minute. Reduce heat to lowest possible setting, cover, and cook for 5 minutes. Whisk polenta to smooth out lumps, then cover and continue to cook, without stirring, until polenta is tender but slightly al dente, about 20 minutes. Off heat, stir in Parmesan and ¾ teaspoon pepper; cover and let sit for 5 minutes.

4. Chop ¼ cup basil, stir into eggplant mixture, and season with salt and pepper to taste. Serve over polenta with extra Parmesan and chopped basil.

Skillet Pizza with Broccolini and Sun-Dried Tomatoes

SERVES 4

4 **garlic cloves**

¾ cup
oil-packed sun-dried tomatoes,
plus ¼ cup packing oil

8 ounces **broccolini**

½ cup pitted **kalamata olives**

1 pound **pizza dough**

1½ cups (6 ounces) shredded
mozzarella cheese

**INGREDIENT SPOTLIGHT
PIZZA DOUGH**

Instead of spending the time mixing, kneading, and proofing homemade yeast dough, we went straight for the ready-made pizza dough that every supermarket carries nowadays. Not only does it save valuable prep time, but it is also super easy to roll out. Unlike homemade dough which needs to rest and relax before it can be rolled out (or else it will snap back), store-bought dough is well rested and ready to go. We find it best to let the dough sit out at room temperature while preparing the remaining ingredients and heating the oven.

WHY THIS RECIPE WORKS It isn't hard to imagine a basic cheese pizza made with only six ingredients, but a veggie pizza is a different story. Broccolini, with its small florets and tender stalks, was the perfect choice for a hearty, low-prep veg, and it paired well with lots of minced garlic. Rather than reach for store-bought pizza sauce, we created a simple yet assertive sun-dried tomato spread that made a great base for our easy skillet pizzas (no baking stone required). Using oil-packed sun-dried tomatoes here was key, not only for the bright, piquant notes of the tomatoes, but also because we used the flavorful packing oil to brown the bottom of the pizzas in the skillet before transferring them to the oven. A sprinkling of kalamata olives and mozzarella cheese rounded out our hearty veggie pizzas. It's important that the pizza dough be at room temperature so that it will stretch and stay put in the skillet to create a beautifully thin and crisp crust.

1. Adjust oven rack to upper-middle position and heat oven to 500 degrees. Mince garlic. Process one garlic clove, tomatoes, 2 tablespoons tomato packing oil, and ¼ cup warm water in food processor until smooth, about 30 seconds.

2. Trim broccolini and cut into 1-inch pieces. Combine broccolini, remaining garlic, and ¼ cup water in large bowl, cover, and microwave until tender, about 3 minutes; drain well. Chop olives.

3. Divide dough in half. Press and roll 1 piece of dough (keep other piece covered) into 11-inch round on lightly floured counter. Grease 12-inch ovensafe skillet with 1 tablespoon tomato packing oil, then lay dough in skillet and reshape as needed. Spread half of tomato sauce over dough, leaving ½-inch border at edge, and sprinkle with half each of mozzarella, broccolini, and olives.

4. Set skillet over high heat and cook until edge of crust has set and bottom is spotty brown, about 3 minutes. Transfer skillet to oven and bake pizza until edges are brown and cheese is melted and spotty brown, 7 to 10 minutes. Carefully (skillet handle will be hot) remove skillet from oven and slide pizza onto cutting board. Let cool slightly before serving. Wipe skillet clean, let cool slightly, and repeat with remaining 1 tablespoon tomato packing oil, dough, tomato sauce, mozzarella, broccolini, and olives.

Orzo Primavera with Feta

SERVES 4
1 pound **leeks**
1 pound **asparagus**
1½ cups **orzo**
1½ cups (6 ounces) crumbled **marinated feta,** plus 2 tablespoons marinade
½ cup **frozen peas**
1 **lemon**

INGREDIENT SPOTLIGHT ORZO

Orzo is a short, rice-shaped pasta that pairs nicely with vegetables and seafood; it also works well in many soups. To improve its flavor, we usually toast orzo before cooking it. Just a few minutes over the heat gives orzo a deep caramel color and rich, nutty flavor.

✓ WHY THIS RECIPE WORKS We wanted to make the most of a handful of spring vegetables that didn't require excessive peeling, chopping, and blanching for a creamy orzo dish that rivaled pasta primavera. With our eye on the ingredient count, we bypassed the store-bought broth and made our own by simmering the tough leek greens and asparagus stalks in salted water. Following our standard method for making risotto, we toasted the orzo, sautéed the leek whites in the olive oil for an aromatic backbone, and then added our homemade broth to cook the orzo. Adding the asparagus to the skillet partway through cooking and stirring in the peas at the end ensured they were perfectly done and retained their color. While our orzo and vegetable dish was good, a sprinkling of marinated feta put it over the top—and we were able to swap out the olive oil for some of the marinade, which added even more flavor.

1. Chop leek greens and halve and thinly slice leek whites; keep greens and whites separate and wash both thoroughly using salad spinner (see page 207). Chop tough ends of asparagus and slice spears ½ inch thick on bias; keep tough ends and spears separate. Bring leek greens, asparagus ends, 4 cups water, and ¼ teaspoon salt to simmer in medium saucepan, then lower heat to medium-low and simmer gently for 10 minutes. Strain through fine-mesh strainer into 4-cup measuring cup, pressing on solids to extract liquid; discard solids. (You should have 3½ cups broth; add water as needed.)

2. Toast orzo in 12-inch nonstick skillet over medium-high heat until golden, 3 to 5 minutes; transfer to bowl. Combine feta marinade, leek whites, and ½ teaspoon salt in now-empty skillet and cook over medium heat until softened, about 5 minutes.

3. Stir in toasted orzo and 3 cups strained broth, cover, and simmer gently for 5 minutes. Stir in asparagus spears, cover, and continue to cook, stirring often, until asparagus is nearly tender, about 7 minutes. Stir in peas, cover, and cook until heated through, about 1 minute; remove from heat.

4. Squeeze lemon for 2 teaspoons juice, stir into skillet, and season with salt and pepper to taste. Loosen consistency of orzo with remaining ½ cup broth as needed. Sprinkle with feta and serve.

Roasted Poblano and Black Bean Enchiladas

SERVES 4

3 **poblano chiles**

1 (15-ounce) can **black beans**

Fresh cilantro

2 cups (8 ounces) shredded
Monterey Jack cheese

2 (10-ounce) cans
red enchilada sauce

10 (6-inch) **corn tortillas**

INGREDIENT SPOTLIGHT
POBLANO CHILES

Poblano chiles are deep-green, medium-size Mexican chiles. They taste slightly bitter, similar to green bell peppers but with a spicier finish. Sold both fresh and dried (the dried are called anchos), they are used in many Mexican dishes, most famously in the United States in deep-fried, cheese-stuffed chiles rellenos.

☑ **WHY THIS RECIPE WORKS** Preparing enchiladas can be a labor-intensive endeavor requiring a mile-long ingredient list—but it doesn't have to be. We streamlined this dish and turned it into a meatless weeknight meal. First, we needed to select the filling for the enchiladas. Black beans were a given for their protein and heft. Zucchini, corn, and tomatoes were all in the running, but poblano chiles won over our tasters with their noticeable, but mild, kick. For the best texture and flavor, we decided to roast the poblanos before mixing them with the beans and cheese. Broiling the chiles brought out a nice smokiness and slightly sweet quality that paired nicely with the earthy black beans. To soften the tortillas for rolling, we simply microwaved them. Placing the enchiladas seam side down in the baking dish ensured that they wouldn't fall apart in the oven. Topped with sauce and cheese, these easy enchiladas were baked to perfection in just 30 minutes. A light sprinkling of cilantro added freshness and visual appeal. You can substitute 2 medium green bell peppers and 1 jalapeño for the poblanos if desired.

1. Adjust oven rack 6 inches from broiler element and heat broiler. Place poblanos on rimmed baking sheet and broil, turning poblanos as needed, until skin is charred, 10 to 15 minutes. Let poblanos cool slightly, then seed and chop.

2. Adjust oven rack to middle position and reduce oven temperature to 400 degrees. Rinse beans and mince ½ cup cilantro. Mash half of beans in large bowl with fork until mostly smooth. Stir in remaining beans, ⅓ cup cilantro, 1 cup Monterey Jack, ½ cup enchilada sauce, and poblanos; season with salt and pepper to taste.

3. Stack tortillas on plate, cover, and microwave until pliable, about 1 minute. Top each tortilla with ¼ cup bean mixture, roll up tightly, and place, seam side down, in greased baking dish. Top with 1 cup enchilada sauce and remaining 1 cup Monterey Jack.

4. Cover with aluminum foil and bake 20 minutes. Remove foil and continue to bake until Monterey Jack is completely melted and beginning to brown, about 5 minutes. Let cool slightly; sprinkle with remaining cilantro. Microwave remaining enchilada sauce in covered bowl until hot, about 1 minute, and serve with enchiladas.

Baked Quinoa with Roasted Kale and Chickpeas

SERVES 4
6 ounces **kale**
1½ cups (6 ounces) crumbled **marinated feta,** plus 3 tablespoons marinade
1 cup **quinoa**
1 (14-ounce) can **chickpeas**
1 **lemon**
2 **plum tomatoes**

INGREDIENT SPOTLIGHT QUINOA

Quinoa originated in the Andes Mountains of South America, and while it is generally treated as a grain, it is actually the seed of the goose-foot plant. Sometimes referred to as a "super-grain" for its well-touted nutritional values (it is a complete protein and has an impressive amino acid profile), we love quinoa for its addictive crunch, nutty taste, and ease of preparation. Unless your quinoa is labeled as "prewashed," it should always be rinsed to remove its protective layer, called saponin, which is unpleasantly bitter. You can find quinoa with the other grains at the supermarket.

✔ WHY THIS RECIPE WORKS Quinoa makes a stellar side dish, but we wanted this grain to be at the center of a robust, flavorful vegetarian casserole with layers of flavor and a cheesy topping. At first, we baked a simple mixture of quinoa, chickpeas, lemon zest, and scallions. Tasters liked the flavors, but wanted more texture and volume. Kale proved to be the perfect solution, and by roasting it briefly before baking it with the quinoa, we boosted its earthy flavor and eliminated some excess moisture. Trading the scallions for fresh tomatoes and adding a splash of fresh lemon juice ensured our dish was bright-tasting and colorful. Topped with a generous sprinkling of tangy marinated feta cheese, this hearty baked quinoa was ready to take center stage.

1. Adjust oven rack to middle position and heat oven to 450 degrees. Stem and chop kale. Toss kale with 1 tablespoon feta marinade, spread in even layer on aluminum foil–lined baking sheet, and roast until crisp and lightly browned at edges, 6 to 8 minutes. Rinse quinoa and chickpeas; combine with roasted kale, remaining 2 tablespoons marinade, ½ teaspoon salt, and ¼ teaspoon pepper in 8-inch square baking dish.

2. Grate lemon for 1 teaspoon zest, then squeeze for 2 teaspoons juice. Microwave zest and 1½ cups water in covered bowl until just boiling, about 2 minutes. Pour hot water over quinoa mixture and cover dish tightly with double layer of foil. Bake until quinoa is tender and no liquid remains, 20 to 25 minutes.

3. Core and finely chop tomatoes. Remove dish from oven and fluff quinoa with fork. Gently fold in tomatoes and lemon juice and sprinkle with feta. Continue to bake casserole, uncovered, until feta is heated through, 6 to 8 minutes. Serve.

TEST KITCHEN TIP
RINSING QUINOA

Place quinoa in fine-mesh strainer and rinse under cool water until water runs clear, occasionally stirring quinoa around lightly with your hand. Let drain briefly.

Easy Stuffed Zucchini

SERVES 4

4 (8-ounce) **zucchini**

2 tablespoons **olive oil**

Fresh basil

12 ounces **soy crumbles**

1½ cups (6 ounces) shredded **Italian cheese blend**

1 cup jarred **arrabbiata sauce**

INGREDIENT SPOTLIGHT
SOY CRUMBLES

Made of seasoned, textured soy protein, soy crumbles make a great stand-in for ground beef and require no prep at all. Note that they can be a bit salty, so season recipes with a light hand when cooking with them. You may see several brands at the supermarket; any of them will work here, but be sure to select plain, not flavored, soy crumbles. You can find them in the freezer or the refrigerated section with veggie burgers, veggie dogs, and other meatless products.

WHY THIS RECIPE WORKS For a vegetarian take on stuffed zucchini, we nixed the usual ground beef and swapped in soy crumbles, which delivered a hearty texture. Jarred arrabbiata sauce worked well to bind the crumbles and added an appealing kick to the filling, while preshredded Italian cheese blend added good depth of flavor. To ensure that the zucchini cooked up tender, not crunchy, we hollowed them out and roasted them on a preheated baking sheet before mounding them with the filling. Topped with a bit more cheese, our stuffed zucchini went back into the oven for a final warm-through, and emerged with an appealing aroma and tender and cohesive filling that more than met our expectations. Soy crumbles can be a bit salty, so we found it unnecessary to salt the mixture before stuffing the zucchini.

1. Adjust oven rack to middle position, place rimmed baking sheet on rack, and heat oven to 400 degrees. Halve each zucchini lengthwise and use soupspoon to remove seeds and flesh until walls of zucchini are ¼ inch thick. Brush cut sides of zucchini with oil and season with salt and pepper. Lay zucchini, cut side down, on hot baking sheet and roast until slightly softened and skins are wrinkled, 10 to 12 minutes. Remove from oven and flip zucchini cut side up.

2. Chop ¼ cup basil. Combine 3 tablespoons basil, soy crumbles, 1 cup Italian cheese blend, and arrabbiata sauce in bowl until crumbles are fully moistened. Spoon filling evenly into zucchini, packing lightly with back of spoon, and sprinkle with remaining ½ cup cheese. Bake until filling is heated through and Italian cheese blend is melted, 8 to 10 minutes. Sprinkle with remaining 1 tablespoon basil and serve.

TEST KITCHEN TIP
SEEDING ZUCCHINI

To make room for filling, use a soupspoon to scrape out seeds and flesh until walls of each zucchini half are ¼ inch thick.

Crispy Tofu with Coconut-Lime Rice

SERVES 4
28 ounces **firm tofu**
1½ cups **long-grain white rice**
2 **scallions**
2 **limes**
3 tablespoons **coconut oil**
⅓ cup **sweet chili sauce**

INGREDIENT SPOTLIGHT
COCONUT OIL

Coconut oil is sold in two forms, both solid at room temperature: refined, which has virtually no taste or aroma, and virgin, which retains a strong coconut flavor. We prefer refined coconut oil for cooking because of its neutral flavor. Because of its high smoke point, coconut oil is a good choice for sautéing and pan-frying. In our recipe, we had good luck using Spectrum Organic Refined Coconut Oil.

✓ WHY THIS RECIPE WORKS Think crispy fried tofu always requires some type of coating? Think again. With the right techniques, it requires no more than tofu, oil, and a smoking-hot skillet. Coconut oil was key because of its high smoke point. However, the temperature of the oil still dropped when the tofu was added, so we needed to let the first side fry a bit longer to ensure a crisp coating. Pressing thick slabs of firm tofu between layers of paper towels underneath a baking sheet was crucial for removing excess liquid before frying. Frying the tofu without a coating freed up ingredients so we could create a flavorful rice side dish and dipping sauce for our tofu sticks. Limes played double-duty here: The zest flavored the rice, while the juice added bright acidity to sweet chili sauce, giving us a fresh-tasting, slightly spicy sauce for dipping. If you don't have a 12-inch nonstick skillet, you can use a smaller skillet to fry the tofu in two batches. Keep the first batch warm in a 200-degree oven, and add 1 tablespoon more oil to the skillet for the second batch. The skillet will seem very full when you start frying the tofu, but it shrinks as it cooks.

1. Slice tofu crosswise into ¾-inch-thick slabs, then slice each slab in half into two fingers. Spread tofu out over paper towel–lined baking sheet, then top with more paper towels and weight with second baking sheet; let sit for 30 minutes. Uncover and pat tofu dry with fresh paper towels.

2. Rinse rice until water runs clear. Thinly slice scallion whites and scallion greens on bias; keep whites and greens separate. Grate 1 lime for 2 teaspoons zest, then squeeze for 2 tablespoons juice. Heat 1 tablespoon oil in medium saucepan over medium heat until shimmering. Cook scallion whites until softened, about 2 minutes. Stir in rice; cook until edges of rice become translucent, about 3 minutes. Stir in lime zest, 2½ cups water, and ½ teaspoon salt; bring to boil. Reduce heat to low, cover, and cook until rice is tender, about 20 minutes. Remove pot from heat, keep covered, and let stand 10 minutes. Fluff rice with fork, season with salt and pepper to taste, and sprinkle with scallion greens.

3. Heat remaining 2 tablespoons oil in 12-inch nonstick skillet over high heat until just smoking. Cook tofu until crisp on first side, 5 to 7 minutes. Flip tofu and continue to cook, flipping as needed, until crisp on all sides, about 10 minutes; transfer to paper towel–lined plate. Combine chili sauce and lime juice in bowl, cut remaining lime into wedges, and serve with tofu and rice.

WHITE LASAGNA WITH ZUCCHINI AND TOMATOES

Fast-Lane Casseroles

225   Unstuffed Shells with Sausage and Fennel

226   Easiest-Ever Lasagna

227   White Lasagna with Zucchini and Tomatoes

229   Baked Penne with Roasted Red Peppers, Artichokes, and Goat Cheese

230   Simple Baked Ziti | FAST RECIPE

231   Chorizo and Black Bean Sopa Seca | FAST RECIPE

233   Spicy Spaghetti Pie

234   Smoky Eggplant Casserole

237   Beef Taco Bake

238   Cheesy Shrimp and Grits

240   Polenta Casserole with Sausage and Peppers | FAST RECIPE

242   Chicken Enchilada Casserole

243   Egg, Ham, and Hash Brown Pie | FAST RECIPE

245   Spanish Tortilla with Roasted Red Peppers and Peas

246   Easy Egg Casserole with Boursin and Sun-Dried Tomatoes | FAST RECIPE

247   Apple and Cheddar Strata

Unstuffed Shells with Sausage and Fennel

SERVES 6 TO 8

12 ounces **jumbo pasta shells**

2 **fennel bulbs**

12 ounces **hot Italian sausage**

2 (25-ounce) jars **vodka sauce**

4 ounces (4 cups) **baby spinach**

1½ cups (6 ounces) shredded **Italian cheese blend**

INGREDIENT SPOTLIGHT
JARRED VODKA SAUCE

This sweet and spicy tomato sauce gets its kick from a bit of vodka and its rich, creamy texture from heavy cream. We found that this multi-tasker gave us a saucy base for our casserole, and also added richness, tangy flavor, and herbal notes. Note that you can use any brand of vodka sauce here.

✓ **WHY THIS RECIPE WORKS** Making stuffed shells can be tedious and time-consuming. After all, each precooked shell has to be painstakingly filled by hand, which usually leads to a good number of them being torn in the process. We wanted a much easier path to this hearty, satisfying casserole, so we started by taking out the filling and turning it into a simple sauce for cooked shells. Rather than combine tomato sauce with the standard ricotta cheese, we found one convenience product that delivered both a creamy texture and bright, tangy flavor: jarred vodka sauce. Hot Italian sausage offered a spicy punch; anise-scented fennel worked well with the sausage and added more substance. To cook the fennel, we jump-started it in the microwave while the sausage browned in our Dutch oven, then tossed it into the pot—with the vodka sauce—to pick up the meaty, savory flavors. Baby spinach contributed freshness to our rich casserole. Finishing the dish was as easy as combining the sauce, sausage, and vegetables with cooked pasta and topping the mix with a layer of Italian shredded cheese before baking. Our easy casserole delivers all the flavor and richness of the original—but without all the work.

1. Adjust oven rack to middle position and heat oven to 375 degrees. Bring 4 quarts water to boil in large pot. Add pasta and 1 table-spoon salt and cook, stirring often, until nearly al dente. Reserve 1 cup cooking water, then drain pasta and return it to pot.

2. Meanwhile, trim fennel stalks and fronds (see page 177); mince fronds and reserve. Trim bulb, cut in half, core, and cut crosswise into ½-inch-thick slices. Microwave fennel and 2 tablespoons water in bowl, covered, until softened, 6 to 8 minutes. Drain well.

3. Remove sausage from casing (see page 199) and cook in Dutch oven over medium heat until no longer pink, about 5 minutes. Stir in fennel and vodka sauce and bring to simmer. Season with salt and pepper to taste.

4. Stir sausage-fennel mixture and spinach into shells and toss to coat, adding reserved cooking water as needed to adjust consistency. Transfer mixture to 13 by 9-inch baking dish, sprinkle with Italian cheese blend, and cover tightly with greased aluminum foil. Bake until bubbling around edges, 35 to 45 minutes. Let cool slightly, sprinkle with fennel fronds, and serve.

Easiest-Ever Lasagna

SERVES 4

8 ounces
hot or sweet Italian sausage

1 (25-ounce) jar **tomato sauce**

2 cups (8 ounces) shredded
mozzarella cheese

½ cup (1 ounce) grated
Parmesan cheese

1 cup (8 ounces)
whole-milk ricotta cheese

6 **no-boil lasagna noodles**

INGREDIENT SPOTLIGHT
NO-BOIL NOODLES

No-boil (also called oven-ready) lasagna noodles are precooked at the factory; during baking, the moisture from the sauce softens, or rehydrates, them. The most common no-boil noodle measures 7 inches long and 3½ inches wide; 3 noodles fit perfectly in a 13 by 9-inch pan, and 2 noodles fit nicely in an 8-inch square pan. Our favorite brand is **Barilla No-Boil Lasagne**; we found these delicate, flat noodles closely resembled fresh pasta in texture.

WHY THIS RECIPE WORKS A prep-free (no chopping required) lasagna—with rich, meaty flavor and a bubbling, cheesy topping? No problem. We developed a scaled-down, six-ingredient weeknight lasagna so this classic doesn't have to be relegated to Sunday-only status. We relied on convenient store-bought pasta sauce to take the place of simmered-all-day sauce and added spicy Italian sausage to give it deep flavor. We didn't even have to get out a pan to cook the sausage—we just crumbled it into small pieces and added it to the dish to cook through right in the sauce. Instead of the traditional time-consuming layering of individual ingredients, we devised a smart, streamlined assembly that takes mere minutes—we simply stirred the sauce, cheeses, and sausage together, then added the mixture to the baking dish, alternating it with no-boil noodles. Leaving some clumps of ricotta cheese in the mixture ensured creamy bites throughout, and a sprinkling of extra mozzarella on top gave the lasagna that picture-perfect browned cheesy blanket. Do not use nonfat ricotta or fat-free mozzarella here.

1. Adjust oven rack to middle position and heat oven to 375 degrees. Remove sausage from casing (see page 199), crumble into ½-inch pieces, and combine with tomato sauce, 1½ cups mozzarella, and Parmesan in large bowl. Gently fold in ricotta, leaving some clumps.

2. Spread ½ cup sauce into greased 8-inch square baking dish. Lay 2 noodles in dish and top with 1½ cups sauce. Repeat layering of noodles and sauce two more times. Top with remaining ½ cup mozzarella.

3. Cover dish tightly with greased aluminum foil, place on foil-lined baking sheet, and bake until bubbling around edges, about 20 minutes. Remove foil and continue to bake until cheese is spotty brown, about 35 minutes. Let cool for 15 minutes. Serve.

TEST KITCHEN TIP
SHREDDING SEMISOFT CHEESES

Mozzarella and other semisoft cheeses can stick to a grater and cause a mess. To prevent the grater from becoming clogged, use vegetable oil spray to lightly coat the holes, then shred away.

White Lasagna with Zucchini and Tomatoes

SERVES 4

3 **plum tomatoes**

1 pound **zucchini**

Fresh basil

1 cup (8 ounces)
whole-milk ricotta cheese

1 (15-ounce) jar **Alfredo sauce**

8 **no-boil lasagna noodles**

INGREDIENT SPOTLIGHT ZUCCHINI

Zucchini works well in any number of dishes, both raw and cooked, savory and sweet. When shopping, try to select zucchini that weigh less than 8 ounces; these are more flavorful and less watery than larger zucchini. In the test kitchen, we often call for salting zucchini to draw off its excess moisture; however, in this recipe we found the moisture to be an asset and skipped this step.

WHY THIS RECIPE WORKS Most béchamel-based white lasagnas tend to suffer from stodgy, flavorless sauces and overcooked vegetables. To keep things simple, we skipped the béchamel (made by adding milk to a butter-flour roux) and reached for store-bought Alfredo sauce. Next, we chose summery vegetables—zucchini and tomatoes—that would add bright color, moisture, and freshness. We cut the zucchini into thin slices and layered them with chopped tomatoes between no-boil lasagna noodles. Though we normally call for salting zucchini to remove excess moisture, we were able to skip that step here; we found that the juices from the zucchini helped to soften the noodles and ensure the Alfredo sauce was ultrasaucy. To add cohesion to the layers, we included some ricotta cheese. Chopped basil gave the ricotta freshness and reinforced the summery flavors of the vegetables. A relatively high oven temperature shortened the cooking time. After 45 minutes and a brief rest, we were met with perfectly cooked pasta, juicy, tender vegetables, and a rich, creamy sauce. Do not use part-skim or nonfat ricotta here.

1. Adjust oven rack to middle position and heat oven to 425 degrees. Chop tomatoes into ½-inch pieces and slice zucchini into ¼-inch-thick rounds. Chop ¼ cup basil and combine with ricotta and ¼ teaspoon pepper in bowl.

2. Spread ¼ cup Alfredo sauce into greased 8-inch square baking dish. Lay 2 noodles in dish and top with one-third ricotta mixture, one-third tomatoes, one-third zucchini, pinch salt, and pinch pepper. Repeat layering of noodles, ricotta mixture, tomatoes, zucchini, salt, and pepper two more times. Place remaining 2 noodles on top and cover with remaining Alfredo sauce.

3. Cover dish tightly with greased aluminum foil and place on foil–lined baking sheet. Bake until casserole is bubbling and zucchini is tender, about 45 minutes. Let cool for 15 minutes. Chop 1 tablespoon basil, sprinkle over top, and serve.

Baked Penne with Roasted Red Peppers, Artichokes, and Goat Cheese

SERVES 4
8 ounces (2½ cups) **penne**
6 ounces **goat cheese**
⅓ cup **heavy cream**
3 cups jarred **roasted red peppers**
½ cup **prepared basil pesto**
1¼ cups **marinated artichokes**

INGREDIENT SPOTLIGHT
ROASTED RED PEPPERS

Roasted red peppers add a sweet, subtly smoky flavor to many dishes—and they help cut down on prep time (no need to roast your own). To find the best roasted red peppers, we sampled eight brands, straight out of the jar and in roasted red pepper soup. Peppers that were packed with flavorful ingredients like garlic, herbs, and vinegar tasted good plain, but those flavors weren't appreciated when incorporated into a sauce or dish. In the end, our favorite peppers were **Dunbars Sweet Roasted Peppers**; the label lists only red bell peppers, water, salt, and citric acid in the ingredient list. No matter which brand you buy, just be sure to rinse and pat the peppers dry before using them to drain off their packing liquid.

WHY THIS RECIPE WORKS In this effortless weeknight casserole, the only thing we precooked was the pasta. Jarred roasted red peppers provided the perfect big, bold flavor base for a simple no-cook sauce. All we had to do was rinse them first to wash away the brining liquid before patting them dry and chopping them. For a bright, balanced sauce, we processed the peppers with prepared pesto, a powerhouse ingredient that combines basil, Parmesan, garlic, and olive oil in one. After tossing our robustly flavored (and richly colored) sauce with the cooked pasta (tubular penne worked well here), we stirred in chopped marinated artichokes, which helped ensure our great-tasting pasta dish was filling, too. Dollops of goat cheese, thinned slightly with a small amount of heavy cream, made for a creamy, tangy topping.

1. Adjust oven rack to middle position and heat oven to 450 degrees. Bring 4 quarts water to boil in large pot. Add pasta and 1 tablespoon salt and cook, stirring often, until nearly al dente. Reserve ½ cup cooking water, then drain pasta and return it to pot.

2. Meanwhile, pulse goat cheese, cream, ⅛ teaspoon salt, and ⅛ teaspoon pepper together in food processor until smooth, about 8 pulses; transfer to bowl. Rinse, pat dry, and coarsely chop roasted red peppers. Process peppers and pesto together in food processor (no need to clean processor bowl) until smooth, about 25 seconds, scraping down sides of bowl as needed. Drain artichokes and cut into ½-inch pieces.

3. Stir red pepper–pesto mixture into pasta and toss to coat, adding reserved cooking water as needed to adjust consistency. Fold in artichokes and season with salt and pepper to taste. Transfer mixture to greased 8-inch square baking dish and dollop goat cheese mixture over top. Bake until bubbling around edges and cheese is spotty brown, about 15 minutes. Let cool slightly and serve.

Simple Baked Ziti

SERVES 4

1 (25-ounce) jar **vodka sauce**

12 ounces (3¾ cups) **ziti**

4 ounces
hot or sweet Italian sausage

Fresh basil

½ cup (4 ounces)
whole-milk ricotta cheese

1 cup (4 ounces) shredded
Italian cheese blend

INGREDIENT SPOTLIGHT
ITALIAN CHEESE BLEND

Bags of preshredded cheese blends are available at every grocery store across the country in a variety of flavors. The Italian cheese blend typically includes mozzarella, provolone, Parmesan, fontina, Romano, and Asiago. We use it to boost the flavor of our casseroles without having to purchase—or prep—multiple ingredients. You can find Italian cheese blends with the block cheeses at any supermarket; note that any brand will work well here.

WHY THIS RECIPE WORKS For an inspired—not tired—baked ziti, we kept things simple and focused on streamlining this family favorite without sacrificing flavor. Instead of spending extra time making a tomato sauce, we turned to jarred vodka sauce for our base. Not only did its bold flavors eliminate the need for garlic and other aromatics, but the creamy sauce also added a cohesive element to the casserole. To cook the pasta, we simmered it right in the sauce with some water until it was al dente and then transferred the whole pot to the oven. Italian sausage, added to the pot before baking, amped up the heartiness of our dish, and dollops of ricotta added further richness. Finally, instead of calling for the traditional mozzarella and grated Parmesan, we cut our ingredient list and prep time by using preshredded Italian cheese; sprinkled over the top of the ziti, it delivered a nicely browned crust and well-rounded flavor. Do not use nonfat ricotta here. Penne can be substituted for the ziti. Scraping the sides of the pot before baking will prevent any sauce clinging to the pot sides from scorching.

1. Adjust oven rack to middle position and heat oven to 475 degrees. Combine vodka sauce, 3 cups water, and pasta in large Dutch oven. Cover and cook, stirring often and adjusting heat as needed to maintain vigorous simmer, until pasta is almost tender, 15 to 18 minutes.

2. Remove sausage from casing (see page 199) and crumble into ½-inch pieces. Chop ¼ cup basil. Season ricotta with ⅛ teaspoon salt and ⅛ teaspoon pepper in bowl.

3. Stir sausage and 3 tablespoons basil into pot. Scrape down sides of pot with rubber spatula. Dollop ricotta mixture evenly over top and sprinkle with Italian cheese blend. Transfer pot to oven and bake, uncovered, until cheese is melted and brown, about 10 minutes. Let cool slightly, sprinkle with remaining 1 tablespoon basil, and serve.

TEST KITCHEN TIP
PARCOOKING ZITI IN SAUCE

Combine vodka sauce, water, and ziti in large Dutch oven, then cover pot and simmer vigorously, stirring often, until ziti is almost tender, 15 to 18 minutes; it will finish cooking through in the oven.

Chorizo and Black Bean Sopa Seca

SERVES 4

8 ounces **vermicelli**

1 tablespoon **vegetable oil**

4 ounces **chorizo sausage**

1 (15-ounce) can **black beans**

2 cups **fresh hot salsa**

½ cup (2 ounces) shredded
Monterey Jack cheese

INGREDIENT SPOTLIGHT
MONTEREY JACK CHEESE

Monterey Jack is a mild cow's-milk
cheese that was originally produced
in Monterey, California. It's sometimes
called Cali Jack or just Jack cheese,
and it is rarely aged. We reach for
Monterey Jack when we need a good
melting cheese. Because of its mild
flavor, it works well when we want
to add a creamy texture to potently
flavored dishes.

WHY THIS RECIPE WORKS Its name might mean "dry soup,"
but sopa seca is a really saucy Mexican dish made with thin, coiled
strands of toasted pasta, known as fideos, that are baked in broth
with tomatoes and capped with melted cheese. To create our
own version of this satisfying dish, our first move was finding a
supermarket-friendly substitute for the fideos. Vermicelli, broken
into pieces and toasted in a hot skillet, worked just fine. Most
recipes call for tomatoes plus a variety of dried chiles, but we
decided that hot salsa covered all the bases for our six-ingredient
recipe. Thin sliced chorizo and black beans added savory, meaty
notes and heft. For the cooking liquid, chicken broth gave us an
overly salty dish, so we stuck with water, which we added right
to the skillet, turning this into an easy, one-pan dinner. Shredded
Monterey Jack, which we sprinkled over the hot pasta before
covering the pan, added creamy richness and balanced the spicy
flavors of the dish. Serve with diced avocado and thinly sliced
scallions, if desired.

1. Break vermicelli into 2-inch lengths, then toss with 2 teaspoons
oil in 12-inch nonstick skillet. Toast vermicelli over medium–high
heat, stirring constantly, until browned and resembles color of
peanut butter, 6 to 10 minutes; transfer to paper towel–lined plate.

2. Halve chorizo lengthwise, then slice crosswise into ¼-inch-
thick pieces. Heat remaining 1 teaspoon oil in now–empty skillet
over medium heat until shimmering. Add chorizo and cook until
browned, 5 to 7 minutes. Rinse beans and stir into skillet with
toasted vermicelli, salsa, and 2 cups water. Bring to rapid simmer,
cover, and simmer vigorously, stirring often, until vermicelli is
tender, 8 to 10 minutes.

3. Off heat, season with salt and pepper to taste and sprinkle
cheese over top. Cover and let stand until cheese melts, 2 to
4 minutes. Serve.

TEST KITCHEN TIP
TOASTING VERMICELLI

Cooking the vermicelli pieces in
a skillet with oil until browned
works to develop a deep, nutty
flavor. To ensure even browning, be sure to stir the pasta
constantly as it toasts.

Spicy Spaghetti Pie

SERVES 4

12 ounces
vermicelli or thin spaghetti

4 ounces sliced **pepperoni**

1 (25-ounce) jar **arrabbiata sauce**

Fresh basil

2 cups (8 ounces) shredded
Mexican cheese blend

INGREDIENT SPOTLIGHT **VERMICELLI**

Vermicelli is a very thin, long-strand pasta (in Italian, the name translates to "little worms"). Vermicelli is about the same thickness as thin spaghetti or spaghettini; any of these will work here. To measure vermicelli and thin spaghetti without a scale, bunch it into a tight circle with your fingers and measure the diameter; 12 ounces of pasta should measure about 1¾ inches.

✓ **WHY THIS RECIPE WORKS** This pasta dish takes the classic flavors of spaghetti and tomato sauce and turns them into a family-friendly, sliceable pie. Thinner versions of spaghetti (vermicelli or thin spaghetti) proved a better choice than spaghetti itself, which didn't stick together well when we cut into the pie. For bold flavor, we swapped the standard tomato sauce for peppery arrabbiata sauce; finely chopped pepperoni reinforced its kick. To make the most of the pepperoni's richness and flavor, we sautéed it until crisp and its fat was rendered, then added our sauce so it could take on the spicy, savory flavors. Mozzarella didn't stand up to the heat and punch of the sauce, so we turned to a preshredded Mexican cheese blend (a combination of Monterey Jack, cheddar, and asadero cheeses) instead. Using a spatula to press the pasta into the pie plate ensured that the baked pie sliced neatly. This dish is spicy; if you would like it less spicy, you can substitute tomato sauce for the arrabbiata sauce.

1. Adjust oven rack to upper-middle position and heat oven to 475 degrees. Bring 4 quarts water to boil in large pot. Add pasta and 1 tablespoon salt and cook, stirring often, until nearly al dente. Drain pasta and return it to pot.

2. Finely chop pepperoni and cook in 12-inch skillet over medium-high heat until crisp, about 2 minutes. Stir in 2 cups arrabbiata sauce and bring to simmer. Chop ½ cup basil.

3. Add pepperoni sauce, Mexican cheese blend, and basil to pasta and toss to combine. Transfer pasta to greased 9-inch pie plate and press with spatula to flatten surface. Bake until golden and bubbling around edges, about 15 minutes. Let cool for 10 minutes. Reheat remaining arrabbiata sauce in microwave, slice pie into wedges, and serve with sauce.

TEST KITCHEN TIP
PRESSING PASTA INTO A PIE PLATE

Transfer pasta mixture to pre-pared pie plate and press with spatula to flatten surface so it can be sliced into tidy pieces for serving.

Smoky Eggplant Casserole

SERVES 6 TO 8

4 medium **eggplant**

¼ cup **olive oil**

¾ cup **panko bread crumbs**

1 (15-ounce) container
whole-milk ricotta cheese

1 (25-ounce) jar **arrabbiata sauce**

4 cups (1 pound) shredded
smoked mozzarella cheese

INGREDIENT SPOTLIGHT PANKO

In recipes where we want an extra-crispy coating, we turn to panko bread crumbs. These light, flaky crumbs, which originated in Japan, add big crunch to dishes. Once the domain of specialty shops and Asian markets, panko bread crumbs are now available in most supermarkets. Our favorite brand is **Ian's Panko Bread Crumbs**, which tasters found to be much crunchier than other brands.

✓ WHY THIS RECIPE WORKS For a more hands-off and less tedious take on eggplant Parmesan, we ditched the deep-fryer and instead roasted our eggplant to evaporate its liquid and concentrate its flavor. So the eggplant slices didn't stick to the baking sheets, we brushed them with a bit of olive oil first. Jarred arrabbiata sauce made a lively, spicy alternative to tomato sauce, and big dollops of ricotta added an ultracreamy texture. Rather than stick with the usual mozzarella, we opted for the smoked variety, which contributed deep, smoky flavor and gooey, cheesy richness. Finally, in a nod to the traditional dish, we sprinkled the casserole with crisp, toasted panko for a big crunch. Leaving the skins on the eggplant keeps the slices intact during roasting, so be sure you don't peel them.

1. Adjust oven racks to upper-middle and lower-middle positions and heat oven to 450 degrees. Slice eggplants into ¾-inch-thick rounds. Line 2 large rimmed baking sheets with aluminum foil and brush each with 1½ teaspoons oil. Toss eggplant with 2 table-spoons oil and 1 teaspoon salt, lay on prepared sheets, and roast until golden, 35 to 50 minutes, flipping eggplant over halfway through roasting; let cool.

2. Toast panko with remaining 1 tablespoon oil in 12-inch nonstick skillet over medium-high heat, stirring often, until golden, about 3 minutes. Season ricotta with ½ teaspoon salt and ½ teaspoon pepper in bowl.

3. Reduce oven temperature to 375 degrees. Spread ¾ cup arrabbiata sauce over bottom of 13 by 9-inch baking dish. Fit half of eggplant into dish in single layer and top with ¾ cup arrabbiata sauce. Dollop half of ricotta mixture over top and flatten dollops with back of spoon. Sprinkle with 2 cups mozzarella and top with ¾ cup arrabbiata sauce. Repeat layering process with remaining eggplant, arrabbiata sauce, ricotta mixture, and mozzarella.

4. Cover dish tightly with greased aluminum foil. Bake on upper-middle rack until filling is bubbling and eggplant is tender, about 40 minutes. Remove foil, sprinkle with panko, and continue to bake until topping is spotty brown, about 15 minutes. Let cool for 10 minutes and serve.

Beef Taco Bake

SERVES 6

2 (10-ounce) cans
**Ro-tel Diced Tomatoes
& Green Chilies**

1½ pounds 90 percent lean
ground beef

1 (1-ounce) package
taco seasoning mix

1 (16-ounce) can **refried beans**

2 cups (8 ounces) shredded
Colby Jack cheese

8 **taco shells**

INGREDIENT SPOTLIGHT
TACO SEASONING MIX

This spice blend combines chili powder, cumin, oregano, and other spices
typically found in Southwestern or
Tex-Mex cuisine. Rather than rum-
mage through our spice cabinet looking for flavorings for our casserole, we
landed on this one potent spice blend
that offered all the flavors we were
after. There are several brands of taco
seasoning mix on the market; any of
them will work here.

✓ WHY THIS RECIPE WORKS This dish combines the crisp,
crunchy, corny flavor of taco shells with a spicy ground beef filling and melted cheese—all in one hearty casserole. For robust
flavor, without a laundry list of spices, we turned to a supermarket
staple: taco seasoning mix. To make the most of its spicy flavors,
we cooked the seasoning mix with the ground beef; this worked
to bloom, or deepen, the flavors of the spices. Ro-tel tomatoes, a
spicy blend of tomatoes and green chiles, contributed both potent
flavor and much-needed moisture to the beef filling. For more
heartiness, we added a layer of refried beans to our casserole;
combining the refried beans with more Ro-tel tomatoes gave them
a spicy kick. Because no taco is complete without the cheese, we
included a good amount of shredded Colby Jack, which offered a
sharp tang and melted to gooey perfection. Finally, we turned to
the taco shells. Crushing them into bite-size pieces and scattering
them on top of the beef before finishing the dish with more cheese
promised big, crunchy bites with every forkful. You can substitute
4 ounces each of Colby and Jack cheeses for the Colby Jack cheese.

1. Adjust oven rack to upper-middle position and heat oven to
475 degrees. Drain tomatoes, reserving ½ cup juice. Cook beef
in 12-inch nonstick skillet over medium heat, breaking up meat
with wooden spoon, until no longer pink, 5 to 8 minutes. Stir in
taco seasoning and cook until fragrant, about 30 seconds. Stir in
half of tomatoes and reserved juice and simmer until thickened,
about 10 minutes. Season with salt and pepper to taste.

2. Combine refried beans with remaining tomatoes; smooth mixture
evenly over bottom of 13 by 9-inch baking dish. Sprinkle with 1 cup
Colby Jack, top with beef mixture, then sprinkle with ½ cup Colby
Jack. Break taco shells into 1-inch pieces; scatter over top. Top with
remaining ½ cup Colby Jack. Bake until filling is bubbling and
topping is spotty brown, about 15 minutes. Let cool slightly; serve.

TEST KITCHEN TIP
**RESERVING JUICE FROM
CANNED TOMATOES**

Drain both cans of Ro-tel
tomatoes using fine-mesh
strainer set over bowl. Then
measure out ½ cup drained
juice and discard extra.

Cheesy Shrimp and Grits

SERVES 4

3 **scallions**

2 teaspoons
Asian chili-garlic sauce

½ cup **whole milk**

1 cup **old-fashioned grits**

1 pound **extra-large shrimp**
(21 to 25 per pound)

1 cup (4 ounces) shredded
cheddar cheese

INGREDIENT SPOTLIGHT
ASIAN CHILI-GARLIC SAUCE

This chile-based sauce is made from garlic, vinegar, and coarsely ground chiles, which give it a slightly chunky texture. Used both in cooking and as a condiment in Asian cuisine, it contributes subtle heat and well-rounded flavor to dishes. You can find it in the supermarket with the Asian ingredients. Once opened, this sauce will keep for several months in the refrigerator.

☑ WHY THIS RECIPE WORKS Most versions of this Southern classic offer intense richness but are light on flavor. We wanted the best of both worlds, and started out building a potent flavor base by adding scallions, garlic, and hot sauce to our grits. We were on the right track, but realized we could swap two ingredients for one—the garlic and hot sauce for Asian chili-garlic sauce—to achieve the same bright, spicy flavor. Instead of the usual heavy cream, we opted for whole milk, which gave our grits a rich creaminess without making them too heavy. When it came to the cheese, cheddar won out for the tangy, savory notes it added to the grits; we also sprinkled more cheese on top. As for the shrimp, we simply assembled the grits in a casserole dish and nestled in the shellfish so it could cook through while the cheesy topping browned, eliminating the need for another dish (or an extra step to sauté the shrimp). Do not substitute instant grits here.

1. Adjust oven rack to middle position and heat oven to 450 degrees. Thinly slice scallion whites and scallion greens; keep whites and greens separate. Cook scallion whites and 2 tablespoons water together in medium saucepan over medium heat until softened, about 2 minutes. Stir in chili-garlic sauce, 4 cups water, and milk; bring to boil. Slowly whisk in grits. Reduce heat to low and cook, stirring often, until grits are thick and creamy, about 15 minutes.

2. Peel and devein shrimp (see page 37). Off heat, stir ½ cup cheddar into grits, season with salt and pepper to taste, and transfer to 4½-cup gratin dish. Nestle shrimp into grits, leaving tails exposed. Sprinkle with remaining ½ cup cheddar. Bake until shrimp are cooked through, about 15 minutes. Let cool slightly, sprinkle with scallion greens, and serve.

TEST KITCHEN TIP
SEPARATING SCALLION
WHITES AND GREENS

To get the most out of scallions, we often separate the more pungent, oniony white part from the more delicate, herblike green part. The scallion whites can then be sautéed to soften their texture and temper their raw bite, leaving the more subtle greens to be added to the dish at the end.

Polenta Casserole with Sausage and Peppers

SERVES 4 TO 6

1½ pounds **hot Italian sausage**

3 **red and/or green bell peppers**

1 **red onion**

1 (25-ounce) jar **tomato sauce**

1 (18-ounce) tube **precooked polenta**

1 cup (2 ounces) grated **Asiago cheese**

INGREDIENT SPOTLIGHT
ITALIAN SAUSAGE

Italian sausages are either hot or sweet. Both are made with coarsely ground fresh pork flavored with garlic and fennel seed; the hot variety is also seasoned with red pepper flakes. Though Italian sausages are great grilled or sautéed, we also like to crumble them and sauté them in pasta sauces and casseroles. The browned sausage contributes not just meaty notes, but also aromatic flavors from the seasonings.

✔ WHY THIS RECIPE WORKS Creamy polenta is classically served with deeply flavored Italian ragu, but making a long-simmered ragu and then making polenta from scratch takes more time and effort than we typically have on a busy weeknight. Prepared polenta, which we sliced into thin rounds and placed on the bottom of a baking dish, made the perfect stand-in for the long-stirred version. Next, we needed a quick ragu with big flavor that we could use to top our polenta. Hot Italian sausage offered robust, spicy flavor and provided plenty of rendered fat to brown our vegetables—tasters like the mix of peppers and onions. To give our speedy ragu bright acidity and depth of flavor, we stirred in a jar of tomato sauce. For a final flavor boost, we sprinkled grated Asiago over the dish. This nutty, firm cheese melted beautifully and contributed a sharp, tangy flavor to our hearty casserole. We like a mix of red and green bell peppers for this dish. We prefer the spicy heat of hot Italian sausage, but sweet Italian sausage can be substituted. Parmesan can be substituted for the Asiago here.

1. Adjust oven rack to middle position and heat oven to 450 degrees. Remove sausage from casing (see page 199), slice peppers into ¼-inch-thick strips, and halve and thinly slice onion. Cook sausage, peppers, onion, and ¼ teaspoon salt together in Dutch oven over medium-high heat, breaking up meat with wooden spoon, until vegetables are softened and lightly browned, about 10 minutes. Stir in tomato sauce and bring to simmer, then remove from heat.

2. Slice polenta into ⅓-inch-thick rounds and arrange in single layer in 13 by 9-inch baking dish. Spread sausage mixture evenly over polenta and sprinkle with Asiago. Bake until polenta has heated through and Asiago has melted, 10 to 15 minutes. Let cool slightly and serve.

TEST KITCHEN TIP
PREPARING POLENTA FOR CASSEROLE

Remove tube of precooked polenta from its package and slice it into ⅓-inch-thick rounds, then arrange in a single layer in 13 by 9-inch baking dish.

Chicken Enchilada Casserole

SERVES 4 TO 6

2 **red and/or green bell peppers**

1 pound
boneless, skinless chicken breasts and/or thighs

2 (10-ounce) cans
red or green enchilada sauce Fresh cilantro

4 ounces **tortilla chips**

1½ cups (6 ounces) shredded
Mexican cheese blend

INGREDIENT SPOTLIGHT
TORTILLA CHIPS

This snack-aisle staple isn't just a carrier for salsa; it adds rich, corny flavor and big crunch to our Chicken Enchilada Casserole. To find the best tortilla chips, we recently sampled nine brands, rating chips on texture, freshness, salt levels, and of course, flavor. In the end, **Santitas Authentic Mexican Style White Corn Tortilla Chips** won us over with their "mild and salty" flavor and "great crunch."

WHY THIS RECIPE WORKS Boasting softened tortillas wrapped around tender, slow-cooked chicken, a rich-tasting, long-simmered sauce, and lots of gooey cheese, authentic Mexican enchiladas are incredibly satisfying—and equally fussy. We wanted to know if we could both trim the ingredient list *and* streamline the procedure. Starting with canned enchilada sauce saved loads of time and slashed our shopping list, and poaching the chicken right in the sauce infused it with deep flavor. For more substance, we included bell peppers; roasting them under the broiler gave our dish intense, smoky flavor in no time. We then mixed the lot together with shredded cheese and crushed tortilla chips, which took the place of the usual tortillas, and transferred it all to a casserole dish. The chips softened nicely in the oven and absorbed the other flavors—but tasters wanted some crunch. So we added more chips to the top and sprinkled them with cheese. They stayed crisp during baking, ensuring a satisfying crunch and bold cheesy flavor. We like using a combination of red and green bell peppers. You can substitute 6 ounces of shredded Monterey Jack, shredded pepper Jack, or crumbled *queso fresco* for the cheese blend. Serve with sour cream, diced avocado, shredded romaine lettuce, and lime wedges.

1. Core and flatten bell peppers (see page 201). Adjust oven rack 6 inches from broiler element and heat broiler. Lay peppers on aluminum foil–lined baking sheet and broil until skin is charred but flesh is still firm, 8 to 10 minutes. Let peppers cool slightly, then cut into ¼-inch-wide slices, leaving charred skin intact.

2. Trim chicken, pat dry, and combine with enchilada sauce in medium saucepan. Cover and simmer gently over medium-low heat until breasts register 160 degrees and thighs register 175 degrees, about 15 minutes. Remove chicken from pot, let cool slightly, then shred into bite-size pieces.

3. Adjust oven rack to middle position and heat oven to 450 degrees. Mince ½ cup cilantro and break tortilla chips into ½-inch pieces. Combine roasted peppers, shredded chicken, enchilada sauce, 1 cup tortilla chips, ⅓ cup cilantro, and 1 cup Mexican cheese blend in large bowl. Season with salt and pepper to taste.

4. Transfer mixture to 8-inch square baking dish. Sprinkle with remaining tortilla chips and top with remaining ½ cup Mexican cheese blend. Bake until casserole is heated through and bubbling, 15 to 20 minutes. Let cool slightly, sprinkle with remaining cilantro, and serve.

Egg, Ham, and Hash Brown Pie

SERVES 4

1 pound (5 cups)
frozen shredded hash browns

4 **scallions**

⅓ cup **olive oil**

4 ounces **ham steak**

4 **large eggs**

1½ cups (6 ounces) shredded
pepper Jack cheese

INGREDIENT SPOTLIGHT
FROZEN SHREDDED POTATOES

This convenience product makes it easy to pull our casserole together in short order, because the potatoes have already been peeled and shredded and are ready to use. We had good luck using Alexia Organic Hashed Browns in our recipe; these potatoes are seasoned with sea salt, onion, garlic, and white pepper, so they add depth of flavor, in addition to slashing significant prep time.

✔ **WHY THIS RECIPE WORKS** For a satisfying breakfast casserole that's light on effort, we started with shredded frozen potatoes and fried them in a hot skillet before adding eggs, spicy pepper Jack cheese, and rich, savory ham. Scallions, sautéed with the potatoes, rounded out the flavor of our hash brown pie. You can substitute other types of deli meat or cooked sausage for the ham. To thaw the potatoes quickly, microwave them in a covered bowl for about four minutes, tossing occasionally.

1. Thaw potatoes. Mince scallion whites and thinly slice scallion greens; keep whites and greens separate. Cook scallion whites, oil, and ⅛ teaspoon salt in 10-inch nonstick skillet over medium-high heat until softened, 3 to 5 minutes. Stir in potatoes and cook, turning often, until potatoes are crisp and browned, about 15 minutes.

2. Cut ham into ½-inch cubes. Whisk eggs, cheese, scallion greens, and ¼ teaspoon pepper together in large bowl, then stir in ham and cooked potato mixture. Pour mixture into now-empty skillet and cook over medium-high heat, gently shaking pan occasionally, until bottom is golden and top is lightly set, about 5 minutes.

3. Off heat, run heatproof rubber spatula around edge of pan and shake pan gently to loosen pie; it should slide around freely in pan. Slide pie onto large plate, then invert onto second large plate and slide back into skillet browned side up. Continue to cook over medium heat, gently shaking pan occasionally, until second side is golden and eggs are cooked through, about 2 minutes. Slide pie onto cutting board, let cool slightly, and serve.

TEST KITCHEN TIP **FLIPPING HASH BROWN PIE**

1. After browning first side, run heatproof rubber spatula around edge of pan and shake pan gently to loosen pie. Slide pie onto large plate.

2. Place second plate face down over pie. Invert pie onto second plate so it is browned side up; slide pie back into pan. Tuck edges into pan with spatula.

Spanish Tortilla with Roasted Red Peppers and Peas

1½ pounds **Yukon Gold potatoes**

1 **small onion**

6 tablespoons plus 1 teaspoon **extra-virgin olive oil**

½ cup **frozen peas**

½ cup jarred **roasted red peppers**

8 **large eggs**

INGREDIENT SPOTLIGHT
FROZEN PEAS

Green peas are quite delicate, and lose a substantial portion of their nutrients within 24 hours of being picked. This rapid deterioration is the reason for the starchy, bland flavor of most "fresh" peas found at the grocery store—these not-so-fresh peas might be several days old, depending on where they came from and how long they were kept in the cooler. Frozen peas, on the other hand, are picked, cleaned, sorted, and frozen within several hours of harvest, which helps to preserve their delicate sugars and flavors. So unless you grow your own or can stop by your local farm stand for fresh picked, you're better off opting for frozen peas. Any brand will work fine; when we sampled three national brands, all of the peas were sweet and fresh, with a bright green color.

✔ **WHY THIS RECIPE WORKS** This tapas bar favorite boasts meltingly tender potatoes in a dense, creamy omelet. But the typical recipe for Spanish tortilla calls for simmering the potatoes in a quart of extra-virgin olive oil, which seemed excessive (and costly) for this simple dish. We found that we could cut down the amount of oil to just 6 tablespoons for a richly flavorful, but not greasy, tortilla. We also found that firmer, less starchy Yukon Gold potatoes worked much better than the standard russets; the russets tended to fall apart when flipped in the pan. To keep prep time to a minimum, we turned to jarred roasted red peppers, which added intense, smoky flavor and an appealing, bright color. A handful of vibrant green peas offered sweet, fresh flavor. This dish can be served warm or at room temperature.

1. Peel potatoes, quarter lengthwise, then slice crosswise ⅛ inch thick. Halve and thinly slice onion. Toss ¼ cup oil, potatoes, onion, ½ teaspoon salt, and ¼ teaspoon pepper in large bowl. Heat 2 tablespoons oil in 10-inch nonstick skillet over medium-high heat until shimmering, then add potato mixture. Reduce heat to medium-low, cover, and cook, stirring every 5 minutes, until potatoes are tender, about 25 minutes.

2. Thaw peas. Rinse roasted red peppers, pat dry, and cut into ½-inch pieces. Whisk eggs and ½ teaspoon salt in large bowl, then gently fold in cooked potato mixture, red peppers, and peas. (Make sure to scrape all of potato mixture out of skillet.)

3. Heat remaining 1 teaspoon oil in now-empty skillet over medium-high heat until just smoking. Add egg mixture and cook, shaking pan and folding mixture constantly for 15 seconds. Reduce heat to medium and smooth top of egg mixture. Cover and cook, gently shaking occasionally, until bottom is golden and top is lightly set, about 2 minutes.

4. Off heat, run heatproof rubber spatula around edge of pan and shake pan gently to loosen tortilla (see page 243); it should slide around freely in pan. Slide tortilla onto large plate, then invert onto second large plate and slide back into skillet browned side up. Tuck edges of tortilla into skillet with rubber spatula. Continue to cook over medium heat, gently shaking pan occasionally, until second side is golden and eggs are cooked through, about 2 minutes. Slide tortilla onto cutting board, let cool slightly, and serve.

Easy Egg Casserole with Boursin and Sun-Dried Tomatoes

SERVES 4

¼ cup
oil-packed sun-dried tomatoes

Fresh basil

24 **Ritz crackers**

10 **large eggs**

⅓ cup **half-and-half**

1 (5.2-ounce) package
Boursin Garlic and Fine Herbs cheese

INGREDIENT SPOTLIGHT **EGGS**

Although perishable, properly stored eggs will last up to three months, but both the yolks and the whites will become looser and their flavor will begin to fade. To be sure that you have fresh eggs, check the sell-by date on the side of the carton; by law, the sell-by date must be no more than 30 days after the packing date. To ensure freshness, store eggs in the back of the refrigerator (the coldest area), not in the door (which is actually the warmest part of your refrigerator), and keep them in the carton. It holds moisture and keeps eggs from drying out; the carton also protects the eggs from odors.

✓ WHY THIS RECIPE WORKS Easy egg brunch casseroles that rely on a baking mix, such as Bisquick, are a dime a dozen; they're often heavy and dense and their flavors are pedestrian. We wanted an egg casserole that was almost as easy, with a lighter texture and a lively mix of flavors. Swapping out the baking mix for cracker crumbs gave the casserole structure without weighing it down, and Ritz crackers proved ideal for their sweet, buttery flavor and easy-to-crush texture. Adding a little half-and-half enriched the dish and helped prevent it from tasting dry. As for the cheese, we tried several before landing on Boursin, whose garlic and herb flavors melted into creamy pockets throughout the dish. A handful of sun-dried tomatoes added further flavor and a hefty dose of fresh basil provided brightness. You can substitute whole milk for the half-and-half in this recipe, but the texture of the casserole will be less tender.

1. Adjust oven rack to lower-middle position and heat oven to 400 degrees. Pat sun-dried tomatoes dry and chop. Chop ½ cup basil.

2. Coarsely crush crackers into large bowl. Add eggs, half-and-half, and ¼ teaspoon pepper and whisk together until fully incorporated. Crumble Boursin into mixture, then fold in basil and sun-dried tomatoes, leaving clumps of cheese intact.

3. Pour mixture into greased 1-quart gratin dish (or deep-dish pie plate). Bake until top is just set and lightly golden, about 15 minutes. Let sit for 2 minutes before serving.

TEST KITCHEN TIP
CRACKING AN EGG

Always aim to crack an egg cleanly; it eliminates those annoying bits of shell that can wind up in a batter. For a clean break, it's best to crack the side of the egg against the flat surface of a counter or cutting board, rather than the edge of the counter or mixing bowl.

Apple and Cheddar Strata

SERVES 6 TO 8

12 slices **bacon**

12 slices
hearty white sandwich bread

2 **McIntosh or Golden Delicious apples**

2 cups (8 ounces) shredded
sharp cheddar cheese

3 cups **whole milk**

6 **large eggs**

INGREDIENT SPOTLIGHT CHEDDAR

Traditionally, cheddar is made by a process called cheddaring: The curd (made by adding acid-producing cultures and clotting agents to unpasteurized whole milk) is cut into slabs, then stacked, cut, pressed, and stacked again. Along the way a large amount of liquid, called whey, is extracted. The remaining compacted curd is what gives farmhouse cheddars their hard and fine-grained characteristics. When it comes to flavor and sharpness, the longer a cheddar is aged, which can be anywhere from a couple months to a couple years, the firmer in texture and more concentrated in flavor (and sharper) it gets. Our favorite brand is **Cabot Sharp Vermont Cheddar Cheese**, which is aged 5 to 8 months. This cheese boasted a "sharp," "clean," and "tangy" flavor.

✓ **WHY THIS RECIPE WORKS** The ultimate breakfast dish, strata is easy to make, feeds a crowd, and can be assembled ahead of time. Plus, with its tender custard and rich flavors, this savory bread pudding is incredibly satisfying. For ours, we started by building big flavor with sharp cheddar, crisped bacon, and thinly sliced apples. After placing slices of hearty sandwich bread on the bottom of a baking dish, we layered these add-ins on top, then capped it all off with more bread slices and poured the custard (eggs and whole milk) over the top. Weighting the bread and custard with a second baking dish and heavy cans before baking ensured that the custard completely soaked all of the bread, for a strata that was cohesive and creamy throughout.

1. Chop bacon and cook in 12-inch nonstick skillet over medium heat until very crisp, about 10 minutes; transfer to paper towel–lined plate. Trim crusts from bread. Peel, core, and thinly slice apples.

2. Arrange six slices trimmed bread in single layer in greased 13 by 9-inch baking dish, cutting bread as needed to fit. Top with half of apples, bacon, 1 cup cheddar, and remaining apples. Arrange remaining bread slices in single layer over top, cutting bread as needed to fit.

3. Whisk milk, eggs, ½ teaspoon salt, and ¼ teaspoon pepper together, then pour over bread. Press gently on bread to submerge. Cover baking dish with plastic wrap pressed flush with custard, then top with another 13 by 9-inch baking dish weighted with heavy canned goods. Refrigerate for at least 2 hours or up to 24 hours.

4. Adjust oven rack to middle position and heat oven to 350 degrees. Remove plastic and sprinkle strata with remaining 1 cup cheddar. Bake until strata is puffed and golden brown, 50 to 60 minutes. Let cool slightly and serve.

TEST KITCHEN TIP
WEIGHTING STRATA

After assembling strata, wrap it tightly with plastic wrap. Then top it with second baking dish weighted with heavy cans.

MARYLAND-STYLE GRILLED SHRIMP AND CORN

Easy Grilling

251 Grilled Pizza Margherita | FAST RECIPE

252 Grilled Chicken Breasts with Cherry Tomatoes

256 Grilled Indian-Spiced Chicken with Raita

257 Grilled Southwestern Drumsticks with Charred Coleslaw

259 Grilled Chicken alla Diavola

260 Grilled Chicken Soft Tacos

261 Grilled Asian Beef Kebabs | FAST RECIPE

263 Grilled Sirloin Steak with Grilled Tomato Salad | FAST RECIPE

264 Grilled Flank Steak with Herb Sauce | FAST RECIPE

265 Grilled Margarita Steak

266 Grilled Free-Form Beef Wellington with Balsamic Reduction

269 Grilled Italian Sausages and Polenta with Pepper Relish | FAST RECIPE

270 Grilled Spice-Rubbed Pork Tenderloin with Peaches | FAST RECIPE

271 Smoked Double-Thick Pork Chops with
Cranberry-Thyme Applesauce

272 Grilled Lamb Chops with Shaved Zucchini Salad | FAST RECIPE

274 Grilled Scallops with Fennel and Orange Salad | FAST RECIPE

275 Maryland-Style Grilled Shrimp and Corn | FAST RECIPE

277 Grill-Smoked Salmon with Creamy Cucumber-Dill Salad

278 Grilled Red Curry Mahi-Mahi with Pineapple Salsa | FAST RECIPE

279 Grilled Swordfish Skewers with Basil Oil | FAST RECIPE

Grilled Pizza Margherita

SERVES 4

4 (8-inch) **naan breads**

2 tablespoons **olive oil**

6 ounces
fresh mozzarella cheese

¾ cup **pizza sauce**

1 cup (2 ounces) grated
Parmesan cheese

Fresh basil

INGREDIENT SPOTLIGHT **NAAN**

Baked naan (available in most super-markets) is not just a piece of bread meant to accompany your chicken tikka masala or vegetable curry. It makes a great base for an easy pizza, because it has already been parbaked and is easy to maneuver around the grill. Most of the time, you'll find it next to the rolls, bagels, and pita bread, but naan is sometimes found in the freezer section at your supermarket. If frozen, be sure to thaw before using.

WHY THIS RECIPE WORKS Moving pizza from the oven to the grill delivers an ultracrispy, nicely charred crust. But who wants to wait for dough (homemade or otherwise) to rise, or deal with getting the floppy rounds onto a super-hot grill? For our grilled pizza, we turned to an Indian staple, naan bread, which required no rising and was easy to maneuver on the hot grill. Plus, each naan provided just enough for one diner. To ensure a nicely browned exterior and crisp crust, we started by brushing the naan with olive oil and placing it directly over the hot coals. Once both sides were browned, we moved the naan to the cooler side of the grill, topped each one with sauce (we turned to store-bought pizza sauce) and cheese, and then covered the grill so the cheese would melt. For these Margherita-style pizzas, fresh mozzarella and chopped basil were a given; the cheese offered gooey bites and the basil provided a fresh, sweet touch. Tasters also liked the addition of a little grated Parmesan cheese, which contributed a nutty, salty tang to our easy grilled pizzas.

1. Brush both sides of naan with olive oil. Slice mozzarella thinly.

2A. FOR A CHARCOAL GRILL: Open bottom vent completely. Light large chimney starter three-quarters filled with charcoal briquettes (4½ quarts). When top coals are partially covered with ash, pour evenly over half of grill. Set cooking grate in place, cover, and open lid vent completely. Heat grill until hot, about 5 minutes.

2B. FOR A GAS GRILL: Turn all burners to high, cover, and heat grill until hot, about 15 minutes. Turn primary burner to medium-high and turn other burner(s) to medium-low.

3. Clean and oil cooking grate. Place 2 naan breads on hotter side of grill. Cook, turning as needed, until both sides are browned and crisp, about 3 minutes.

4. Slide breads to cooler side of grill. Top each bread with 3 table-spoons pizza sauce, one-quarter of sliced mozzarella, and ¼ cup Parmesan. Cover and cook until cheese is melted and sauce is warmed through, 4 to 6 minutes. Transfer to cutting board and tent with aluminum foil. Repeat with remaining 2 naan breads. Chop ¼ cup fresh basil, sprinkle over pizzas, and serve.

Grilled Chicken Breasts with Cherry Tomatoes

SERVES 4

Fresh basil

2 **garlic cloves**

½ cup **extra-virgin olive oil**

2 tablespoons **red wine vinegar**

1½ pounds **cherry tomatoes**

4 (10- to 12-ounce)
bone-in split chicken breasts

INGREDIENT SPOTLIGHT
RED WINE VINEGAR

Red wine vinegar has a sharp but clean flavor, making it the most versatile choice for salad dressings. While acidity is the obvious key factor in vinegar, it is actually the inherent sweetness of the grapes used to produce the vinegar that makes its flavor appealing to the palate. Our favorite brand is French import **Laurent du Clos Red Wine Vinegar**, which tasters described as having a "good red wine flavor."

✓ **WHY THIS RECIPE WORKS** Ideally, bone-in, skin-on chicken breasts should come off the grill moist and tender. After all, the bone insulates the meat, and the skin protects it from drying out. But when we tried grilling our bone-in breasts over a single-level fire, they dried out every time. We found our solution in a half-fire grill set-up. After a quick sear on the hotter side of the grill to give them color, we placed the breasts on the cooler side to finish cooking through; covering the grill trapped the heat and kept the meat moist. To round out the meal, we tossed cherry tomatoes with a little olive oil, skewered them, and grilled them. A quick dressing of garlic, basil, olive oil, and red wine vinegar added big flavor to our easy supper. You will need four or five 12-inch metal skewers for this recipe, depending on the size of the tomatoes.

1. Chop ¼ cup basil, mince garlic, and combine with 6 tablespoons oil, vinegar, ½ teaspoon salt, and ¼ teaspoon pepper in bowl; set aside for serving. Toss tomatoes with remaining 2 tablespoons oil and thread through stem ends onto 12-inch metal skewers. Trim chicken, pat dry with paper towels, and season with salt and pepper.

2A. FOR A CHARCOAL GRILL: Open bottom vent completely. Light large chimney starter filled with charcoal briquettes (6 quarts). When top coals are partially covered with ash, pour evenly over half of grill. Set cooking grate in place, cover, and open lid vent completely. Heat grill until hot, about 5 minutes.

2B. FOR A GAS GRILL: Turn all burners to high, cover, and heat grill until hot, about 15 minutes. Leave primary burner on high and turn other burner(s) to medium-low. (Adjust burners as needed to maintain grill temperature around 350 degrees.)

3. Clean and oil cooking grate. Place chicken, skin side down, on hotter side of grill. Cook (covered if using gas) until lightly browned on both sides, about 5 minutes. Slide chicken to cooler side of grill, with skin side down and thicker ends facing hotter side of grill. Cover and cook, turning as needed, until chicken is well browned on both sides and registers 160 degrees, 20 to 30 minutes.

4. Transfer chicken to platter, tent with aluminum foil, and let rest while finishing tomatoes. Place tomatoes on hotter side of grill. Cook, turning as needed, until skins begin to blister and wrinkle, about 5 minutes; transfer to platter and remove from skewers. Drizzle chicken and tomatoes with vinaigrette and serve.

Grilling 101

The hot fire of a grill is a great way to add flavor to food, especially when you're working with just a handful of ingredients. Here are some tips for successful grilling every time.

Lighting a Gas Grill

Gas grills are less complicated than charcoal grills, but nevertheless there are a few important points to keep in mind before you get going. First and foremost, read all the instructions in your owner's manual thoroughly and follow the directions regarding the order in which the burners must be lit. On most grills, an electric igniter lights the burners, though we have found that electric igniters can fail occasionally, especially in windy conditions. For these situations, most models have a hole for lighting the burners with a match. Be sure to wait several minutes (or as directed) between attempts at lighting the grill. This waiting time allows excess gas to dissipate and is an important safety measure.

Lighting a Fire with a Chimney Starter

We prefer to start a charcoal fire with a chimney starter, or flue starter. Fill the starter's bottom section with crumpled newspaper, set it on the grill grate, and fill the top with charcoal. When you light the newspaper, the charcoal easily ignites. Once the coals are coated with an even layer of fine gray ash, turn them out into the grill.

Lighting a Fire without a Chimney Starter

If you don't have a chimney starter, use the following technique.

1. Place enough sheets of crumpled newspaper, about 8 sheets, beneath charcoal grate to fill space loosely.

2. With bottom vents open, pile charcoal on grate and light paper. After about 20 minutes, coals should be covered with gray ash and ready to arrange for cooking.

Is Your Fire Hot Enough?

Whether we're cooking with gas or charcoal, we rely on the same test to determine the heat level of our fire (true, gas grills usually come with a temperature display, but over the years we've found them inconsistent and unreliable). After initially heating up the grill, hold your hand 5 inches above the cooking grate and count how long you can comfortably keep it there. (We preheat gas grills on high heat for 15 minutes with the lid down and charcoal for 5 minutes with the lid on.)

Hot Fire	2 seconds
Medium-Hot Fire	3 to 4 seconds
Medium Fire	5 to 6 seconds
Medium-Low Fire	7 seconds

Cleaning the Cooking Grate

Before placing any food on the grill, it is important to clean and oil the cooking grate, whether you're using a gas or charcoal grill. After you've heated the grill, scrape the grate clean with a grill brush to remove any residue from previous grilling. Then dip a large wad of paper towels in vegetable oil, grab it with tongs, and wipe the cooking grate thoroughly. Repeat multiple times.

Building a Charcoal Fire

When you're cooking on a gas grill, heat is easily adjusted with the turn of a dial, but for a charcoal grill, using the correct amount of charcoal and the right set-up is key (see below). The charcoal amounts in our recipes are based on an 18- to 22-inch kettle charcoal grill. Also, charcoal grills have both bottom vents and lid vents, which can have an effect on how fast and how hot the charcoal burns. Opening the vents to varying degrees is important when using wood chips (or wood chunks) for smoking; vents that are halfway open help trap smoke inside the grill.

SINGLE-LEVEL FIRE

Arrange all of the lit charcoal in an even layer across the bottom of the grill. This fire delivers even, moderate heat and is great for small, quick-cooking foods; we use it for kebabs, sausage, and seafood.

SPLIT FIRE

Arrange the lit charcoal into two piles on opposite sides of the grill, leaving the center of the grill empty. This creates intense heat on either side of the grill and a moderate level of indirect heat in the center. This setup helps avoid flare-ups since the fat from the meat drips down into the center of the grill (sometimes we place a disposable pan there to catch the drips), rather than onto the coals.

HALF-GRILL FIRE

Arrange all of the lit charcoal over half of the grill and leave the other half of the grill empty. This fire, like a two-level fire, creates two cooking zones, but the difference is more dramatic. It allows searing over the coals and then slow cooking over indirect heat. We use it to make a super-hot fire for fast searing and to make the cooler cooking zone more controlled for lean and easily overcooked meats.

TWO-LEVEL FIRE

Arrange two-thirds of the lit charcoal evenly over half the grill, and the remaining coals evenly over the other half of the grill. This creates two cooking zones—a hotter area for searing and a slightly cooler area to cook food through more gently. Charcoal burns quite hot, so having a cooler area to slide food to if it begins to char is necessary.

Making a Foil Packet

Whether working on a charcoal or gas grill, wood chips can add great smoky flavor to grilled foods. In general, we prefer to use chips rather than chunks since they're easier to handle and don't take as long to soak before they're put on the fire. We've found that how the chips are used can play a big part in the final flavor of grilled or bar-becued meat; it's important not to sear the meat directly over a fresh packet of smoking wood chips because it can leave the meat tasting like the inside of a chimney.

After soaking wood chips in water for 15 minutes, drain and spread them in center of 15 by 12-inch piece of heavy-duty aluminum foil. Fold to seal edges, then cut three or four slits to allow smoke to escape.

Grilled Indian-Spiced Chicken with Raita

SERVES 4

1½ cups **plain yogurt**

1 tablespoon **curry powder**

1 tablespoon **garam masala**

4 (10- to 12-ounce)
bone-in split chicken breasts

Fresh cilantro

1 small **garlic clove**

INGREDIENT SPOTLIGHT
PLAIN YOGURT

Yogurt isn't just a snack anymore. In the test kitchen, we use yogurt in sauces and dips when we want a creamy texture and subtly tangy flavor, but not the heavy richness of sour cream. We also use it in marinades, where it helps to keep meat moist. Our favorite brand is **Brown Cow Cream Top Plain Yogurt**, which tasters found to be especially "creamy" and "smooth," and have a "rich," "well-rounded" flavor.

✓ WHY THIS RECIPE WORKS Inspired by yogurt-marinated chicken cooked in an Indian tandoor oven, this dish packs in surprising flavor in spite of its short ingredient list. As with authentic tandoori recipes, we marinated the chicken in yogurt. For the spice rub, curry powder alone tasted harsh and one-dimensional. Garam masala added complexity, but the raw taste remained. Adding the spices to the yogurt marinade solved the problem—the yogurt kept the chicken moist and tender, plus it helped to bloom, or deepen, the flavor of the spices once they hit the grill. To prevent the yogurt marinade from burning, we started the chicken on the cooler side of the grill, then finished it on the hotter side so it would brown slightly. More yogurt, plus some garlic and cilantro, provided a cool, creamy counterpoint to the grilled meat. See page 286 for more information on garam masala.

1. Combine ¾ cup yogurt, curry powder, garam masala, 1 teaspoon salt, and ¼ teaspoon pepper in gallon-size zipper-lock bag. Trim chicken, pat dry with paper towels, and add to bag with yogurt marinade. Seal bag tightly and toss to coat chicken. Refrigerate for 1 to 6 hours, flipping bag occasionally.

2. Mince 2 tablespoons cilantro and mince garlic; combine with remaining ¾ cup yogurt in bowl and season with salt and pepper to taste. Cover and refrigerate until ready to serve.

3A. FOR A CHARCOAL GRILL: Open bottom vent completely. Light large chimney starter filled with charcoal briquettes (6 quarts). When top coals are partially covered with ash, pour evenly over half of grill. Set cooking grate in place, cover, and open lid vent completely. Heat grill until hot, about 5 minutes.

3B. FOR A GAS GRILL: Turn all burners to high, cover, and heat grill until hot, about 15 minutes. Leave primary burner on high and turn other burner(s) to medium-low. (Adjust burners as needed to maintain grill temperature around 350 degrees.)

4. Clean and oil cooking grate. Remove chicken from marinade and place, skin side down, on cooler side of grill with thicker ends facing hotter side of grill. Cover and grill until chicken begins to brown and registers 155 degrees, 25 to 35 minutes.

5. Slide chicken to hotter side of grill and cook, turning as needed, until well browned and registers 160 degrees, 3 to 5 minutes. Transfer chicken to platter and rest for 5 to 10 minutes. Serve with cilantro-yogurt sauce.

Grilled Southwestern Drumsticks with Charred Coleslaw

SERVES 4

½ head **green cabbage**
(1 pound)

½ cup **mayonnaise**

8 (6-ounce) **chicken drumsticks**

3½ teaspoons **chili powder**

1 **carrot**

4 teaspoons **cider vinegar**

INGREDIENT SPOTLIGHT
CIDER VINEGAR

Apple cider vinegar adds a potent hit of flavor to many dishes. Though cider vinegars can range in flavor from sweet to puckeringly tart, we prefer sweeter vinegars, and we like them to have a notable apple flavor. Our favorite, French-produced **Maille Apple Cider Vinegar**, was praised by our tasters for its "deep, warm" flavor profile and "definite apple" taste.

✓ WHY THIS RECIPE WORKS Drumsticks are a good match for the grill: Their skin becomes golden and crisp, and the bone insulates the meat to keep it moist and tender. To turn our drumsticks into a complete meal, we paired them with a charred cabbage slaw. A bit of chili powder gave our chicken and slaw a Southwestern bent. But without some oil to help bloom, or deepen, the flavor of the chili powder, it tasted dry and dusty on our chicken. Combining the chili powder with a bit of mayonnaise, which we needed for our slaw, before applying it to the drumsticks solved the problem. The fat in the mayo helped rid the spice of its raw taste and ensured the skin crisped nicely. A quick brush of more mayo on our cabbage before grilling kept the veggie moist, too. Do not remove the core from the cabbage; it will keep the leaves intact on the grill.

1. Cut cabbage into 4 wedges through stem end, brush with 2 tablespoons mayonnaise, and season with salt and pepper. Trim drumsticks; pat dry with paper towels. Combine 2 tablespoons mayonnaise with 1 tablespoon chili powder and brush evenly over drumsticks.

2A. FOR A CHARCOAL GRILL: Open bottom vent completely. Light large chimney starter filled with charcoal briquettes (6 quarts). When top coals are partially covered with ash, pour evenly over half of grill. Set cooking grate in place, cover, and open lid vent completely. Heat grill until hot, about 5 minutes.

2B. FOR A GAS GRILL: Turn all burners to high, cover, and heat grill until hot, about 15 minutes. Leave primary burner on high and turn other burner(s) to medium-low. (Adjust burners as needed to maintain grill temperature around 350 degrees.)

3. Clean and oil cooking grate. Place chicken, skin side down, on cooler side of grill. Cover and cook until skin is crisp and golden, 20 to 30 minutes. Meanwhile, place cabbage on hotter side of grill and cook, turning as needed, until lightly charred on all sides, 8 to 12 minutes; transfer to bowl and cover to keep warm.

4. Slide chicken to hotter side of grill and cook, turning as needed, until well browned and drumsticks register 175 degrees, 5 to 10 minutes. Transfer chicken to platter; let rest while finishing slaw. Slice cabbage into thin strips, discarding core. Peel and shred carrot. Whisk remaining ¼ cup mayonnaise, vinegar, and remaining ½ teaspoon chili powder together in large bowl, then stir in cabbage and carrot and season with salt and pepper to taste. Serve coleslaw with chicken.

Grilled Chicken alla Diavola

SERVES 3 TO 4

2 heads plus 4 cloves **garlic**

3 **bay leaves**

1 (3- to 4-pound) **whole chicken**

¼ cup **olive oil**

2 teaspoons **red pepper flakes**

Lemon wedges

INGREDIENT SPOTLIGHT
WHOLE CHICKEN

At the supermarket, you might see birds labeled "all-natural," "organic," and "free-range," among other things. But we think the most important thing to look for is that the chicken you're buying is air-chilled. In a recent tasting of whole birds, our top two brands were both air-chilled, not water-chilled like many brands; air-chilling leads to better flavor and texture, and meat that is juicy rather than soggy. Our favorite brands are **Bell & Evans Air Chilled Premium Fresh Chicken** (shown) and **Mary's Free Range Air Chilled Chicken**.

✓ WHY THIS RECIPE WORKS Butterflying a chicken is a win-win when it comes to grilling. Not only does it allow the chicken to cook through more quickly and evenly, but it also exposes more skin to the heat of the grill so it can brown and become ultracrisp. But crisp skin and tender meat are only half the battle—the chicken has to be flavorful, too. To that end, we set out to infuse our grilled bird with bold heat and garlicky flavor. Adding two heads of garlic to the brine was our first move. Next, we created a potent garlic-pepper oil and brushed some under the skin of the chicken before tossing it on the grill. For one last punch of flavor, we reserved some of the garlicky oil and served it alongside the chicken. If using a kosher chicken, do not brine. This dish is very spicy; for milder heat, reduce the amount of red pepper flakes. Note you will need a disposable aluminum roasting pan for this recipe if using charcoal.

1. Combine 2 garlic heads, bay leaves, and ½ cup salt in zipper-lock bag, crush gently with meat pounder, and transfer to large container. Stir in 2 quarts water to dissolve salt. Trim chicken, butterfly (see page 126), immerse in brine, and refrigerate for 2 hours.

2. Mince remaining 4 cloves garlic and cook with oil, pepper flakes, and 2 teaspoons pepper in small saucepan over medium heat until fragrant, about 3 minutes. Off heat, let garlic oil cool, then measure out and set aside 2 tablespoons for serving.

3. Remove chicken from brine and pat dry with paper towels. Gently loosen skin covering breast and thighs and apply remaining garlic oil beneath skin. Tuck wingtips behind back (see page 125).

4A. FOR A CHARCOAL GRILL: Open bottom vent completely and place disposable aluminum pan in center of grill. Light large chimney starter filled with charcoal briquettes (6 quarts). When top coals are partially covered with ash, pour into 2 even piles on either side of disposable pan. Set cooking grate in place, cover, and open lid vent completely. Heat grill until hot, about 5 minutes.

4B. FOR A GAS GRILL: Turn all burners to high, cover, and heat grill until hot, about 15 minutes. Turn all burners to medium-low.

5. Clean and oil cooking grate. Place chicken, skin side down, in center of grill (over disposable pan if using charcoal). Cover and cook until skin is crisp, breast registers 160 degrees, and thighs register 175 degrees, 30 to 45 minutes.

6. Transfer chicken to carving board; let rest for 5 to 10 minutes. Carve chicken and serve with reserved garlic oil and lemon wedges.

Grilled Chicken Soft Tacos

SERVES 4

8 ounces **cherry tomatoes**

Canned **chipotle chiles**

½ cup **sour cream**

4 (6- to 8-ounce)
**boneless, skinless
chicken breasts**

8–12 (6-inch) **flour tortillas**

Fresh cilantro

**INGREDIENT SPOTLIGHT
FLOUR TORTILLAS**

Typically made with just five ingredients—flour, water, fat, salt, and (often) baking powder—homemade tortillas have a pliancy and clean flavor that can be hard to come by in their store-bought counterparts. But in a recent tasting, we did find one supermarket brand that boasted both a "soft and pliable" texture and "nice, mild, wheaty flavor." Tasters liked **Old El Paso 6-Inch Flour Tortillas**, which offered a "flaky yet substantial texture" and "rich" flavor.

☑ **WHY THIS RECIPE WORKS** For satisfying chicken soft tacos that delivered tender bites of chicken and appealing flavor, without an armload of toppings, we started with boneless, skinless chicken breasts, which needed little prep, cooked quickly, and picked up rich, smoky flavor from the grill. Toasting our tortillas on the grill gave them some color and flavor. For the toppings, we started with chopped cherry tomatoes, which offered sweetness and moisture. But for even more oomph, we combined tangy sour cream with spicy chipotle chiles, then tossed our sliced chicken in this creamy, smoky sauce. With a sprinkling of grassy cilantro leaves, our minimalist tacos delivered maximum flavor.

1. Chop tomatoes, transfer to bowl, and season with salt and pepper to taste; set aside for serving. Mince 2 teaspoons chipotle and whisk together with sour cream and ½ teaspoon salt together in large bowl; set aside for serving. Trim chicken, pat dry with paper towels, and season with salt and pepper.

2A. FOR A CHARCOAL GRILL: Open bottom vent completely. Light large chimney starter filled with charcoal briquettes (6 quarts). When top coals are partially covered with ash, pour evenly over half of grill. Set cooking grate in place, cover, and open lid vent completely. Heat grill until hot, about 5 minutes.

2B. FOR A GAS GRILL: Turn all burners to high, cover, and heat grill until hot, about 15 minutes. Leave primary burner on high and turn other burner(s) to low. (Adjust burners as needed to maintain grill temperature around 350 degrees.)

3. Clean and oil cooking grate. Place chicken on cooler side of grill with thicker ends facing hotter side of grill. Cover and cook, turning as needed, until chicken registers 140 degrees, 12 to 18 minutes.

4. Slide chicken to hotter side of grill and cook, turning as needed, until nicely browned on both sides and chicken registers 160 degrees, 2 to 6 minutes. Transfer to carving board, tent with aluminum foil, and let rest while grilling tortillas.

5. Place tortillas on hotter side of grill and cook until warm and lightly charred, about 20 seconds per side; transfer to plate and cover to keep warm. Slice chicken thinly on bias, add to sour cream mixture, and toss to coat. Serve chicken with tortillas, tomatoes, and cilantro leaves.

Grilled Asian Beef Kebabs

SERVES 4
Fresh ginger
4 **garlic cloves**
½ cup **hoisin sauce**
1½ pounds **sirloin steak tips**
1½ pounds **shiitake mushrooms**
1 pound **sugar snap peas**

INGREDIENT SPOTLIGHT
SHIITAKE MUSHROOMS

Once native to only Japan, China, and Korea, shiitake mushrooms are now cultivated all over the world; they are grown on either natural hardwood logs or on man-made sawdust logs. Mushrooms grown this way are called wood-decomposing fungi, a family of mushrooms in which tough, woody stems are characteristic. The woody stems are a necessity since a tender, flimsy stem would not be able to establish growth in the tough environment of a log. So, unlike white mushrooms which have delicate stems with a similar texture as the cap when cooked, shiitake stems should be trimmed away before cooking or else their tough, chewy texture will stand out. When buying fresh shiitakes, look for those that have smooth, brown caps without any bruising.

✔ **WHY THIS RECIPE WORKS** In these Asian-inspired skewers, we combined meaty steak tips, earthy shiitake mushrooms, and crisp snap peas, which all picked up a nice char and smoky flavor from the grill. Though they had a lot going for them, our kebabs needed a flavorful marinade to really bring the components together. While we usually turn to soy sauce for the base of our meat marinades, we couldn't afford the lengthy list of ingredients that we use to amp up soy's flavor. Plus, we needed a base with more body to cling to the kebabs. The answer? Unctuous, complex hoisin sauce. Thick enough to baste the meat and full of warm, pungent notes, hoisin, thinned with a little water—plus some ginger and garlic for freshness and zing—really made our kebabs come alive, and its sugars helped the steak tips brown nicely. Sirloin steak tips are sometimes sold as whole steaks labeled "flap meat." To ensure even-size chunks, we prefer to purchase whole steaks and cut them ourselves. You will need eight 12-inch metal skewers for this recipe. See page 141 for more information on hoisin sauce.

1. Grate 2 tablespoons ginger and mince garlic; combine with hoisin sauce, ⅓ cup water, ½ teaspoon salt, and ½ teaspoon pepper in medium bowl. Trim steak, cut into 1½-inch pieces, and toss with marinade. Stem shiitakes and halve if large. Remove strings from snap peas. Thread marinated beef, mushrooms, and snap peas onto eight 12-inch metal skewers, then brush with leftover marinade.

2A. FOR A CHARCOAL GRILL: Open bottom vent completely. Light large chimney starter filled with charcoal briquettes (6 quarts). When top coals are partially covered with ash, pour evenly over grill. Set cooking grate in place, cover, and open lid vent completely. Heat grill until hot, about 5 minutes.

2B. FOR A GAS GRILL: Turn all burners to high, cover, and heat grill until hot, about 15 minutes. Leave all burners on high.

3. Clean and oil cooking grate. Place kebabs on grill and cook (covered if using gas), turning as needed, until lightly charred on all sides and meat registers 130 to 135 degrees (for medium), about 10 minutes. Transfer kebabs to platter, tent with aluminum foil, and let rest for 5 to 10 minutes before serving.

Grilled Sirloin Steak with Grilled Tomato Salad

SERVES 4

1 pound **cherry tomatoes**

6 tablespoons **extra-virgin olive oil**

1 (2-pound) **boneless shell sirloin steak,** 1 to 1¼ inches thick

1 **garlic clove**

6 ounces (6 cups) **baby spinach**

Shaved **Parmesan cheese**

INGREDIENT SPOTLIGHT
SHELL SIRLOIN STEAK

One of our favorite inexpensive steaks is the shell sirloin, also known as top butt, butt steak, top sirloin butt, top sirloin steak, and center-cut roast; do not confuse it with the top loin steak, which is sometimes called sirloin strip steak. We find that this cut delivers great beefy flavor and a tender texture at a price point that won't break the bank.

WHY THIS RECIPE WORKS For the perfect centerpiece to our grilled steak salad, we opted for a boneless shell sirloin steak, which boasts big beefy flavor at a reasonable price. Baby spinach, grilled cherry tomatoes, and shaved Parmesan rounded out the salad, but the dressing was still up in the air. As we took our olive oil–brushed tomatoes off the grill, we realized we had the makings of a flavorful vinaigrette right in front of us. We reserved half of the tomatoes for the salad, then blitzed the other half with more olive oil and a clove of garlic in the blender, for a simple dressing that brought bright flavor to both the salad and the steak. You will need four or five 12-inch metal skewers for this recipe, depending on the size of the tomatoes. We prefer this steak cooked to medium-rare, but if you prefer it more or less done, see our guidelines on page 100.

1. Toss tomatoes with 2 tablespoons oil and thread through stem ends onto 12-inch metal skewers. Trim steak, pat dry with paper towels, and season with salt and pepper.

2A. FOR A CHARCOAL GRILL: Open bottom vent completely. Light large chimney starter mounded with charcoal briquettes (7 quarts). When top coals are partially covered with ash, pour two-thirds evenly over half of grill, then pour remaining coals over other half of grill. Set cooking grate in place, cover, and open lid vent completely. Heat grill until hot, about 5 minutes.

2B. FOR A GAS GRILL: Turn all burners to high, cover, and heat grill until hot, about 15 minutes. Leave primary burner on high and turn other burner(s) to medium.

3. Clean and oil cooking grate. Place steak on hotter side of grill and tomatoes on cooler side of grill. Cook (covered if using gas), turning steak and tomatoes as needed, until steak registers 120 to 125 degrees (for medium-rare) and tomato skins begin to blister, 6 to 10 minutes. Transfer steak to carving board, tent with aluminum foil, and let rest for 5 to 10 minutes. Transfer tomatoes to bowl.

4. Mince garlic; add to blender with half of tomatoes and remaining ¼ cup oil. Blend until smooth, about 30 seconds; season with salt and pepper to taste. Add spinach to bowl with remaining grilled tomatoes, toss with ½ cup tomato vinaigrette, and top with Parmesan. Slice meat thinly against grain and drizzle with remaining tomato vinaigrette. Serve with salad.

Grilled Flank Steak with Herb Sauce

SERVES 4 TO 6

1 (2-pound) **flank steak**

1 teaspoon **sugar**

Fresh parsley

3 **garlic cloves**

1 **lemon**

⅓ cup **extra-virgin olive oil**

INGREDIENT SPOTLIGHT
FLANK STEAK

Flank steak is a large, thin, flat cut with a distinct longitudinal grain; it is cut from the underside of a cow in the area nearest the hind legs. It is best cooked either rare or medium-rare. We always recommend slicing flank steak against the grain because this shortens the tough muscle fibers, thus ensuring more tender meat.

✓ WHY THIS RECIPE WORKS For an easy, economical steak for a backyard barbecue, we turn to flank steak. With a little salt, pepper, and sugar (to aid in browning), ours was ready to hit the grill. For this quick-cooking steak, we used a half-fire grill setup: We spread the coals over half of the grill to concentrate the heat for optimal char on the steak, and left the other side of the grill cooler so we could move the steak over if it started to burn. In about 10 minutes, it was perfectly done. For a bright counterpoint, we combined a few flavorful ingredients to make a quick herb sauce. Fresh parsley contributed a grassy, herbal element, pungent garlic stood up to the meaty flavor of the steak, and lemon juice added a touch of acidity. A bit of sugar contributed sweetness and helped to mellow out the potent garlic-herb sauce. We prefer this steak cooked to medium-rare, but if you prefer it more or less done, see our guidelines on page 100.

1. Trim steak, pat dry with paper towels, sprinkle with ¾ teaspoon sugar, and season with salt and pepper. Mince 1 cup parsley, mince garlic, and squeeze lemon for 2 tablespoons juice; combine in bowl with oil, remaining ¼ teaspoon sugar, ¼ teaspoon salt, and ¼ teaspoon pepper and set aside for serving.

2A. FOR A CHARCOAL GRILL: Open bottom vent completely. Light large chimney starter filled with charcoal briquettes (6 quarts). When top coals are partially covered with ash, pour evenly over half of grill. Set cooking grate in place, cover, and open lid vent completely. Heat grill until hot, about 5 minutes.

2B. FOR A GAS GRILL: Turn all burners to high, cover, and heat grill until hot, about 15 minutes. Leave primary burner on high and turn other burner(s) to medium.

3. Clean and oil cooking grate. Place steak on hotter side of grill. Cook (covered if using gas), turning as needed, until lightly charred and meat registers 120 to 125 degrees (for medium-rare), 8 to 12 minutes.

4. Transfer steak to carving board, tent with aluminum foil, and let rest for 5 to 10 minutes. Slice steak thinly against grain and serve with garlic-herb sauce.

Grilled Margarita Steak

SERVES 4
4 **limes**
½ cup **tequila**
2 tablespoons **sugar**
2 tablespoons **vegetable oil**
Fresh cilantro
1 (1½-pound) **flank steak**

INGREDIENT SPOTLIGHT **TEQUILA**

Tequila is distilled from blue agave, and it comes in two general types. Mixed (*mixto*) tequila often has added cane or corn sugar. Super-premium tequila, on the other hand, is distilled from 100 percent blue agave sugar, and will say so on the bottle. There are also several styles of tequila, from more economical choices that are bottled immediately upon distillation or stored for just a few months, to the more expensive styles that are aged and cost a pretty penny. Though we wouldn't use the high-end stuff in a marinade, this recipe will work with any kind of tequila you have on hand.

☑ **WHY THIS RECIPE WORKS** For another take on grilled flank steak, we soaked it in a tequila-spiked marinade. Scoring the surface of the meat ensured it absorbed the flavors of the marinade. Adding sugar to a mixture of tequila, lime juice, and oil helped the steak brown and form a satisfying crust on the grill. For more flavor, we set aside a portion of the marinade, stirred in chopped cilantro, and drizzled this sauce over the steak before serving. Don't marinate the steak for longer than 4 hours or it will turn gray and mushy.

1. Squeeze limes for ½ cup juice; combine with tequila, sugar, oil, ¾ teaspoon salt, and ½ teaspoon pepper in bowl. Measure out ¼ cup mixture for steak marinade. Mince 1 tablespoon cilantro, stir into remaining mixture, and set aside for serving.

2. Using sharp knife, lightly score both sides of steak at 1½-inch intervals. Combine steak and marinade in gallon-size zipper-lock bag and refrigerate for 1 to 4 hours, flipping bag often. Just before cooking, remove steak from marinade and pat dry with paper towels.

3A. FOR A CHARCOAL GRILL: Open bottom vent completely. Light large chimney starter filled with charcoal briquettes (6 quarts). When top coals are partially covered with ash, pour evenly over half of grill. Set cooking grate in place, cover, and open lid vent completely. Heat grill until hot, about 5 minutes.

3B. FOR A GAS GRILL: Turn all burners to high, cover, and heat grill until hot, about 15 minutes. Leave primary burner on high and turn other burner(s) to medium.

4. Clean and oil cooking grate. Place steak on hotter side of grill. Cook (covered if using gas), turning as needed, until lightly charred and meat registers 120 to 125 degrees (for medium-rare), 8 to 12 minutes. Transfer steak to carving board, tent with aluminum foil, and let rest for 5 to 10 minutes. Slice steak thinly against grain and serve with lime-cilantro mixture.

TEST KITCHEN TIP
SCORING A FLANK STEAK

Using a sharp knife, lightly score both sides of the steak at 1½-inch intervals; do not cut through steak. This allows the marinade to flavor the meat more deeply.

Grilled Free-Form Beef Wellington with Balsamic Reduction

| SERVES 4 |

½ cup **balsamic vinegar**

3 (8-ounce) **filets mignons,**
about 2 inches thick

4 large
portobello mushroom caps,
about 4 inches in diameter

2 tablespoons **olive oil**

4 thick slices
rustic or country bread

4 ounces **smooth duck liver pâté**

INGREDIENT SPOTLIGHT
BALSAMIC VINEGAR

True balsamic vinegar is made in just two provinces of Emilia-Romagna, Italy, sold in an official bottle, and labeled with the word *tradizionale*—and is very expensive. Fortunately, we found an affordable, and flavorful, balsamic vinegar at the supermarket that we liked both on its own and in prepared dishes. **Lucini Gran Riserva Balsamico** offers a "nice compromise between sweet and tangy" and has a "sweet, nuanced flavor."

✔ **WHY THIS RECIPE WORKS** For a streamlined, modern-day twist on beef Wellington, that classic combination of tender meat, sautéed mushrooms, and rich pâté wrapped in flaky puff pastry, we decided to not only pare back the ingredient list, but also move the cooking outside. First, we grilled our filets mignons and mushrooms, then sliced them thinly. Before layering them on thick pieces of grilled country bread—our answer to puff pastry—we applied a thin coating of duck liver pâté. Reduced balsamic vinegar, drizzled over each beef Wellington, was the perfect finishing touch. We found that three steaks was ample for serving four. See page 100 for our meat doneness guidelines.

1. Simmer vinegar in small saucepan over medium heat until reduced to 3 tablespoons, about 5 minutes; transfer to bowl. Trim steaks, pat steaks and mushrooms dry with paper towels, brush with oil, and season with salt and pepper.

2A. FOR A CHARCOAL GRILL: Open bottom vent completely. Light large chimney starter filled with charcoal briquettes (6 quarts). When top coals are partially covered with ash, pour two-thirds evenly over grill, then pour remaining one-third over half of grill. Set cooking grate in place, cover, and open lid vent completely. Heat grill until hot, about 5 minutes.

2B. FOR A GAS GRILL: Turn all burners to high, cover, and heat grill until hot, about 15 minutes. Leave primary burner on high and turn other burner(s) to medium.

3. Clean and oil cooking grate. Place steaks on hotter side of grill and cook (covered if using gas) until well browned on first side, 2 to 3 minutes. Slide steaks to cooler side of grill and cook, turning as needed, until meat registers 120 to 125 degrees (for medium-rare), 5 to 9 minutes. Transfer steaks to carving board, tent with aluminum foil, and let rest while grilling mushrooms and bread.

4. Place mushrooms on hotter side of grill. Cook, turning once, until tender and lightly browned, 8 to 10 minutes; transfer to platter. Place bread slices on cooler side of grill until golden brown on both sides, 1 to 1½ minutes; transfer to platter.

5. Spread pâté over grilled bread. Slice mushrooms; lay on top of pâté. Slice steaks ¼ inch thick and lay on top of portobellos. Drizzle with reduced balsamic vinegar and serve.

Grilled Italian Sausages and Polenta with Pepper Relish

SERVES 4 TO 6

3 **red bell peppers**

1 (18-ounce) tube
precooked polenta

3 tablespoons
extra-virgin olive oil

1½ pounds
sweet or hot Italian sausage links

Fresh parsley

2 tablespoons **balsamic vinegar**

**INGREDIENT SPOTLIGHT
PRECOOKED POLENTA**

Available in supermarkets everywhere, these tubes of shelf-stable precooked polenta are handy to have in your pantry. You can cut them into rounds and grill or broil them for an easy, unexpected side dish. Before using, we found it important to brush the polenta with oil to prevent it from sticking. Also, some brands may be saltier than others; be sure to taste yours before seasoning with salt.

✓ **WHY THIS RECIPE WORKS** Grilled sausages and peppers are a time-honored combination, but they're usually destined for a crusty roll at a street fair or tailgating party. To elevate this duo from casual to classy, we opted to pair them with polenta. While often cooked into a creamy porridge, this Italian staple is also available precooked in shelf-stable rolls. Sliced into rounds and brushed with extra-virgin olive oil, the polenta grilled up nicely—crunchy on the outside and creamy on the inside. The flavors and textures were working, but tasters thought the dish lacked cohesion. To bring everything together, we chopped our grilled peppers and tossed them with fresh parsley and balsamic vinegar for a quick, piquant relish that stood up to the spicy sausage and enlivened the milder polenta. Liberally pricking the sausages with a fork prior to cooking ensures that they won't burst open. Handle the polenta minimally once it is on the grill; to avoid sticking, let the polenta char lightly before trying to turn it, and use a thin spatula.

1. Core and flatten bell peppers (see page 201). Slice polenta into ½-inch-thick rounds, brush with 1 tablespoon oil, and season with salt and pepper. Prick sausages all over with fork.

2A. FOR A CHARCOAL GRILL: Open bottom vent completely. Light large chimney starter filled with charcoal briquettes (6 quarts). When top coals are partially covered with ash, pour evenly over grill. Set cooking grate in place, cover, and open lid vent completely. Heat grill until hot, about 5 minutes.

2B. FOR A GAS GRILL: Turn all burners to high, cover, and heat grill until hot, about 15 minutes. Leave all burners on high.

3. Clean and oil cooking grate. Place sausages, bell peppers, and polenta on grill. Cook (covered if using gas), turning as needed, until sausages and polenta are lightly charred on all sides and sausages are no longer pink in center, 6 to 10 minutes. (Handle polenta gently to avoid breaking.) Transfer sausages and polenta to platter. Continue to cook bell peppers until softened and lightly charred, 4 to 6 minutes longer; transfer to platter.

4. Cut bell peppers into ¼-inch pieces and mince 1 tablespoon parsley; combine in bowl with remaining 2 tablespoons oil and vinegar. Season bell peppers with salt and pepper to taste and serve with sausages and polenta.

Grilled Spice-Rubbed Pork Tenderloin with Peaches

SERVES 4

2 tablespoons packed **brown sugar**

2 teaspoons **smoked paprika**

¼ teaspoon **ground allspice**

2 (1-pound) **pork tenderloins**

1 tablespoon **vegetable oil**

4 **peaches**

INGREDIENT SPOTLIGHT
SMOKED PAPRIKA

Paprika is a generic term for a spice made from ground dried red peppers. Smoked paprika, a Spanish favorite, is made by drying red peppers over an oak fire. It has a distinctive rich and smoky taste. Smoked paprika comes in three varieties: sweet (*dulce*), bittersweet or medium hot (*agridulce*), and hot (*picante*). For this recipe, we prefer the sweet kind.

✓ **WHY THIS RECIPE WORKS** Pork tenderloin is known for its tender texture, but when it comes to flavor, this ultralean cut comes up short. For a quick fix, we decided a flavor-packed spice rub that enhanced, but didn't overpower, the mild-tasting meat was in order. Most rubs utilize several different spices, but we had to narrow ours down to just two or three. We liked the flavor and crust promoted by brown sugar, but we needed a savory element to add flavor and identity. Chili powder was promising, but we preferred the smoky sweetness imbued by smoked paprika. A small amount of allspice added warm notes. To round out our dish and play up the mild, sweet flavor of the pork, we tossed a few peaches on the grill as well. After splitting them in half and pitting them, we sprinkled them with brown sugar, which ensured nice caramelization once they hit the hot grate.

1. Mix 1 tablespoon sugar, paprika, allspice, 1 teaspoon salt, and 1 teaspoon pepper together in bowl. Trim pork, pat dry with paper towels, rub with 1 teaspoon oil, and coat evenly with spice mixture. Halve and pit peaches, then brush with remaining 2 teaspoons oil and sprinkle cut sides with remaining 1 tablespoon sugar, salt, and pepper.

2A. FOR A CHARCOAL GRILL: Open bottom vent completely. Light large chimney starter three-quarters filled with charcoal briquettes (4½ quarts). When top coals are partially covered with ash, pour evenly over grill. Set cooking grate in place, cover, and open lid vent completely. Heat grill until hot, about 5 minutes.

2B. FOR A GAS GRILL: Turn all burners to high, cover, and heat grill until hot, about 15 minutes. Turn all burners to medium-high.

3. Clean and oil cooking grate. Place pork on grill and cook (covered if using gas), turning as needed, until browned on all sides and pork registers 145 degrees, 12 to 15 minutes. Transfer pork to carving board, tent with aluminum foil, and let rest while grilling peaches.

4. Place peaches, cut side down, on grill and cook until well caramelized, 3 to 4 minutes. Flip peaches, cut side up, and continue to cook until they are slightly softened, about 3 minutes longer; transfer to platter. Cut pork into ½-inch-thick slices and serve with peaches.

Smoked Double-Thick Pork Chops with Cranberry-Thyme Applesauce

SERVES 6 TO 8

4 (1¼- to 1½-pound)
bone-in blade-cut pork chops,
about 2 inches thick

¼ cup **sugar,**
plus extra as needed

4 pounds
**Jonagold, Jonathan, Pink Lady,
or Macoun apples**

Fresh thyme

1 cup **dried cranberries**

2 tablespoons **unsalted butter**

INGREDIENT SPOTLIGHT
APPLES FOR APPLESAUCE

We tested 18 apple varieties to find the best ones for our applesauce. The flavor of the apples, more than their texture or color, influenced our judgment. Our favorites were Jonagold (shown), Jonathan, Pink Lady, and Macoun; all four varieties produced a sauce with a pleasing balance of tart and sweet.

✓ WHY THIS RECIPE WORKS Smoking pork chops on the grill gives them an intensely flavored crust that contrasts nicely with the tender, juicy meat. Starting our chops on the cooler side of the grill allowed them to cook through gently, while finishing them on the hotter side ensured they had a well-browned exterior. To complete our pork chop dinner, we made a rustic, hearty applesauce with sweet-tart dried cranberries. If your chops are less than 2 inches thick, the cooking time will be shorter.

1. Soak 2 cups wood chips in water for 15 minutes; drain. Using large piece of heavy-duty aluminum foil, wrap soaked chips in foil packet, and cut several vent holes in top. Trim pork chops, dry with paper towels, and sprinkle with 1 tablespoon sugar.

2A. FOR A CHARCOAL GRILL: Open bottom vent halfway. Light large chimney starter filled with charcoal briquettes (6 quarts). When top coals are partially covered with ash, pour evenly over half of grill. Place wood chip packet on coals. Set cooking grate in place, cover, and open lid vent halfway. Heat grill until hot and wood chips are smoking, about 5 minutes.

2B. FOR A GAS GRILL: Place wood chip packet over primary burner. Turn all burners to high, cover, and heat grill until hot and wood chips are smoking, about 15 minutes. Leave primary burner on high and turn off other burner(s). (Adjust burners as needed to maintain grill temperature of 350 degrees.)

3. Clean and oil cooking grate. Place pork chops on cooler side of grill, with bone sides facing hotter side of grill. Cover (positioning lid vent over pork if using charcoal) and cook until pork registers 140 degrees, 50 to 60 minutes. Slide pork chops to hotter side of grill and cook, turning as needed, until well browned on both sides, about 4 minutes. Transfer pork chops to platter, tent with aluminum foil, and let rest until meat reaches 150 degrees, about 15 minutes.

4. Meanwhile, peel, core, and chop apples into 1½-inch pieces and mince 1 tablespoon thyme; combine with cranberries, 1 cup water, remaining 3 tablespoons sugar, and ½ teaspoon salt in Dutch oven. Cover and cook over medium heat until apples begin to break down and cranberries soften, 15 to 20 minutes. Off heat, mash apples with potato masher, stir in butter, and season with extra sugar and salt to taste. Cut pork off bones, cut crosswise into ½-inch-thick slices, and serve with applesauce.

Grilled Lamb Chops with Shaved Zucchini Salad

SERVES 4

1 pound **zucchini**

1 **lemon**

Fresh mint or basil

¼ cup **extra-virgin olive oil**

Shaved **Parmesan cheese**

8 (4-ounce)
lamb rib or loin chops,
¾ to 1 inch thick

INGREDIENT SPOTLIGHT
LAMB CHOPS

When shopping for lamb chops, look for those that come from the rib area or loin, but avoid shoulder chops—they can be tough and are best braised or cut off the bone and used in stews. In a rib chop (shown), the bone runs along the edge, with all the meat on one side; we find the rib chop to be juicier and more flavorful than the loin chop. A loin chop looks like a T-bone steak, with the bone running down the center and meat on either side.

☑ **WHY THIS RECIPE WORKS** We usually reserve leg of lamb for special occasions, when we have time to monitor the oven. For an easy weeknight dinner, we turn to quick-cooking chops. To keep our chops moist, we grilled them for just a few minutes. A simple zucchini salad, seasoned with lemon juice and mint, paired nicely with the rich meat. Slicing the zucchini into ribbons gave us tender pieces that didn't need any cooking. A drizzle of extra-virgin olive oil and shaved Parmesan rounded out this simple salad. Look for small zucchini, which are younger and have thinner skins. You can shave the zucchini into ribbons using either a mandoline or a vegetable peeler. See page 100 for our meat doneness guidelines.

1. Using vegetable peeler, shave zucchini into thin ribbons. Season with salt and pepper; arrange on platter. Squeeze lemon for 1 tablespoon juice and chop 2 tablespoons mint; sprinkle over zucchini with 3 tablespoons oil and Parmesan. Trim chops, pat dry with paper towels, rub with remaining 1 tablespoon oil, and season with salt and pepper.

2A. FOR A CHARCOAL GRILL: Open bottom vent completely. Light large chimney starter filled with charcoal briquettes (6 quarts). When top coals are partially covered with ash, pour evenly over grill. Set cooking grate in place, cover, and open lid vent completely. Heat grill until hot, about 5 minutes.

2B. FOR A GAS GRILL: Turn all burners to high, cover, and heat grill until hot, about 15 minutes. Leave all burners on high.

3. Clean and oil cooking grate. Place lamb chops on grill and cook (covered if using gas) until well browned on both sides and meat registers 120 to 125 degrees (for medium-rare), 2 to 4 minutes per side. Transfer chops to platter, tent with aluminum foil, and let rest for 5 to 10 minutes. Serve with zucchini salad.

TEST KITCHEN TIP
MAKING ZUCCHINI RIBBONS

Using vegetable peeler or mandoline, slice zucchini lengthwise into very thin ribbons.

Grilled Scallops with Fennel and Orange Salad

SERVES 4
2 **oranges**
Fresh mint
¼ cup **olive oil**
2 **fennel bulbs**
4 teaspoons **pink peppercorns**
16 **large sea scallops**
(1 pound)

INGREDIENT SPOTLIGHT
PINK PEPPERCORNS

Not a true peppercorn, this spice is the dried berry from the *Baies* rose plant. These berries hail from Madagascar and are pungent and floral in flavor, with a distinctly sweet aftertaste. Although they are typically sold whole, they can be ground and used in much the same way as true peppercorns.

✔ WHY THIS RECIPE WORKS Grilled scallops need little embellishment—their sweet, briny richness becomes even more intense on a hot grill, and their exterior develops a flavorful, nicely charred crust. With just a bit of oil, salt, and pepper, plus a sprinkling of ground pink peppercorns for color and fruity flavor, our scallops were ready for the grate. To turn our tender scallops into a satisfying supper, we created a simple salad to go with them. The trio of grilled fennel, orange pieces, and chopped mint kept our dish bright and fresh-tasting. A quick stint in the microwave helped soften the fennel so it didn't need too long on the grill. You will need four 12-inch metal skewers for this recipe.

1. Cut away peel and pith from oranges, then quarter fruit and cut into ¼-inch-thick pieces. Chop 2 tablespoons mint; combine with oranges and 1 tablespoon oil in bowl and set aside. Trim fennel bulb, discarding stalks, and cut vertically into ¼-inch-thick slices. Toss fennel with 2 tablespoons oil in bowl, season with salt, cover, and microwave until softened, about 6 minutes, tossing halfway through cooking; drain well.

2. Crush pink peppercorns in zipper-lock bag with meat pounder. Remove and discard tendons from scallops (see page 164), pat dry with paper towels, and thread onto four 12-inch metal skewers. Brush skewers with remaining 1 tablespoon oil and season with pink peppercorns, salt, and pepper.

3A. FOR A CHARCOAL GRILL: Open bottom vent completely. Light large chimney starter mounded with charcoal briquettes (7 quarts). When top coals are partially covered with ash, pour evenly over grill. Set cooking grate in place, cover, and open lid vent completely. Heat grill until hot, about 5 minutes.

3B. FOR A GAS GRILL: Turn all burners to high, cover, and heat grill until hot, about 15 minutes. Leave all burners on high.

4. Clean and oil cooking grate. Place scallop skewers and fennel on grill. Cook (covered if using gas), turning as needed, until lightly charred and cooked through, about 6 minutes for scallops and 8 minutes for fennel; transfer to platter and tent with aluminum foil.

5. Chop fennel into 1-inch pieces, discarding cores; gently stir into orange mixture. Season with salt and pepper to taste. Serve with scallops.

Maryland-Style Grilled Shrimp and Corn

SERVES 4

1 pound **small red potatoes**

4 ears **corn**

8 tablespoons **unsalted butter**

1 tablespoon **Old Bay seasoning**

1½ pounds **extra-large shrimp**
(21 to 25 per pound)

Fresh parsley

INGREDIENT SPOTLIGHT
OLD BAY SEASONING

Old Bay seasoning is a spice mix that's essential for many shrimp and crab dishes. Created in the 1940s, this spice mix is a regional favorite in Maryland and Virginia along the coast. The predominant flavors in Old Bay are celery, mustard, and paprika. At your local supermarket, you can find it in the spice aisle or near the seafood department; many fish markets carry it as well.

✓ **WHY THIS RECIPE WORKS** Shrimp are often grilled in their shells to protect their delicate flesh, but this means you have to remove the shells before eating—a task that can be messy. For easier access to our grilled shrimp, we peeled them first, then crowded the shrimp onto skewers to prevent them from overcooking. A very hot fire ensured they were cooked to perfection in just minutes. We took advantage of the rest of the space on the grate to grill corn, and since we seemed to be on our way to a seaside supper, we combined butter and Old Bay seasoning for a flavor-packed sauce. To complete our Chesapeake-inspired meal, we microwaved tender red potatoes and then tossed everything into our buttery sauce. We prefer to use extra-large shrimp (21 to 25 per pound) for this recipe; if your shrimp are smaller or larger, they will have slightly different cooking times. We prefer potatoes no larger than 2 inches in length here to ensure that they cook evenly. You will need four 12-inch metal skewers for this recipe.

1. Halve potatoes, combine with 1 tablespoon water in bowl, cover, and microwave until potatoes are tender, 5 to 7 minutes; keep warm. Remove husks and silk from corn and halve crosswise. Cook butter and Old Bay together in medium saucepan over medium heat until butter melts, about 2 minutes.

2. Peel and devein shrimp (see page 37), pat dry with paper towels, and toss with 1 tablespoon butter mixture. Thread shrimp onto four 12-inch metal skewers, alternating direction of heads and tails.

3A. FOR A CHARCOAL GRILL: Open bottom vent completely. Light large chimney starter mounded with charcoal briquettes (7 quarts). When top coals are partially covered with ash, pour evenly over grill. Set cooking grate in place, cover, and open lid vent completely. Heat grill until hot, about 5 minutes.

3B. FOR A GAS GRILL: Turn all burners to high, cover, and heat grill until hot, about 15 minutes. Leave all burners on high.

4. Clean and oil cooking grate. Place shrimp skewers and corn on grill. Cook (covered if using gas), turning as needed, until lightly charred and cooked through, about 6 minutes for shrimp and 8 minutes for corn; transfer to platter and tent with aluminum foil.

5. Toss shrimp, corn, and potatoes with remaining melted butter; arrange on platter. Mince 2 tablespoons parsley, sprinkle over top, and serve.

Grill-Smoked Salmon with Creamy Cucumber-Dill Salad

SERVES 6

6 (6- to 8-ounce)
center-cut skin-on salmon fillets

2 tablespoons **sugar**

3 **cucumbers**

Fresh dill

1 cup whole or 2 percent
plain Greek yogurt

3 tablespoons **rice vinegar**

INGREDIENT SPOTLIGHT CUCUMBERS

At the supermarket, you'll see standard American cucumbers and long, skinny, seedless cucumbers (though they do contain small seeds), which are also sold as English or European cucumbers. Is one better than the other? In taste tests, we've found that American cucumbers have a crisper texture and more concentrated cucumber flavor than the seedless variety, which is much milder and more watery. However, the American cucumbers have a tougher skin due to a food-safe wax coating (seedless cucumbers are wrapped in plastic). In general, we prefer the American cucumbers, even though they do require peeling and seeding, in salads, as they hold up much better to dressings and vinaigrettes and retain their crispness.

WHY THIS RECIPE WORKS Wanting to take simple grilled salmon up a notch, we decided to grill-smoke our fillets. Quick-curing the fish with a mixture of salt and sugar worked to draw moisture from the flesh and help firm it up, and also ensured it was well seasoned inside and out. Cooking the fish indirectly over a gentle fire with ample smoke produced salmon that was sweet, smoky, and tender. To complement the salmon and cut its richness, we added a creamy cucumber salad flavored with fresh dill and rice vinegar. Using Greek yogurt for the dressing gave our salad a tangy flavor and nice richness.

1. Lay salmon on wire rack set in rimmed baking sheet. Combine sugar and 1 tablespoon kosher salt and sprinkle over salmon flesh. Refrigerate, uncovered, for 1 hour. Using paper towels, brush excess salt and sugar off salmon; keep refrigerated.

2. Peel cucumbers, halve lengthwise, remove seeds, and slice ¼ inch thick; toss with ½ teaspoon salt and drain in colander for 15 minutes. Chop ¼ cup dill; combine with yogurt and vinegar in bowl. Stir in drained cucumbers and season with salt and pepper.

3. Soak 1 cups wood chips in water for 15 minutes; drain and toss with 1 cup unsoaked chips. Using large piece of heavy-duty aluminum foil, wrap chips in foil packet; cut several vent holes in top.

4A. FOR A CHARCOAL GRILL: Open bottom vent halfway. Light large chimney starter one-third filled with charcoal briquettes (2 quarts). When top coals are partially covered with ash, pour into steeply banked pile against side of grill. Place wood chip packet on coals. Set cooking grate in place, cover, and open lid vent halfway. Heat grill until hot and wood chips are smoking, about 5 minutes.

4B. FOR A GAS GRILL: Place wood chip packet over primary burner. Turn primary burner to high (leave other burners off), cover, and heat grill until hot and wood chips begin to smoke, 15 to 25 minutes. Turn primary burner to medium. (Adjust primary burner as needed to maintain grill temperature of 275 to 300 degrees.)

5. Clean and oil cooking grate. Fold piece of foil into 18 by 6-inch rectangle and place on cooler side of grill. Place salmon fillets on foil, spaced ½ inch apart. Cover grill (positioning lid vent over fish if using charcoal) and cook until flesh flakes apart when gently prodded with paring knife and registers 125 degrees (for medium-rare), 30 to 40 minutes. Transfer to platter; serve with cucumber salad.

Grilled Red Curry Mahi-Mahi with Pineapple Salsa

SERVES 4

12 ounces
fresh peeled and cored pineapple

1 **scallion**

Fresh cilantro

1 tablespoon **vegetable oil**

4 (6-ounce)
skin-on mahi-mahi fillets,
1 to 1½ inches thick

1 tablespoon **red curry paste**

INGREDIENT SPOTLIGHT PINEAPPLE

When it comes to pineapple, we prefer Costa Rican–grown pineapples, also labeled "extra-sweet" or "gold." We find this fruit to be consistently "honey-sweet" in comparison to the "acidic" Hawaiian pineapples with greenish, not yellow, skin. Pineapples will not ripen further once picked, so be sure to purchase golden, fragrant fruit that gives slightly when pressed. Unpeeled pineapples should be stored at room temperature.

WHY THIS RECIPE WORKS Mahi-mahi boasts a hearty, meaty texture that makes it a great candidate for the grill, plus the flavorful char contributes rich, smoky notes to this mild-tasting fish. To give ours even more flavor, we coated it with a thin layer of red curry paste before tossing it on the hot grate. Now all we needed was an exotic fruit salsa to sweeten things up. Pineapple, cut into small pieces and combined with a sliced scallion and minced cilantro, gave us a sweet but still bright and zingy salsa. We prefer the flavor of red curry paste here (see page 53 for more information), but you can substitute green curry paste if you prefer.

1. Cut pineapple into ¼-inch pieces, slice scallion thinly, and mince 1 tablespoon cilantro; combine in bowl with 1 teaspoon oil, season with salt and pepper to taste, and set aside for serving. Pat fish dry with paper towels. Combine curry paste with remaining 2 teaspoons oil and brush over flesh of fish.

2A. FOR A CHARCOAL GRILL: Open bottom vent completely. Light large chimney starter filled with charcoal briquettes (6 quarts). When top coals are partially covered with ash, pour evenly over grill. Set cooking grate in place, cover, and open lid vent completely. Heat grill until hot, about 5 minutes.

2B. FOR A GAS GRILL: Turn all burners to high, cover, and heat grill until hot, about 15 minutes. Leave all burners on high.

3. Clean and oil cooking grate. Place fish, skin side up, on grill. Cook (covered if using gas) until well browned, about 3 minutes. Gently flip fish over and continue to grill until flesh flakes apart when gently prodded with paring knife and registers 140 degrees, 3 to 8 minutes longer. Transfer fish to platter and serve with pineapple relish.

TEST KITCHEN TIP
OILING A GRILL GRATE

To prevent fish from sticking to the grill, rub the grill grates with paper towels dipped in vegetable oil until they look dark and glossy, about 10 times. This should be done just before cooking, after the grill has been heated and cleaned.

Grilled Swordfish Skewers with Basil Oil

SERVES 4
3 **lemons**
1 large **red onion**
1 (1½-pound) **skinless swordfish steak**
4 teaspoons **ground coriander**
¼ cup **extra-virgin olive oil**
Fresh basil

INGREDIENT SPOTLIGHT CORIANDER

This light brown spherical seed is the dried fruit of the herb cilantro, a member of the parsley family. Coriander possesses a sweet, almost fruity flavor with just a hint of the distinctive character of mature cilantro. Ground coriander works well in spice crusts for meat and fish, while whole seeds can be used for pickling.

WHY THIS RECIPE WORKS Swordfish has a robust taste all its own and needs co-starring ingredients with just as much oomph. For these skewers, we paired our swordfish with big pieces of red onion and chunks of lemon. Once grilled, the onion pieces softened slightly yet retained some texture, and the lemon flavor went from tart and acidic to intensely sweet and rich. A simple basil oil, brushed over our skewers once they came off the grill, complemented the bright lemon flavor. Tossing the swordfish in a bit of ground coriander added complexity and provided a base of flavor that popped with the lemon and basil. We like the flavor of swordfish here but you can substitute other sturdy, firm-fleshed fish such as mahi-mahi or halibut. You will need four 12-inch metal skewers for this recipe.

1. Halve lemons crosswise, then quarter each half. Cut onion into 1-inch squares. Pat fish dry with paper towels, and cut into 1¼-inch pieces. Rub fish with coriander and season with salt and pepper. Thread fish, lemons, and onion evenly onto four 12-inch metal skewers, in alternating pattern. Brush skewers with 1 tablespoon oil.

2A. FOR A CHARCOAL GRILL: Open bottom vent completely. Light large chimney starter three-quarters filled with charcoal briquettes (4½ quarts). When top coals are partially covered with ash, pour evenly over grill. Set cooking grate in place, cover, and open lid vent completely. Heat grill until hot, about 5 minutes.

2B. FOR A GAS GRILL: Turn all burners to high, cover, and heat grill until hot, about 15 minutes. Turn all burners to medium-high.

3. Clean and oil cooking grate. Place skewers on grill and cook (covered if using gas), turning as needed, until fish is opaque and flakes apart when gently prodded with paring knife, 5 to 8 minutes.

4. Transfer skewers to platter, tent with aluminum foil, and let rest for 5 to 10 minutes. Chop 2 tablespoons basil; combine with remaining 3 tablespoons oil and season with salt and pepper to taste. Brush skewers with basil oil before serving.

NUTELLA TART

No-Fuss Desserts

283   Speedy Trifle with Cookies and Berries | FAST RECIPE

284   Fresh Berry and Croissant Gratins | FAST RECIPE

285   Apple Turnovers

286   French Caramel Apple Tart

288   Lemon Tart

289   Nutella Tart

290   Chocolate Pots de Crème

293   Chocolate Mousse Parfaits | FAST RECIPE

295   No-Bake Rocky Road Bars

296   Pound Cake

297   Easy Chocolate-Nut Torte

299   Caramel Turtle Ice Cream Pie

Speedy Trifle with Cookies and Berries

SERVES 8

8 ounces (1 cup)
mascarpone cheese

½ cup (3½ ounces) **sugar**

1 teaspoon **vanilla extract**

2 cups **heavy cream,**
chilled

30 ounces (6 cups)
**blackberries, blueberries,
raspberries, and/or hulled and
quartered strawberries**

12 ounces **gingersnap cookies**

**INGREDIENT SPOTLIGHT
MASCARPONE CHEESE**

This rich and velvety Italian-style cream cheese is essentially a soft triple-crème cheese made from fresh cream and thickened with an acid; it has a texture similar to clotted cream. Best known for its role in the popular Italian dessert tiramisù, mascarpone is also often simply served with fruit. Though once a hard-to-find item, this Italian cheese can be found in just about every supermarket these days in a small, round tub near the specialty cheeses.

TO MAKE AHEAD
Trifle can be assembled and refrigerated for up to 4 hours before serving.

✓ WHY THIS RECIPE WORKS To update and streamline the classic British trifle, a layered dessert composed of sponge cake, fresh fruit, custard, and jam, we started by ditching the homemade cake. Fortunately, we discovered that crumbled store-bought cookies were a great substitute and ready to use right out of the box. We experimented with different varieties and preferred the crisp texture and subtly spiced flavor of gingersnaps. For a simple, no-cook custardlike filling, we whipped together mascarpone cheese with heavy cream; a bit of sugar sweetened the mixture. Juicy fresh berries provided enough sweetness in our trifle that we didn't need any jam. This modern-day take on trifle delivered the rich, creamy filling and bright, fruity bites of the classic version—but with a lot less effort. You can substitute an equal amount of amaretti cookies or chocolate wafer cookies for the gingersnaps. You can use any combination of berries here; just be sure to have 30 ounces of fruit in total. Do not use frozen berries.

1. Using stand mixer fitted with whisk, whip mascarpone, sugar, vanilla, and ⅛ teaspoon salt together on medium-high speed until smooth, about 1 minute, scraping down bowl as needed. Reduce speed to low and gradually add cream until combined. Increase speed to medium-high and whip until stiff peaks form, about 2 minutes.

2. Measure out and reserve ½ cup mascarpone mixture for garnish. Gently toss berries together. Crumble gingersnap cookies.

3. Arrange 2 cups berries in bottom of 14- to 16-cup trifle bowl. Spread half of remaining mascarpone mixture evenly over top, then sprinkle with half of crumbled cookies. Repeat with 2 cups berries, remaining mascarpone mixture, and remaining crumbled cookies. Sprinkle remaining 2 cups berries over top. Dollop reserved mascarpone mixture attractively on top and serve.

Fresh Berry and Croissant Gratins

SERVES 8

2 tablespoons **unsalted butter**

3 plain **croissants**

⅓ cup packed (2⅓ ounces)
brown sugar

Pinch **ground cinnamon**

30 ounces (6 cups)
**blackberries, blueberries,
raspberries, and/or hulled and
quartered strawberries**

1 tablespoon
kirsch or other eau de vie
(optional)

INGREDIENT SPOTLIGHT
BROWN SUGAR

Brown sugar is essentially white
sugar that has been flavored with
molasses. Dark brown sugar contains
more molasses than light brown
sugar, so it has a darker color and
slightly stronger flavor. If your brown
sugar has hardened, spread it out
onto a pie plate and heat it gently
in a 250-degree oven until softened,
about 5 minutes, then break apart
with a fork and let cool before using.

TO MAKE AHEAD

Gratins can be assembled and held at
room temperature for up to 4 hours
before baking.

✓ WHY THIS RECIPE WORKS Quicker and dressier than a crisp,
a gratin is a layer of fresh fruit piled into a shallow baking dish and
dressed up with sweetened bread crumbs. In the oven, the topping
browns and the fruit is warmed just enough to release a bit of juice.
We wanted to find the quickest, easiest route to this pleasing dessert. For the topping, we borrowed a page from the French, grinding
croissants with sugar, cinnamon, and butter in the food processor;
the croissants contributed more richness and buttery flavor than
the usual bread crumbs. Using brown sugar instead of granulated
sugar added extra flavor and a small splash of kirsch enhanced the
fruity flavor of our filling. Either light or dark brown sugar will work
here. You can use any combination of berries here; just be sure to
have 30 ounces of fruit in total. Do not use frozen berries. You will
need eight 6-ounce ramekins for this recipe.

1. Adjust oven rack to lower–middle position and heat oven to
400 degrees. Soften butter and tear croissants into quarters. Pulse
butter, croissants, ¼ cup sugar, and cinnamon in food processor
until mixture resembles coarse crumbs, about 10 pulses.

2. Gently toss berries with remaining sugar, pinch salt, and kirsch,
if using, in bowl. Divide mixture evenly among eight 6-ounce
ramekins. Place ramekins on rimmed baking sheet and sprinkle
evenly with croissant crumbs.

3. Bake gratins until crumbs are deep golden brown and fruit is
hot, 15 to 20 minutes. Cool for 5 minutes before serving.

TEST KITCHEN TIP
MAKING CROISSANT CRUMBS

Pulse croissants, butter, brown
sugar, and salt together in food
processor until combined and
crumbs have a coarse tex-
ture, about 10 pulses. Do not
overprocess.

Apple Turnovers

MAKES 8

2 **Granny Smith apples**

1 **lemon**

¾ cup (5¼ ounces) **sugar**

1 teaspoon **ground cinnamon**

½ cup **applesauce**

2 (9½ by 9-inch) sheets
puff pastry, thawed

INGREDIENT SPOTLIGHT
GRANNY SMITH APPLES

Granny Smith apples are a relative newcomer to the American apple orchard, and have only been cultivated on U.S. soil since 1972. Since then, however, they have become a staple in our supermarkets. Here in the test kitchen, they're one of our top picks for baking; they have a sturdy texture that holds up well in the oven and a strong, tart flavor that stands up to the sugar and butter in desserts.

TO MAKE AHEAD
Turnovers can be assembled, chilled, and topped with cinnamon sugar, then allowed to freeze completely on baking sheet; transfer to zipper-lock freezer bag and freeze for up to 1 month. To bake, let turnovers sit at room temperature for 20 minutes, then bake as directed.

✓ **WHY THIS RECIPE WORKS** For a no-fuss take on apple turnovers, we skipped the from-scratch puff pastry and finicky filling. Frozen puff pastry dough, which we thawed and rolled out into squares, gave us the light, flaky, buttery pastry layers we were after. Chopped Granny Smith apples and applesauce delivered complex apple flavor, and processing the apples with sugar and draining them first removed excess liquid that would have made the crust soggy. For more flavor, we brushed our turnovers with the drained apple juices and sprinkled them with cinnamon sugar. If you don't have a food processor, you can grate the apples on the coarse side of a box grater before mixing them with the lemon juice, sugar, and salt. To thaw frozen puff pastry, allow it to sit either in the refrigerator for 24 hours or on the counter for 30 minutes to 1 hour. If the dough becomes too warm and sticky to work with, cover it with plastic wrap and chill in the refrigerator until firm.

1. Adjust oven rack to middle position and heat oven to 400 degrees. Peel, core, and coarsely chop apples. Squeeze lemon for 1 tablespoon juice. Combine ¼ cup sugar and cinnamon in bowl.

2. Pulse apples, lemon juice, remaining ½ cup sugar, and ⅛ teaspoon salt together in food processor until apples are no larger than ½ inch, about 6 pulses. Let mixture sit for 5 minutes, then drain through fine-mesh strainer, reserving juices. Combine drained apples and applesauce in bowl.

3. Working with 1 sheet pastry at a time, roll into 10-inch square on lightly floured counter, then cut into four 5-inch squares. Mound 2 tablespoons apple mixture in center of each square and brush edges with reserved juice. Fold dough over apple filling into triangle-shaped turnovers and crimp edges with fork to seal. Place turnovers on baking sheet and freeze until firm, about 15 minutes. Once chilled, brush tops with more reserved juice and sprinkle with cinnamon sugar.

4. Transfer turnovers to parchment paper–lined baking sheet and bake until well browned, 20 to 26 minutes, rotating sheet halfway through baking. Let cool slightly before serving. Serve warm or at room temperature.

French Caramel Apple Tart

SERVES 6

1 (9-inch) round store-bought **pie dough**

2 pounds **Granny Smith apples**

¾ cup **caramel sauce**

1 teaspoon **vanilla extract**

½ teaspoon **garam masala**

4 cups (2 pints) **vanilla ice cream**

INGREDIENT SPOTLIGHT
GARAM MASALA

Garam masala comes in many variations but consistently includes black pepper, cinnamon, coriander, cardamom, and dried chiles; it may also have cumin, cloves, fennel, mace, or nutmeg. It's commonly used in curries and stews, but we found it also added warm spice notes and complexity to our French Caramel Apple Tart. Our favorite brand is **McCormick Gourmet Collection Garam Masala**, which tasters praised for its "mellow," "well-balanced" aroma.

TO MAKE AHEAD
Baked and cooled tart can be held at room temperature for up to 8 hours before serving.

✔ **WHY THIS RECIPE WORKS** For an impressive yet effortless French apple tart, we started with two supermarket staples: store-bought pie dough and jarred caramel sauce. The pie dough gave us a light, flaky tart shell, while the caramel sauce provided a sweet, glazy coating for our apple slices. For complexity, we added a bit of vanilla, plus a rather unexpected ingredient: garam masala. Microwaving the apples drove off moisture that would have made the bottom of the crust soggy. Glazing our baked tart with more caramel gave it an elegant shine, and vanilla ice cream made the perfect garnish. Any brand of jarred caramel sauce will work fine here. See page 289 for more information on our favorite pie dough.

1. Adjust oven rack to middle position and heat oven to 375 degrees. Press dough into 9-inch tart pan with removable bottom; push dough down pan sides to rest ¼-inch below rim (see page 288). Place tart pan on baking sheet and bake until pale golden and just set, 15 to 20 minutes; let cool.

2. Peel and core apples, cut in half, and slice ¼ inch thick. Toss with pinch salt in bowl, cover, and microwave at 50 percent power, stirring occasionally, until beginning to soften, 10 to 12 minutes; drain juice.

3. Starting at edge and working toward center, shingle apples in overlapping rows over tart shell bottom. Repeat with remaining apples in second layer on top of first layer. Microwave ½ cup caramel sauce, vanilla, and garam masala together in bowl until melted, about 20 seconds; pour evenly over apples. Bake until filling is bubbling at edges and topping is golden, about 35 minutes; let cool 30 minutes.

4. Melt 1 tablespoon caramel sauce in microwave, about 10 seconds, then brush over tart; let cool. To serve, remove outer metal ring of tart pan, slide thin metal spatula between tart and pan bottom, and carefully slide tart onto serving platter. Serve with remaining caramel sauce and ice cream.

TEST KITCHEN TIP
MAKING FRENCH APPLE TART

Starting at edge and working toward center, shingle apple slices in overlapping rows over tart shell bottom. Repeat with remaining apples in second layer on top of first layer. Be sure to use any very soft or broken apples in bottom layer.

Lemon Tart

SERVES 8 TO 10

1 (9-inch) round store-bought
pie dough

4 **lemons**

2 **large eggs**
plus 7 **large egg yolks**

1 cup (7 ounces) **sugar**

4 tablespoons **unsalted butter**

3 tablespoons **heavy cream,**
chilled

INGREDIENT SPOTLIGHT LEMONS

Buying good, juicy lemons will save you valuable prep time, especially if you need lots of juice. We found that certain shapes and sizes can give a hint as to the amount of juice inside. Round lemons are slightly juicier than elliptical ones, and bigger lemons yield more juice than smaller ones. But the best way to find the lemons with the most juice is to squeeze while you shop. In our tests, we found that whole lemons that yielded under pressure contained more juice, even when the lemons were nearly identical in size, shape, and weight. Also, before juicing the lemon, roll it back and forth on the counter while pressing on it with your palm to help release the juice from the fruit.

TO MAKE AHEAD

Baked and cooled tart can be held at room temperature for up to 8 hours before serving.

✔ WHY THIS RECIPE WORKS A good lemon tart should have a bright and balanced filling—it shouldn't be too sweet, too cloying, or too thick. After baking store-bought pie dough in a tart pan, we got to work making our own perfectly balanced lemon curd. For just enough sugar to offset the acidity of the lemons, we used 3 parts sugar to 2 parts lemon juice, plus a whopping ¼ cup of lemon zest for a bright, lemony flavor. To achieve a curd that was creamy and dense with a vibrant yellow color, we used a combination of whole eggs and egg yolks. A few pats of butter, whisked in as we cooked the curd over gentle heat, contributed more richness. For a smooth, light texture, we strained the curd, then stirred in heavy cream before pouring the filling into the tart shell and baking it until set. Dust with confectioners' sugar before serving, if desired. See page 289 for more information on our favorite pie dough.

1. Adjust oven rack to middle position and heat oven to 375 degrees. Press dough into 9-inch tart pan with removable bottom; push dough down pan sides until just below rim. Place tart pan on baking sheet and bake until golden and set, 20 to 25 minutes.

2. Grate lemons for ¼ cup zest, then squeeze for ⅔ cup juice. Whisk eggs and egg yolks together in medium saucepan. Whisk in sugar until combined, then whisk in lemon zest and juice and pinch salt. Cut butter into 4 pieces, add to pot, and cook over medium-low heat, stirring constantly, until mixture thickens slightly and registers 170 degrees, about 5 minutes. Immediately pour mixture through fine-mesh strainer into bowl and stir in cream.

3. Pour lemon filling into tart shell and bake until filling is shiny, opaque, and jiggles slightly in very center when shaken, 10 to 15 minutes. Let cool completely, about 1½ hours. To serve, remove outer metal ring of tart pan, slide thin metal spatula between tart and pan bottom, and carefully slide tart onto serving platter.

TEST KITCHEN TIP
MAKING A TART CRUST

Press dough into tart pan, pushing it down pan sides and pulling it across pan bottom until it fits. Continue to push dough down pan sides to desired height as directed in recipe, either just below rim (as shown) or ¼ inch below rim.

Nutella Tart

SERVES 8 TO 10

1 cup **hazelnuts**

1 (9-inch) round store-bought **pie dough**

2 ounces **bittersweet chocolate**

1½ cups **heavy cream**

2 tablespoons **unsalted butter**

1¼ cups **Nutella**

INGREDIENT SPOTLIGHT
STORE-BOUGHT PIE DOUGH

Hands down, homemade pie crust is worth the effort, but we don't always have the time. Enter premade crust—it may not be from scratch, but it's fast and easy. To find the best one on the market, we sampled eight brands, including a mix of frozen and refrigerated doughs. We ate the shells baked plain, in single-crust pumpkin pies, and in double-crust apple pies. One sample clearly outshone the others: **Wholly Wholesome 9-Inch Certified Organic Traditional Bake at Home Rolled Pie Dough**. Tasters found it "subtly sweet," "rich," and "tender." Note that this pie dough is sold frozen and requires 3 hours of defrosting. This is best done on the counter rather than in the refrigerator; you may need to microwave the dough for up to 10 seconds if the center is not fully thawed.

TO MAKE AHEAD
Tart can be refrigerated for up to 24 hours before serving.

✓ **WHY THIS RECIPE WORKS** For an incredibly easy, incredibly irresistible dessert, we started with a flavor-packed base: Nutella. For a dense and velvety filling, we stirred Nutella into a simple ganache made of chocolate and cream. Adding a little butter to the mixture proved important because it ensured the tart was easy to slice once it was chilled. To cook the filling, we turned to the microwave. Using low power and stirring the mixture often was key; when the power was too high, the filling became grainy. A bottom layer of chopped, toasted hazelnuts, sprinkled over our fully baked tart shell (made from store-bought pie dough), contributed more nutty flavor and a nice crunch. Garnishing this easy tart with whole toasted hazelnuts amped up the elegance factor, and adding a dollop of whipped cream helped to cut its richness. Letting the tart chill for a full 1½ hours after assembling is crucial, or else it will not be firm enough to slice.

1. Adjust oven rack to middle position and heat oven to 375 degrees. Toast hazelnuts on rimmed baking sheet until skins begin to blister and crack, 15 to 20 minutes. Wrap warm nuts in dish towel and rub gently to remove skins. Reserve 24 whole nuts for garnish, then chop remaining nuts coarsely.

2. Press dough into 9-inch tart pan with removable bottom; push dough down pan sides until just below rim (see page 288). Place tart pan on baking sheet and bake until golden and set, 20 to 25 minutes. Sprinkle chopped nuts into tart shell.

3. Finely chop chocolate and combine with ½ cup cream, butter, and Nutella in bowl. Cover and microwave at 30 percent power, stirring often, until mixture is smooth and glossy, about 1 minute (do not overheat). Pour warm mixture evenly into tart shell.

4. Refrigerate until filling is just set, about 15 minutes. Arrange reserved whole nuts around edge of tart and continue to refrigerate until filling is firm, about 1½ hours. To serve, remove outer metal ring of tart pan, slide thin metal spatula between tart and pan bottom, and carefully slide tart onto serving platter.

5. Before serving, use stand mixer fitted with whisk to whip remaining 1 cup cream on medium-low speed until foamy, about 1 minute. Increase speed to high and whip until soft peaks form, 1 to 3 minutes. Serve with tart.

Chocolate Pots de Crème

SERVES 6

6 ounces **bittersweet chocolate,** plus extra for garnish

7 **large egg yolks**

⅓ cup plus 2 teaspoons **sugar**

2 cups **heavy cream**

½ cup **whole milk**

1 teaspoon **vanilla extract**

INGREDIENT SPOTLIGHT
BITTERSWEET CHOCOLATE

According to the U.S. Food and Drug Administration, bittersweet chocolate—and semisweet chocolate as well—must contain at least 35 percent cacao (the cocoa solids and cocoa butter from the cacao bean). Looking for the best chocolate to use in our desserts, we gathered 12 brands, each containing around 60 percent cacao, and sampled them raw, in chocolate pots de crème, and baked into brownies. Our top picks were the Belgian **Callebaut Intense Dark Chocolate L-60-40NV**, which was described as being "dark and earthy," and a supermarket staple, **Ghirardelli Bittersweet Chocolate Baking Bar**, which tasters praised for being "creamy, rich, and glossy."

TO MAKE AHEAD
Pots de crème can be refrigerated for up to 3 days before serving.

✔ WHY THIS RECIPE WORKS Classic *pots de crème* can be finicky and laborious, requiring a hot water bath that threatens to splash the custards every time the pan is moved. In addition, the individual custards don't always cook at the same rate in the oven. We wanted a user-friendly recipe that delivered a decadent dessert with a satiny texture and intense chocolate flavor. First we moved the dish out of the oven, concentrating on an unconventional approach: cooking the custard on the stovetop in a saucepan, then pouring it into ramekins. For the right amount of richness and body, we went with a combination of heavy cream and whole milk, enriched with several egg yolks. For intense chocolate flavor, we included bittersweet chocolate—and a lot of it. Be sure to use high-quality chocolate, such as Callebaut or Ghirardelli, in this recipe. If substituting chocolate chips for the chocolate, use a high-quality brand, such as Ghirardelli 60 Percent Bittersweet Chocolate Chips. You will need six 6-ounce ramekins for this recipe.

1. Finely chop chocolate and place in large bowl; set aside. In separate bowl, whisk egg yolks, ⅓ cup sugar, and ⅛ teaspoon salt together until smooth.

2. Bring 1½ cups cream and milk to simmer in medium saucepan over medium heat, stirring occasionally; remove pan from heat. Slowly whisk 1 cup cream mixture into egg yolk mixture to temper, then slowly whisk yolk mixture into pan. Return pan to low heat and cook, whisking constantly, until mixture thickens slightly, thinly coats back of spoon, and registers 175 to 180 degrees, 7 to 9 minutes.

3. Strain cream mixture through fine-mesh strainer into bowl with chocolate and let stand for 2 minutes. Stir in vanilla and gently whisk mixture until thoroughly combined. Divide mixture evenly among six 6-ounce ramekins. Cover with plastic wrap and refrigerate until firm, about 4 hours.

4. Before serving, use stand mixer fitted with whisk to whip remaining ½ cup cream and remaining 2 teaspoons sugar on medium-low speed until foamy, about 1 minute. Increase speed to high and whip until soft peaks form, 1 to 3 minutes. Garnish pots de crème with whipped cream and shaved chocolate (see page 293).

Chocolate Mousse Parfaits

SERVES 6

6 ounces **bittersweet chocolate,**
plus extra for garnish

10 ounces **marshmallows**

¼ cup **milk**

2½ cups **heavy cream,**
chilled

1½ teaspoons **vanilla extract**

6 ounces
chocolate wafer cookies

INGREDIENT SPOTLIGHT
CHOCOLATE WAFER COOKIES

You can find two types of chocolate wafer cookies at the supermarket. The kind that we use in this recipe are thin, round, and super-crisp; be sure to avoid the long, waffle-shaped wafer cookies that have a cream filling (the two are not interchangeable). In our tests, we had good luck using Nabisco Famous Chocolate Wafers.

TO MAKE AHEAD
Parfaits can be assembled and refrigerated for up to 4 hours before serving.

✔ WHY THIS RECIPE WORKS Chocolate mousse parfaits make an impressive dessert, but making the star ingredient from scratch is downright fussy. To streamline our mousse, we reached for marshmallows, which provide a stable and smooth base once microwaved. Bittersweet chocolate, melted with the marshmallows, gave us rich chocolate flavor; milk helped to thin the mixture. Allowing it to cool was essential to achieving a light, airy texture once we folded in the whipped cream. Crushed chocolate cookies, whipped cream, and shaved chocolate completed our streamlined parfaits. Regular or mini marshmallows can be used in this recipe. You will need six 12-ounce parfait or sundae glasses for this recipe.

1. Chop chocolate and microwave with marshmallows and milk in medium bowl, stirring often, until melted and smooth, about 2 minutes. Set bowl over large bowl of ice water and let stand, whisking often, until mixture is cool and thickened, about 10 minutes.

2. Meanwhile, using stand mixer fitted with whisk, whip cream and vanilla together on medium-low speed until foamy, about 1 minute. Increase speed to high and continue to whip until stiff peaks form, 1 to 3 minutes.

3. Fold one-quarter of whipped cream into cooled chocolate mixture to lighten, then fold another quarter of whipped cream into chocolate mixture until just incorporated.

4. Crush cookies into coarse crumbs. Spoon half of chocolate mousse evenly into six 12-ounce parfait or sundae glasses. Sprinkle with half of cookie crumbs and top with all but ½ cup remaining whipped cream. Sprinkle with remaining cookie crumbs and top with remaining chocolate mousse. Garnish with remaining whipped cream and shaved chocolate. Serve.

TEST KITCHEN TIP
SHAVING CHOCOLATE

For chocolate shavings, simply use a vegetable peeler and peel them off a large block of chocolate. Large blocks of chocolate make prettier shavings than thin bars of chocolate, but either will work.

No-Bake Rocky Road Bars

MAKES 16 BARS

1 cup whole **almonds**

6 **graham crackers**

2½ cups lightly packed **mini marshmallows**

8 ounces **semisweet chocolate**

4 tablespoons **unsalted butter**

2 tablespoons **light corn syrup**

INGREDIENT SPOTLIGHT
GRAHAM CRACKERS

The original graham crackers, developed by Sylvester Graham almost 200 years ago, were more like hardtack than like the sweet wafers we know today. Marketed as "Dr. Graham's Honey Biskets," the dense crackers were made largely from coarse whole-wheat flour. Nowadays, they still incorporate graham (or whole-wheat) flour, but white flour is the primary ingredient, with sugar of some sort not far behind. They also contain oil, salt, and leaveners. Our favorite brand for baking is **Keebler Grahams Crackers Original**, which held up well in recipes. However, if you're eating them straight from the box, we prefer **Nabisco Grahams Original** for their wheaty flavor.

TO MAKE AHEAD
Bars can be stored in airtight container at room temperature for up to 4 days.

✔ WHY THIS RECIPE WORKS The combo of chocolate, almonds, and marshmallows is an utterly addictive one, delivering both rich, sweet bites and a big crunch. For easy, no-bake cookie bars that made the most of this trio, we started by melting chopped chocolate with a portion of the marshmallows, which helped to hold the ingredients of our bars together. Toasted, chopped almonds offered nutty flavor and a crunchy texture, and a few pats of butter and a couple spoonfuls of corn syrup firmed up the mixture so the bars were easy to slice. Rather than layer the mixture on a graham cracker crust, we crumbled the graham crackers and incorporated them right into the bars for even more crunch and flavor. Try not to crush the graham crackers into crumbs, but rather break them into large pieces. Peanuts can be substituted for the almonds.

1. Line 8-inch square baking pan with foil sling and grease foil. Toast almonds (see page 297), then chop. Break graham crackers into 1-inch pieces and combine with almonds and 1 cup marshmallows in large bowl.

2. Chop chocolate. Melt butter in medium saucepan over low heat. Add remaining 1½ cups marshmallows and cook, stirring constantly, until melted and smooth, about 2 minutes. Stir in chocolate and corn syrup and continue to cook, stirring constantly, until incorporated, about 30 seconds.

3. Working quickly, pour chocolate mixture over graham cracker mixture and fold gently until evenly coated. Scrape mixture into prepared baking pan and press into even layer with greased rubber spatula. Refrigerate bars until firm, about 2 hours. Using foil overhang, lift bars out of pan, cut into squares, and serve.

TEST KITCHEN TIP
MAKING A FOIL SLING

Fold 2 long sheets of aluminum foil so each is 8 inches wide. Lay sheets of foil in pan perpendicular to each other, with extra foil hanging over edges of pan. Push foil into corners and up sides of pan, smoothing foil flush to pan.

Pound Cake

SERVES 8

1½ cups (6 ounces) **cake flour**

1 teaspoon **baking powder**

16 tablespoons **unsalted butter**

1¼ cups (8¾ ounces) **sugar**

4 **large eggs,**
room temperature

1½ teaspoons **vanilla extract**

INGREDIENT SPOTLIGHT
CAKE FLOUR

Cake flour has a low protein level (6 to 8 percent) and delivers delicate, fine-crumbed cakes and light, airy biscuits. Not all cakes require cake flour; we call for it only in recipes where we feel it delivers decidedly better results than all-purpose flour. If you don't have cake flour on hand, you can substitute all-purpose flour combined with cornstarch. For each cup of cake flour, use ⅞ cup all-purpose flour mixed with 2 tablespoons cornstarch.

TO MAKE AHEAD
This cake tastes best when served on the same day. Leftover cake can be wrapped in plastic wrap and stored at room temperature for up to 3 days.

WHY THIS RECIPE WORKS Pound cake should be the ultimate easy cake—after all, it calls for just a handful of ingredients. The problem is that most recipes use a finicky mixing method in which all the ingredients need to be the same temperature, otherwise the batter turns into a curdled mess—and there's no way to save it. Looking for an easier way, we found the answers to our fussy batter problems: hot, melted (rather than softened) butter and the food processor. The fast-moving blade of the processor, in conjunction with the hot melted butter, emulsified the liquid ingredients quickly before they had a chance to curdle. Plus, it sped up the process so the cake could be in the oven (and on a plate) that much sooner. This recipe makes one 8½-inch loaf, but it will also make four miniature pound cakes; use four 2-cup mini loaf pans and reduce the baking time to 40 minutes.

1. Adjust oven rack to middle position and heat oven to 350 degrees. Grease and flour 8½ by 4½-inch loaf pan. Whisk flour, baking powder, and ½ teaspoon salt together in bowl.

2. Melt butter and keep hot. Process sugar, eggs, and vanilla together in food processor until combined, about 10 seconds. With processor running, add hot melted butter in steady stream until combined, about 30 seconds. Pour mixture into large bowl.

3. Sift one-third of flour mixture over egg mixture and whisk to combine until just a few streaks of flour remain. Repeat twice more with remaining flour mixture, then continue to whisk batter gently until most lumps are gone (do not overmix).

4. Scrape batter into prepared pan and smooth top. Wipe any drops of batter off sides of pan and gently tap pan on counter to release air bubbles. Bake until toothpick inserted in center comes out clean, 50 to 60 minutes, rotating pan halfway through baking.

5. Let cake cool in pan on wire rack for 10 minutes. Run small knife around edge of cake to loosen, then flip it out onto wire rack. Turn cake right side up and let cool completely on rack, about 2 hours.

Easy Chocolate-Nut Torte

SERVES 10 TO 12

3 cups (12 ounces)
pecans or walnuts

6 tablespoons **unsalted butter**

⅓ cup **whole milk**

1 **large egg**

1 (17.5-22.5 ounce) box **brownie mix**

Confectioners' sugar

INGREDIENT SPOTLIGHT
BROWNIE MIX

The convenience of box brownie mix is undeniable. After all, it combines chocolate, cocoa, flour, and leavener, so all the cook has to do is add an egg, oil, and water. But not all of them deliver big chocolate flavor. Our favorite brand is **Ghirardelli Double Chocolate Supreme Brownie Mix**, which gave us moist, chewy brownies with a "balanced chocolate" flavor. But note that you can use any basic brownie mix in this recipe, as long as it measures between 17.5 and 22.5 ounces.

TO MAKE AHEAD
Cooled torte can be wrapped in plastic wrap and refrigerated for up to 24 hours. Bring torte to room temperature, or refresh in 350-degree oven for 10 to 15 minutes, before dusting with confectioners' sugar and serving.

✓ WHY THIS RECIPE WORKS No one will ever suspect this rich and nutty cake started with box brownie mix. The secret was ratcheting up its flavor and texture with a good amount of nuts. Toasting the nuts brought out their flavor, and finely grinding them in the food processor before adding them to the batter made the torte moist and dense. Butter and an egg ensured it was plenty rich and had structure, and a dusting of confectioners' sugar dressed up this shockingly easy dessert.

1. Adjust oven rack to middle position and heat oven to 325 degrees. Grease 9-inch round cake pan and line bottom with parchment paper. Toast nuts, let cool, and process in food processor until very finely ground, about 15 seconds.

2. Melt butter and let cool slightly. Whisk butter, milk, and egg together in large bowl until well combined. Stir in nuts and brownie mix until fully incorporated.

3. Give batter final stir with rubber spatula to make sure it is thoroughly combined. Scrape batter into prepared pan, smooth top, and gently tap pan on counter to release air bubbles. Bake until toothpick inserted in center comes out with a few moist crumbs attached, 35 to 45 minutes, rotating pan halfway through baking.

4. Let torte cool in pan for 10 minutes. Run small knife around edge of torte to loosen, then flip it out onto wire rack. Peel off parchment paper, then flip torte right side up. Serve warm or at room temperature. Dust with confectioners' sugar before serving.

TEST KITCHEN TIP
TOASTING NUTS

To toast a large quantity of nuts, spread them in single layer on rimmed baking sheet; toast in 350-degree oven, shaking every few minutes, until nuts are lightly browned and fragrant, 5 to 10 minutes. To toast 1 cup or less, put nuts in dry skillet over medium heat. Shake skillet occasionally to prevent scorching and toast until nuts are lightly browned and fragrant, 3 to 8 minutes.

Caramel Turtle Ice Cream Pie

SERVES 6 TO 8

1 cup **pecans**

3 cups (1½ pints) **vanilla ice cream**

1 (9-inch)
chocolate crumb pie crust

2 ounces **semisweet chocolate**

2 tablespoons **caramel sauce**

INGREDIENT SPOTLIGHT
VANILLA ICE CREAM

Finding a good vanilla ice cream shouldn't be hard, but with nearly 40 brands on the market, in a slew of different styles (like vanilla bean, natural vanilla, and French vanilla), who knows which one to pick? To find out, we tasted eight brands of vanilla ice cream. Brands straying too far from the authentic, old-fashioned starting points of cream, milk, sugar, eggs, and vanilla extract scored poorly, while ice cream made with real vanilla extract, that wasn't hidden behind artificial or other natural flavors, and a creamy texture, achieved without a ton of emulsifiers and stabilizers, did well. Our winner, **Ben & Jerry's Vanilla**, was buttery-tasting and rich, full of "indulgent" vanilla flavor, sweetened with real sugar, and enriched with egg yolks. Though this ice cream included two stabilizers—way less than some competitors—its texture was still ultra-creamy and silky.

TO MAKE AHEAD
Assembled pie can be wrapped tightly in plastic wrap and kept frozen for up to 1 week.

☑ WHY THIS RECIPE WORKS To transform ice cream into something special, we decided to make an ice cream pie, and looked to incorporate the classic turtle candy flavors of caramel, nuts, and chocolate. Starting with a prepared chocolate pie crust helped us save time. After toasting and chopping a cup of pecans, we stirred some into softened vanilla ice cream and then spread the mixture into the crust. Melted semisweet chocolate and caramel sauce, drizzled over the top of the pie, completed our homage to the sweet caramel and chocolate candy. Topping the pie with more pecans added crunch and guaranteed this effortless dessert was a looker. Freezing the pie for at least 30 minutes before serving gave it time to set up and ensured it was easy to slice.

1. Toast pecans (see page 297), then chop. Scoop ice cream into large bowl and work with wooden spoon (or rubber spatula) to soften. Fold in three-quarters of nuts until incorporated. Using spatula, spread ice cream mixture evenly into pie crust.

2. Chop chocolate and microwave in covered bowl, stirring occasionally, until melted, about 2 minutes. Let cool slightly, then drizzle over top of pie. Melt caramel in microwave, 15 to 30 seconds, then drizzle over top of pie. Sprinkle remaining pecans over top and press to adhere. Freeze pie until ice cream is firm, at least 30 minutes. Serve.

TEST KITCHEN TIP MAKING ICE CREAM PIE

1. Scoop ice cream into large bowl. Then use wooden spoon or rubber spatula to break up scoops of ice cream. Stir and fold to achieve smooth consistency.

2. After folding in three-quarters of nuts until incorporated, spread ice cream mixture evenly into pie crust using spatula. Then drizzle with melted chocolate and caramel.

Conversions & Equivalencies

Some say cooking is a science and an art. We would say that geography has a hand in it, too. Flour milled in the United Kingdom and elsewhere will feel and taste different from flour milled in the United States. So we cannot promise that the loaf of bread you bake in Canada or England will taste the same as a loaf baked in the States, but we can offer guidelines for converting weights and measures. We also recommend that you rely on your instincts when making our recipes. Refer to the visual cues provided. If the bread dough hasn't "come together in a ball," as described, you may need to add more flour—even if the recipe doesn't tell you to. You be the judge.

The recipes in this book were developed using standard U.S. measures following U.S. government guidelines. The charts below offer equivalents for U.S., metric, and imperial (U.K.) measures. All conversions are approximate and have been rounded up or down to the nearest whole number.

EXAMPLE:

1 teaspoon = 4.9292 milliliters, rounded up to 5 milliliters
1 ounce = 28.3495 grams, rounded down to 28 grams

VOLUME CONVERSIONS

U.S.	METRIC
1 teaspoon	5 milliliters
2 teaspoons	10 milliliters
1 tablespoon	15 milliliters
2 tablespoons	30 milliliters
¼ cup	59 milliliters
⅓ cup	79 milliliters
½ cup	118 milliliters
¾ cup	177 milliliters
1 cup	237 milliliters
1¼ cups	296 milliliters
1½ cups	355 milliliters
2 cups (1 pint)	473 milliliters
2½ cups	591 milliliters
3 cups	710 milliliters
4 cups (1 quart)	0.946 liter
1.06 quarts	1 liter
4 quarts (1 gallon)	3.8 liters

WEIGHT CONVERSIONS

OUNCES	GRAMS
½	14
¾	21
1	28
1½	43
2	57
2½	71
3	85
3½	99
4	113
4½	128
5	142
6	170
7	198
8	227
9	255
10	283
12	340
16 (1 pound)	454

CONVERSIONS FOR INGREDIENTS COMMONLY USED IN BAKING

Baking is an exacting science. Because measuring by weight is far more accurate than measuring by volume, and thus more likely to achieve reliable results, in our recipes we provide ounce measures in addition to cup measures for many ingredients. Refer to the chart below to convert these measures into grams.

INGREDIENT	OUNCES	GRAMS
1 cup all-purpose flour*	5	142
1 cup cake flour	4	113
1 cup whole-wheat flour	5½	156
1 cup granulated (white) sugar	7	198
1 cup packed brown sugar (light or dark)	7	198
1 cup confectioners' sugar	4	113
1 cup cocoa powder	3	85
4 tablespoons butter† (½ stick, or ¼ cup)	2	57
8 tablespoons butter† (1 stick, or ½ cup)	4	113
16 tablespoons butter† (2 sticks, or 1 cup)	8	227

* U.S. all-purpose flour, the most frequently used flour in this book, does not contain leaveners, as some European flours do. These leavened flours are called self-rising or self-raising. If you are using self-rising flour, take this into consideration before adding leavening to a recipe.

† In the United States, butter is sold both salted and unsalted. We generally recommend unsalted butter. If you are using salted butter, take this into consideration before adding salt to a recipe.

OVEN TEMPERATURES

FAHRENHEIT	CELSIUS	GAS MARK (IMPERIAL)
225	105	¼
250	120	½
275	135	1
300	150	2
325	165	3
350	180	4
375	190	5
400	200	6
425	220	7
450	230	8
475	245	9

CONVERTING TEMPERATURES FROM AN INSTANT-READ THERMOMETER

We include doneness temperatures in many of the recipes in this book. We recommend an instant-read thermometer for the job. Refer to the above table to convert Fahrenheit degrees to Celsius. Or, for temperatures not represented in the chart, use this simple formula:

Subtract 32 degrees from the Fahrenheit reading, then divide the result by 1.8 to find the Celsius reading.

EXAMPLE:
"Roast chicken until thighs register 175 degrees."
To convert:

$175°F - 32 = 143°$
$143° ÷ 1.8 = 79.44°C$, rounded down to 79°C

Index

A

Almonds

No-Bake Rocky Road Bars, *294,* 295

Smoked, and Dried Fruit, Chicken and Couscous with, 72

Aloha Kebabs with Sesame Rice, 86, *87*

Appetizers

Brie and Jam Phyllo Cups, 27

Broiled Chipotle Shrimp, 37

Caprese Skewers, *18,* 19

Cheese Crisps (Frico), 7

Citrusy Shrimp Cocktail, 36

Crispy Spiced Chickpeas, 16

Endive Cups with Apples and Blue Cheese, *4,* 20

Feta-Dill Dip with Cucumber Chips, 10

Ham and Cheese Palmiers, 30, *31*

Herbed Cheese Coins, 6

Herbed Ricotta Crostini, *14,* 15

Kielbasa Bites, 32

Marinated Feta and Green Olives, 11

Melted Brie with Honey and Herbs, *12,* 13

Naan Tarts with Artichokes, Pesto, and Goat Cheese, 33

Pink Peppercorn–Crusted Goat Cheese Log, *8, 9*

Prosciutto-Wrapped Figs with Gorgonzola, 21

Salami and Provolone–Stuffed Peppers, 26

Serrano and Manchego Crostini with Orange Honey, 17

Smoked Salmon Rolls, *38, 39*

Spicy Shrimp Cocktail Shooters, *34, 35*

Stuffed Mushrooms with Boursin and Prosciutto, *22, 23*

Tomato Tartlets, 28, *29*

Warm Bacon-Wrapped Chorizo and Dates, *24,* 25

Apple(s)

best, for applesauce, 271

and Blue Cheese, Endive Cups with, *4,* 20

and Cheddar Strata, 247

Granny Smith, about, 285

Smoked Double-Thick Pork Chops with Cranberry-Thyme Applesauce, 271

Tart, French Caramel, 286, *287*

Apple(s) *(cont.)*

Turnovers, 285

Artichokes

frozen, about, 147

marinated, about, 170

Marinated, Garlic, and Olive Oil, Spaghetti with, 170

Olives, and Sun-Dried Tomatoes, Baked Cod with, *146,* 147

Pesto, and Goat Cheese, Naan Tarts with, 33

Roasted Red Peppers, and Goat Cheese, Baked Penne with, *228,* 229

Arugula

BLT Pasta, *182,* 183

Roasted Garlic, and Chicken Sausage, Campanelle with, *190,* 191

and Shaved Parmesan, Steak Salad with, 96, *97*

Asian chili-garlic sauce, about, 238

Asparagus

Orzo Primavera with Feta, 216

Avocados, about, 99

B

Bacon

BLT Pasta, *182,* 183

taste tests on, 183

-Wrapped Chorizo and Dates, Warm, *24,* 25

Baked Cod with Artichokes, Olives, and Sun-Dried Tomatoes, *146,* 147

Baked Penne with Roasted Red Peppers, Artichokes, and Goat Cheese, *228,* 229

Baked Quinoa with Roasted Kale and Chickpeas, 218, *219*

Bars, No-Bake Rocky Road, *294,* 295

Basil

Caprese Skewers, *18,* 19

Herbed Ricotta Crostini, *14,* 15

Oil, Grilled Swordfish Skewers with, 279

shredding, 192

Bean(s)

Baked Quinoa with Roasted Kale and Chickpeas, 218, *219*

Bean(s) *(cont.)*

Beef Taco Bake, *236,* 237

Black, and Chorizo Sopa Seca, 231

Black, and Roasted Poblano Enchiladas, 217

black, canned, taste tests on, 55

Black, Soup with Chorizo, *54,* 55

canned, rinsing, 106

chickpeas, canned, taste tests on, 16

Crispy Spiced Chickpeas, 16

Lazy Man's Chili, 106

Beef

Braised, with Red Wine and Cherries, 140

and Broccoli Stir-Fry, 102, *103*

Chipotle Steak Soft Tacos, *98,* 99

cooking temperatures, 100

Easiest Sunday Pot Roast, 142, *143*

Empanadas, Easy, 107

flank steak, about, 264

flank steak, scoring, 265

Ginger and Soy–Braised Short Ribs, 141

Grilled Flank Steak with Herb Sauce, 264

Grilled Free-Form Beef Wellington with Balsamic
    Reduction, 266, *267*

Grilled Margarita Steak, 265

Grilled Sirloin Steak with Grilled Tomato Salad,
    262, 263

Kebabs, Grilled Asian, 261

Kimchi Fried Rice with, *104,* 105

Lazy Man's Chili, 106

Philly Cheesesteak Sandwiches, 101

roast, separating and tying, 142

roast, trimming and cutting, 140

shell sirloin steak, about, 263

Sirloin, Roast, with Caramelized Carrots and
    Potatoes, *138,* 139

sirloin steak tips, about, 100

Sirloin Steak with Boursin Mashed Potatoes, *94,* 95

skirt steak, about, 101

slicing, for stir-fries, 102

Steak Salad with Arugula and Shaved Parmesan,
    96, *97*

strip steaks, about, 96

Taco Bake, *236,* 237

Teriyaki Steak Tips, 100

Beef *(cont.)*

top sirloin, about, 139

see also Meatloaf mix

Belgian endive. *See* Endive

Bell's poultry seasoning, about, 131

Berry(ies)

and Cookies, Speedy Trifle with, *282,* 283

Fresh, and Croissant Gratins, 284

see also Cranberry

Bistro-Style Steamed Mussels with White Wine
    and Garlic, 165

Black Bean Soup with Chorizo, *54,* 55

Bloody Mary mix

about, 35

Spicy Shrimp Cocktail Shooters, *34,* 35

BLT Pasta, *182,* 183

Bok Choy and Sticky Rice, Cola-Glazed Pork
    Chops with, 112, *113*

Boursin

about, 73

Creamy Tortellini with Vegetables, 193

Mashed Potatoes, Sirloin Steak with, *94,* 95

and Prosciutto, Stuffed Mushrooms with, *22, 23*

Simple Stuffed Chicken Breasts with, 73

and Sun-Dried Tomatoes, Easy Egg Casserole with,
    246

Zucchini, and Cherry Tomatoes, Penne with, 175

Braised Beef with Red Wine and Cherries, 140

Braised Chicken with Onions, Mushrooms, and
    Bacon, 84

Braised Cod with Leeks and Cherry Tomatoes, 148

Bratwurst

Brats with Beer and Mustard on Egg Noodles, 200

taste tests on, 200

Bread

Apple and Cheddar Strata, 247

crumbs, panko, taste tests on, 234

toasting quickly, 17

see also Crostini; Naan; Tortillas

Brie and Jam Phyllo Cups, 27

Broccoli

and Beef Stir-Fry, 102, *103*

florets, about, 196

Italian Sausage, and Sun-Dried Tomatoes, Ziti with,
    196

Broccolini and Sun-Dried Tomatoes, Skillet Pizza
    with, *214,* 215
Broiled Chipotle Shrimp, 37
Brownie mix, taste tests on, 297
Brown sugar, about, 284
Brussels Sprouts
    about, 185
    Blue Cheese, and Bacon, Rotini with, *168,* 185
    slicing, 185
Burgers, Chicken and Sun-Dried Tomato, *88,* 89

C

Cabbage & coleslaw mix
    coleslaw mix, about, 118
    Grilled Southwestern Drumsticks with Charred
        Coleslaw, 257
    Mu Shu–Style Pork Wraps, 118
Cajun Roast Chicken with Sautéed Corn and
    Bell Peppers, *124,* 125
Cajun seasoning, about, 125
Cake flour, about, 296
Cakes
    Easy Chocolate-Nut Torte, 297
    Pound, 296
Campanelle with Porcini Cream Sauce, 174
Campanelle with Roasted Garlic, Chicken
    Sausage, and Arugula, *190,* 191
Caprese Skewers, *18,* 19
Caramel Sauce, Salty-Sweet, Catfish in, 153
Caramel Turtle Ice Cream Pie, *298,* 299
Cardamom pods, about, 57
Carrots and Potatoes, Caramelized, Roast Beef
    Sirloin with, *138,* 139
Casseroles
    Apple and Cheddar Strata, 247
    Baked Penne with Roasted Red Peppers,
        Artichokes, and Goat Cheese, *228,* 229
    Beef Taco Bake, *236,* 237
    Cheesy Shrimp and Grits, 238, *239*
    Chicken Enchilada, 242
    Chorizo and Black Bean Sopa Seca, 231
    Easiest-Ever Lasagna, 226
    Easy Egg, with Boursin and Sun-Dried Tomatoes, 246

Casseroles *(cont.)*
    Egg, Ham, and Hash Brown Pie, 243
    Polenta, with Sausage and Peppers, 240, *241*
    Simple Baked Ziti, 230
    Smoky Eggplant, 234, *235*
    Spanish Tortilla with Roasted Red Peppers and
        Peas, *244,* 245
    Spicy Spaghetti Pie, *232,* 233
    Unstuffed Shells with Sausage and Fennel, *224,*
        225
    White Lasagna with Zucchini and Tomatoes, *222,*
        227
Catfish in Salty-Sweet Caramel Sauce, 153
Cauliflower
    cutting up, 44
    Soup, Curried, 44
Chai
    about, 42
    -Infused Butternut Squash Soup, 42, *43*
Cheddar Crumb–Crusted Chicken with Sautéed
    Cherry Tomatoes, *58,* 65
Cheese
    Apple and Cheddar Strata, 247
    Baked Quinoa with Roasted Kale and Chickpeas,
        218, *219*
    Beef Taco Bake, *236,* 237
    Blue, and Apples, Endive Cups with, *4,* 20
    Blue, Brussels Sprouts, and Bacon, Rotini with,
        168, 185
    Blue, Radicchio, and Walnuts, Shells with, 184
    Brie, about, 13
    Brie and Jam Phyllo Cups, 27
    cheddar, taste tests on, 247
    Cheddar Crumb–Crusted Chicken with Sautéed
        Cherry Tomatoes, *58,* 65
    Cheesy Shrimp and Grits, 238, *239*
    Coins, Herbed, 6
    Crisps (Frico), 7
    Easiest-Ever Lasagna, 226
    Easy Stuffed Zucchini, 220
    feta, marinated, about, 121
    feta, taste tests on, 10
    Feta-Dill Dip with Cucumber Chips, 10
    Goat, Artichokes, and Pesto, Naan Tarts with, 33
    Goat, Log, Pink Peppercorn–Crusted, *8,* 9

Cheese *(cont.)*

Goat, Roasted Red Peppers, and Artichokes, Baked Penne with, *228,* 229

goat, taste tests on, 9

Gorgonzola, about, 21

Greek-Style Shrimp with Orzo and Feta, 161

hard, grating, 197

Herbed Ricotta Crostini, *14,* 15

Italian blend, about, 230

Manchego, about, 17

Marinated Feta and Green Olives, 11

mascarpone, about, 283

Melted Brie with Honey and Herbs, *12,* 13

Montasio, about, 7

Monterey Jack, about, 231

Orzo Primavera with Feta, 216

Philly Cheesesteak Sandwiches, 101

Pork Chops with Spicy Pepper Relish and Cheesy Grits, *92,* 115

Prosciutto-Wrapped Figs with Gorgonzola, 21

ricotta, taste tests on, 15

Roasted Poblano and Black Bean Enchiladas, 217

Rustic Chicken and Brie Tart, *90,* 91

Salami and Provolone–Stuffed Peppers, 26

semisoft, shredding, 226

Serrano and Manchego Crostini with Orange Honey, 17

Simple Baked Ziti, 230

Skillet Monterey Chicken with Rice, 68

Smoked Salmon Rolls, *38,* 39

Smoky Eggplant Casserole, 234, *235*

Speedy Trifle with Cookies and Berries, *282,* 283

Spicy Spaghetti Pie, *232,* 233

sticky, cutting, tip for, 27

Unstuffed Chicken Cordon Bleu, *66,* 67

White Lasagna with Zucchini and Tomatoes, *222,* 227

see also Boursin; Mozzarella; Parmesan

Cheese sticks, taste tests on, 47

Cherry(ies)

frozen, taste tests on, 137

and Red Wine, Braised Beef with, 140

Sauce, Slow-Roasted Pork with, 137

Chicken

Abruzzo, Spicy Braised, 69

Chicken *(cont.)*

Bake, Cranberry-Ginger, 64

Braised, with Onions, Mushrooms, and Bacon, 84

breasts, bone-in split, about, 77

breasts, boneless, skinless, taste tests on, 60

Breasts, Grilled, with Cherry Tomatoes, 252, *253*

Breasts, Simple Stuffed, with Boursin, 73

and Brie Tart, Rustic, *90, 91*

broth, taste tests on, 52

Cheddar Crumb–Crusted, with Sautéed Cherry Tomatoes, *58,* 65

Coconut-Curry Braised, *78, 79*

Cordon Bleu, Unstuffed, *66, 67*

and Couscous with Dried Fruit and Smoked Almonds, 72

drumsticks, removing skin from, 82

Enchilada Casserole, 242

with 40 Cloves of Garlic, 127

Grilled, alla Diavola, *258, 259*

Grilled, Soft Tacos, 260

Grilled Indian-Spiced, with Raita, 256

Grilled Southwestern Drumsticks with Charred Coleslaw, 257

Lemon-Braised, with Fennel, 77

Meatballs with Tomatoes and Cilantro, 85

Mustard-Glazed Drumsticks, *82, 83*

Pan-Roasted, with Potatoes, 76

Pan-Roasted, with Tomatoes and Olives, *74, 75*

Pizzaiola with Pasta, 70, *71*

Pomegranate-Glazed, with Couscous, 128, *129*

Porcini-Rubbed, 61

Prosciutto-Wrapped, with Sage, *62, 63*

with Rice, Skillet Monterey, 68

Roast, Cajun, with Sautéed Corn and Bell Peppers, *124, 125*

rotisserie, about, 91

Soup, Hearty Italian, with Kale and Gnocchi, 52

Soup, Thai Red Curry and Coconut, 53

and Sun-Dried Tomato Burgers, *88, 89*

Sweet and Spicy Glazed, 60

Thighs, Five-Spice, with Snap Peas, *80,* 81

whole, butterflying, 126

whole, splitting, 128

whole, taste tests on, 259

Za'atar-Rubbed, with Roasted Shallots, 126

Chicken Sausage(s)
    Aloha Kebabs with Sesame Rice, 86, *87*
    Roasted Garlic, and Arugula, Campanelle with, *190,* 191
Chiles
    Broiled Chipotle Shrimp, 37
    chipotle, in adobo sauce, about, 37
    Chipotle Steak Soft Tacos, *98,* 99
    Grilled Chicken Soft Tacos, 260
    poblano, about, 217
    Roasted Poblano and Black Bean Enchiladas, 217
Chili, Lazy Man's, 106
Chili-garlic sauce, about, 238
Chili powder, taste tests on, 106
Chipotle Steak Soft Tacos, *98, 99*
Chives, about, 95
Chocolate
    bittersweet, taste tests on, 290
    Caramel Turtle Ice Cream Pie, *298,* 299
    Mousse Parfaits, *292,* 293
    No-Bake Rocky Road Bars, *294,* 295
    Nutella Tart, *280,* 289
    -Nut Torte, Easy, 297
    Pots de Crème, 290, *291*
    shaving, 293
    wafer cookies, about, 293
Chorizo
    about, 203
    and Black Bean Sopa Seca, 231
    Black Bean Soup with, *54,* 55
    and Clams, Linguine with, *202,* 203
    and Dates, Warm Bacon-Wrapped, *24, 25*
    Israeli Couscous, and Scallions, Clams with, *166,* 167
Cilantro Sauce, Roast Pork Loin with, 136
Citrusy Shrimp Cocktail, 36
Clams
    and Chorizo, Linguine with, *202,* 203
    with Israeli Couscous, Chorizo, and Scallions, *166,* 167
    scrubbing, 203
Coconut milk
    Coconut-Curry Braised Chicken, *78,* 79
    Curried Cauliflower Soup, 44
    taste tests on, 79

Coconut milk *(cont.)*
    Thai Red Curry and Coconut Chicken Soup, 53
    Thai-Style Fish and Creamy Coconut Rice Packets, 149
Coconut oil, taste tests on, 221
Cod
    about, 151
    Baked, with Artichokes, Olives, and Sun-Dried Tomatoes, *146,* 147
    Braised, with Leeks and Cherry Tomatoes, 148
    Fillets, Roasted, with Crispy Potatoes and Lemon, *150,* 151
Cola-Glazed Pork Chops with Bok Choy and Sticky Rice, 112, *113*
Coleslaw mix. *See* Cabbage & coleslaw mix
Cookies
    and Berries, Speedy Trifle with, *282,* 283
    chocolate wafer, about, 293
Coriander, about, 279
Corn
    about, 181
    and Bell Pepper, Sautéed, Cajun Roast Chicken with, *124,* 125
    kernels, removing from cob, 181
    Mexicorn, about, 68
    and Shrimp, Grilled, Maryland-Style, *248,* 275
    Skillet Monterey Chicken with Rice, 68
    Toasted, Bacon, Cherry Tomatoes, and Basil, Farfalle with, 181
    and Tomato, Roasted, Tostadas, *210,* 211
Cornflake-Crusted Pork Chops, 114
Couscous
    and Chicken with Dried Fruit and Smoked Almonds, 72
    Israeli, about, 167
    Israeli, Chorizo, and Scallions, Clams with, *166,* 167
    Pomegranate-Glazed Chicken with, 128, *129*
Cranberry
    -Ginger Chicken Bake, 64
    sauce, whole berry, about, 64
    -Thyme Applesauce, Smoked Double-Thick Pork Chops with, 271
Creamy Tortellini with Vegetables, 193
Crispy Potato-Crusted Salmon with Herb Salad, 158, *159*

Crispy Spiced Chickpeas, 16
Crispy Tofu with Coconut-Lime Rice, *208*, 221
Crostini
    Herbed Ricotta, *14*, 15
    Serrano and Manchego, with Orange Honey, 17
Cucumber(s)
    about, 277
    Chips, Feta-Dill Dip with, 10
    -Dill Salad, Creamy, Grill-Smoked Salmon with, *276*, 277
Curried dishes
    Coconut-Curry Braised Chicken, *78*, 79
    Curried Cauliflower Soup, 44
    Grilled Indian-Spiced Chicken with Raita, 256
    Grilled Red Curry Mahi-Mahi with Pineapple Salsa, 278
    Thai Red Curry and Coconut Chicken Soup, 53
    Thai-Style Fish and Creamy Coconut Rice Packets, 149
Curry paste, Thai green, about, 149
Curry paste, Thai red, about, 53
Curry powder, taste tests on, 44

D

Dates
    and Chorizo, Warm Bacon-Wrapped, *24*, 25
    Medjool, about, 25
Desserts
    Apple Turnovers, 285
    Caramel Turtle Ice Cream Pie, *298*, 299
    Chocolate Mousse Parfaits, *292*, 293
    Chocolate Pots de Crème, 290, *291*
    Easy Chocolate-Nut Torte, 297
    French Caramel Apple Tart, 286, *287*
    Fresh Berry and Croissant Gratins, 284
    Lemon Tart, 288
    No-Bake Rocky Road Bars, *294*, 295
    Nutella Tart, *280*, 289
    Pound Cake, 296
    Speedy Trifle with Cookies and Berries, *282*, 283
Dip, Feta-Dill, with Cucumber Chips, 10

E

Easiest-Ever Lasagna, 226
Easiest Sunday Pot Roast, 142, *143*
Easy Beef Empanadas, 107
Easy Chocolate-Nut Torte, 297
Easy Egg Casserole with Boursin and Sun-Dried Tomatoes, 246
Easy Stuffed Pork Loin with Sun-Dried Tomato Vinaigrette, *134*, 135
Easy Stuffed Zucchini, 220
Easy Tortellini Gratin, 192
Eggplant
    about, 213
    Casserole, Smoky, 234, *235*
    Ragu, Parmesan Polenta with, 213
Egg(s)
    about, 246
    Casserole, Easy, with Boursin and Sun-Dried Tomatoes, 246
    cracking, tip for, 246
    Fried, and Bread Crumbs, Spaghetti with, *178*, 179
    Ham, and Hash Brown Pie, 243
    Kimchi Fried Rice with Beef, *104*, 105
    and Lemon Soup with Rice, Greek, 57
    Spanish Tortilla with Roasted Red Peppers and Peas, *244*, 245
    tempering, 57
Empanadas, Easy Beef, 107
Enchiladas, Roasted Poblano and Black Bean, 217
Endive
    Belgian, about, 20
    Cups with Apples and Blue Cheese, *4*, 20

F

Farfalle
    with Bacon, Toasted Corn, Cherry Tomatoes, and Basil, 181
    with Fennel, Cream, and Herbs, *176*, 177
    with Salmon and Leeks, *206*, 207
    with Sautéed Mushrooms and Truffle Oil, 180
Fennel
    about, 177

Fennel *(cont.)*
Cream, and Herbs, Farfalle with, *176, 177*
and Italian Sausage, Ziti with, 197
Lemon-Braised Chicken with, 77
and Orange Salad, Grilled Scallops with, 274
and Pesto, Swordfish en Cocotte with, 152
preparing, 177
Salad, Warm, and Roast Pork Tenderloin with
Herbes de Provence, 132
and Sausage, Unstuffed Shells with, *224, 225*
Feta-Dill Dip with Cucumber Chips, 10
Fettuccine with Shrimp, Tarragon, and Cream,
205
Fig(s)
-Glazed Pork Loin with Roasted Potatoes and
Bacon, *122, 133*
jam or preserves, about, 133
Prosciutto-Wrapped, with Gorgonzola, 21
Fish
Baked Cod with Artichokes, Olives, and Sun-Dried
Tomatoes, *146, 147*
Braised Cod with Leeks and Cherry Tomatoes, 148
Catfish in Salty-Sweet Caramel Sauce, 153
cod, about, 151
and Creamy Coconut Rice Packets, Thai-Style, 149
fillets, cooking tip, 147
Grilled Red Curry Mahi-Mahi with Pineapple
Salsa, 278
Grilled Swordfish Skewers with Basil Oil, 279
Mediterranean Penne with Tuna and Niçoise
Olives, 204
Roasted Cod Fillets with Crispy Potatoes and
Lemon, *150, 151*
Sesame-Crusted Tuna with Wasabi Dressing, 154,
155
swordfish, about, 152
Swordfish en Cocotte with Fennel and Pesto, 152
tuna, premium, taste tests on, 204
see also Salmon
Fish sauce, about, 153
Five-spice powder
Five-Spice Chicken Thighs with Snap Peas, *80, 81*
taste tests on, 81
Flour, cake, about, 296

Foil sling, preparing, 295
French Caramel Apple Tart, 286, *287*
French onion soup, condensed, about, 142
Fresh Berry and Croissant Gratins, 284
Fruit
Dried, and Smoked Almonds, Chicken and
Couscous with, 72
dried, mix, about, 72
see also specific fruits
Fusilli with Giardiniera and Sausage, *198,* 199

G

Garam masala, taste tests on, 286
Garlic
about, 127
40 Cloves of, Chicken with, 127
Grilled Chicken alla Diavola, *258, 259*
mincing to a paste, 10
Olive Oil, and Marinated Artichokes, Spaghetti
with, 170
prepeeled, about, 191
Roasted, Chicken Sausage, and Arugula,
Campanelle with, *190,* 191
slicing thinly, 11
and White Wine, Bistro-Style Steamed Mussels
with, 165
Gemelli with Caramelized Onions, Kale, and
Bacon, 188
Giardiniera
and Sausage, Fusilli with, *198,* 199
and Sausage–Stuffed Peppers, 119
taste tests on, 199
Ginger
-Cranberry Chicken Bake, 64
grating, 60
and Soy–Braised Short Ribs, 141
Gnocchi and Kale, Hearty Italian Chicken Soup
with, 52
Graham crackers
No-Bake Rocky Road Bars, *294,* 295
taste tests on, 295
Grains. *See* Grits; Polenta; Quinoa; Rice

Grapefruit
    Citrusy Shrimp Cocktail, 36
Greek Egg and Lemon Soup with Rice, 57
Greek-Style Shrimp with Orzo and Feta, 161
Greens
    Crispy Potato-Crusted Salmon with Herb Salad,
        158, *159*
    radicchio, about, 184
    radicchio, preparing, 184
    Shells with Blue Cheese, Radicchio, and Walnuts,
        184
    see also Arugula; Kale; Spinach
Grilled
    Asian Beef Kebabs, 261
    Chicken alla Diavola, *258,* 259
    Chicken Breasts with Cherry Tomatoes, 252, *253*
    Chicken Soft Tacos, 260
    Flank Steak with Herb Sauce, 264
    Free-Form Beef Wellington with Balsamic
        Reduction, 266, *267*
    Grill-Smoked Salmon with Creamy Cucumber-
        Dill Salad, *276, 277*
    Indian-Spiced Chicken with Raita, 256
    Italian Sausages and Polenta with Pepper Relish,
        268, 269
    Lamb Chops with Shaved Zucchini Salad, 272, *273*
    Margarita Steak, 265
    Pizza Margherita, *250,* 251
    Red Curry Mahi-Mahi with Pineapple Salsa, 278
    Scallops with Fennel and Orange Salad, 274
    Shrimp and Corn, Maryland-Style, *248,* 275
    Sirloin Steak with Grilled Tomato Salad, *262,* 263
    Smoked Double-Thick Pork Chops with
        Cranberry-Thyme Applesauce, 271
    Southwestern Drumsticks with Charred Coleslaw,
        257
    Spice-Rubbed Pork Tenderloin with Peaches, 270
    Swordfish Skewers with Basil Oil, 279
Grilling tips and techniques, 254–55, 278
Grits
    Cheesy, and Spicy Pepper Relish, Pork Chops with,
        92, 115
    and Shrimp, Cheesy, 238, *239*
    taste tests on, 115

H

Ham
    and Cheese Palmiers, 30, *31*
    Egg, and Hash Brown Pie, 243
    Serrano and Manchego Crostini with Orange
        Honey, 17
    Unstuffed Chicken Cordon Bleu, *66,* 67
    see also Prosciutto
Hazelnuts
    Nutella Tart, *280,* 289
Hearty Italian Chicken Soup with Kale and
    Gnocchi, 52
Herbes de Provence, about, 6
Herb(s)
    adding flavor with, 2
    Herbed Cheese Coins, 6
    Herbed Ricotta Crostini, *14,* 15
    Salad, Crispy Potato-Crusted Salmon with, 158,
        159
    Sauce, Grilled Flank Steak with, 264
    see also specific herbs
Hoisin, sauce, taste tests on, 141
Hot pepper jelly, taste tests on, 36

I

Ice Cream
    Pie, Caramel Turtle, *298, 299*
    vanilla, taste tests on, 299

J

Jam and Brie Phyllo Cups, 27
Jams and jellies, for glazes, 2–3

K

Kale
    about, 188
    Caramelized Onions, and Bacon, Gemelli with, 188
    and Gnocchi, Hearty Italian Chicken Soup with, 52
    Roasted, and Chickpeas, Baked Quinoa with, 218,
        219

Kielbasa
  Bites, 32
  Rustic Potato-Leek Soup with, *48, 49*
  taste tests on, 32
Kimchi
  about, 105
  Fried Rice with Beef, *104,* 105

L

Lamb
  chops, about, 272
  Chops, Grilled, with Shaved Zucchini Salad, 272,
    273
  Pitas with Roasted Red Pepper Sauce, *120,* 121
Lasagna
  Easiest-Ever, 226
  noodles, no-boil, taste tests on, 226
  White, with Zucchini and Tomatoes, *222,* 227
Lazy Man's Chili, 106
Leek(s)
  about, 148
  and Cherry Tomatoes, Braised Cod with, 148
  Orzo Primavera with Feta, 216
  -Potato Soup, Rustic, with Kielbasa, *48,* 49
  preparing, 49
  and Salmon, Farfalle with, *206,* 207
  washing, 207
Lemon(s)
  about, 288
  -Braised Chicken with Fennel, 77
  and Egg Soup with Rice, Greek, 57
  Tart, 288
Linguine with Clams and Chorizo, *202,* 203

M

Mahi-Mahi, Grilled Red Curry, with Pineapple
    Salsa, 278
Marinated Feta and Green Olives, 11
Marshmallows
  Chocolate Mousse Parfaits, *292,* 293
  No-Bake Rocky Road Bars, *294,* 295

Maryland-Style Grilled Shrimp and Corn, *248,*
    275
Meat. *See* Beef; Lamb; Meatloaf mix; Pork
Meatballs
  Chicken, with Tomatoes and Cilantro, 85
  Spaghetti and, Six-Ingredient, *194,* 195
Meatloaf Florentine, *108,* 109
Meatloaf mix
  Meatloaf Florentine, *108,* 109
  Six-Ingredient Spaghetti and Meatballs, *194,* 195
Mediterranean Penne with Tuna and Niçoise
    Olives, 204
Melted Brie with Honey and Herbs, *12,* 13
Mexicorn, about, 68
Miso
  about, 157
  -Glazed Salmon, 157
  -Mushroom Soup with Shrimp and Udon, 50, *51*
Mozzarella
  balls, baby, about, 19
  Caprese Skewers, *18, 19*
  Chicken Pizzaiola with Pasta, 70, *71*
  Easiest-Ever Lasagna, 226
  Easy Tortellini Gratin, 192
  Grilled Pizza Margherita, *250,* 251
  Skillet Pizza with Broccolini and Sun-Dried
    Tomatoes, *214,* 215
  smoked, about, 187
  Smoked, Fire-Roasted Tomatoes, and Pepperoni,
    Ziti with, *186,* 187
  Smoky Eggplant Casserole, 234, *235*
  Tomato Tartlets, 28, *29*
Mushroom(s)
  Campanelle with Porcini Cream Sauce, 174
  dried porcini, about, 174
  dried porcini, rehydrating, 174
  Grilled Asian Beef Kebabs, 261
  Grilled Free-Form Beef Wellington with Balsamic
    Reduction, 266, *267*
  -Miso Soup with Shrimp and Udon, 50, *51*
  Mu Shu–Style Pork Wraps, 118
  Onions, and Bacon, Braised Chicken with, 84
  Porcini-Rubbed Chicken, 61
  Portobello and Spinach Strudel, 212

Mushroom(s) *(cont.)*
    Sautéed, and Truffle Oil, Farfalle with, 180
    shiitake, about, 261
    Stuffed, with Boursin and Prosciutto, *22, 23*
    white, about, 23
Mu Shu–Style Pork Wraps, 118
Mussels
    about, 165
    Bistro-Style Steamed, with White Wine and Garlic, 165
    debearding, 165
Mustard
    Dijon, taste tests on, 30
    -Glazed Drumsticks, 82, *83*
    whole-grain, taste tests on, 82

N

Naan
    about, 251
    Grilled Pizza Margherita, *250,* 251
    Tarts with Artichokes, Pesto, and Goat Cheese, 33
No-Bake Rocky Road Bars, *294, 295*
Noodles
    Egg, Brats with Beer and Mustard on, 200
    lasagna, no-boil, taste tests on, 226
    Mushroom-Miso Soup with Shrimp and Udon, 50, *51*
    udon, about, 50
Nutella Tart, *280, 289*
Nut(s)
    Caramel Turtle Ice Cream Pie, *298,* 299
    Chicken and Couscous with Dried Fruit and Smoked Almonds, 72
    -Chocolate Torte, Easy, 297
    Herbed Cheese Coins, 6
    No-Bake Rocky Road Bars, *294,* 295
    Nutella Tart, *280,* 289
    Shells with Blue Cheese, Radicchio, and Walnuts, 184
    toasting, 297

O

Old Bay seasoning, about, 275
Olive oil, extra-virgin, taste tests on, 11
Olives
    Artichokes, and Sun-Dried Tomatoes, Baked Cod with, *146, 147*
    Green, and Feta, Marinated, 11
    kalamata, about, 75
    Niçoise, and Tuna, Mediterranean Penne with, 204
    pitting, 204
    Roast Pork Tenderloin with Herbes de Provence and Warm Fennel Salad, 132
    and Tomatoes, Pan-Roasted Chicken with, *74,* 75
Olive tapenade
    about, 135
    Easy Stuffed Pork Loin with Sun-Dried Tomato Vinaigrette, *134,* 135
Onions
    about, 84
    Caramelized, Kale, and Bacon, Gemelli with, 188
    Mushrooms, and Bacon, Braised Chicken with, 84
Orange(s)
    and Fennel Salad, Grilled Scallops with, 274
    and Radish Salad, Sesame Pork Chops with, 110, *111*
    Sweet and Spicy Glazed Chicken, 60
    zest, grating, 64
Orzo, about, 216
Orzo Primavera with Feta, 216
Oyster sauce, taste tests on, 102

P

Palmiers, Ham and Cheese, 30, *31*
Panko bread crumbs, taste tests on, 234
Pan-Roasted Chicken with Potatoes, 76
Pan-Roasted Chicken with Tomatoes and Olives, *74,* 75
Pan-Seared Scallops with Butternut Squash Puree, *162,* 163
Pan-Seared Scallops with Tomato-Ginger Relish, 164
Paprika, smoked, about, 270

Parfaits, Chocolate Mousse, *292, 293*

Parmesan

Chicken Pizzaiola with Pasta, *70,* 71

Grilled Pizza Margherita, *250,* 251

Ham and Cheese Palmiers, 30, *31*

Polenta with Eggplant Ragu, 213

shaving, 96

Tomato Tartlets, 28, *29*

Parsley, about, 33

Pasta

BLT, *182, 183*

with Cajun Shrimp, Andouille Sausage, and Bell Pepper, 201

Campanelle with Porcini Cream Sauce, 174

Campanelle with Roasted Garlic, Chicken Sausage, and Arugula, *190, 191*

Chorizo and Black Bean Sopa Seca, 231

cooking water, reserving, 171

Creamy Tortellini with Vegetables, 193

Easiest-Ever Lasagna, 226

Easy Tortellini Gratin, 192

Fettuccine with Shrimp, Tarragon, and Cream, 205

Fusilli with Giardiniera and Sausage, *198,* 199

Gemelli with Caramelized Onions, Kale, and Bacon, 188

Greek-Style Shrimp with Orzo and Feta, 161

Hearty Italian Chicken Soup with Kale and Gnocchi, 52

Linguine with Clams and Chorizo, *202, 203*

no-boil lasagna noodles, about, 226

orzo, about, 216

Orzo Primavera with Feta, 216

Rotini with Brussels Sprouts, Blue Cheese, and Bacon, *168,* 185

Sausage and Tortellini Florentine Soup, *40,* 56

Shells with Blue Cheese, Radicchio, and Walnuts, 184

tortellini, taste tests on, 192

Unstuffed Shells with Sausage and Fennel, *224,* 225

vermicelli, about, 233

White Lasagna with Zucchini and Tomatoes, *222,* 227

see also Couscous; Farfalle; Penne; Noodles; Spaghetti; Ziti

Peaches, Grilled Spice-Rubbed Pork Tenderloin with, 270

Peas

Creamy Tortellini with Vegetables, 193

frozen, about, 245

Grilled Asian Beef Kebabs, 261

Snap, Five-Spice Chicken Thighs with, *80,* 81

Penne

Baked, with Roasted Red Peppers, Artichokes, and Goat Cheese, *228,* 229

with Fire-Roasted Tomato and Roasted Red Pepper Sauce, *172, 173*

Mediterranean, with Tuna and Niçoise Olives, 204

taste tests on, 175

with Zucchini, Cherry Tomatoes, and Boursin Cheese, 175

Pepperoni

Chicken Pizzaiola with Pasta, 70, *71*

Fire-Roasted Tomatoes, and Smoked Mozzarella, Ziti with, *186, 187*

Spicy Spaghetti Pie, *232, 233*

Stuffed Cherry Peppers, and Tomato Sauce, Ziti with, 189

taste tests on, 70

Pepper(s)

Aloha Kebabs with Sesame Rice, 86, *87*

Bell, and Corn, Sautéed, Cajun Roast Chicken with, *124,* 125

Bell, Cajun Shrimp, and Andouille Sausage, Pasta with, 201

bell, cutting up, 201

cherry, stuffed, about, 189

Cherry, Stuffed, Pepperoni, and Tomato Sauce, Ziti with, 189

hot cherry, sliced, about, 69

Peppadew, about, 26

Relish, Grilled Italian Sausages and Polenta with, *268,* 269

Relish, Spicy, and Cheesy Grits, Pork Chops with, *92,* 115

Roasted Red, and Fire-Roasted Tomato Sauce, Penne with, *172, 173*

Roasted Red, and Peas, Spanish Tortilla with, *244,* 245

Pepper(s) *(cont.)*

Roasted Red, Artichokes, and Goat Cheese, Baked Penne with, *228,* 229

roasted red, preparing, 47

Roasted Red, Sauce, Lamb Pitas with, *120,* 121

Roasted Red, Soup with Smoked Paprika and Basil Cream, *46,* 47

roasted red, taste tests on, 229

Salami and Provolone–Stuffed, 26

and Sausage, Polenta Casserole with, 240, *241*

Sausage and Giardiniera–Stuffed, 119

Spicy Braised Chicken Abruzzo, 69

see also Chiles

Pesto

Artichokes, and Goat Cheese, Naan Tarts with, 33

and Fennel, Swordfish en Cocotte with, 152

Six-Ingredient Spaghetti and Meatballs, *194,* 195

taste tests on, 109

Philly Cheesesteak Sandwiches, 101

Phyllo

Cups, Brie and Jam, 27

frozen, about, 212

Portobello and Spinach Strudel, 212

shells, mini, taste tests on, 27

Pie dough, taste tests on, 289

Pies

Caramel Turtle Ice Cream, *298,* 299

Egg, Ham, and Hash Brown, 243

Spicy Spaghetti, *232,* 233

Pineapple

about, 278

Aloha Kebabs with Sesame Rice, 86, *87*

Salsa, Grilled Red Curry Mahi-Mahi with, 278

Salsa, Spicy Pork Tacos with, *116,* 117

Pink Peppercorn–Crusted Goat Cheese Log, *8,* 9

Pink peppercorns, about, 274

Pizza

dough, about, 215

Margherita, Grilled, *250,* 251

Skillet, with Broccolini and Sun-Dried Tomatoes, *214,* 215

Polenta

Casserole with Sausage and Peppers, 240, *241*

and Italian Sausages, Grilled, with Pepper Relish, *268,* 269

Polenta *(cont.)*

Parmesan, with Eggplant Ragu, 213

precooked, about, 269

Pomegranate molasses

about, 128

Pomegranate-Glazed Chicken with Couscous, 128, *129*

Porcini-Rubbed Chicken, 61

Pork

chops, boneless, about, 114

Chops, Cola-Glazed, with Bok Choy and Sticky Rice, 112, *113*

Chops, Cornflake-Crusted, 114

chops, curled, preventing, 110

chops, scoring, 114

Chops, Sesame, with Orange and Radish Salad, 110, *111*

Chops, Smoked Double-Thick, with Cranberry-Thyme Applesauce, 271

Chops with Spicy Pepper Relish and Cheesy Grits, *92,* 115

loin, butterflying, 135

Loin, Easy Stuffed, with Sun-Dried Tomato Vinaigrette, *134,* 135

Loin, Fig-Glazed, with Roasted Potatoes and Bacon, *122,* 133

Loin, Roast, with Cilantro Sauce, 136

removing silverskin from, 132

slicing, for stir-fries, 118

Slow-Roasted, with Cherry Sauce, 137

Tacos, Spicy, with Pineapple Salsa, *116,* 117

tenderloin, about, 132

Tenderloin, Grilled Spice-Rubbed, with Peaches, 270

Tenderloin, Roast, with Herbes de Provence and Warm Fennel Salad, 132

Wraps, Mu Shu–Style, 118

see also Bacon; Ham; Meatloaf mix; Pork sausages

Pork sausages

andouille, taste tests on, 201

Brats with Beer and Mustard on Egg Noodles, 200

bratwurst, taste tests on, 200

Easiest-Ever Lasagna, 226

Fusilli with Giardiniera and Sausage, *198,* 199

Grilled Italian Sausages and Polenta with Pepper Relish, *268,* 269

Pork sausage *(cont.)*
Italian sausage, about, 240
Pasta with Cajun Shrimp, Andouille Sausage, and Bell Pepper, 201
Polenta Casserole with Sausage and Peppers, 240, *241*
removing from casing, 199
Salami and Provolone–Stuffed Peppers, 26
Sausage and Giardiniera–Stuffed Peppers, 119
Sausage and Tortellini Florentine Soup, *40,* 56
Simple Baked Ziti, 230
Unstuffed Shells with Sausage and Fennel, *224,* 225
Ziti with Fennel and Italian Sausage, 197
Ziti with Italian Sausage, Broccoli, and Sun-Dried Tomatoes, 196
see also Chorizo; Kielbasa; Pepperoni
Portobello and Spinach Strudel, 212
Potato chips, kettle-cooked, about, 158
Potato(es)
Boursin Mashed, Sirloin Steak with, *94,* 95
and Carrots, Caramelized, Roast Beef Sirloin with, *138,* 139
Crispy, and Lemon, Roasted Cod Fillets with, *150,* 151
-Crusted Salmon, Crispy, with Herb Salad, 158, *159*
Easiest Sunday Pot Roast, 142, *143*
Egg, Ham, and Hash Brown Pie, 243
frozen shredded, taste tests on, 243
-Leek Soup, Rustic, with Kielbasa, *48, 49*
Maryland-Style Grilled Shrimp and Corn, *248,* 275
Pan-Roasted Chicken with, 76
red, about, 49
Roasted, and Bacon, Fig-Glazed Pork Loin with, *122,* 133
Spanish Tortilla with Roasted Red Peppers and Peas, *244, 245*
Pots de Crème, Chocolate, 290, *291*
Poultry. *See* Chicken; Turkey
Pound Cake, 296
Prosciutto
and Boursin, Stuffed Mushrooms with, *22,* 23
taste tests on, 193
-Wrapped Chicken with Sage, *62, 63*

Prosciutto *(cont.)*
-Wrapped Figs with Gorgonzola, 21
Puff pastry
Apple Turnovers, 285
Ham and Cheese Palmiers, 30, *31*
Kielbasa Bites, 32
taste tests on, 28
Tomato Tartlets, 28, *29*

Q

Quinoa
about, 218
Baked, with Roasted Kale and Chickpeas, 218, *219*
rinsing, 218

R

Radicchio
about, 184
Blue Cheese, and Walnuts, Shells with, 184
preparing, 184
Radish and Orange Salad, Sesame Pork Chops with, 110, *111*
Rice
Coconut-Lime, Crispy Tofu with, *208,* 221
Creamy Coconut, and Fish Packets, Thai-Style, 149
Fried, Kimchi, with Beef, *104,* 105
Greek Egg and Lemon Soup with, 57
long-grain white, taste tests on, 86
precooked, taste tests on, 119
Sausage and Giardiniera–Stuffed Peppers, 119
Sesame, Aloha Kebabs with, 86, *87*
Skillet Monterey Chicken with, 68
Sticky, and Bok Choy, Cola-Glazed Pork Chops with, 112, *113*
sushi, about, 112
Thai Red Curry and Coconut Chicken Soup, 53
Ritz crackers, about, 67
Roast Beef Sirloin with Caramelized Carrots and Potatoes, *138,* 139
Roasted Cod Fillets with Crispy Potatoes and Lemon, *150,* 151
Roasted Poblano and Black Bean Enchiladas, 217

Roasted Red Pepper Soup with Smoked Paprika and Basil Cream, *46, 47*

Roasted Salmon with Tangerine Relish, *144,* 156

Roasted Tomato and Corn Tostadas, *210, 211*

Roasted Tomato Soup, 45

Roast Pork Loin with Cilantro Sauce, 136

Roast Pork Tenderloin with Herbes de Provence and Warm Fennel Salad, 132

Rose's sweetened lime juice, about, 136

Rotini with Brussels Sprouts, Blue Cheese, and Bacon, *168,* 185

Rustic Chicken and Brie Tart, *90, 91*

Rustic Potato-Leek Soup with Kielbasa, *48,* 49

S

Saffron, about, 161

Sage, about, 63

Salami and Provolone–Stuffed Peppers, 26

Salmon
  about, 156
  Crispy Potato-Crusted, with Herb Salad, 158, *159*
  fillets, cutting, 158
  fillets, scoring, 156
  Grill-Smoked, with Creamy Cucumber-Dill Salad, *276, 277*
  and Leeks, Farfalle with, *206,* 207
  Miso-Glazed, 157
  Roasted, with Tangerine Relish, *144,* 156
  smoked, about, 39
  Smoked, Rolls, *38,* 39

Salsa, tomato, taste tests on, 107

Sandwiches, Philly Cheesesteak, 101

Sauces, store-bought, cooking with, 2

Sausages. *See* Chicken Sausage(s); Pork sausages

Scallion whites and greens, separating, 238

Scallops
  about, 164
  Grilled, with Fennel and Orange Salad, 274
  Pan-Seared, with Butternut Squash Puree, *162,* 163
  Pan-Seared, with Tomato-Ginger Relish, 164
  preparing, 164

Seafood. *See* Clams; Fish; Mussels; Scallops; Shrimp

Serrano and Manchego Crostini with Orange Honey, 17

Sesame-Crusted Tuna with Wasabi Dressing, 154, *155*

Sesame Pork Chops with Orange and Radish Salad, 110, *111*

Shallots, Roasted, Za'atar-Rubbed Butterflied Chicken with, 126

Shellfish. *See* Clams; Mussels; Scallops; Shrimp

Shells with Blue Cheese, Radicchio, and Walnuts, 184

Sherry, dry, taste tests on, 61

Shrimp
  about, 160
  Broiled Chipotle, 37
  Cajun, Andouille Sausage, and Bell Pepper, Pasta with, 201
  Cocktail, Citrusy, 36
  Cocktail Shooters, Spicy, *34, 35*
  and Corn, Grilled, Maryland-Style, *248,* 275
  deveining, 37
  Greek-Style, with Orzo and Feta, 161
  and Grits, Cheesy, 238, *239*
  Spicy Pan-Seared, with Tomatoes and Scallions, 160
  Tarragon, and Cream, Fettuccine with, 205
  and Udon, Mushroom-Miso Soup with, 50, *51*

Simple Baked Ziti, 230

Simple Stuffed Chicken Breasts with Boursin, 73

Sirloin Steak with Boursin Mashed Potatoes, *94,* 95

Six-ingredient cooking
  cooking techniques for, 1–3
  flavorful fats for, 1
  international condiments for, 3
  jams and jellies for, 2–3
  marinated and pickled vegetables for, 3
  pantry snacks for, 3
  seasoning and tasting dishes, 3
  spice blends for, 2
  store-bought sauces for, 2

Six-Ingredient Spaghetti and Meatballs, *194,* 195

Skillet Monterey Chicken with Rice, 68

Skillet Pizza with Broccolini and Sun-Dried Tomatoes, *214,* 215

Slow-Roasted Pork with Cherry Sauce, 137

Smoked paprika, about, 270

Smoked Salmon
   about, 39
   Rolls, *38,* 39
Smoky Eggplant Casserole, 234, *235*
Soups
   Black Bean, with Chorizo, *54, 55*
   Cauliflower, Curried, 44
   Chai-Infused Butternut Squash, *42, 43*
   Chicken, Hearty Italian, with Kale and Gnocchi, 52
   Egg and Lemon, Greek, with Rice, 57
   Mushroom-Miso, with Shrimp and Udon, 50, *51*
   Potato-Leek, Rustic, with Kielbasa, *48,* 49
   Roasted Red Pepper, with Smoked Paprika and
      Basil Cream, *46,* 47
   Roasted Tomato, 45
   Sausage and Tortellini Florentine, *40,* 56
   Thai Red Curry and Coconut Chicken, 53
Soy crumbles
   about, 220
   Easy Stuffed Zucchini, 220
Spaghetti
   Chicken Pizzaiola with Pasta, 70, *71*
   with Fried Eggs and Bread Crumbs, *178,* 179
   with Garlic, Olive Oil, and Marinated Artichokes,
      170
   and Meatballs, Six-Ingredient, *194,* 195
   Pie, Spicy, *232, 233*
   with Quickest Tomato Sauce, 171
   taste tests on, 179
**Spanish Tortilla with Roasted Red Peppers and
   Peas,** *244,* **245**
Speedy Trifle with Cookies and Berries, *282,* **283**
Spices, cooking with, 2
Spicy Braised Chicken Abruzzo, 69
**Spicy Pan-Seared Shrimp with Tomatoes and
   Scallions, 160**
Spicy Pork Tacos with Pineapple Salsa, *116,* **117**
Spicy Shrimp Cocktail Shooters, *34,* **35**
Spicy Spaghetti Pie, *232,* **233**
Spinach
   Creamy Tortellini with Vegetables, 193
   Grilled Sirloin Steak with Grilled Tomato Salad,
      262, 263
   Meatloaf Florentine, *108,* 109

Spinach *(cont.)*
   and Portobello Strudel, 212
   Rustic Chicken and Brie Tart, *90,* 91
   Sausage and Tortellini Florentine Soup, *40,* 56
Squash
   butternut, cutting up, 42
   butternut, precut, about, 163
   Butternut, Puree, Pan-Seared Scallops with, *162,*
      163
   Butternut, Soup, Chai-Infused, *42, 43*
   see also Zucchini
Strata, Apple and Cheddar, 247
Strudel, Portobello and Spinach, 212
Stuffed Mushrooms with Boursin and Prosciutto,
   22, 23
Sugar, brown, about, 284
Sweet and Spicy Glazed Chicken, 60
Sweet chili sauce, about, 110
Swordfish
   about, 152
   en Cocotte with Fennel and Pesto, 152
   Skewers, Grilled, with Basil Oil, 279

T

Tacos
   Soft, Chipotle Steak, *98,* 99
   Soft, Grilled Chicken, 260
   Spicy Pork, with Pineapple Salsa, *116,* 117
Taco seasoning mix, about, 237
Taco shells
   Beef Taco Bake, *236, 237*
   Spicy Pork Tacos with Pineapple Salsa, 116, 117
   taste tests on, 117
Tangerine Relish, Roasted Salmon with, *144,* **156**
Tarragon, about, 205
Tarts
   Chicken and Brie, Rustic, *90,* 91
   French Caramel Apple, 286, *287*
   Lemon, 288
   Naan, with Artichokes, Pesto, and Goat Cheese, 33
   Nutella, *280,* 289
   preparing crust for, 288
   Tomato Tartlets, 28, *29*

Tequila

about, 265

Grilled Margarita Steak, 265

Spicy Shrimp Cocktail Shooters, *34,* 35

Teriyaki Steak Tips, 100

Thai Red Curry and Coconut Chicken Soup, 53

Thai-Style Fish and Creamy Coconut Rice Packets, 149

Thyme, about, 76

Tofu, Crispy, with Coconut-Lime Rice, *208,* 221

Tomato(es)

BLT Pasta, *182,* 183

canned whole, taste tests on, 45

Caprese Skewers, *18,* 19

cherry, about, 65

Cherry, and Leeks, Braised Cod with, 148

Cherry, Bacon, Toasted Corn, and Basil, Farfalle with, 181

Cherry, Grilled Chicken Breasts with, 252, *253*

Cherry, Sautéed, Cheddar Crumb–Crusted Chicken with, *58,* 65

Cherry, Zucchini, and Boursin Cheese, Penne with, 175

and Cilantro, Chicken Meatballs with, 85

and Corn, Roasted, Tostadas, *210,* 211

crushed canned, taste tests on, 171

diced, with garlic and onion, about, 85

fire-roasted, about, 173

Fire-Roasted, and Roasted Red Pepper Sauce, Penne with, *172,* 173

Fire-Roasted, Pepperoni, and Smoked Mozzarella, Ziti with, *186,* 187

-Ginger Relish, Pan-Seared Scallops with, 164

Grilled, Salad, Grilled Sirloin Steak with, *262, 263*

Grilled Chicken Soft Tacos, 260

and Olives, Pan-Roasted Chicken with, *74,* 75

paste, taste tests on, 197

removing core from, 28

Roasted, Soup, 45

salsa, jarred, taste tests on, 107

sauce, jarred, taste tests on, 195

Sauce, Quickest, Spaghetti with, 171

and Scallions, Spicy Pan-Seared Shrimp with, 160

Tomato(es) *(cont.)*

sun-dried, about, 89

Sun-Dried, and Broccolini, Skillet Pizza with, *214,* 215

Sun-Dried, and Chicken Burgers, *88,* 89

Sun-Dried, Italian Sausage, and Broccoli, Ziti with, 196

Sun-Dried, Vinaigrette, Easy Stuffed Pork Loin with, *134,* 135

Tartlets, 28, *29*

Tortellini, taste tests on, 192

Tortilla chips

Chicken Enchilada Casserole, 242

taste tests on, 242

Tortillas

Chipotle Steak Soft Tacos, *98,* 99

corn tostadas, taste tests on, 211

flour, taste tests on, 260

Grilled Chicken Soft Tacos, 260

Mu Shu–Style Pork Wraps, 118

Roasted Poblano and Black Bean Enchiladas, 217

Spicy Pork Tacos with Pineapple Salsa, *116,* 117

taco shells, taste tests on, 117

see also Tortilla chips

Tostadas

corn, taste tests on, 211

Roasted Tomato and Corn, *210,* 211

Trifle, Speedy, with Cookies and Berries, *282,* 283

Truffle oil, about, 180

Tuna

and Niçoise Olives, Mediterranean Penne with, 204

premium, taste tests on, 204

Sesame-Crusted, with Wasabi Dressing, 154, *155*

Turkey Breast en Cocotte with Pan Gravy, *130,* 131

Turnovers, Apple, 285

U

Unstuffed Chicken Cordon Bleu, *66,* 67

Unstuffed Shells with Sausage and Fennel, *224,* 225

V

Vanilla ice cream, taste tests on, 299
Vegetables
    marinated, cooking with, 3
    pickled, cooking with, 3
    see also Giardiniera; specific vegetables
Vegetarian main dishes
    Baked Quinoa with Roasted Kale and Chickpeas, 218, 219
    Crispy Tofu with Coconut-Lime Rice, 208, 221
    Easy Stuffed Zucchini, 220
    Orzo Primavera with Feta, 216
    Parmesan Polenta with Eggplant Ragu, 213
    Portobello and Spinach Strudel, 212
    Roasted Poblano and Black Bean Enchiladas, 217
    Roasted Tomato and Corn Tostadas, 210, 211
    Skillet Pizza with Broccolini and Sun-Dried Tomatoes, 214, 215
Vermicelli, about, 233
Vinegar
    balsamic, taste tests on, 266
    cider, taste tests on, 257
    Grilled Free-Form Beef Wellington with Balsamic Reduction, 266, 267
    red wine, taste tests on, 252
V8 juice
    about, 56
    Sausage and Tortellini Florentine Soup, 40, 56
Vodka sauce, about, 225

W

Walnuts
    Blue Cheese, and Radicchio, Shells with, 184
    Easy Chocolate-Nut Torte, 297
    Herbed Cheese Coins, 6
Warm Bacon-Wrapped Chorizo and Dates, 24, 25
Wasabi paste, about, 154
White Lasagna with Zucchini and Tomatoes, 222, 227
Wine
    Red, and Cherries, Braised Beef with, 140
    red, for cooking, 140

Wine (cont.)
    White, and Garlic, Bistro-Style Steamed Mussels with, 165
    white, for cooking, 207

Y

Yogurt
    Feta-Dill Dip with Cucumber Chips, 10
    Grilled Indian-Spiced Chicken with Raita, 256
    Grill-Smoked Salmon with Creamy Cucumber-Dill Salad, 276, 277
    plain, taste tests on, 256

Z

Za'atar-Rubbed Butterflied Chicken with Roasted Shallots, 126
Za'atar seasoning, about, 126
Ziti
    with Fennel and Italian Sausage, 197
    with Fire-Roasted Tomatoes, Pepperoni, and Smoked Mozzarella, 186, 187
    with Italian Sausage, Broccoli, and Sun-Dried Tomatoes, 196
    Pasta with Cajun Shrimp, Andouille Sausage, and Bell Pepper, 201
    Simple Baked, 230
    with Stuffed Cherry Peppers, Pepperoni, and Tomato Sauce, 189
Zucchini
    about, 227
    Cherry Tomatoes, and Boursin Cheese, Penne with, 175
    Easy Stuffed, 220
    ribbons, creating, 272
    seeding, 220
    Shaved, Salad, Grilled Lamb Chops with, 272, 273
    and Tomatoes, White Lasagna with, 222, 227